On the
Stigma of
Mental Illness

On the Stigma of Mental Illness

Practical Strategies for Research and Social Change

Edited by Patrick W. Corrigan

American Psychological Association
Washington, DC

Published by
American Psychological Association
750 First Street, NE
Washington, DC 20002
www.apa.org

To order
APA Order Department
P.O. Box 92984
Washington, DC 20090-2984

Tel: (800) 374-2721; Direct: (202) 336-5510
Fax: (202) 336-5502; TDD/TTY: (202) 336-6123
Online: www.apa.org/books/
E-mail: order@apa.org

In the U.K., Europe, Africa, and the Middle East, copies may be ordered from
American Psychological Association
3 Henrietta Street
Covent Garden, London
WC2E 8LU England

Typeset in Goudy by MacAllister Publishing Services, Indianapolis, IN

Printer: Sheridan Books, Ann Arbor, MI
Cover Designer: Aqueous Studio, Arlington, VA
Project Manager: MacAllister Publishing Services, Indianapolis, IN

The opinions and statements published are the responsibility of the authors, and such opinions and statements do not necessarily represent the policies of the American Psychological Association.

Library of Congress Cataloging-in-Publication Data
On the stigma of mental illness : practical strategies for research and social change / [edited by] Patrick W. Corrigan.— 1st ed.
    p. cm.
   Includes bibliographical references and index.
   ISBN 1-59147-189-3
  1 Mental illness—Public opinion.   2. Mental illness—Social aspects.
3. Discrimination against the mentally ill.   4. Stigma (Social psychology)   I. Corrigan, Patrick W.

    RC455.2.P85O5 2005
    305.9'084—dc22

2004013800

British Library Cataloguing-in-Publication Data
A CIP record is available from the British Library.

Printed in the United States of America
First Edition

If one advances confidently in the direction of his dreams and endeavors
to live the life he has imagined, he will meet with
a success unexpected in common hours.

—Henry David Thoreau

CONTENTS

CONTRIBUTORS

Herbert Allen, Department of Marketing Communications, Columbia
College, Chicago

Beth Angell, School of Social Service Administration, University of
Chicago

Galen V. Bodenhausen, Department of Psychology, Northwestern
University, Evanston, IL

Joseph D. Calabrese, Committee on Human Development, University of
Chicago

Andrea Cooke, Chicago Consortium for Stigma Research

Amy E. Cooper, Department of Psychiatry, University of Chicago

Patrick W. Corrigan, University of Chicago Center for Psychiatric
Rehabilitation, Tinley Park, IL

Thomas Hamilton, Department of Marketing Communications, Columbia
College, Chicago

Mark Heyrman, Mandell Legal Aid Clinic, University of Chicago

Petra Kleinlein, Center for Cognitive Medicine, University of Illinois at
Chicago

Kelly Kovac, School of Social Work, University of Wisconsin—Madison

Robert Lundin, University of Chicago Center for Psychiatric
Rehabilitation, Tinley Park, IL

Arthur Lurigio, Department of Criminal Justice, Loyola University of
Chicago

Fred E. Markowitz, Department of Sociology, Northern Illinois University,
DeKalb, IL

Leonard S. Newman, Psychology Department, University of Illinois at
Chicago

Colm O'Muircheartaigh, Irving B. Harris School of Public Policy
Research, University of Chicago

Victor Ottati, Department of Psychology, Loyola University of Chicago

Kenneth A. Rasinski, Substance Abuse, Mental Health, and Criminal Justice Division, NORC at the University of Chicago

L. Philip River, University of Chicago, School of Social Service Administration, Chicago

Margaret Sullivan, Department of Marketing Communications, Columbia College, Chicago

Peter Viechnicki, American Management Systems, Lanham, MD

Amy C. Watson, University of Chicago Center for Psychiatric Rehabilitation, Tinley Park, IL

Pamela Woll, Great Lakes Addiction Technology Transfer Center, Chicago, IL

FOREWORD

ROBERT LUNDIN

The more I become immersed in the study of the stigma attached to mental illness, the more it astonishes me that any such phenomenon should exist at all. I believe that serious and persistent mental illnesses, like the one I live with, are clearly and inexorably no-fault phenomena. They fully warrant being treated with the same gentleness and respect as multiple sclerosis, testicular cancer, or sickle-cell anemia. No doubt some people will cry foul at this assertion, but I offer no apologies. Fie on the elements of society that would put me in emotional turmoil, have me feel guilt, and be broadly disliked, merely for having a psychiatric disorder. These people have tried, and failed, to wreck my life.

The phenomenon of stigma warrants careful and thorough examination. In this volume, some of the leading stigma researchers in the nation present their data and findings. There is cause for hope; there is cause for distress. Although some studies reviewed in this book point to a growing acceptance of people with certain types of mental illness—most notably depression—other data describe continued negative labeling, ridicule, prejudice, resistant public attitudes, and discrimination.

I hadn't been ill with a psychosis more than 24 hours before I felt the sting of stigma. My first major break, and subsequent suicide attempt, came as a terrible shock to me only a few days after I graduated from high school in 1974. While in high school, due in large part to my school's no-tolerance drug policy, I had refrained from using marijuana or any other street drug. After graduation, with the school's authority no longer looming, I imbibed in an illegal smoke with Walter, a friend I knew fairly well, and a friend of his I hardly knew at all. The pot was potent and soon after I became high, my mind expanded into a fierce psychosis. My distorted thinking led to a grim and distorted action: I tried to end my life with a dull penknife.

It will be a long time before I'll forget the horrified looks of the other people waiting in the emergency room. If I had broken my arm in a motorcycle accident or had a laceration from an industrial accident, there would have been no such revulsion. But a self-inflicted wound was perverted and disgusting. I felt this deeply. Everyone looked at me accusingly. I spent the following few days in the adult psychiatric ward, and my friends were nowhere to be seen. They didn't communicate, they didn't visit, they didn't call, they showed no concern. The stigma was so grave that it was 15 years before I spoke with Walter again. Moreover, news of my behavior reached other friends of mine, and I was, for all practical purposes, shunned from my social group. That was a very lonely summer in 1974.

Twenty-seven years later, this ugly experience is largely forgotten. I find myself a member of the Chicago Consortium for Stigma Research, listening to presentations and partaking in discourse with the nation's leading authorities on the stigma of mental illness. With Dr. Patrick Corrigan I have written a book on the subject, *Don't Call Me Nuts! Coping With the Stigma of Mental Illness*. I've assembled talented creative writers from Maine to California to publish three editions of *The Awakenings Review*, a truly stigma-busting literary journal. Every author published in it has an intimate relationship to mental illness; nearly every member of the editorial board is a consumer. It's been a long journey from the emergency room in 1974 to sitting at a seminar table listening to the exchange of ideas between members and faculty of the consortium and such notables as Otto Wahl, David Penn, Jo Phelan, and Howard Goldman.

Over the years I've grown to accept my illness, and in following, I've carved out a personal niche among fellow consumers and people comfortable with mental illnesses. As a result, stigma has become less of an issue for me. But in my first years of coping with what was then a diagnosis of manic depression, stigma haunted me in virtually every facet of my life: intimate relationships, casual relationships, and work relationships. A few examples: It was decided for me that, after becoming ill, a particularly suitable, low-pressure job was teaching at a prep school. So, I was enrolled in math and computer courses at the nearby college with the intention that I would find a job teaching math and computer, because people who taught them were particularly sought after. After making a lot of applications I was offered a job by a well-regarded prep school in the Washington, DC, area. In the meantime I had been working at a summer camp in North Carolina. The school called the director of the camp, who divulged that I was taking lithium. Thereafter, the school spoke to me only once: to withdraw its offer of employment.

In 1991, fortified with anti-stigma messages from groups like the National Alliance for the Mentally Ill, I organized a small protest of a movie I found particularly offensive, *Misery*. The heinous villain is a woman who is clearly depicted as mentally ill, and she (Kathy Bates) convincingly mimics symptoms of manic depression. My friends and I called for a picket in front of the small theater in my hometown where it was playing, and I posted a flyer in a small restaurant. A few days later, I received a letter from a lawyer complaining that his client was receiving harassing and stigmatizing telephone calls that were intended for me. Inadvertently, I had inverted two numbers on the flyer so that the angry, intimidating calls went to this hapless man. In 1980 I had to leave graduate school after a serious psychotic episode; by now my psychoses were no longer triggered by mind-expanding drugs. This set in motion a severe depression, but then after several months it lifted and I was feeling well. The admissions director at the nearby college —a highly ranked institution—had for years been following my academic career. Perhaps with a few misgivings he nonetheless offered me an assistant's job. Several months into the job my delusions began afresh. While on my first recruiting trip in South Carolina, I could no longer function, and I cut it short to fly back to the office. Although I was suffering from a medical illness, I arrived at home to find that I was summarily fired and instructed to have my belongings out of my office by that evening.

In the following years my medical expenses were substantial, with the costs of both medications and intense psychotherapy being in the thousands. Because I was disabled, I was permitted to remain on my father's health insurance policy after the cut-off period at age 23. Then his employer, the same college from which I had been fired, abruptly and inexplicably dropped me from their coverage. I had no job; I had no medical insurance. My family threatened to sue. So, a deal was struck in which I would work again for the college for three months and then my outstanding medical bills would be paid. After that I was on my own. The job for which I was deemed suitable was cleaning garbage from around the dormitories and other menial tasks.

Today I work in research and publications at the University of Chicago Center for Psychiatric Rehabilitation, a far cry from weed-eating lawns and picking up litter for $4.85 an hour. In 1992 my recovery was such that I was able to begin work as a freelance reporter for small weekly newspapers, which eventually led to stringing for the *Chicago Tribune*. In 1997 I began my career at the University of Chicago.

The Chicago Consortium for Stigma Research (CSSR) is an exciting undertaking. The meetings are small, intimate, and are held in a book-lined seminar room at the University of Chicago Law School. These are well-attended groups. The attendees—psychologists, social workers, lawyers, anthropologists, sociologists, media experts, students—hear presentations that are on the leading edge of stigma research. I believe the future of the CCSR is exhilarating in its enormity. The chapters in this book represent much thought, research, and scholarship, both pure science and clinical practice. It can be an invaluable tool to other researchers and clinicians, as well as persons like myself who live in these conditions, who likewise say fie to the purveyors of stigma.

ACKNOWLEDGMENTS

The list for acknowledgments for this book is straightforward: my colleagues and friends from the Chicago Consortium whom I have worked with these past several years to better understand the stigma of mental illness. Many of these folks authored the chapters in this book.

We also wish to thank the members of our national advisory board who have worked with us in various capacities. These include Mahzarin Banaji, Jennifer Crocker, Susan Fiske, Howard Goldman, Bruce Link, John Monahan, Steve Morse, David Penn, Bernice Pescosolido, Jo Phelan, Otto Wahl, and Bernard Weiner. Thanks to Amy Warpinski for helping me assemble the final draft of the manuscript.

Thanks also to the National Institute of Mental Health (NIMH; and Emeline Otey) for infrastructure funding of the consortium as well as specific project support from NIMH, the National Institute on Alcohol Abuse and Alcoholism, the Fogarty International Center, the Center for Substance Abuse Treatment, the Center for Mental Health Services, the U.S. Department of Labor, the Rehabilitation Services Administration, the Pew Trust, the Boeing Foundation, and the MacArthur Foundation.

Finally, many thanks to my wife, Georgeen Carson, and my children, Abe and Liz, for their continuing love and for providing a critical sounding board for my ideas around the dinner table.

On the
Stigma of
Mental Illness

INTRODUCTION

PATRICK W. CORRIGAN

Much of my professional life has focused on helping people with serious mental illness achieve their life goals. To do this, I have been a member of service teams that have provided the gamut of evidence-based pharmacological and psychosocial services: symptom monitoring, medication management, assertive community treatment, supported employment, skills training, cognitive rehabilitation, and family services. Common to the mission of most of these approaches is the effort to help people manage their symptoms and disabilities so they can better accomplish the personal goals that are essential to a satisfactory life. Two of the most important of these goals are (a) to live independently in a setting that is comfortable to them and (b) to obtain employment in real-world work sites with a living wage.

The mission seems clear and achievable: Help people to overcome their disabilities so they can get back to work and live on their own. The reality is not. Several times I assisted individuals in finding jobs only to have employers notice their psychiatric history and balk at having a potentially dangerous person on the job. In other instances, I aided people in obtaining housing only to encounter the landlord who was certain that the "ex-mental patient" would trash the apartment. The lesson was jarring: Helping people find jobs or apartments is not solely a matter of treatment and rehabilitation. The community's response to people with psychiatric disabilities is also an essential part of the equation. Members of the general public who endorse the stigma of mental illness are likely to avoid these people and rob them of their opportunities.

This kind of realization forces mental health services investigators to broaden their research program from a focus on what people with mental illness need so they can fit into their community and achieve their goals to also

3

include the changes that are necessary in the community so it is appropriately responsive to these treatment and rehabilitation efforts. The community's role in disabilities is a complex issue that requires study at many levels of social analysis. Clearly, one important aspect of the community's response is stigma: the view that an attribute such as having a mental illness is deeply discrediting and justifies a hostile response from society (Goffman, 1963). Mental health researchers have completed some descriptive research on the prevalence and effect of stigma on people with mental illness. Missing from this literature, however, is a bridge to the work of basic behavioral scientists —most notably social psychologists and sociologists—who have delved into the experience of stereotype, prejudice, and discrimination. Hence, our understanding of the stigma of mental illness would be greatly advanced by partnering with the basic behavioral researchers working in the area of prejudice and discrimination. This kind of partnership is consistent with the translational research agenda recently highlighted by the National Institute of Mental Health (2000): namely, the promotion of research paradigms that seek to expand the conceptual and methodological base of mental health services by using the wisdom gained from basic behavioral sciences.

Recognizing this state of affairs, in 2000 a handful of researchers began to meet at the University of Chicago's Quadrangle Club over lunch to discuss the needed infrastructure for a research center addressing the stigma of mental illness. After monthly meetings for more than a year and funding from the NIMH, we developed the Chicago Consortium for Stigma Research (CCSR). CCSR is a group of about 25 researchers from seven local Universities—the University of Chicago, Columbia College, Northwestern University, the University of Illinois at Chicago, Northern Illinois University, Illinois State University, and Loyola University—plus the National Opinion Research Center. Consortium participants include basic behavioral scientists in a variety of fields (social psychology, sociology, anthropology, history, and public policy) partnering with services researchers from clinical psychology, psychiatry, social work, and law. Also active in the consortium is a collection of public partners from the Chicago area. This group represents a variety of advocates from consumer and other groups, including the Mental Health Consumer Education Consortium, the National Alliance for the Mentally Ill (NAMI) of Illinois, the Mental Health Association in Illinois, Equip for Equality, the Community Behavioral Health Association, and the Illinois Office of Mental Health.

Now active for 4 years, CCSR has more than 60 projects on the stigma of mental illness in various states of completion. In the process, we have developed core conceptual models and related methodological strategies that guide our work. The chapters in this book are authored by CCSR members and represent our gathered wisdom related to theory and methods. Our intended audience for the book is diverse. First, we write to the advocates who seek to eradicate the barriers thrown up by the stigma of mental illness.

We also authored the text with the research community in mind, seeking to advance knowledge about mental illness stigma. The book is also written for service providers: clinical psychologists, rehabilitation psychologists, psychiatrists, social workers, psychiatric nurses, and other professionals who witness the pain of stigma and may be in a position to change it. Finally, this book may serve as a useful text for graduate school classes in both clinical and rehabilitation psychology (for students seeking to reduce the life barriers of people with mental illness) and social psychology (for students seeking to better understand prejudice and discrimination.

Book chapters are divided into four parts. The overview in Part I of the book has two components. First, Pat Corrigan and Petra Kleinlein provide an overview of the effect of stigma on people with mental illness. Chapter 1 shows the breadth and depth of the egregious effects that stigma of mental illness has—not only on people labeled with the disorder, but also on people associated with the labeled and on society as a whole. An implicit goal of this book is to outline research strategies for studying the stigma of mental illness. Ken Rasinski and colleagues provide an overview of various methodological issues and approaches in chapter 2.

Part II examines a variety of perspectives that answer the question, "What is the stigma of mental illness?" The first few chapters of this section answer the question from various disciplines. Perhaps paramount among these is the consumers' perspective and approach to the question. Hence, Beth Angell and colleagues review the research as well as the methodological issues related to first person accounts in chapter 3. The next two chapters specifically highlight basic behavioral approaches to mental illness stigma. Vic Ottati and colleagues describe social psychological models in chapter 4, with special focus on the social–cognitive and motivational models that have been used to explain stereotypes, prejudice, and discrimination. Fred Markowitz provides a review of the extensive research using sociological models of stigma in chapter 5. The remaining chapters of part II further describe specific components of the experience of stigma. Amy Watson and Phil River examine the effect of stigma on people labeled with mental illness in chapter 6, on self-stigma and empowerment. Note that they construe personal empowerment on the same continuum as self-stigma, though obviously at the opposite extreme.

Many advocates and researchers believe that concerns related to dangerousness are most likely to cause the stigma of mental illness. Hence, the next three chapters examine aspects of the dangerousness issue. In chapter 7, Pat Corrigan and Amy Cooper examine the epidemiological evidence regarding the relationship between dangerousness and mental illness as well as the size of the problem. The dangerousness issue becomes especially poignant when a heinous crime that seems to be due to mental illness dominates the news media (e.g., Andrea Yates drowning her five children in the Houston area). In chapter 8, Pat Corrigan and Amy Watson address the issues of senseless crimes and their relationship to mental illness or evil. Amy Watson and colleagues address the role of police as first responders in chapter 9, examining how stigmatizing attitudes may influence their work. The last chapter of part II examines the stigma of mental illness in one important domain. Ken Rasinski and colleagues discuss the stigma related to substance abuse in chapter 10.

Part III reviews different ways in which stigma might be changed. In chapter 11, Pat Corrigan and Joe Calabrese review strategies for diminishing self-stigma (i.e., What can people labeled with mental illness do for themselves to diminish the harmful impact of prejudice and discrimination?). One important question related to self-stigma is whether people with mental illness should disclose to others aspects of their mental health history. Pat Corrigan discusses the costs and benefits to coming out of the closet in chapter 12.

Note that focusing on self-stigma may suggest that stigma is the problem of people labeled with mental illness. In no way do we mean to imply this. Hence, the last two chapters discuss how stigma might be changed in the public arena. In chapter 13, Amy Watson and Pat Corrigan discuss ways to challenge public stigma. Key to their approach is a focus on groups that are in positions of power vis-à-vis those labeled with mental illness (e.g., landlords, employers, police, health care providers, and legislators). Finally, Margaret Sullivan and colleagues take a comprehensive look at the role of the media in stigma. Their chapter 14 includes a range of marketing strategies which have been shown successful in promoting other social agendas and which might be applied to improve media approaches to the stigma of mental illness.

Society has been moved by great thinkers and activists who have sought to shake the foundations on which our world is built to remove the various injustices that rob groups of people of their rightful life opportunities. The stigma of mental illness is one of many examples of social injustices that advocates dream will be eventually erased. Part IV, chapter 15 by Pat Corrigan concludes this book by summarizing where we must go to make the dream of "no more" a reality.

A FINAL WORD

Stigma is of concern to social scientists largely because of the egregious effects it has on almost all levels of society. Stigma represents a social injustice that deprives people of their humanity, leads to violence, and results in robbing individuals of the opportunities that are rightfully theirs. Correcting the injustice is an important motivation for many researchers working in this area. Although the authors of this text recognize that stigma is a social evil worthy of significant correction, our book chooses, for the most part, to eschew the righteous argument, instead focusing on data that informs the argument and points to resolutions. Sometimes this may yield information that is at odds with various social movements. However, we believe that change will more effectively be realized when it can rely on information that is inferred from rigorous theory development and methodological testing. Our job is to provide the empirical ammunition so that all those concerned about the effect of stigma can attack it wisely and effectively.

REFERENCES

Goffman, E. (1963). *Stigma: Notes on the management of spoiled identity*. New York: Simon & Schuster.

National Institute of Mental Health. (2000). *Translating behavioral science into action* (NIH Publication No. 00-4699). Washington, DC: Superintendent of Documents, Government Printing Office.

I
OVERVIEW OF THE PROBLEM

1

THE IMPACT OF MENTAL ILLNESS STIGMA

PATRICK W. CORRIGAN AND
PETRA KLEINLEIN

THE IMPACT OF MENTAL ILLNESS STIGMA

Perhaps one truism permeating this book is that stigma is a complex phenomenon that is understandable at many levels. The goal of research is to make stigma and stigma change a bit more understandable. The motivation for this book, however, is not scientific speculation for its own sake. Rather, it is concern about the impact of stigma on the lives of people affected by mental illness: How do we help people from being victimized by the prejudice and discrimination that arises from stigma? Note that this chapter focuses on the impact of stigma on a generic category called people *affected* by mental illness; although consumers of mental health services most likely experience the most harsh consequences of stigma, it also harms their family members and friends, the other stakeholders involved in any aspect of services to this group, and the public as a whole. The review in this chapter attempts to highlight these different experiences.

This chapter begins with a simple question: What is mental illness? After a brief review of the phenomenology and epidemiology, we more directly address a question relevant to stigma: Do the problems that seemingly arise from stigma actually represent the results of prejudice, or a "normal" response to eccentric or dangerous behavior of people with mental illness? We review Bruce Link's work on the modified labeling theory to answer this question. The remainder of the chapter describes the ways in which stigma impacts people affected by mental illness. We distinguish between public stigma (the results of a naive public endorsing the stereotypes of mental illness) and self-stigma (the consequences of people with mental illness applying stigma to themselves). The discussion of public stigma considers how key power groups negatively impact the lives of people affected by mental illness: landlords, employers, members of the criminal justice system, and health providers, to name a few. Self-stigma examines the impact on the person's psychological well-being, health care choices, and decisions about life goals. We end the chapter with a discussion of societal manifestations of stigma and its impact on people with mental illness.

WHAT IS MEANT BY MENTAL ILLNESS AND ITS CORRESPONDING STIGMA?

Understanding the nosology and etiology of mental illness is a complex and ever-evolving enterprise that is embodied in the American Psychiatric Association's (APA's) *Diagnostic and Statistical Manual of Mental Disorders* (DSM) and the World Health Organization's *International Classification of Diseases* (ICD). Several aspects of psychiatric diseases lead to a definition of mental illness, including a clinically significant behavioral pattern that leads to distress (e.g., a painful symptom), disability (an impairment in an important life function), or potential loss of freedom (American Psychiatric Association, 2000). Five axes have emerged to sort out the various disorders that arise from these criteria including clinical disorders, personality disorders, and mental retardation. The multiaxial system has led to the identification of more than a dozen sets of disorders distinguishing childhood from adult illnesses and, among adult disorders, identifying relatively less serious syndromes like the adjustment disorders to more serious diseases like schizophrenia and other psychotic disorders. Adding to the complexity are considerations about development, general medical conditions, trauma, and substance use.

An interesting question that will be revisited in this book is whether and how stigma changes across the various parameters that distinguish psychiatric illnesses; for example, do people who abuse substances experience greater stigma than those with a developmental disability? The issue addressed in this chapter is more general: What are the signals that lead to mental illness stigma? Given that stigma has been equated with a mark that

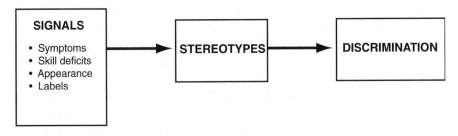

Figure 1.1. How signals lead to stereotypes and discrimination. Note that this model parallels a cognitive–behavioral model with discriminative stimuli, cognitive mediators, and behavior.

yields negative, often hostile, reactions from the majority, what characterizes the mark that produces mental illness stigma (Goffman, 1963; Jones et al., 1984)? The importance of mental illness stigma as signal or mark may be understood in terms of a social–cognitive model like the one in Figure 1.1. This model seeks to explain the relationship between discriminative stimuli and consequent behavior by identifying the cognitions that mediate these constructs. In a simple version, persons with severe mental illness signal the public about their mental illness: "That person talking to himself on the park bench must be crazy." These signals yield stereotypes about persons with mental illness: "Crazy people are dangerous." Stereotypes lead to behavioral reactions or discrimination: "I'm not going to allow dangerous people like that move into my neighborhood."

Signals That Lead to Stigma

The general public must infer mental illness from four signals: psychiatric symptoms, social skills deficits, physical appearance, and labels (Corrigan, 2000; Penn & Martin, 1998). Many of the symptoms of severe mental illness, such as inappropriate affect, bizarre behavior, language irregularities, and talking to self aloud, are manifest indicators of psychiatric illness that frighten the public. Research has shown that symptoms like these tend to produce stigmatizing reactions (Link, Cullen, Frank, & Wozniak, 1987; Penn, Guynan, Daily, & Spaulding, 1994; Socall & Holtgraves, 1992). Moreover, poor social skills that are a function of psychiatric illness also lead to stigmatizing reactions. Deficits in eye contact, body language, and choice of discussion topics (Bellack, Morrison, Mueser, & Wade, 1990; Mueser, Bellack, Douglas, & Morrison, 1991) potentially mark a person as mentally ill and lead to stigmatizing attitudes. Finally, research suggests personal appearance may lead to stigmatizing attitudes (Eagly, Ashmore, Makhijani, & Longo, 1991; Penn, Mueser, & Doonan, 1997). In particular, physical attractiveness and personal hygiene may be manifest indicators of mental illness leading to stereotypic responses from one's community; for example, "that unkempt person on the park bench must be a mental patient."

Note, however, the potential for misattributing someone as mentally ill on the basis of these three signals. What might be eccentric behavior that is not pathgnomonic of a psychiatric disorder could be misunderstood as mental illness. Social skills vary on a continuum such that low skills may represent a shy person rather than mental illness. Physical appearance may also lead to false positives about judging someone as mentally ill. Many street people with slovenly appearance are believed to be mentally ill when, in actuality, they are poor and homeless (Koegel, 1992; Mowbray, 1985). Just as these three signs may yield false positives, so the absence of these signs will often lead to false negatives. Many people are able to conceal their experiences with mental illness without peers being aware. Goffman (1963) more fully developed this point when he distinguished between discredited and discreditable stigma. The former occurs when people have a mark that is readily perceivable. Examples of the discredited group include persons from a cultural minority with an apparent physical trait which leads them to believe that their differentness is obvious to the public; for example, Africans have dark skin. Persons with discreditable stigma, on the other hand, can hide their condition; they have no readily manifest mark that identifies them as part of a stigmatized group. The public sometimes cannot determine whether a person is mentally ill.

Juxtaposing concerns about false positives that many signals provoke with the idea that the stigma of mental illness may be hidden begs the question, what, then, is the mark that leads to stigmatizing responses? Several carefully constructed studies suggest labeling as the key variable (Jones et al., 1984; Link, 1987; Scheff, 1974). People who are known as mentally ill will likely be the victims of mental illness stigma. Labels can be obtained in various ways: others can tag people with a label (a psychiatrist can inform someone that Ms. X is mentally ill), individuals can label themselves (a person can decide to introduce himself as a psychiatric survivor), or labels can be obtained by association (a person observed coming out of a psychologist's office may be assumed to be mentally ill).

IS IT DISEASE OR LABEL?

During the 1960s, questions arose regarding whether the disabilities associated with mental illness originate entirely from medical conditions, or whether the labels attached to mental illness exacerbate the problem. This divided many mental health providers and researchers into factions supporting the medical model versus labeling theory. Thomas Scheff, a leading proponent of the latter, described the difference in perspectives by stating that "Labeling theory is a sociologistic theory, in that it deals only with social processes. . . . Labeling theory is the antithesis of the medical model thesis" (1975, pp. 75–76).

The key principle in Scheff's labeling theory is that the *label* "deviant" (i.e., mentally ill) leads society to treat the labeled individual as deviant (Scheff, 1966, 1972). Common responses to the label "mental illness" included fear and disgust, leading people to minimize contact and socially distance themselves from anyone displaying undesirable behaviors. Once the label is applied, the person with mental illness is exposed to adverse reactions (such as prejudice and discrimination) from others, which facilitates the process of his or her socialization into the role of the mental patient (Goffman, 1961). This causes the individual with mental illness to exhibit continued deviant behavior (secondary deviance), fitting the label and stabilizing the mental illness (Scheff, 1966).

Critics have countered labeling theory on several grounds. Some argue that aberrant behavior, and not the label per se, is the source of negative responses from the public (Gove, 1982; Huffine & Clausen, 1979; Lehman, Joy, Kreisman, & Simmens, 1976). Others have argued that the impact of stereotypes on persons with mental illness is temporary, posing only a minor and brief problem for the person with mental illness (Gove, 1980, Gove & Fain, 1973; Karmel, 1969). Gove and Fain (1973) counter labeling theory's concept of secondary deviance arguing that psychiatric relapse is due solely to the recurrence of the mental disorder; it is not impacted by the label. According to Gove (1975), the label does not elicit negative societal reactions. Rather, negative reactions are due to bizarre behavior displayed by persons with mental illness (1975). Other researchers concluded that there generally is no negative reaction toward people labeled mentally ill (Crocetti, Spiro, Herzl, & Siassi, 1971).

In an effort to resolve differences between labeling theory and the medical model, Link (1987) conducted a study in which label and aberrant behavior were manipulated in a series of vignettes. Results indicated that members of the general public were likely to stigmatize a person labeled mentally ill even in the absence of any aberrant behavior. Subsequent studies have replicated this finding (Link, Cullen, Frank, & Wozniak, 1987; Link, Phelan, Bresnahan, Stueve, & Pescosolido, 1999). Link and colleagues (1987, 1989) posed a modified labeling theory to make sense of the diverse literature, concluding that psychiatric labels are associated with negative societal reactions that exacerbate the course of the person's disorder. This represents a middle ground between Scheff's original labeling theory and Gove's medical explanation. Aberrant behavior causes negative reactions from society, which lead the public (and the individual himself) to label mental illness negatively; this can lead to exacerbation of the existing disorder for the individual. Although the debate over the mechanics of labeling remain unresolved, it seems clear that stigmatization worsens the lives of people experiencing mental illness. (Link & Cullen, 1986; Mechanic, McAlpine, Rosenfield, & Davis, 1994).

Public stigma is distinguished from self-stigma as the reaction that the general population has to people with mental illness. Three components make up this model as outlined in Figure 1.2: stereotypes, prejudice, and discrimination. Social psychologists view *stereotypes* as knowledge structures that are learned by most members of a social group (Augoustinos, Ahrens, & Innes, 1994; Esses, Haddock, & Zanna, 1994; Hilton & von Hippel, 1996; Judd & Park, 1993; Krueger, 1996; Mullen, Rozell, & Johnson, 1996). Stereotypes are especially efficient means of categorizing information about social groups. Stereotypes are considered "social" because they represent collectively agreed upon notions of groups of persons. They are "efficient" because people can quickly generate impressions and expectations of individuals who belong to a stereotyped group (Hamilton & Sherman, 1994). As discussed more fully in later chapters of this text, stereotypes about mental illness include dangerousness, incompetence, and character weakness.

Just because most people have knowledge of a set of stereotypes does not imply that they agree with them (Jussim, Nelson, Manis, & Soffin, 1995). For example, many persons can recall stereotypes about different racial groups but do not agree that the stereotypes are valid. People who are *prejudiced*, on the other hand, endorse these negative stereotypes ("That's right; all persons with mental illness are violent!") and generate negative emotional reactions as a result ("They all scare me!") (Devine, 1988, 1989, 1995; Hilton & von Hip-

Public Stigma	Self-Stigma
• **Stereotype:** Negative belief about a group e.g., dangerous incompetence character weakness	• **Stereotype:** Negative belief about the self e.g., character weakness incompetence
• **Prejudice:** Agreement with belief and/or negative emotional reaction e.g., anger fear	• **Prejudice:** Agreement with belief Negative emotional reaction e.g., low self-esteem low self-efficacy
• **Discrimination:** Behavior response to prejudice e.g., avoidance of work and housing opportunities withhold help	• **Discrimination:** Behavior response to prejudice e.g., fails to pursue work and housing opportunities

Figure 1.2. The distinction between public stigma and self-stigma.

pel, 1996; Krueger, 1996). Prejudice is also viewed as a general attitude toward a group. In contrast to stereotypes, which are beliefs, prejudicial attitudes involve an evaluative (generally negative) component (Allport, 1954/1979; Eagly & Chaiken, 1993). According to some social psychological models of attitude structure, prejudice may arise from sources other than stereotypes about members of a group. Affect and past behavior toward members of a group may also form the basis of prejudice (Zanna & Rempel, 1988).

Prejudice, which is fundamentally a cognitive and affective response, leads to *discrimination*, the behavioral reaction (Crocker, Major, & Steele, 1998). Prejudice that yields anger can lead to hostile behavior (e.g., physically harming a member of a minority group) (Weiner, 1995). In terms of mental illness, angry prejudice may lead to withholding help or replacing health care with services provided by the criminal justice system (Corrigan, 2000). Fear leads to avoidance; for example, employers do not want persons with mental illness nearby so they do not hire them (Corrigan, Backs, Green, Diwan, & Penn, 2001). As outlined in Figure 1.1, stereotype, prejudice, and discrimination manifest differently depending on whether the public is considering stigma or the self. The specific impact of public and self-stigma is reviewed in the remainder of this chapter.

THE IMPACT OF PUBLIC STIGMA

The public endorsement of stigma impacts many people; our discussion here examines four groups. Perhaps of greatest concern is the harm which public stigma causes on people who are labeled mentally ill. Rather than broadly considering the effect of general stigma, our review is focused on key power groups, people in functional roles that have significant implications for the life goals of people with mental illness. These include landlords, employers, members of the criminal and civil justice system, health care providers, legislators, and policy makers. Although this review largely focuses on the impact of stigma on the person with mental illness, research suggests public stigma impacts three other key groups. Research suggests family members and friends are impacted by public stigma. Moreover, representatives of many of the various provider groups involved in mental health services have reported harm from public stigma. Finally, public stigma negatively impacts the public, too. Ways in which these various problems occur are briefly reviewed in this chapter.

The Impact on People With Mental Illness

Most researchers and advocates agree: people with mental illness suffer the greatest impact from stigma. In this section, we focus on three such examples of negative impact. First, stigma robs people of rightful life opportunities. Two opportunities that are especially relevant to the lives of people with mental illness are employment and housing. Second, stigma interacts with violence issues to cause people with mental illness to have a distorted experience with the criminal justice system. Third, the general health care system seems to withhold appropriate medical procedures because of mental illness stigma. We consider each of these areas in turn.

The Loss of Rightful Life Opportunity

Stereotype, prejudice, and discrimination can rob people labeled mentally ill of important life opportunities that are essential for achieving life goals. Two goals, in particular, are central to the concerns of people with serious mental illness (Corrigan, 2002): (a) obtaining competitive employment and (b) living independently in a safe and comfortable home. Before considering the role of stigma in employment and housing, it is important to understand the extent of problems in these areas. Surveys consistently estimate that less than 15% of people with serious and persistent mental illness are employed (Anthony & Blanch, 1987; Louis Harris & Associates, 1986), even though the majority desire regular work (Rogers, Walsh, Masotta, & Danley, 1991). In a more recent national survey Sturm and colleagues (1999) found that unemployment rates among persons with mental disorders were three to five times higher than among those with no psychiatric disorder. Similarly, recent data from the Substance Abuse and Mental Health Services Administration (SAMHSA) suggested that more than 60% of people with mental or emotional problems are unemployed and almost a quarter of this group are below the poverty level (Willis, Willis, Male, Henderson, & Manderscheid, 1998). These numbers are particularly disturbing given that work fulfills an essential contribution to personal satisfaction, health, and well-being (Lehman, 1988). It has also been shown to be therapeutic and reduce symptoms for individuals with mental illness (Markowitz, 2001; Russert & Frey, 1991).

The housing situation faced by people with mental illness is similarly disconcerting. According to a United States Department of Health and Human Services (1983) report to Congress, a majority of the approximately 2 million Americans considered "long-term mentally ill" live in inadequate housing, lack needed supports, or are homeless. Similar sobering findings were reported in a 1998 SAMHSA report (Willis et al., 1998). Often, their only options are in low-income neighborhoods with substandard housing and high crime rates. Even in these neighborhoods, individuals with mental illness must compete for housing with other low-income groups that are considered "more suitable tenants" (Carling, 1990). Federal initiatives related to community-based mental health services have mandated that an individual should have as much choice and control over his or her living environment as possible (NIMH, 1987). Research on housing preferences suggests that most consumers with severe and persistent mental illness prefer their own residence (Ridgeway & Zipple, 1990; Tanzman, 1993) and that housing satisfaction and community housing options may be related to the extent to which the consumer's home lends to a sense of self-mastery (Markowitz, 2001; Rosenfield, 1992).

Inability to obtain good jobs and housing can best be understood in terms of the modified labeling theory. In part, these problems occur because of the disabilities that result from serious mental illness (Corrigan, 2001). Many people with serious mental illness lack the social and coping skills to meet the demands of the competitive work force and independent housing. Nevertheless, the problems of many people with psychiatric disability are exacerbated by labels and stigma. People with mental illness are frequently unable to obtain good jobs or find suitable housing because of the prejudice of key members in their communities: employers and landlords. Several studies have documented the public's widespread endorsement of stigmatizing attitudes (Bhugra, 1989; Brockington, Hall, Levings, & Murphy, 1993; Greenley, 1984; Hamre, Dahl, & Malt, 1994; Link, 1987; Madianos, Madianou, Vlachonikolis, & Stefanis, 1987; Rabkin, 1974; Roman & Floyd, 1981). These attitudes have a deleterious impact on obtaining and keeping good jobs (Bordieri & Drehmer, 1986; Farina, Felner, & Boudreau, 1973; Link, 1982, 1987; Olshansky, Grob, & Ekdahl, 1960; Wahl, 1999; Webber & Orcutt, 1984) and leasing safe housing (Aviram & Segal, 1973; Farina, Thaw, Lovern, & Mangone, 1974; Hogan, 1985a, 1985b; Page, 1977, 1983, 1995; Segal, Baumohl, & Mayles, 1980; Wahl, 1999). Classic research by Farina (Farina & Felner, 1973) poignantly illustrates the nature of the problem. A male confederate, posing as an unemployed worker, sought jobs at 32 businesses. The same work history was reported at each of the job interviews except 50% also included information about a past psychiatric hospitalization. Subsequent analyses found interviewers were less friendly and less supportive of hiring the confederate when he mentioned his psychiatric hospitalization.

Two considerations could conceivably mitigate conclusions from this body of research. First, although some landlords and employers show stigma, this prejudice has no meaningful effects on the housing and work problems of people with mental illness. Instead, these problems solely arise from the cognitive and behavioral dysfunctions that result from the disorders. Although research has not tested this assumption directly, studies have shown a parallel connection between attitudes and behavior; namely, stigmatizing attitudes about mental illness impact access to care. First, stigma has been shown to decrease participation in rehabilitation and other services that assist people in obtaining their life goals (Leaf, Bruce, & Tischler, 1986; Leaf, Bruce, Tischler, & Holzer, 1987; Sirey, Bruce, et al., 2001). Second, whereas some might believe that prejudice was a problem 10 to 30 years ago when many of these studies were completed, but that stigma has greatly diminished because of more public knowledge about mental illness, analyses of 1996 General Social Survey data actually showed the opposite! A U.S. probability sample in 1996 was more likely to endorse stigmatizing attitudes than a similar group from 1956 (Phelan, Link, Stueve, & Pescosolido, 2000). Hence, the potential for landlords and employers discriminating against people with mental illness is exceedingly present.

The Reaction of the Criminal Justice System

With the stigma attached to mental illness intensifying over the last four decades (Martin, Pescosolido, & Tuch, 2000; Surgeon General, 2000), the number of people with mental illness entangled in the criminal justice system also rose significantly. The prevalence rate of serious mental illness in jails, currently between 6% and 15% (Ditton, 1999; Lamb & Weinberger, 1998; Teplin, 1990, 1984; Teplin, Abran, & McClelland, 1996), has risen 154% over the past 20 years (Travis, 1997). Recent studies have shown that as many as 6% of individuals considered suspects by police have a serious mental illness (Engel & Silver, 2001; Teplin & Pruett, 1992). LaGrange (2000) surveyed police officers of a large metropolitan area police department and found that 89% had had contact with citizens with mental illness in the previous year. For a person with mental illness, police officers are often the first point of contact with the criminal justice system. The officer's determination impacts whether persons with mental illness receive adequate psychiatric care or are further processed into the criminal justice system. A common outcome from this kind of interaction is involuntary psychiatric hospitalization and the concomitant loss of liberty.

Criminalizing mental illness is a way in which the criminal justice system reacts to people with mental illness, contributing to the increasing prevalence of serious mental illness in jail (Watson, Ottati, Corrigan, & Heyrman, in press). As Teplin (1984) points out, persons exhibiting symptoms and signs of serious mental illness (like psychoses) are more likely than others to be arrested by the police. The selective process continues if the person is taken to jail. Someone experiencing a mental illness tends to spend more time incarcerated than persons without mental illness (Steadman, McCarty, & Morrisey, 1989). Treating a person with mental illness like a criminal instead of a like someone who is sick and in need of treatment has implications not only for the life, liberty, and well-being of individuals with mental illness, but also affects the larger community. As noted before, public fear of individuals with mental illness has increased over the past 40 years (Martin, Pescosolido, & Tuch, 2000; Phelan, Link, Moore, & Stueve, 1997; Phelan et al., 2000), resulting in a higher degree of preferred social distance from persons with mental illness. The growing intolerance of offenders in general has led to harsher laws and hampered effective treatment planning for mentally ill offenders (Jemelka, Trupin, & Chiles, 1989; Lamb & Weinberger, 1998).

Persons with mental illness are not always encountered as the perceived wrong-doers by members of the criminal justice system; they are also witnesses or victims of crime. Research on helping behavior suggests that officers who believe that individuals are responsible for their illness may be less willing to provide appropriate assistance (Weiner, 1995). This may occur in situations in which an individual needs help accessing mental health or other social services. If an offense has occurred, officers who blame individuals for their illness may be more inclined to arrest the person, even if a deferral to mental health services would be more appropriate. Officers may also be less willing to assist individuals with mental illness who are victims of crime (Mastrofski, Snipes, & Parks, 2000). Similarly, officers who view individuals with mental illness as incompetent may be less willing to accept the information they provide as credible. This may cause police to disregard useful information from witnesses and potential suspects. It may also cause them to fail to believe and assist victims of crime. As this review shows, attitudes and beliefs held about mental illness by police officers, the gatekeepers of the criminal justice system, may have significant consequences in terms of safety and quality of life for both the general public and the individual with mental illness.

The Reaction of the General Health Care System

A research program by Benjamin Druss and colleagues seems to indicate that people with mental illness are less likely to benefit from the depth and breadth of the American health care system than people without these illnesses. Druss and colleagues completed two studies on large archival data that suggested people with mental illness receive fewer medical services that those not labeled in this manner (Desai, Rosenheck, Druss, & Perlin, 2002; Druss & Rosenheck, 1997). Moreover, studies by Druss and colleagues suggest individuals with mental illness are less likely to receive the same range of insurance benefits as people without mental illness (Druss, Allen, & Bruce, 1998; Druss & Rosenheck, 1998). Clearly, data by his group and others (Berk, Schur, & Cantor, 1995; Mark & Mueller, 1996) identifies a disparity in services across groups that are identified as mentally ill or not mentally ill. Unclear from this research is whether this disparity is due to stigma on the part of health care providers and insurers or represents economic and sociocultural variables that interact with the experience of mental illness. One study by Druss, Bradford, Rosenheck, Bradford, and Krumholz (2000) seems to implicate stigma more directly.

Previous research has used rates of procedures for cardiovascular disorders as an index of differential service rate by race (Ayanian, Udvarhelyi, Gatsonis, Pashos, & Epstein, 1993; Wenneker & Epstein, 1989) and gender (Ayanian & Epstein, 1991; Krumholz, Douglas, Lauer, & Pasternak, 1992) bias. For this reason, Druss and colleagues (2000) examined the likelihood of a range of medical procedures after myocardial infarction in a sample of 113,653. Compared to the remainder of the sample, Druss et al. found that people with comorbid psychiatric disorder were significantly less likely to undergo percutaneous transluminal coronary angioplasty. Once again, mental illness is indicated as a barrier to receiving appropriate care.

Nevertheless, the body of research by Druss and colleagues illustrates the difficulty of research that seeks to examine the impact of stigma. Although it is not unreasonable to conclude that people with mental health diagnoses receive less quality health care and coverage because of stigma, we cannot exclude a variety of other variables that also might account for this distinction. People with mental illness, for example, often find themselves in impoverished socioeconomic classes that traditionally receive less adequate care. Note, however, that these socioeconomic variables do not rule out stigma as a relevant variable. Link and Phelan (2001) argued that some socio-cultural differences between people with mental illness and the rest of the population may represent *structural stigma*. Namely, because of a history of stigma against mental illness, certain social structures develop that represent prejudice against this group. Research to examine the impact of social structures needs to include more macro social science theories and methods to illustrate these effects.

The Impact on Family Members, Providers, and Others

Stigma not only affects people with mental illness, but also those closely associated with the mentally ill. This phenomenon is alternatively called *courtesy stigma* (Goffman, 1963) or *associative stigma* (Mehta & Farina, 1988) and reflects the idea that the prejudice and discrimination experienced by persons with psychiatric disorders also affects family, providers, and others associated with the person with mental illness, albeit in muted form. The majority of research in this area has examined the impact of stigma on parents, spouses, siblings, and other family members. Hence, we will examine these studies in depth. There is also some mostly conjectural literature examining the stigma perceived by mental illness treatment providers. These reviews will be briefly summarized, too.

The Stigma Experienced by Family Members

Several studies have attempted to document the stigma experienced by family members of people with mental illness by surveying them directly (Lefley, 1987; Phelan, Bromet, & Link, 1998, Thompson & Doll, 1982; Wahl & Harman, 1989; Yarrow, Schwartz, Murphy, & Deasy, 1955) and have uncovered some recurring trends. The majority of family members in these studies reported that they were personally impacted by stigma. Wahl and Harman's (1989) study of 487 National Alliance for the Mentally Ill (NAMI) members, for example, showed that about a fifth of the sample reported stigma had impeded the quality of relationships with other family members and diminished their self-esteem. In a subsequent study of 156 parents and spouses of people with mental illness, Phelan and colleagues (1998) found that about a third of the sample actively tried to conceal the mental illness of their family member and about a quarter of the group at least occasionally experienced others trying to avoid them because of their relative.

Phelan and her colleagues concluded, from an analysis of both their data and previous studies, that families are currently experiencing greater courtesy stigma than 20 years earlier. Just as we need to be mindful of changing the stigma experienced by people with mental illness, so we need to consider the prejudice experienced by family members, too. Wahl and Harman's (1989) survey uncovered several aids to coping with courtesy stigma. Most prominent among these included factual information about mental illness, interaction with other families who have an individual with mental illness, and mutual support from within the family.

The Stigma Experienced by Treatment Providers

Several authors have expressed concern about the impact of mental illness stigma on mental health providers and their corresponding disciplines (Dichter, 1992; Dickstein & Hinz, 1992; Fink, 1986; Gabbard & Gabbard, 1992; Persaud, 2000). Because of stigma, authors have opined that undergraduates are less likely to pursue training in psychiatry and other mental health disciplines, residents and graduate level trainees experience stigma and demoralization as professionals, and actual practitioners feel underappreciated by their patients and by society as a whole. Moreover, treatment providers assert that mental health services receive fewer financial resources because of the stigma of mental illness. Although these viewpoints seem reasonable, the literature in this area is notable by the absence of empirical data. It is important, therefore, for researchers to develop and test hypotheses that reflect the impact of stigma on mental health providers. Interesting questions might include how stigma influences provider-level variables like job burnout or how stigma's effects on providers trickle down to the quality of care they provide consumers.

The Impact on the At-Large Public

Stigma also harms society and those in it (Corrigan & Lundin, 2001). It promotes injustices which undermine some of the basic assumptions of a community. It robs society of an important resource: persons with mental illness who could be gainful members of the neighborhood. Stigma perpetuates the personal fears of all citizens about becoming mentally ill and losing control. These areas have been highlighted more by advocates than studied by behavioral scientists. Hence, we briefly outline each area here as targets for future research.

The Injustice of Stigma Infects a Community

Clearly, citizens who agree with stereotypes about mental illness and choose to act on those stereotypes harm persons with psychiatric disorders. By no means, however, does the damage end there. Any kind of prejudice undermines ethical assumptions of the entire culture. For example, citizens of many societies believe individuals should have a fair opportunity to prove themselves on the basis of their actions and accomplishments. Stereotypes like those experienced by persons with mental illness challenge this fundamental belief. Stereotypes mean persons lose their chance to be successful because they belong to marked groups.

Stereotypes about mental illness are just one of many concrete examples of limited, categorical thinking about groups of people (Allport, 1988). This kind of naive categorizing ignores the unique and interesting differences among people. Instead, it paints all members of a group the same. Once these groups are identified, they can be quickly segregated from the majority. Black persons are different than White. Women are different from men. Mentally ill are different from "normals." Some may argue that recognizing these distinctions is nothing more than reflecting physical characteristics. Persons who promote these arguments, however, forget that the advancement of distinctions and differences undermines the sharing of resources.

Stigma Robs Communities of an Important Resource

Communities lose out from discrimination, too (Corrigan & Lundin, 2001). Instead of being productive members of society, many persons with mental illness unnecessarily must rely on handouts from their neighbors. They could be out working, earning a reasonable wage, and living independently. Instead, because of society's ignorance, they are deprived of job and housing opportunities and must be supported by government assistance.

There is also a more intangible loss that results from this kind of discrimination. Segregating persons with mental illness robs the community of the possible kind of interactions these individuals might bring. Persons with mental illness are kept from becoming active participants in the interchange among people. One of the wonders of melting pot societies like the United States is the diversity of perspectives represented by cultural and other differences. Through history, humans have discovered that excluding groups deprives society of vital segments.

Stigma Maintains Personal Fears

Fear of mental illness is personal; almost everyone worries at some time in their life about having a "nervous breakdown." People believe they are able to cope because of some personal strength and that mental illness is moral weakness. Persons with mental illness, so the theory goes, failed to choose a healthy lifestyle. This kind of logic is reflected in the "just world" hypothesis

(Lerner, 1965). Persons who experience significant life problems like mental illness must have a character flaw. A just world would never deal people such an unfair hand. Hence, persons with mental illness have earned the disrespect of their community.

Stigma maintains personal fears (Corrigan & Lundin, 2001). "If I were weak, I would become mentally ill like that homeless guy talking to himself." This kind of ignorance limits citizens' understanding of mental illness. In addition, it distances the general public from its own brushes with anxiety and depression. Instead of trying to understand how life events converged to cause emotional upset, persons steeped in stigmatizing beliefs deny their own woes so they aren't associated with "these weak mentally ill."

THE IMPACT OF SELF-STIGMA

Living in a culture steeped in stigmatizing images, persons with mental illness may accept these notions and experience diminished self-esteem, self-efficacy, and confidence in one's future as a result (Corrigan, 1998; Holmes & River, 1998). Persons with mental illness like Kathleen Gallo have written eloquently about this kind of self-stigma.

> I perceived myself, quite accurately unfortunately, as having a serious mental illness and therefore as having been relegated to what I called "the social garbage heap." . . . I tortured myself with the persistent and repetitive thought that people I would encounter, even total strangers, did not like me and wished that mentally ill people like me did not exist. Thus, I would do things such as standing away from others at bus stops and hiding and cringing in the far corners of subway cars. Thinking of myself as garbage, I would even leave the sidewalk in what I thought of as exhibiting the proper deference to those above me in social class. The latter group, of course, included all other human beings. (Gallo, 1994, pp. 407–408)

First-person narratives such as this one, as well as other subjective data, provide a compelling illustration of the impact of stigma on a person's self-esteem (Davidson, 1992; Estroff, 1989; Strauss, 1989; see also chap. 3, this volume). Qualitative data of this sort have been augmented by quantitative surveys of persons with mental illness. For example, studies of persons with mental illness and their families showed self-esteem to be a significant problem (Wahl, 1999; Wahl & Harman, 1989).

As suggested by the earlier described societal reaction theory, first impressions about the stigma of mental illness suggest that people with psychiatric disability, living in a society that widely endorses stigmatizing ideas, will internalize these ideas and believe that they are less valued because of their psychiatric disorder (Link, 1987; Link & Phelan, 2001). Like public stigma, self-stigma includes prejudice and its components. First, persons who agree with prejudice concur with the stereotype: "That's right; I am weak and unable to care for myself!" In addition, self-prejudice leads to negative emotional reactions. Prominent among these are low self-esteem and self-efficacy. Self-esteem is typically operationalized in this kind of research as the rating of agreement of personal worth on Likert scale items (Corrigan, Faber, Rashid, & Leary, 1999; Rosenberg, 1965). Self-efficacy is defined here as the expectation that one can successfully perform a behavior in a specific situation (Bandura, 1977, 1989) and is often assessed with self-report measures (Sherer & Adams, 1983).

Self-prejudice may also lead to behavioral responses. Low self-efficacy and demoralization has been shown to be associated with failing to pursue work or independent living opportunities at which persons might otherwise succeed (Link, 1982, 1987). Obviously, this kind of self-stereotype, self-prejudice, and self-discrimination will significantly interfere with a person's life goals and quality of life; this impact is discussed more fully below. However, it is also important to remember that self-stigma is not universal.

Diminished Self-Esteem Is Not Inevitable

Many persons with mental illness are aware of the stereotypes that exist about their group. However, awareness of stigma is not synonymous with internalizing it (Crocker & Major, 1989). Many persons with mental illness report being aware of the negative stereotypes about them (Bowden, Schoenfeld, & Adams, 1980; Kahn, Obstfeld, & Heiman, 1979; Shurka, 1983; Wright, Gronfein, & Owens, 2000) but do not necessarily agree with these stereotypes (Hayward & Bright, 1997). Hence, not every person with a mental disorder reacts to the stigma of mental illness with a loss of self-esteem. Quite the contrary, some individuals are energized by prejudice and express righteous anger. Others neither experience lowered self-esteem nor become righteously angry; instead, these individuals seem to ignore the effects of public prejudice altogether.

Long-standing theories have represented self-stigma as the automatic result of being a member of a stigmatized group (Allport, 1954/1979; Erikson, 1956; Jones et al., 1984). Accordingly, African Americans, women, and persons with physical disabilities would all be expected to have lower self-esteem compared to the majority. Several studies have shown, however, that people of color and other ethnic minorities do not have lower self-esteem than the White majority (Hoelter, 1983; Jensen, White, & Gelleher, 1982; Porter & Washington, 1979; Verkuyten, 1994, 1995; Wylie, 1979). Nor are women shown to have lower self-esteem than men (Maccoby & Jacklin, 1974; Wylie, 1979). Similar results have been found in persons with mental illness, in spite of their awareness of the stigmatizing views about them. Despite this awareness, several studies have been unable to find a sharp decline in self-esteem in this group (see Hayward & Bright, 1997, for a review).

Crocker and colleagues (Crocker & Lawrence, 1999; Crocker & Major, 1989) highlight an even more amazing trend in stigma and self-esteem. Several stigmatized groups showed higher self-esteem than the majority; participants in these studies included persons of color (Hoelter, 1983; Jensen, White, & Gelleher, 1982; Porter & Washington, 1979) and people with disabilities (Fine & Caldwell, 1967; Willey & McCandless, 1973). It seems that being stigmatized somehow stimulates psychological reactance (Brehm, 1966), suggesting that rather than complying with the perceived threat of stigma and viewing one's self poorly, an individual opposes the negative evaluation and positive self-perceptions emerge. Research on empowerment supports this concept, showing persons with psychiatric disability who, despite this disability, have positive self-esteem and are not significantly encumbered by a stigmatizing community. Instead, they seem to be energized by the stigma to righteous anger (Corrigan et al., 1999; Rogers, Chamberlin, Ellison, & Crean, 1997). Righteous anger is evident in many of the narratives of persons with serious mental illness: "I was angry that I'd been crazy, but I was even more angry at the inhumane, hurtful, degrading, and judgmental 'treatment' I'd been subjected to" (Unzicker, 1989, p. 71; see also Davidson, Stayner, & Haglund, 1998; Estroff, 1995).

In addition to those who view mental illness stereotypes as unjust, persons who find them irrelevant will also experience no reduction in self-esteem due to stigma. Persons with intact self-esteem will respond to stigma with indifference or indignation depending on their identification with the generic group of people with mental illness. Those with high group identification will show righteous anger. Those who do not identify with the group will be indifferent to stigma.

The Impact on Accessing Services

Self-stigma may have another unfortunate effect: people may opt to not seek out treatment so they are not identified with this stigmatized group. Research has shown that the psychiatric symptoms, psychological distress, and life disabilities caused by many mental illnesses are significantly remedied by a variety of psychopharmacological and psychosocial treatments. Unfortunately, research also suggests that many people who meet criteria for treatment, and who are likely to improve after participation, either opt not to seek services or fail to fully adhere to treatments once they are prescribed. Results from the Epidemiologic Catchment Area (ECA) Study show that only 60% of people with schizophrenia participated in treatment (Regier, Narrow, Rae,

& Manderscheid, 1993). Taking into account the severity of one's mental disorder, Narrow and colleagues (2000) found that people with serious mental illness were no more likely to participate in treatment than those with relatively minor disorders. A subsequent study, the National Comorbidity Survey, on the epidemiology of adult psychopathologies showed similar results (Kessler et al., 2001). Fewer than 40% of the 6.2% of respondents with serious mental illness received stable treatment in the past year, with young adults and individuals living in more urban/suburban areas more likely to have unmet needs.

Many people choose not to pursue mental health services because they do not want to be labeled a "mental patient" or experience the prejudice and discrimination that the label entails. Early research on this matter (cf. Lorion, 1974 for a review) tried to distinguish the effects of stigmatizing attitudes related to treatment (e.g., I must be weak if I need counseling) from other kinds of misconceptions about treatment (e.g., psychotherapists don't believe in God and discourage spiritual concerns) (Garfield & Bergin, 1971). Some support for the relationship between stigma and participating in mental health care services was provided by epidemiological studies on adult psychopathology. Results gleaned from the Yale arm of the Epidemiological Catchment Area data (Leaf, Bruce, & Tischler, 1986) showed respondents with psychiatric diagnosis were more likely to avoid services if they were unreceptive to treatment (e.g., agreeing that people should not seek care if they have a mental or emotional problem) or believed family members would have a negative reaction to these services. A second study by the same group completed on 3,058 community residents showed similar results; namely, negative attitudes inhibit service utilization in those at risk for psychiatric disorder (Leaf, Bruce, Tischler, & Holzer, 1987). Results from the National Comorbidity Survey suggest several beliefs that might sway people from treatment (Kessler et al., 2001). These include concerns about what others might think and the desire to solve one's own problems. Finally, positive attitudes of family members were associated with greater service use in a sample of more than 1,000 drawn from a representative community sample and a group from a mental health clinic (Greenley, Mechanic, & Clearly, 1987). Using the Scale of Perceived Stigma (Link, Struening, Cullen, & Shrout, 1989), a 20-item scale that represents beliefs about the devaluation and discrimination directed toward persons with mental illness, Sirey and colleagues (2001) found a direct relationship between stigmatizing attitudes and treatment adherence. Scores on the utilized scale were associated with whether 134 adults were compliant with their antidepressant medication regimen 3 months later. Hence, perceptions of and identification with existing stereotypes about mental illness can hinder persons in getting much needed help, which may make their lives unnecessarily more difficult.

UNDERSTANDING STIGMA AT THE SOCIETAL LEVEL

Thus far, this chapter has provided an overview of psychological models of stigma, descriptions of cognitive–behavioral processes engaged in by individuals that harm people with mental illness (public stigma) or themselves (self-stigma). The individual level of analysis only provides half the picture of the egregious impact of stigma. Sociologists have also discussed how political, economic, and historical forces create societal-level phenomena that diminish the life opportunities of people with mental illness and hence become stigma (Link & Phelan, 2001; Pincus, 1999a; Rubinstein, 1994; Wilson, 1987). As outlined in Figure 1.3, two levels of stigma in society have been identified: institutional policies and social structures. The key distinction between this form of stigma, and stigma at an individual level of analysis, is the emergence of societal forms and structures that restrict the life opportunities of people with mental illness. Although concepts related to institutional and structural stigma have a prominent role in understanding racism and sexism, related models have not been well-developed in explaining mental illness stigma except for an important paper by Link and Phelan (2001). This paper illustrates how social structures may impede the opportunities of people with mental illness.

INSTITUTIONAL POLICIES	SOCIAL STRUCTURES
Based on prejudice of people in leadership positions	The effects of prejudice and discrimination: • historically • politically • economically
Translated into laws and regulations that discriminate against people with mental illness	Structures: • Lack of parity in health benefits appropriations

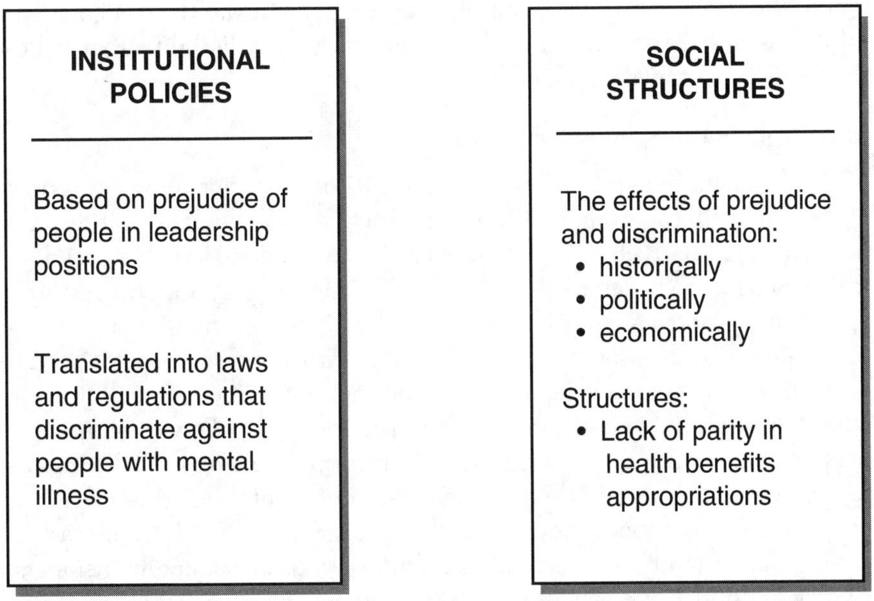

Figure 1.3. Societal levels of stigma: institutional policies and structural stigma.

Institutional Policies and Stigma

Pincus (1999a) argues that stereotypes and prejudice can have a major impact on people of color when they are enacted into rules that impede their opportunities. These can be formal legislation at various levels of government like the Jim Crow laws of the late nineteenth and early twentieth century that robbed African Americans of their right to vote. They can be company policy such as banks that do not provide mortgages to minorities in red line neighborhoods. They can be less formal polices such as restaurant chains like *Denny's* that, in the 1990s, instructed their employees to provide a lesser grade of service to people of color. In each case, there is one person (e.g., the CEO of a company) or a group of people (e.g., a legislative bloc) in positions of power with a prejudicial agenda who promote this agenda by enacting policies that discriminate against a group.

Similar examples are evident for people with mental illness, especially in government institutions. Research has shown that there are state laws in effect that restrict the rights of people with mental illness in terms of such fundamental opportunities and privileges as jury service, voting, holding public office, marriage, and parenting (Hemmens, Miller, Burton, & Milner, 2002). In fact, findings from this survey suggest restriction of familial rights may be worsening for people with mental illness, despite an increasing concern about prejudice in this arena. Another study shows that mental illness continues to be used as a rationale for restricting medical licensure (Hansen, Goetz, Bloom, & Fenn, 1997). Results suggested that it was the label of mental illness, rather than evidence of current psychiatric disability, that led to the restriction of medical practice.

Methods for Studying Institutional Stigma

Although there is some evidence of institutional stigma toward people with mental illness, comprehensive empirical data documenting the phenomenon are relatively scarce. However, the few studies as well as sociological paradigms that describe institutional stigma suggest a useful research approach for more carefully documenting the phenomenon. Given that virtually all of state legislation is now accessible through the Internet, a search of the Lexis and Westlaw databases for existing statutes by state will provide a historical record of that state's characterization of people with mental illness. Examining the state's perspective on mental illness is especially important given its dominant role in the provision of mental health services for children and adults with serious disorders. To complete this research task, a focus group of multiple stakeholders including consumers, family members, providers, and legislators will need to generate a comprehensive list of key words to guide the search of the database. Candidates for these key words include psychiatric terms like *mental illness* and *disability* as well as legal terms like *lunatic* and *insanity*.

Although this kind of comprehensive search will provide a historical picture of each state's set of laws, it may generate some false positives in terms of institutional stigma. Most states in the Union have outdated (seemingly silly) laws that have never been removed from the books; for example, Illinois defines vagrancy as individuals who do not have at least one dollar bill on their person and requires contacting the police before entering their city in an automobile. Hence, finding a law that discriminates against people with mental illness in State A does not mean it is actively followed in that state. One way to avoid this "antiquated status effect" is to complete a Lexis and Westlaw survey of all bills that were proposed to each state's legislature in the past year. This kind of analysis not only shows the products of a carefully deliberated political process but also the "on the floor" musings of individual legislative blocs vis-à-vis mental illness. A similar snapshot can be obtained of the judiciary by examining Lexis and Westlaw for findings of the appellate courts in each state.

Not every governmental action involving mental illness represents institutional stigma. Hence, the products of these database surveys must then be coded in terms of stigma. Two elements of this interpretation are required. (a) Do the legislation or court findings result in lost opportunities for people with mental illness; for example, can people with mental illness not obtain certain kinds of jobs? (b) Do these lost opportunities represent the stigma of the label ("People who are mentally ill cannot") or the disability commensurate with the label ("People who are currently disabled because of mental illness cannot do X until the disability remits.")? Our group is currently working on a subset of this research agenda with the NAMI TRIAD project; TRIAD is the Treatment/Recovery Information and Advocacy Database which, among its many goals, has determined to obtain indicators of each state's success and failures in the public mental health system. Not only is the proposed research fruitful for reasons of scholarship, but documenting statutes, bills, and rules by state will also serve the advocacy agenda of groups like NAMI. For example, the National Office and local affiliates can write to State A, notify them of recent and specific governmental activity that restricts the opportunities of people with mental illness (e.g., "HB XXX restricts the voting rights of people with mental illness"), and ask for correction of this bias.

Social Structures and Stigma

Typically, institutional stigma arises from the prejudices of individuals in power who enact legislation and administrative rules that discriminate against people with mental illness (Pincus, 1996, 1999a; Wilson, 1987). Sociologists have also identified structural stigma that develops historically as the result of the economic and political injustices wrought by prejudice and discrimination. Once again, this concept has mostly been used to explain racism and sexism. Pincus (1999a), for example, describes the disparity of insurances rates across White and Black communities. Although agents might explain this as the result of higher rates of street crime in lower-income Black communities, it nevertheless results in higher premiums for people of color. The key element of structural stigma is not the intent but rather the effect of keeping certain groups in a subordinate position. Hence, there is not clearly a prejudicial group in power maintaining structural stigma; rather, it is the product of historical trends in discrimination.

Inability to achieve parity in mental health insurance with general medical coverage may be an example of structural stigma related to mental illness (Feldman, Bachman, & Bayer, 2002). Although failure of legislatures to endorse parity may be affected by the individual prejudices of some representatives and senators (Corrigan & Watson, 2003), it also represents the insidious effects of structural stigma. Namely, several decades of history where insurance benefits for physical illness have surpassed those for mental illness leads to the assumption that greater benefits for mental health will produce diminished benefits for physical health, an assumption, by the way, that may not be borne out by actual evidence. The significantly lower rate of federal monies for mental health research, compared to other areas of health research, is another example of structural stigma (Link & Phelan, 2001). The latter example also shows the circular nature of structural stigma. Knowledge about mental illness that will diminish stigma, and hence lead to more enlightened policies about funding research, cannot be increased because funding agencies are not supporting studies in the psychiatric arena at the same rate as other general medical conditions.

The Role of Affirmative Actions

Pincus (1999b) believes that affirmative actions are needed to resolve structural discrimination and stigma. Affirmative action was originally thrust on the American political scene as an Executive Order signed by Lyndon Johnson directing Federal contractors to develop a hiring plan that would increase the number of women and minorities in all job categories of their business. This plan was seeking to resolve the historical disparities in hiring practices that kept people of color and women out of better jobs. More broadly put, affirmative action might be construed as any official effort that seeks to decrease structural stigma by purposively and strategically increasing the opportunities of a stigmatized group. Two examples come to mind in terms of mental illness. Reasonable accommodations for people with psychiatric disabilities are the first. An important clause of the Americans With Disabilities Act (ADA), reasonable accommodations are those provisions that employers must supply to employees with disabilities so these employees can competently do their job. The provision of these accommodations may not cause undue burden to employers and their business. Common examples of these kinds of accommodations include wheelchair-accessible work environments so that people with ambulatory disabilities can easily navigate their offices. More difficult to define have been accommodations for people with psychiatric disabilities (MacDonald-Wilson, Rogers, Massaro, Lyass, & Crean, 2002; Mechanic, 1998). They have included the provision of flexible schedules and job coaching so people with mental illness can cope with the stress of job demands.

The U.S. Supreme Court's ruling in Olmstead versus L.C. is a second example where court decisions have led to affirmative actions for people with mental illness. In this case, the State of Georgia was found to be in limited violation of the ADA because it did not provide community services to psychiatric inpatients (Cohen, 2001; Herbert & Young, 1999). In particular, the High Court found that the state could not avoid its duties under the ADA because the legislature did not appropriate sufficient funds to support community programs for people with psychiatric disabilities in need of these services. To comply with the ruling, states must develop comprehensive plans to end unnecessary institutionalization (Bazelon Center, 1999). Hence, the Supreme Court is requiring affirmative actions that challenge the kinds of structural stigmas that have evolved over time.

CONCLUSION

We hoped to illustrate in this opening chapter that stigma is a complex phenomenon which has a broad and harmful impact on people with mental illness. Sense was made of the complex phenomenon by distinguishing public stigma from self-stigma and examining social cognitive concepts that are implicated in each. Full understanding of the experience of stigma is going to require a variety of social scientific models; additional paradigms examined in this book include social psychological, sociological, and historical models. We expect that information that emerges from scientific efforts in each of these paradigms will uncover ways to effectively address public and self-stigma. Advocates may then call on this body of knowledge to put into practice the kind of ideas outlined through this enterprise. Service providers including psychologists, psychiatrists, social workers, and psychiatric nurses may use this information to help people with mental illness better deal with stigma.

REFERENCES

Allport, A. (1988). What concept of consciousness? In A. J. Marcel & E. Bisiach (Ed.), *Consciousness in contemporary science* (pp. 159–182). Oxford, England: Clarendon Press.

Allport, G. W. (1979). *The nature of prejudice*. New York: Doubleday. (Original work published 1954)

American Psychiatric Association. (2000). *Diagnostic and statistical manual of mental disorders* (4th ed., text rev.). Washington, DC: Author.

Anthony, W., & Blanch, A. (1987). Supported employment for persons who are psychiatrically disabled: An historical and conceptual perspective. *Psychosocial Rehabilitation Journal, 11,* 5–23.

Augoustinos, M., Ahrens, C., & Innes, J. (1995). Stereotypes and prejudice: The Australian experience. *British Journal of Social Psychology, 33,* 125–141.

Aviram, U., & Segal, S. (1973). Exclusion of the mentally ill: Reflection on an old problem in a new context. *Archives of General Psychiatry, 29,* 126–131.

Ayanian, J. Z., & Epstein, A. M. (1991). Differences in the use of procedures between women and men hospitalized for coronary heart disease. *New England Journal of Medicine, 325,* 221–225.

Ayanian, J. Z., Udvarhelyi, I. S., Gatsonis, C. A., Pashos, C. L., & Epstein, A. M. (1993). Racial differences in the use of revascularization procedures after coronary angiography. *Journal of the American Medical Association, 269,* 2642–2646.

Bandura, A. (1977). Self-efficacy: Toward a unifying theory of behavioral change. *Psychological Review, 84,* 191–215.

Bandura, A. (1989). Regulation of cognitive processes through perceived self-efficacy. *Developmental Psychology, 25,* 729–735.

Bazelon Center. (1999). *Under court order: What the community integration mandate means for people with mental illnesses* [On-line]. Retrieved June 9, 2004 from http://www.bazelon.org/issues/disabilityrights/resources/olmstead/under/

Bellack, A. S., Morrison, R. L., Mueser, K. T., & Wade, J. H. (1990). Role play for assessing the social competence of psychiatric patients. *Psychological Assessment, 2,* 248–255.

Berk, M. L., Schur, C. L., & Cantor, J. C. (1995). Ability to obtain health care: recent estimates from the Robert Wood Johnson Foundation National Access to Care Survey. *Health Affairs, 14*(3), 139–146.

Bhugra, D. (1989). Attitudes towards mental illness: A review of the literature. *Acta Psychiatrica Scandinavica, 80,* 1–12.

Bordieri, J., & Dremer, D. (1986). Hiring decisions for disabled workers: Looking at the cause. *Journal of Applied Social Psychology, 16,* 197–208.

Bowden, C. L., Schoenfeld, L. S., & Adams, R. L. (1980). Mental health attitudes and treatment expectations as treatment variables. *Journal of Clinical Psychology, 36,* 653–657.

Brehm, J. W. (1966). *A theory of psychological reactance.* New York: Academic Press.

Brockington, I., Hall, P., Levings, J., & Murphy, C. (1993). The community's tolerance of the mentally ill. *British Journal of Psychiatry, 162,* 93–99.

Carling, P. (1990). Major mental illness, housing, and supports: The promise of community integration. *American Psychologist, 45,* 969–975.

Cohen, P. S. (2001). Being "reasonable": Defining and implementing a right to community-based care for older adults with mental disabilities under the Americans with Disabilities Act. *International Journal of Law and Psychiatry, 24,* 233–252.

Corrigan, P. W. (1998). The impact of stigma on severe mental illness. *Cognitive and Behavioral Practice*, 5, 201–222.

Corrigan, P. W. (2000). Mental health stigma as social attribution: Implications for research methods and attitude change. *Clinical Psychology: Science and Practice*, 7, 48–67.

Corrigan, P. W. (2001). Place-then-train: An alternative paradigm for psychiatric disabilities. *Clinical Psychology: Science and Practice*, 8, 334–349.

Corrigan, P. W. (2002). Testing social psychological models of mental illness stigma: The Prairie State Stigma Studies. *Psychiatric Rehabilitation Skills*, 6, 232–254.

Corrigan, P., Backs, A., Green, A., Diwan, S., & Penn, D. (2001). Prejudice, social distance, and familiarity with mental illness. *Psychiatric Service*, 27, 219–226.

Corrigan, P. W., Faber, D., Rashid, F., & Leary, M. (1999). The construct validity of empowerment among consumers of mental health services. *Schizophrenia Research*, 38, 77–87.

Corrigan, P. W., & Lundin, R. (2001). *Don't call me nuts: Coping with the stigma of mental illness.* Tinley Park, IL: Recovery Press.

Corrigan, P. W., & Watson, A. C. (2003). Factors explaining how policy makers distribute resources to mental health services? *Psychiatric Services*, 54, 501–507.

Crocetti, G., Spiro, Herzl, R., & Siassi, I. (1971). Are the ranks closed? Attitudinal social distance and mental illness. *American Journal of Psychiatry*, 127, 1121–1127.

Crocker, J., & Lawrence, J. S. (1999). Social stigma and self-esteem: The role of contingencies of worth. In D. A. Prentice & D. T. Miller (Eds.), *Cultural divides: Understanding and overcoming group conflict* (pp. 364–392). New York: Russell Sage Foundation.

Crocker, J., Major, B. (1989). Social stigma and self-esteem: The self-protective properties of stigma. *Psychological Review*, 96, 608–630.

Crocker, J., Major, B., & Steele, C. (1998). Social stigma. In D. Gilbert, S. T. Fiske, & G. Lindzey (Eds.), *The handbook of social psychology* (4th ed., Vol. 2, pp. 504–553). New York: McGraw-Hill.

Davidson, L. (1992). Developing an empirical-phenomenological approach to schizophrenia research. *Journal of Phenomenological Psychology*, 23, 3–15.

Davidson, L., Stayner, D., & Haglund, K. E. (1998). Phenomenological perspectives on the social functioning of people with schizophrenia. In K. T. Mueser & N. Tarrier (Eds.), *Handbook of social functioning in schizophrenia* (pp. 97–120). Needham Heights, MA: Allyn & Bacon.

Desai, M. M., Rosenheck, R. A., Druss, B. G., & Perlin, J. B. (2002). Mental disorders and quality of care among postacute myocardial infarction outpatients. *Journal of Nervous and Mental Disease*, 190, 51–53.

Devine, P. G. (1988). *Stereotype assessment: Theoretical and methodological issues.* Madison: University of Wisconsin–Madison Press.

Devine, P. G. (1989). Stereotypes and prejudice: Their automatic and controlled components. *Journal of Personality and Social Psychology*, 56, 5–18.

Devine, P. G. (1995). Getting hooked on research in social psychology: Examples from eyewitness identification and prejudice. In G. G. Brannigan & M. R. Merrens (Eds.), *The social psychologists: Research adventures* (pp. 161–184). New York: McGraw-Hill.

Dichter, H. (1992). The stigmatization of psychiatrists who work with chronically mentally ill persons. In P. J. Fink & A. Tasman (Eds.), *Stigma and mental illness* (pp. 203–215). Washington, DC: American Psychiatric Press.

Dickstein, L. J., & Hinz, L. D. (1992). The stigma of mental illness for medical students and residents. In P. J. Fink & A. Tasman (Eds.), *Stigma and mental illness* (pp. 153–165). Washington, DC: American Psychiatric Press.

Ditton, P. M. (1999, July). *Mental health and treatment of inmates and probationers.* Washington, DC: U.S. Department of Justice, Office of Justice Programs, Bureau of Justice Statistics.

Druss, B. G., Allen, H. M., Jr., & Bruce, M. L. (1998). Physical health, depressive symptoms, and managed care enrollment. *American Journal of Psychiatry, 155,* 878–882.

Druss, B. G., Bradford, D. W, Rosenheck, R. A., Radford, M. J., & Krumholz, H. M. (2000). Mental disorders and use of cardiovascular procedures after myocardial infarction. *Journal of the American Medical Association, 283,* 506–511.

Druss, B. G., & Rosenheck, R. A. (1997). Use of medical services by veterans with mental disorders. *Psychosomatics, 38,* 451–458.

Druss, B. G., & Rosenheck, R. A. (1998). Mental disorders and access to medical care in the United States. *American Journal of Psychiatry, 155,* 1775–1777.

Eagly, A. H., Ashmore, R. D., Makhijani, M. G., & Longo, L. C. (1991). What is beautiful is good, but . . .: A meta-analytic review of research on the physical attractiveness stereotype. *Psychological Bulletin, 110,* 109–128.

Eagly, A., & Chaiken, S. (1993). *The social psychology of attitudes.* Fort Worth, TX: Harcourt.

Engel, R. S., & Silver, E. (2001). Policing mentally disordered suspects: A reexamination of the criminalization hypothesis. *Criminology, 39,* 225–252.

Erikson, E. (1956). The problem of ego-identity. *Journal of the American Psychoanalytic Association, 4,* 56–121.

Esses, V., Haddock, G., & Zanna, M. (1994.) The role of mood in the expression of intergroup stereotypes. In M. Zanna & J. Olson (Eds.), *The psychology of prejudice: The Ontario Symposium* (Vol. 7, pp. 77–101). Hilldale, NJ: Erlbaum.

Estroff, S. E. (1989). Self, identity, and subjective experiences of schizophrenia: In search of the subject. *Schizophrenia Bulletin, 15,* 189–196.

Estroff, S. E. (1995). Whose story is it anyway? Authority, voice, and responsibility in narratives of chronic illness. In S. K. Toombs & D. Barnard (Eds.), *Chronic illness: From experience to policy.* (pp. 77–102). Bloomington: Indiana University Press.

Farina, A., & Felner, R. (1973). Employment interviewer reactions to former mental patients. *Journal of Abnormal Psychology, 82,* 268–272.

Farina, A., Felner, R. D., & Boudreau, L. A. (1973). Reactions of workers to male and female mental patient job applicants. *Journal of Consulting and Clinical Psychology, 41,* 363–372.

Farina, A., Fisher, J., & Fischer, E. (1992). Societal factors in the problems faced by deinstitutionalized psychiatric patients. In P. Fink & A. Tasman (Eds.), *Stigma and mental illness* (pp. 167–184). Washington, DC: American Psychiatric Press.

Farina, A., Thaw, J., Lovern, J., & Mangone, D. (1974). People's reactions to a former mental patient moving to their neighborhood. *Journal of Community Psychology, 2,* 108–112.

Feldman, S., Bachman, J., & Bayer, J. (2002). Mental health parity: A review of research and a bibliography. *Administration and Policy in Mental Health, 29,* 215–228.

Fine, M. J., & Caldwell, T. E. (1967). Self evaluation of school related behavior of educable mentally retarded children: A preliminary report. *Exceptional Children, 33,* 324.

Fink, P. J. (1986). Dealing with psychiatry's stigma. *Hospital and Community Psychiatry, 37,* 814–818.

Gabbard, G. O., & Gabbard, K. (1992). Cinematic stereotypes contributing to the stigmatization of psychiatrists. In P. J. Fink & A. Tasman (Eds.), *Stigma and mental illness* (pp. 113–126). Washington, DC: American Psychiatric Press.

Gallo, K. M. (1994). First person account: Self-stigmatization. *Schizophrenia Bulletin, 20,* 407–410.

Garfield, S. L., & Bergin, A. E. (1971). Personal therapy, outcome and some therapist variables. *Psychotherapy: Theory, Research and Practice, 8,* 251–253.

Goffman, E. (1961). *Asylums.* New York: Doubleday.

Goffman, E. (1963). *Stigma: Notes on the management of spoiled identity.* Englewood Cliffs, NJ: Prentice Hall.

Gove, W. R. (Ed). (1975). *The labeling of deviance: Evaluating a perspective.* New York: Wiley.

Gove, W. R. (1980). Labeling and mental illness: A critique. In W. Gove (Ed.), *Labeling deviant behavior* (pp. 53–109). Beverly Hills, CA: Sage.

Gove, W. R. (1982). Labeling theory's explanation of mental illness: An update of recent evidence. *Deviant Behavior, 3,* 307–327.

Gove, W. R., & Fain, T. (1973). The stigma of mental hospitalization: An attempt to evaluate its consequences. *Archives of General Psychiatry, 29,* 494–500.

Greenley, J. (1984). Social factors, mental illness, and psychiatric care: Recent advances from a sociological perspective. *Hospital and Community Psychiatry, 35,* 813–820.

Greenley, J. R., Mechanic, D., & Cleary, P. (1987). Seeking help for psychological problems: A replication and extension. *Medical Care, 25,* 1113–1128.

Hamilton, D. L., & Sherman, J. W. (1994). Stereotypes. In R. S. Wyer & T. K. Srull (Eds.), *Handbook of social cognition, Vol. 1: Basic processes; Vol. 2: Applications,* (2nd ed., pp. 1–68). Hillsdale, NJ: Erlbaum.

Hamre, P., Dahl, A., & Malt, U. (1994). Public attitudes to the quality of psychiatric treatment, psychiatric patients, and prevalence of mental disorders. *Norwegian Journal of Psychiatry, 4,* 275–281.

Hansen, T. E., Goetz, R. R., Bloom, J. D., & Fenn, D. S. (1997). Changes in questions about psychiatric illness asked on medical licensure applications between 1993 and 1996. *Psychiatric Services, 49,* 202–206.

Hayward, P., & Bright, J. A. (1997). Stigma and mental illness: A review and critique. *Journal of Mental Health, 6,* 345–354.

Hemmens, C., Miller, M., Burton, V. S., & Milner, S. (2002). The consequences of official labels: An examination of the rights lost by the mentally ill and mentally incompetent ten years later. *Community Mental Health Journal, 38,* 129–140.

Herbert, P. B., & Young, K. A. (1999). The Americans with Disabilities Act and deinstitutionalization of the chronically mentally ill. *Journal of the American Academy of Psychiatry and the Law, 27,* 603–613.

Hilton, J., & von Hippel, W. (1996). Stereotypes. *Annual Review of Psychology, 47,* 237–271.

Hoelter, J. W. (1983). Factorial invariance and self-esteem: Reassessing race and sex differences. *Social Forces, 61,* 834–846.

Hogan, R. (1985a). *Gaining community support for group homes.* Unpublished manuscript, Purdue University.

Hogan, R. (1985b). *Not in my town: Local government in opposition to group homes.* Unpublished manuscript, Purdue University.

Holmes, P. E., & River, L. P. (1998). Individual strategies for coping with the stigma of severe mental illness. *Cognitive and Behavioral Practice, 5,* 231–239.

Huffine, C., & Clausen, J. (1979). Madness and work: Short- and long-term effects of mental illness on occupational careers. *Social Forces, 57,* 1049–1062.

Jemelka, R., Trupin, E., & Chiles, J. A. (1989). The mentally ill in prisons: A review. *Hospital and Community Psychiatry, 40,* 481–491.

Jensen, G. F., White, C. S., & Gelleher, J. M. (1982). Ethnic status and adolescent self-evaluations: An extension of research on minority self-esteem. *Social Problems, 30,* 226–239.

Jones, E. E., Farina, A., Hastorf, A. H., Markus, H., Miller, D. T., & Scott, R. A. (1984). *Social stigma: The psychology of marked relationships.* New York: Freeman.

Judd, C., & Park, B. (1993). Definition and assessment of accuracy in stereotypes. *Psychological Review, 100,* 109–128.

Jussim, L., Nelson, T. E., Manus, M., & Soffin, S. (1995). Prejudice, stereotypes, and labeling effects: Sources of bias in person perception. *Journal of Personality and Social Psychology, 68,* 228–246.

Kahn, M. W., Obstfeld, L., & Heiman, E. (1979). Staff conceptions of patients' attitudes toward mental disorder and hospitalization as compared to patients' and staff's actual attitudes. *Journal of Clinical Psychology, 35,* 415–420.

Karmel, M. (1969). Total institution and self-mortification. *Journal of Health and Social Behavior, 10*(2), 134–141.

Kessler, R. C., Berglund, P. A., Bruce, M. L., Koch, R., Laska, E. M., Leaf, P. J., et al. (2001). The prevalence and correlates of untreated serious mental illness. *Health Services Research, 36,* 987–1007.

Koegel, P. (1992). Through a different lens: An anthropological perspective on the homeless mentally ill. *Culture, Medicine and Psychiatry, 16*, 1–22.

Krueger, J. (1996). Personal beliefs and cultural stereotypes about racial characteristics. *Journal of Personality and Social Psychology, 71*, 536–548.

Krumholz, H. M., Douglas, P. S., Lauer, M. S., & Pasternak, R. C. (1992). Selection of patients for coronary angiography and coronary revascularization early after myocardial infarction: Is there evidence for a gender bias? *Annals of Internal Medicine, 116*, 785–790.

LaGrange, T. (2000, November). *Distinguishing between the criminal and the "crazy": Decisions to arrest in police encounters with mentally disordered.* Paper presented at the American Society of Criminology, San Francisco, CA.

Lamb, H. R., & Weinberger, L. E. (1998). Persons with severe mental illness in jails and prisons: A review. *Psychiatric Services, 49*, 483–492.

Leaf, P. J., Bruce, M. L., & Tischler, G. L. (1986). The differential effect of attitudes on the use of mental health services. *Social Psychiatry, 21*, 187–192.

Leaf, P. J., Bruce, M. L., Tischler, G. L., & Holzer, C. E. (1987). The relationship between demographic factors and attitudes toward mental health services. *Journal of Community Psychology, 15*, 275–284.

Lefley, H. P. (1987). Impact of mental illness in families of mental health professionals. *Journal of Nervous and Mental Disease, 175*, 613–619.

Lehman, A. (1988). A Quality of Life Interview for the chronically mentally ill. *Evaluation and Program Planning, 11*, 51–62.

Lehman, S., Joy, V., Kreisman, D., & Simmens, S. (1976). Responses to viewing symptomatic behaviors and labeling or prior mental illness. *Journal of Community Psychology, 4*, 327–334.

Lerner, M. (1965). Evaluation of performance as a function of performer's reward and attractiveness. *Journal of Personality and Social Psychology, 1*, 355–360.

Lerner, M. (1980). *The belief in a just world: A fundamental delusion.* New York: Plenum Press.

Link, B. G. (1982). Mental patient status, work and income: An examination of the effects of a psychiatric label. *American Sociological Review, 47*, 202–215.

Link, B. G. (1987). Understanding labeling effects in the area of mental disorders: An assessment of the effects of expectations of rejection. *American Sociological Review, 52*, 96–112.

Link, B. G., & Cullen, F. T. (1986). Contact with the mentally ill and perceptions of how dangerous they are. *Journal of Health and Social Behavior, 27*, 289–302.

Link, B. G., Cullen, F. T., Frank, J., & Wozniak, J. (1987). The social rejection of former mental patients: Understanding why labels matter. *American Journal of Sociology, 92*, 1461–1500.

Link, B. G., Cullen, F. T., Struening, E. L., & Shrout, P. E. (1989). A modified labeling theory approach to mental disorders: An empirical assessment. *American Sociological Review, 54*, 400–423.

Link, B. G., Cullen, F. T., Struening, E. L., Shrout, P. E., & Dohrenwend, B. (1989). A modified labeling theory approach to mental disorders: An empirical assessment. *American Sociological Review, 54*, 400–423.

Link, B. G., & Phelan, J. (1999). Labeling and stigma. In C. Aneshensel & J. Phelan (Eds.), *Handbook of sociology of mental health. Handbooks of sociology and social research* (pp. 481–494). New York: Kluwer Academic/Plenum Publishers.

Link, B. G., & Phelan, J. C. (2001). Conceptualizing stigma. *Annual Review of Sociology, 27*, 363–385.

Link, B. G., Phelan, J. C., Bresnahan, M., Stueve, A., & Pescosolido, B. A. (1999). Public conceptions of mental illness: Labels, causes, dangerousness, and social distance. *American Journal of Public Health, 89*, 1328–1333.

Lorion, R. P. (1974). Patient and therapist variables in the treatment of low-income patients. *Psychological Bulletin, 81*, 344–354.

Louis Harris & Associates, Inc. (1986). *The ICD survey of disabled Americans*. New York: International Center for the Disabled.

Maccoby, E. E., & Jacklin, C. N. (1974). Myth, reality and shades of gray: What we know and don't know about sex differences. *Psychology Today, 8*, 109–112.

MacDonald-Wilson, K. L., Rogers, E. S., Massaro, J. M., Lyass, A., & Crean, T. (2002). An investigation of reasonable workplace accommodations for people with psychiatric disabilities: Quantitative findings from a multi-site study. *Community Mental Health Journal, 38*, 35–50.

Madianos, M., Madianou, D., Vlachonikolis, J., & Stefanis, C. (1987). Attitudes toward mental illness in the Athens area: Implications for community mental health intervention. *Acta Psychiatrica Scandinavia, 75*, 158–165.

Mark, T., & Mueller, C. (1996). Access to care in HMOs and traditional insurance plans. *Health Affairs, 15*, 81–87.

Markowitz, F. (2001). Modeling processes in recovery from mental illness: An analysis of the relationships between symptoms, life satisfaction, and self-concept. *Journal of Health and Social Behavior, 42*, 64–79.

Martin, J., Pescosolido, B., & Tuch, S. (2000). Of fear and loathing: The role of "disturbing behavior," labels, and causal attributions in shaping public attitudes toward people with mental illness. *Journal of Health and Social Behavior, 41*, 208–223.

Mastrofski, S. D., Snipes, J. B., & Parks, R. B. (2000). The helping hand of the law: Police control of citizens on request. *Criminolgy, 38*, 307–342.

Mechanic, D. (1998). Cultural and organizational aspects of applications of the Americans with Disabilities Act to persons with psychiatric disabilities. *Milbank Quarterly, 76*, 5–23.

Mechanic, D., McAlpine, D., Rosenfield, S., & Davis, D. (1994). Effects of illness attribution and depression on the quality of life among persons with serious mental illness. *Social Science & Medicine, 39*, 155–164.

Mehta, S. I., & Farina, A. (1988). Associative stigma: Perceptions of the difficulties of college-aged children of stigmatized fathers. *Journal of Social and Clinical Psychology, 7*, 192–202.

Mowbray, C. T. (1985). Homelessness in America: Myths and realities. *American Journal of Orthopsychiatry, 55*, 4–8.

Mueser, K. T., Bellack, A. S., Douglas, M. S., & Morrison, R. L. (1991). Prevalence and stability of social skill deficits in schizophrenia. *Schizophrenia Research, 5,* 167–176.

Mullen, B., Rozell, D., & Johnson, C. (1996). The phenomenology of being in a group: Complexity approaches to operationalizing cognitive representation. In J. Nye & A. Brower (Eds.), *What's social about social cognition? Research on socially shared cognition in small groups* (pp. 205–229). Thousand Oaks, CA: Sage.

Narrow, W. E., Regier, D. A., Norquist, G., Rae, D. S., Kennedy, C., & Arons, B. (2000). Mental health service use by Americans with severe mental illnesses. *Social Psychiatry and Psychiatric Epidemiology, 35,* 147–155.

National Institute of Mental Health. (1987). *Toward a model plan for a comprehensive, community-based mental health system.* Washington, DC: Superintendent of Documents, U.S. Government Printing Office.

Olshansky, S., Grob, S., & Ekdahl, M. (1960). Survey of employment experience of patients discharged from three mental hospitals during the period 1951–1953. *Mental Hygiene, 44,* 510–521.

Page, S. (1977). Effects of the mental illness label in attempts to obtain accommodation. *Canadian Journal of Behavioral Sciences, 9,* 85–90.

Page, S. (1983). Psychiatric stigma: Two studies of behavior when the chips are down. *Canadian Journal of Mental Health, 2,* 13–19.

Page, S. (1995). Effects of the mental illness label in 1993: Acceptance and rejection in the community. *Journal of Health and Social Policy, 7,* 61–68.

Penn, D. L., Guynan, K., Daily, T., & Spaulding, W. (1994). Dispelling the stigma of schizophrenia: What sort of information is best? *Schizophrenia Bulletin, 20,* 567–578.

Penn, D. L., & Martin, J. (1998). The stigma of severe mental illness: Some potential solutions for a recalcitrant problem. *Psychiatric Quarterly, 69,* 235–247.

Penn, D. L., Mueser, K. T., & Doonan, R. (1997). Physical attractiveness in schizophrenia: The mediating role of social skill. *Behavior Modification, 21,* 78–85.

Persaud, R. (2000). Psychiatrists suffer from stigma too. *Psychiatric Bulletin, 24,* 284–285.

Phelan, J. C., Bromet, E. J., & Link, B. G. (1998). Psychiatric illness and family stigma. *Schizophrenia Bulletin, 24,* 115–126.

Phelan, J. C., Link, B. G., Moore, R. E., & Stueve, A. (1997). The stigma of homelessness: The impact of the label "homeless" on attitudes toward poor persons. *Social Psychology Quarterly, 60,* 323–337.

Phelan, J. C., Link, B., Stueve, A., & Pescosolido, B. (2000). Public conceptions of mental illness in 1950 and 1996: What is mental illness and is it to be feared? *Journal of Health and Social Behavior, 41,* 188–207.

Pincus, F. L. (1996). Discrimination comes in many forms: Individual, institutional, and structural. *American Behavioral Scientist, 40,* 186–194.

Pincus, F. L. (1999a). From individual to structural discrimination. In F. L. Pincus & H. J. Ehrlich (Eds.), *Race and ethnic conflict: Contending views on prejudice, discrimination, and ethnoviolence* (pp. 120–124). Boulder, CO: Westview Press.

Pincus, F. L. (1999b). The case for affirmative action. In F. L. Pincus & H. J. Ehrlich (Eds.), *Race and ethnic conflict: Contending views on prejudice, discrimination, and ethnoviolence* (pp. 205–222). Boulder, CO: Westview Press.

Porter, J. R., & Washington, R. E. (1979). Black identity and self-esteem: A review of studies of Black self-concept, 1968–1978. *Annual Review of Sociology, 5*, 53–74.

Rabkin, J. (1974). Public attitudes toward mental illness: A review of the literature. *Psychological Bulletin, 10*, 9–33.

Regier, D. A., Narrow, W. E., Rae, D. S., & Manderscheid, R. W. (1993). The de facto U.S. mental and addictive disorders service system. Epidemiologic catchment area prospective 1-year prevalence rates of disorders and services. *Archives of General Psychiatry, 50*, 85–94.

Ridgway, P., & Zipple, A. (1990). Challenges and strategies for implementing supported housing. *Psychosocial Rehabilitation Journal, 13*, 115–120.

Rogers, E. S., Chamberlin, J., Ellison, M. L., & Crean, T. (1997). A consumer-constructed scale to measure empowerment among users of mental health services. *Psychiatric Services, 48*, 1042–1047.

Rogers, E. S., Walsh, D., Masota, L., & Danley, K. (1991). *Massachusetts survey of client preferences for community support services* (Final Report). Boston, MA: Center for Psychiatric Rehabilitation.

Roman, P., & Floyd, H. (1981). Social acceptance of psychiatric illness and psychiatric treatment. *Social Psychiatry, 16*, 16–21.

Rosenberg, M. (1965). *Society and the adolescent self image*. Princeton, NJ: Princeton University Press.

Rosenfield, S. (1992). Factors contributing to the subjective quality of life of the chronic mentally ill. *Journal of Health and Social Behavior, 33*, 299–315.

Rubinstein, D. (1994). The social construction of opportunity. *Journal of Socio-Economics, 23*, 61–79.

Russert, M., & Frey, J. (1991). The PACT vocational model: A step into the future. *Psychosocial Rehabilitation Journal, 14*, 7–18.

Satcher, D. (1999). *Mental health: A report of the Surgeon General*. Washington, DC: Office of the U.S. Surgeon General.

Scheff, T. J. (1966). *Being mentally ill: A sociology theory*. Chicago: Aldine.

Scheff, T. J. (1972). On reason and sanity: Political dimensions of psychiatric thought. In W. P. Lebra (Ed.), *Transcultural research in mental health*. Honolulu: University Press of Hawaii.

Scheff, T. J. (1974). The labeling theory of mental illness. *American Sociological Review, 39*, 444–452.

Scheff, T. J. (1975). Labeling, emotion, and individual change. In T. Scheff (Ed.), *Labeling madness* (pp. 75–89). Englewood Cliffs, NJ: Prentice-Hall.

Segal, S., Baumohl, J., & Moyles, E. (1980). Neighborhood types and community reaction to the mentally ill: A paradox of intensity. *Journal of Health and Social Behavior, 21*, 345–359.

Sherer, M., & Adams, C. (1983). Construct validation of the self-efficacy scale. *Psychological Reports, 53*, 899–902.

Shurka, E. (1983). The evaluation of ex-mental patients by other ex-mental patients. *International Journal of Social Psychiatry, 29*, 286–291.

Sirey, J. A., Bruce, M. L., Alexopoulos, G. S., Perlick, D. A., Friedman, S. J., & Meyers, B. S. (2001). Stigma as a barrier to recovery: Perceived stigma and patient-rated severity of illness as predictors of antidepressant drug adherence. *Psychiatric Services, 52*, 1615–1620.

Sirey, J. A., Bruce, M. L., Alexopoulos, G. S., Perlick, D. A., Raue, P., Friedman, S. J., et al. (2001). Perceived stigma as a predictor of treatment discontinuation in young and older outpatients with depression. *American Journal of Psychiatry, 158*, 479–481.

Socall, D., & Holtgraves, T. (1992). Attitudes toward the mentally ill: The effects of label and beliefs. *Sociological Quarterly, 33*, 435–445.

Steadman, H. J., McCarty, D., & Morrisey, J. (1989). *The mentally ill in jail.* New York: Guilford Press.

Strauss, J. S. (1989). Subjective experiences of schizophrenia: Toward a new dynamic psychiatry: II. *Schizophrenia Bulletin, 15*, 179–187.

Sturm, R., Gresenz, C., Pacula, R., & Wells, K. (1999). Labor force participation by persons with mental illness. *Psychiatric Services, 50*, 1407.

Tanzman, B. (1993). An overview of surveys of mental health consumers' preferences for housing and support services. *Hospital and Community Psychiatry, 44*, 450–455.

Teplin, L. A. (1984). Criminalizing mental disorder: The comparative arrest rate of the mentally ill. *American Psychologist, 39*, 794–803.

Teplin, L. A. (1990). The prevalence of severe mental disorders among male urban jail detainees: Comparison with the epidemiologic catchment area program. *American Journal of Public Health, 80*, 663–669.

Teplin, L. A., Abram, K. M., & McClelland, G. M. (1996). Prevalence of psychiatric disorders among incarcerated women. *Archives of General Psychiatry, 53*, 505–512.

Teplin, L. A., & Pruett, N. S. (1992). Police as street-corner psychiatrist: Managing the mentally ill. *International Journal of Law and Psychiatry, 15*, 139–156.

Thompson, E. H., & Doll, W. (1982). The burden of families coping with the mentally ill: An invisible crisis. *Family Relations: Journal of Applied Family and Child Studies, 31*, 379–388.

Travis, J. (1997, September 3). *The mentally ill offender: Viewing crime and justice through a different lens.* Speech to the National Association of State Forensic Mental Health Directors.

Unzicker, R. (1989). On my own: A personal journey through madness and re-emergence. *Psychosocial Rehabilitation Journal, 13*, 71–77.

U.S. Department of Health and Human Services. (1983). *Report to Congress on shelter and basic living needs of chronically mentally ill individuals.* Washington, DC: Author.

Verkuyten, M. (1994). Self-esteem among ethnic minority youth in Western countries. *Social Indicators Research, 32*, 21–47.

Verkuyten, M. (1995). Self-esteem, self-concept stability, and aspects of ethnic identity among minority and majority youth in the Netherlands. *Journal of Youth and Adolescence, 24*, 155–175.

Wahl, O. (1999). Mental health consumers' experience of stigma. *Schizophrenia Bulletin, 25*, 467–478.

Wahl, O., & Harman, C. (1989). Family views of stigma. *Schizophrenia Bulletin, 15*, 131–139.

Watson, A., Ottati, V., Corrigan, P., & Heyrman, M. (in press). Mental illness stigma and police decision making. *Community Mental Health Journal.*

Webber, A., & Orcutt, J. (1984). Employers' reactions to racial and psychiatric stigma: A field experiment. *Deviant Behavior, 5*, 327–336.

Weiner, B. (1995). *Judgments of responsibility: A foundation for a theory of social conduct.* New York: Guilford Press.

Wenneker, M. B., & Epstein, A. M. (1989). Racial inequalities in the use of procedures for patients with ischemic heart disease in Massachusetts. *Journal of the American Medical Association, 261*, 253–257.

Willey, N. R., & McCandless, B. R. (1973). Social stereotypes for normal, educable mentally retarded, and orthopedically handicapped children. *Journal of Special Education, 7*, 283–288.

Willis, A. G., Willis, G. B., Male, A., Henderson, M., & Manderscheid, R. W. (1998). Mental illness and disability in the U.S. adult household population. In R. W. Manderscheid & M. J. Henderson (Eds.), *Mental Health, United States, 1998* (pp. 113–123). Washington, DC: Government Printing Office.

Wilson, W. J. (1987). *The truly disadvantaged: The inner city, the underclass, and public policy.* Chicago: The University of Chicago Press.

Wright, E. R., Gronfein, W. P., & Owens, T. J. (2000). Deinstitutionalization, social rejection, and the self-esteem of former mental patients. *Journal of Health and Social Behavior, 41*, 68–90.

Wylie, G. (1979). A study to identify and compare the personal, social and academic adjustment problems experienced by minority Black and Caucasian graduate students enrolled at Virginia Polytechnic Institute and State University, a predominantly White institution, and Virginia State College, a predominantly Black institution. *Dissertation Abstracts International. 40*, 2408–2409.

Yarrow, M. R., Schwartz, C. G., Murphy, H. S., & Deasy, L. C. (1955). The psychological meaning of mental illness in the family. *Journal of Social Issues, 11*, 12–24.

Zanna, M., & Rempel, J. (1988). Attitudes: A new look at an old concept. In D. Bar-Tal & A. Kruglanski (Eds.), *The social psychology of knowledge* (pp. 315–334). Cambridge, MA: Cambridge University Press.

2

METHODS FOR STUDYING STIGMA
AND MENTAL ILLNESS

KENNETH A. RASINSKI, PETER VIECHNICKI, AND
COLM O'MUIRCHEARTAIGH

In this chapter, we examine methods used to study stigma and mental illness. We discuss the strengths and weaknesses of each method and offer examples, commenting on choice of methodology and what it brings to the study of stigma. We also suggest possibilities based on tried and true methods and methods that are new but that have not been widely exploited. We will focus on four general techniques: laboratory experiments, surveys, ethnography, and linguistic analysis.

SOME FUNDAMENTAL CONCERNS

Before describing each method in detail, it is worthwhile to discuss some general issues in social science research with reference to how they may apply to the study of stigma and mental illness. *Validity* is a ubiquitous concept throughout social science. Whereas many subtypes of validity exist, a general distinction in quantitative research is between internal and external validity (Brewer, 2000). Roughly speaking, *internal validity* refers to the researcher's ability to make claims about causal mechanisms. The internal validity of research in the study of stigma and mental illness is critical for testing psychological mechanisms of stigmatization and response to stigmatization. It is also important in elucidating mechanisms and means of stigma change. Typically, the claim to internal validity is strongest in well-constructed, controlled laboratory experiments.

External validity is a quality of the research design that permits the investigator to generalize study results beyond research participants. It is sometimes associated with collecting information from respondents who were scientifically sampled from a population but can also be associated with the robustness of findings of an experiment (Brewer, 2000); that is, the presence of a hypothesized relationship in different settings under different conditions. In the area of stigma and mental illness, the claim to external validity is crucial because of the real-world consequences attached to stigmatization.

These general descriptions of validity do not tell the entire story of this important concept. Different research paradigms make different assumptions and claims about validity. For example, psychologists who conduct laboratory studies may assume that their studies have external validity. This is because, they might argue, the study is designed to test hypotheses related to a general law or theory of human behavior. If the theory is supported then it should apply to everyone, or at least to all people specified by the theory (e.g., some theories may apply only to women or to men or, in our case, to judgments about people with mental illness). In contrast, survey researchers are more formal in their conceptualization of external validity. They have developed mathematical models that demonstrate that the results from their samples will generalize to a population. They have also developed methods and a logic to test causal mechanisms, but it is different from, and generally not as rigorous as, those used in experiments.

Ethnographic researchers are also concerned with validity but have a different view of it. According to Miles and Huberman (1994), the concept of internal validity is related most to concerns about authenticity, or credibility. They stress that results of a study must make sense to the researcher, the informants (i.e., those that are being studied), and the reader. Ethnographic researchers state that results of ethnographic studies should pass the tests of apparency, verisimilitude, plausibility, and adequacy (Van Maanen, 1988). These concepts are obviously of critical concern to the study of stigma and mental illness.

Validity is also important in the *measurement* of stigma. Social scientists who create measurement tools are concerned with a type of validity called construct validity that, in a broad sense, is the relationship of the measurement instrument to the underlying theoretical construct (Cronbach & Meehl, 1955; Loevinger, 1957). Establishing construct validity is a fairly time consuming process, and is probably not done as often as it should be. For the study of stigma and mental illness, scales purporting to measure stigmatization or its effects should be subjected to some of the standard tests of construct validation.

Construct validity is also important in experimental design and in the study of stigma and mental illness in our culture through linguistic analysis. In the former, experimenters must demonstrate that their operations are, indeed, manifestations of the theoretical constructs they purport to study (Rakover, 1981). In the latter, we shall see that it is possible in linguistic analysis to build a model of stigma from the ground up. For example, automatic text analysis techniques can be applied to examine how mental illness has been described by counting words and looking for associations among words within documents. But at some point theory must enter into the process to determine which of the potentially stigmatizing statements are related to stigma in an important way and which are not (Bartholomew, Henderson, & Marcia, 2000).

In the next sections we will discuss each of the four methods—experimentation, surveys, ethnography, and linguistic analysis—in some detail, with further elaboration on their strengths and weaknesses. We will also describe and comment on studies related to stigma and mental illness that have used each of these methods. We begin with laboratory experiments.

LABORATORY EXPERIMENTS

Laboratory experiments are the cornerstone of psychological investigation and, because much of the theory and research on stigma is based on psychological research on attitudes and social cognition, it is worth considering the methodology in some detail. The hallmark of social experimentation is that, through the deliberate manipulation of events and the assignment of people to conditions, one can make inferences about causality. This manipulation does not have to be conducted in the laboratory. However, it is in a laboratory that a social scientist has the greatest degree of control. Laboratory experiments have been used to study theories about psychological functioning. This may include theories about how people will act in certain situations, or theories about psychological processes, such as how information is mentally organized, retrieved, and used in judgments.

In its simplest form, an experiment consists of the following activities. Study participants are assigned at random to different conditions. The conditions are manifestations (called *operationalizations* in research terminology) of hypotheses that concern the investigator. The study participant completes a task or undergoes an experience that is designed to elicit a response. Measures are taken. If the measure of response elicited by one condition differs in a predicted way from the measure of response elicited by another, inferences about the hypotheses and about the causes of the responses are made. Responses may be attitudes, judgments, perceptions, or behaviors. Sometimes a number of these are measured and process models are examined.

Many variations to the basic experimental design exist. The assignment of unrelated participants at random to groups, as described, is called a *between-subjects* experimental design. A common variation is where one participant experiences a number of conditions, or is presented with a number of stimuli, sequentially. Measures are taken after each experience. This is called a *within-subject* design and it can be useful for studying change. Between- and within-subjects designs can be combined to form *mixed* designs. Winer (1971) gives an encyclopedic description of different types of experimental design. Smith (2000) discusses a number of interesting conceptual issues related to experimental design and its close cousin, the quasi-experimental design.

EXPERIMENTAL DESIGNS AND STIGMA RESEARCH

A good example of a laboratory experiment on stigmatization is Henderson-King and Nisbett (1996). These investigators used an experiment to demonstrate that observation of a negative behavior performed by a single individual from a stigmatized ethnic group (in this case, African Americans) will generalize to other members of the group. The experiment involved the use of a confederate; some study participants watched an African American confederate behave in a hostile and rude manner. Others watched a Caucasian confederate behave rudely. Then, participants were asked to conduct a mock interview of another student for position of residence hall counselor. Those who observed the rude and hostile African American confederate conducted significantly shorter interviews indicating that they had already formed conclusions about the applicant on the basis of their experience with the confederate.

The strength of this study is the control the researchers had over the study environment. Extraneous effects were eliminated through careful administration of procedures, and the target effects and outcomes were isolated. Studies of this type have advanced the field of social perception immensely. However, they have a substantial limitation. Although they possess internal validity because they allow the experimenters to isolate critical effects, thus establishing the plausibility of the research hypotheses, they are weak in external validity in the sense that the researchers cannot generally claim with any degree of confidence that their results will hold beyond the laboratory setting. This study represents two common obstacles to external validity that are found in most laboratory experiments. First, key aspects of the study may be somewhat artificial. In particular, whereas the study participants, college students, may someday have to make judgments about whether to hire or fire an individual, they knew that the interview was a mock one. The lack of consequences associated with their decision may have played a role in their behavior. Second, participants were a *convenience* sample of students selected in such a way that generalization of the effect could not be made to other students, let alone the adult working population. That is to say, no scientific sampling procedures were used in selecting the students.

Next, we consider experiments that explicitly examine the stigma associated with mental illness. Piner and Kahle (1984) arranged for 30 female undergraduate participants to wait for the performance of a task in a room with a person labeled either as mentally ill or as having a physical impairment. Results indicated that the mere label of mental illness, in absence of bizarre behavior, affected ratings and task performance of the participants. The implication is that the label "mentally ill" affects social judgments of perceivers in ways that are detrimental to people with mental illness.

A study by Desforges and associates (1991) assigned student participants at random to interact or not interact in structured tasks with a person who was described as having had a mental illness in the past. Interaction resulted in more positive attitudes toward the person labeled as having a mental illness. Like most studies of this type, the emphasis was on testing social psychological theory rather than on stigma and mental illness. The only indication the participant had that the target person had a mental illness prior to the study was based on a self-descriptive essay. In fact, the target person did not have a past mental illness, but this was irrelevant to the theory being tested. In addition, there was no control condition in which the target person did not receive a mental illness label. The absence of a control condition did not influence the investigators' complex theoretical goals, which were to examine the effects of structured interpersonal contact on attitudes toward stigmatized others and to examine the influence of category-based judgment on impression formation.

In contrast, an experiment by Corrigan and associates (2001) did focus on real-world applications. They tested the effects of three predominant strategies used by activists to combat stigma—protest, education, and contact. Participants were assigned at random to one of three conditions. In the first two conditions, participants viewed materials drawn from actual documentation or courses dealing with mental illness. In the third condition, participants interacted with one of two people who had recovered from a serious mental illness. Unlike many experiments in psychology, the goal was not to test a prediction about a mental or social process. Rather, the goal was to understand the effectiveness of three methods that are often used in the real world to change attitudes about people with mental illness. Although the study has important implications for policy, it still suffers from the external validity problems that plague most psychological experiments. In this case, the study participants consisted of people attending a junior college. Whereas this group may be more diverse than would be found on most four-year college campuses, it cannot be considered as representing a general population. External validity is strengthened by a second study (Corrigan et al., 2002), also using students from a community college, which replicated and extended the results of the earlier study. A key feature of the second study is that it also tested elements from a theoretical model of stigmatization and stigma change.

Link, Pescosolido, and their associates (Link, Phelan, Bresnahan, Stueve, & Pescosolido, 1999; Pescosolido, Monohan, Link, Stueve, & Kikuzawa, 1999) conducted a vignette experiment embedded in a major national survey. In the vignette methodology, investigators use a random procedure to assign survey respondents to different versions of short descriptions, or vignettes, describing a person, situation, or interaction. The descriptions vary systematically on key characteristics of interest to the investigator. This particular study was embedded in the 1996 General Social Survey, a national social omnibus survey conducted since 1972. A general population probability sample of 1,444 respondents were assigned to receive descriptions of either a person who was alcohol dependent, undergoing a major depression, had symptoms of schizophrenia, was drug dependent, or was described as a "troubled person." The vignette descriptions varied in the sex of the target, the education level (eighth grade, high school, or college), and the target's ethnicity (Caucasian, African American, or Hispanic). The combination of demographic information and disorder type resulted in 90 unique vignettes, and roughly 16 or 17 survey respondents across the country were assigned at random to each vignette. Multiple follow-up questions, including open-ended questions that were subsequently coded, were administered to the respondents after they read the vignettes. Some examples include the perceived cause of the disorder, the dangerousness of the person portrayed in the vignette, and a measure of social distance.

There are two apparent strengths to this study. First, results from the experiment can be generalized to the population at large because they came from a scientifically selected sample. Second, the multiple follow-up questions permit complex modeling of attitudes and judgments as a function of type of disorder and the demographics of the disordered group. As is typical for this type of study, a weakness is that respondents are reacting to a written description rather than a real situation. A second weakness is that the variations in the vignettes appeared to have very little theoretical basis.

The experiments described previously illustrate the strengths and weaknesses of the experimental method and show the tradeoffs between internal validity (careful theory testing) and external validity (the ability to generalize beyond the experimental sample). However, the major conclusion we draw from our review is not that the experimental method is flawed, but that it is underused as a means to study the stigma of serious mental illness. Whether it is in controlled laboratory settings or in survey-based vignette studies, much opportunity exists to use the powerful tool of experimentation to understand more about the structure and function of stigma about people with mental illness. Many of the experiments conducted on the sources of stigmatization of other groups could be replicated in studying stigma and mental illness. It may also be desirable to use as participants in the study people with mental illness, testing theories about their reactions to stigmatizing conditions. It should be noted that research on people with mental illness must be thoroughly reviewed by institutional review boards to assure that the potential gain in knowledge would outweigh any risk to the participants.

As we have seen, surveys can contain experimental manipulations. As survey data collection methodology becomes more technologically sophisticated, members of the general public can be exposed to experimental stimuli that were once limited to laboratories. For example, surveys using computers to collect information and surveys using data collected via the World Wide Web will permit the administration of video-clips in an experimental design and the collection of response times in addition to overt responses to questions.

SURVEYS

The use of surveys can go a long way to overcome the external validity limitations of the laboratory experiment. However, this is only the case when surveys are conducted in conjunction with scientific sampling. Unfortunately, survey research on stigma and mental illness suggests this goal is more the exception than the rule. Many surveys have been conducted with convenience samples. Also, as we have seen, experiments can be embedded in surveys, but they are usually limited in scope. For example, it would be difficult to imagine acting out a scenario such as the one presented in the study by Henderson-King and Nisbett (1996) in a household survey.

Generally, data collected by surveys fall under the rubric of correlational research. That is, the investigator is concerned more about the relationships among variables rather than about inferences of cause and effect. Many researchers may think of a survey solely as a questionnaire administered to a conveniently available group, and that is, indeed, one type of survey. However, a major purpose of survey research, and one of its great strengths, is to provide estimates of population values from scientifically designed samples. Results from population-based surveys are strong in external validity; to the extent that the survey sample was well-designed and the data collection was implemented carefully, we can have confidence that the attitudes and behaviors measured in the sample represent those in the population.

Because sample surveys are so important in social science research, we present a short description of the methodology. A sample survey is a standardized and systematic method for obtaining information about a population using a questionnaire to measure elements sampled from that population. Modalities include face-to-face administration; administration by telephone, mail, and computerized self-administered questionnaires; and, most recently, surveys via the Internet. Three general types of surveys exist, each of which can be applied to a convenience sample or, better when possible, to a scientific sample. A *cross-sectional survey* studies one group of people at a given point in time. When cross-sectional surveys are based on the scientific sampling of a population over a number of years, and they include the same questions year after year, the entire set of surveys is called a *repeated, cross section design*. This is useful for assessing trends in the population. Another type is the *longitudinal survey*. In this type of survey, the same respondents are interviewed repeatedly over time. Respondents may or may not be selected using scientific sampling methods. They may be a cross section of some broader group (e.g., a sample from the general population) or an age cohort or special group (e.g., a treatment group). Scientific survey sample design can be an important part of the survey process. As we will see later, sampling is not limited to a population of individuals, but can apply to a set of media material in preparation for semi-automated content analysis of media. Because of its dual importance, we present a brief description of typical scientific sample designs.

First one defines a population as the total set of elements to which one wishes to theoretically generalize. The population may be small, such as the total number of state psychiatric hospitals in Illinois, or large, such as the total number of households in the United States. The goal of a sample survey is to obtain unbiased estimates of population information without having to collect information from all of the elements of the population.

Sample surveys may be conducted using a variety of research designs. A scientifically designed sample, at minimum, specifies a method for choosing elements from a population with known selection probability. A simple random sample is the most elementary form of a scientifically designed sample. One common level of complexity is stratification. In a stratified design, elements in the population (or strictly speaking, the sample frame, which is the most complete list of population elements that can be obtained) are grouped according to one or more characteristics and a simple random sample is selected from each stratum. Statistics derived from the sample must take into account the sampling rate in each stratum, or erroneous population estimates will be calculated.

Another level of complexity is called clustering. Sometimes it is impractical to obtain a good sample frame of the elements one wishes to study. If these elements are grouped hierarchically, one has a list of all of the higher order groupings; a probability sample of these groupings can be selected and used to generate a list of elements within each selected grouping. Stratification and clustering can be combined to create complex survey designs.

Application of Survey Design to Stigma Research

We mentioned that two general conceptualizations of survey research exist, distinguished by whether measures were taken from a scientifically selected sample or from respondents who were available by convenience. Many surveys of the second type have been used to study stigma. One example is a study by Weiner, Perry, and Magnuson (1988). These researchers administered questionnaires to convenience samples of students in California to test relationships between attributions of responsibility and stigmatization of mental illness. Lin (1993) administered the same questionnaire to students in the People's Republic of China. In both studies, afflictions such as Alzheimer's disease, cancer, and blindness, which typically are not associated with stigma, were rated as being less under the control of the one afflicted than afflictions such as AIDS, drug abuse, and obesity, which typically are associated with stigma. The samples used by these investigators were adequate to test their theories about the relationship between control and stigma but, strictly speaking, the results cannot be generalized to a population in either country. Because of this, it is difficult to make the argument (as Weiner [1995] does) that this relationship holds across cultures. Indeed, it may be that both groups of students are similar in their views because of the communality of the higher-education experience. This leaves open the possibility that comparing groups of Americans and Chinese who have not been exposed to higher eductation may hold vastly different views. This is not a criticism of these particular studies. Much work in cross-cultural psychology has been conducted by comparing responses of students in different societies. This is understandable, given the expense and difficulty of conducting population-based surveys. However, interpretation of the results as representing cultural similarities or differences must be made with the limitations of the samples in mind.

Other surveys have used probability sampling, or a combination of probability sampling and convenience sampling, to study stigma and mental illness. One example of the latter is a complicated study conducted by Link and his associates (Link, 1987; Link, Cullen, Struening, Shrought, & Dohrenwend, 1989) in the Washington Heights, New York City area. The study was designed to compare attitudes, perceptions, and outcomes of people with and without mental illness. The "without" group was drawn mostly from an area-probability sample of households in Washington Heights. Less information is given about the construction of the "with" sample, except that patients were "selected from outpatient clinics and inpatient facilities in the same general area of New York City" (Link, 1987, p. 100). This leads one to suppose that there was no scientific sampling strategy in place. However, given the purpose of the study and the care taken to select patients in the same geographic area as the community residents, this does not appear to be a substantial liability. Indeed, though the study was designed to develop and test sociological theory about the effects of labeling on the self-image of people with a mental illness, a substantial amount of external validity was built into the design. Still, it is possible that results were somehow related to living in the Washington Heights, New York area, and that an adequate cross section of patients was not obtained.

The Analysis of Survey Data

Because of the topical breadth of most surveys, in contrast to the narrowness of most experiments, it is worthwhile to discuss some of the analytic possibilities. Although it is common for a research publication to report the results of one or more experiments, it is not uncommon for a single survey to result in a number of publications. For example, the 1996 Mental Health Module in the General Social Survey has already generated several articles and will, no doubt, be the source of several more. At the simplest level, survey data has been analyzed by observing point estimates (overall totals, means, or percentages). Slightly more complicated is the comparison of differences in point estimates among demographic groups. Correlational analysis, from the examination of simple co-occurrences of responses between two variables to the construction and estimation of complex causal models, has been a favored way of exploiting the richness of survey data. Is not always the case that the best results are obtained through the most complicated methods. In any research, it is the theoretical underpinnings of the analysis that are most important.

Many researchers who work with survey data have taken advantage of statistical techniques that allow partitioning of relationships among sets of variables. These techniques range from multiple regression to structural equation causal modeling of latent variables. Some of these models have been applied to good effect in the study of stigma and mental illness. For example, Link (1987) used multiple regression analysis to test hypotheses generated from the labeling theory of mental illness. Corrigan and associates (2002) used latent variable structural equation modeling to test a theory of stigma based on perceptions of responsibility and dangerousness. Watson (2001) used structural equation modeling to test a complex model of stigma using the 1996 General Social Survey Mental Health Module, and Markowitz (2001) estimated elegant reciprocal causation models using structural equation modeling of a panel survey.

Earlier we suggested that experimental methods could be used with greater frequency to study stigma and mental illness. Because it is easy to do surveys of poor quality, we hesitate to make this suggestion about survey research. The literature is replete with examples of poorly constructed surveys conducted on small samples. In our estimation, application of these substandard methods to the study of stigma and mental illness does not serve the field well. Rather, those who wish to use survey methods to study this topic should take time to learn proper survey techniques, enlist the aid of an expert in the field, and invest the resources necessary to obtain meaningful samples and high-quality data.

ETHNOGRAPHY

Ethnographic methods enable the researcher to capture a detailed picture of the experience of a person or group. Though surveys may cover a broad range of topics, as mentioned earlier, the level of detail captured in an ethnographic study is far greater than could possibly be obtained through a survey. Unlike experiments, which tend to have a narrow focus and test specific parts of a theory, ethnographic studies attempt to understand through description and build theory from the "ground up." Ethnographic research methods include participant (or unobtrusive, non-participant) observation; unstructured, open-ended interviews; analysis of archival material and autobiographical reports; and viewing videotapes or other images (Creswell, 2003). Focus groups have also been used effectively as an ethnographic research tool (Morgan, 1988). The distinguishing feature of the focus group is that it creates an environment whereby participants can interact. Aspects of the interaction are often as important as the narrative data that are obtained.

Ethnographic methods differ philosophically from the quantitative methods discussed earlier. Whereas quantitative social scientists are presumed to be objective and impartial, ethnographers strive to be explicit about their biases, so as not to let them taint their interpretations of the data. Quantitative social scientists are generally doing something to people: for example, manipulating experimental variables or collecting responses on a survey. Ethnographers often include study participants in the creation of the research design and interpretation of the data, validating results through "triangulation," which is the process of examining evidence from several sources and points of view to extract a coherent theme. Gathering complete and thorough information is extremely important to the ethnographer lest a distorted picture of the phenomenon under study be drawn. Possibly the most famous ethnographic study on stigma is the work by Erving Goffman (1963). Goffman draws on secondary sources to obtain autobiographical accounts of individuals with different stigmatized conditions and assembles them masterfully into a social philosophy of stigmatization.

Ethnographic research allows study participants to tell their own stories in a natural, confidential setting. This is a substantial contrast to the structured approach of the psychological laboratory. Assuming the informant trusts the ethnographer, sensitive topics can be discussed in great detail. Cain

(2000) interviewed 10 psychotherapists and explored the effect of their psychiatric hospitalizations on subsequent psychotherapy with clients. In-depth interviews of the psychotherapists captured nuances of this sensitive topic, including the stigma that these "wounded healers" faced. Three studies have similarly examined the experiences of families of people with a mental illness. One of these involved focus groups (Bassett, Lampe, & Lloyd, 1999) and the other was conducted using in-depth interviews (Muhlbauer, 2002). A study by Nicholson, Sweeney, and Geller (1998a, 1998b) used focus groups to examine difficulties of mothers with mental illness.

Most ethnographic studies are either purely descriptive or attempt to develop grounded theory (i.e., theory that emerges from the narratives) through studying narratives and extrapolating themes from them. Ethnographic research has been used to test theories about stigma and mental illness and to explore practical, consequential issues. As an example of theory testing, Camp, Finlay, and Lyons (2002) examined modified labeling theory as it relates to self-esteem in women with chronic mental illness.

Ethnographic studies have been used to study many different aspects of mental illness and the stigmatization that accompanies it. One study examined barriers to employment (Bassett, Lloyd, & Bassett, 2001); another described the experiences of mothers with mental illness (Bassett, Lampe, & Lloyd, 1999). Two of the studies focused on education (Weiner, 1999; Dougherty & Campana, 1996). The study by Weiner (1999) explored the different meanings of achieving a college education to people with psychiatric illness, while the study by Dougherty and Campana (1996) documented the experiences of college students with a history of psychiatric illness in a "supported education" program that tried to help them deal with problems associated with the illness. One study examined relationship-based needs of women with a mental illness (Cogan, 1998). Most of the studies used open-ended or semi-structured interviewing techniques.

It is interesting to note that of all the qualitative studies found mentioning stigma as a factor in dealing with mental illness, only the study by Muhlbauer (2002) was designed explicitly to address the issue of stigma. The other studies were designed to explore other topics and reported stigmatization when it was mentioned as a topic by one or more of the study participants. This suggests that the ethnographic method is underused as a tool to investigate stigma within the context of mental illness.

LINGUISTIC ANALYSIS

Cultural stigma of mental illness is reflected in language. Recognition of this is one of the reasons that there is a push among activists and professionals to do away with popular labels for people with an illness such as "disabled" or "handicapped," in favor of the expressions "person with a disability" or "person with a handicap." The first type of label reduces the person to his or her affliction, implicitly ignoring that people are multidimensional and that no single label can sum up a person. The alternative label recognizes first the humanity of the afflicted person and thus avoids the reduction of the person to their problem. In similar fashion, the way in which mental illness is portrayed in public discourse is important to understanding the stigma associated with mental illness, and may suggest ways of alleviating that stigma. This section describes a successful body of research that has grown up around the linguistic study of portrayals of mental illness and its associated stigma in public discourse, particularly in the popular media. As we will see, however, the same concerns over internal and external validity that we have seen in experimental, survey-based, and ethnographic studies hold true in the linguistic analysis of mental illness stigma. Because of problems of internal and external validity, it is often difficult to generalize from such studies.

Two Types of Linguistic Analyses of Stigma

Within the quantitative linguistic study of stigma and mental illness, at least two types of questions may be addressed. First, one may use linguistic analysis to define or describe the properties of stigma associated with mental illness. Note that in this first type of study, if the source of the texts to be studied is the popular media, then the subsequent analysis is based on the assumption that information on stigma and mental illness found in a media document can be used to make inferences about the underlying conceptual frameworks shared by the creators and recipients of those media messages. This is a bottom-up, empirically driven process, one that allows understanding of stigma and mental illness to proceed from the data, rather than looking for confirmation of some prior theory in a particular dataset. In pursuing such analyses, researchers must be careful to appreciate the relationship between media language and culture (Bakhtin 1975/1981).

One such bottom-up methodology that has successfully used linguistic analysis to study stigma in mental illness is concept mapping (Trochim, 1989). Concept mapping begins with the generation of a number of statements about stigma and mental illness. These may be generated by focus group participants, or may be drawn from a sample of relevant media documents. Next, the statements are sorted into piles by members of population groups such as mental health administrators, service providers, people with mental illness, or family members. The sorting is used to determine conceptual similarities and differences among the statements. Special statistical techniques are used to analyze the similarities and differences. The end result is a set of clustered statements that show something about concepts shared by the group members. As an example of successful use of concept mapping to understand mental illness stigma, Trochim, Cook, and Setze (1994) use this technique to delineate obstacles facing persons with mental illness in a supported employment program.

Whereas concept mapping of stigma has increased our understanding of how victims of mental illness and their associates perceive its effects, this technique must nevertheless be used with care, if it is to overcome the same concerns of internal and external validity as are described throughout this chapter. Internal validity becomes a concern for concept mapping in two main areas. First is the potential arbitrariness of the statistical methods used to obtain the final clustering. They are sensitive to idiosyncrasies in the statements and to the choice of statistical models. Often the same set of statements can result in dramatically different concept maps if different statistical models are applied. Second, human judgment must be used in the final delineation and definitions of clusters.

Concerns about external validity of concept mapping studies would focus on the representativeness of the participants for the target population. Typical population samples used in concept mapping studies have been convenience samples (though Onken, 2002 used a rational sampling strategy for a concept mapping task). It is therefore difficult to assess the general applicability of the maps of mental illness stigma which are generated by such procedures, however intuitively appealing they may seem.

A second major type of linguistic analysis of mental illness stigma is the quantitative measurement of relative levels of stigma in media portrayals.[1] Such a study is top-down in nature, and theory-driven. That is, to accomplish such a study the researcher must possess a set of theoretical prior assumptions, hypotheses, or categories, which can then be applied to the data through testing, classification, or similar means. Here the goal of the research is to chart the magnitude, history, or distribution of stigma as it is associated with mental illness; hence a different set of methodologies are appropriate (Francis, Pirkis, Dunt, & Blood, 2001). In such cases, a definition of stigma as it relates to mental illness is determined and is applied to a sample document set, rather than being developed out of a set of documents, as in concept mapping. Themes are determined from the definition and the documents are coded for the presence of themes.

This type of linguistic analysis need not be particularly complex to achieve important findings; in fact, much of the quantitative research on mental illness and stigma has employed simple techniques such as counting occurrences of certain themes that relate to stigma. For example, Philo (1996) studied print and television depictions of mental illness (both factual and fictional) from Britain during the month of April 1993 by counting the number

---

[1]Because this second type of study examines relative levels of stigma in media portrayals rather than the absolute properties of those messages, it does not depend on assumptions about the relationship between media messages and the attitudes of their creators and recipients; that relationship can be safely assumed to be the same for all groups under study.

of occurrences of five major thematic treatments of mental illness. The frequency of negative (stigmatizing) themes greatly outweighed positive ones.

At a slightly more sophisticated level, given a sample of documents and a set of themes relating to mental illness, it is possible to count co-occurrences of themes that are deemed to convey negative affect together with terms for mental illness. For example, Ward (1997) examined the portrayal of mental health issues in United Kingdom print media. Themes were extracted that related to mental illness and their co-occurrence with themes of danger and fear was noted. The study concluded that almost half of the media coverage at that time implicitly or explicitly connected mental illness with violent crime.

It is also possible to combine quantitative and qualitative methods in the analysis of a sample of media documents. Rose (1989), for example, studied a sample of television shows from the United Kingdom from 1992. Three months of television shows were taped and screened for relevance to mental illness. Those that mentioned mental illness were then analyzed for the presence or absence of certain themes. The unit of analysis was the camera shot. Narrative structure was also analyzed. Rose also found a preponderance of themes and narrative structures that connect mental illness and violence (Francis et al., 2001).

One of the most powerful extensions of this type of method involves the analysis of repeated cross-sectional samples of media documents that will allow inferences about changing patterns of media representations of mental illness and stigma over time. For example, Signorielli (1989) studied representations of mental illness in prime-time television from the United States in 1969 and 1985. The study concluded that there was little change either in the extent of mental illness portrayed in prime-time television between the two periods, or in the nature of the portrayals themselves.

It is possible to envision certain improvements and extensions to the top-down quantitative linguistic methodologies described here. The coding of themes is often the area of such studies where human intuition is most relied on, and yet the assumptions that drive the themes are rarely made explicit in the final study. This situation could be alleviated by automating some aspects of thematic selection using techniques described in the concept mapping section.

A computational linguistic technique called Automated Text Categorization (ATC) can be used if a large body of text is to be coded. ATC "learns" from a body of texts labeled with categories, and then is able to classify unlabeled texts using its learned categories (Yang & Liu, 1999). ATC typically achieves high accuracy rates when compared to human coders, sometimes up to 90% (Dumais, Platt, Heckerman, & Sahami, 1998).

Although using ATC to automate the coding process would introduce classification errors into the data, the disadvantages that would accrue from these errors would likely be overshadowed by increased reliability. Manual coding of large document sets typically requires great care to ensure sufficient reliability of coding. Many carefully designed and successful studies, such as those conducted by Matas, el-Guebaly, Peterkin, Green, and Harper (1985) or Day and Page (1986), nevertheless suffer from unclear reliability ratings for their code frames (Francis et al., 2001). ATC, though of variable accuracy depending on the task, will have perfect reliability within the document sample and near-perfect reliability across repeated classifications of the same sample. Furthermore, by preserving the classification parameters, it will be possible to replicate the coding process as many times as is necessary.

SAMPLING STRATEGIES

For both top-down and bottom-up studies, it is generally appropriate to select a sample of media documents rather than attempting to study the entire universe. Possible exceptions to this statement include targeted, small-scale studies of media documents concerning temporally and topically well-defined issues (Altheide, 1981). For such studies, a purposive sampling strategy may be most appropriate and an ethnographic analysis that seeks to understand the full context of the sampled documents may yield a much richer understanding than the quantitative analysis described earlier in this chapter (Altheide, 1996). Sampling as it relates to content analysis of media documents is discussed in greater detail in Neuendorf (2002).

The same designs used in survey sampling can be used to sample media materials. The majority of quantitative analyses of mental illness in the media have attempted to select samples of documents that are representative of those created during a particular time or in a particular place. Typically, this is accomplished by screening a large collection of documents for relevance to mental illness and stigma, and then selecting some sample from within the relevant documents. An example of such a procedure can be found in Williams and Taylor (1995), who study the portrayal of people with mental illness in Australian newspapers. The document frame that undergoes the initial screening is usually a convenience set rather than a complete list of all documents across various media channels. Furthermore, the relevance screening procedure (discussed later, this chapter) is often labor-intensive. These factors have conspired to make it difficult to generalize from such samples to the "effective media environment," even within a particular modality such as print or television. Limitations on sample selection in media studies of mental illness have diminished in recent years.

CONCLUSION

In this chapter we examined major research methodologies as they have been used, or could be used, to study stigma and mental illness. This phenomenon is pervasive and complex, as the literature suggests, and, as our review of the different methodologies used to study it reveals, can be studied at different levels. Experiments can be used to test psychological factors that cause stigmatization and the effects that stigmatization has on those stigmatized. Experiments can also be used to evaluate programs designed for stigma change. Program-based experiments with careful attention to the collection of theoretically relevant information can provide useful insights into why different procedures work, as well as provide support for the theories.

Surveys can be used to test theories that specify relationships among variables or can be used to describe populations. Although survey research does not permit the level of control that is possible in experimentation, it allows the researcher to include a broad range of questions on a topic and is generally collected on larger samples than those used in experiments. This gives the researcher the ability to test complex theories, although establishing cause and effect relationships is more difficult. In many cases, survey research is abused because of its apparent simplicity. However, for results to have their greatest impact, researchers who use surveys to study stigma and mental illness should pay careful attention to question writing, scale construction, administration, and response rates, each of which can bias responses and lead to false conclusions.

Because of its ability to capture the richness of the human experience, ethnography has a good deal of potential in the study of stigma and mental illness. In general, we would like to see more studies that are explicitly designed to study stigma, rather than uncover stigma. These studies would give us a sophisticated understanding of the human experience of stigmatization. Ethnographic studies that examine the source of stigmatization would also be useful. Studies, perhaps using focus group methodology, that examine interactions between individuals who hold stigmatizing attitudes toward people with mental illness and who are in a position of power to affect their lives (e.g., employers, case workers, health care professionals, or, in some cases, the general public) and those who are stigmatized may be of some value in understanding the dynamics of stigmatization and its effects.

Relatively new developments in the analysis of text information present interesting possibilities for understanding stigma and mental illness at the cultural level through the analysis of media text. The current state-of-the-art techniques require a great deal of sophistication to use and the hope is that linguists will become more interested in this important topic.

Which methodology is the right one for a given researcher? That is partly determined by the methodology in which one has the most training. It is also important that the selected methodology should match the level at which the problem is being studied. Carefully controlled experiments that examine the effects of subtle stimuli on social judgments must be done under laboratory conditions and may not be replicable using a survey methodology, ethnography, or media analysis. The investigator who wishes to have detailed descriptive information about the experience of a few individuals will not be satisfied with the relatively limited amount of detail that can be garnered from survey data. However, the researcher who wants to have more or less broad findings that can be applied to a population at large can do no less than conduct a population-based survey. Examining cultural themes related to mental illness may only be possible by studying the way people with mental illness are portrayed in the media or by examining legislation.

A social phenomenon such as the stigmatization of people with mental illness is complex enough to where it may be thoroughly understood only after sophisticated teams of researchers attempt to use multiple methods to get at different aspects of it. Like the story of the blind men and the elephant, each detects his own part of the phenomenon. In this chapter it was not our intention to draw a composite picture of the elephant. Rather, we attempted to explore some characteristics of the blind men.

REFERENCES

Altheide, D. (1981). Iran vs. U.S. TV news: The hostage story out of context. In W. Adams (Ed.), *TV coverage of the Middle East* (pp. 128–158). Norwood, NJ: Ablex.

Altheide, D. (1996). *Qualitative media analysis.* Thousand Oaks, CA: Sage.

Bakhtin, M. (1981). Discourse in the novel. In M. Holquist (Ed.), *The dialogic imagination* (C. Emerson & M. Holquist, Trans.). Austin: University of Texas Press. (Original work published 1975)

Bartholomew, K., Henderson, A. J. Z., & Marcia, J. E. (2000). Coded semistructured interviews in social psychological research. In H. T. Reis & C. M. Judd (Eds.), *Handbook of research methods in social and personality psychology* (pp. 286–312). Cambridge, England: Cambridge University Press.

Bassett, H., Lampe, J., & Lloyd, C. (1999). Parenting: Experiences and feelings of parents with a mental illness. *Journal of Mental Health, 8,* 597–604.

Bassett, J., Lloyd, C., & Bassett, H. (2001). Work issues for young people with psychosis: Barriers to employment. *British Journal of Occupational Therapy, 64*(2), 66–72.

Brewer, M. B. (2000). Research design and issues of validity. In H. T. Reid & C. M. Judd (Eds.), *Handbook of research methods in social and personality psychology* (pp. 3–16). Cambridge, England: Cambridge University Press.

Cain, N. M. (2000). Psychotherapists with personal histories of psychiatric hospitalization: Countertransference in wounded healers. *Psychiatric Rehabilitation Journal, 24*(1), 22–28.

Camp, D. L., Finlay, W. M. L., & Lyons, E. (2002). Is low self-esteem an inevitable consequence of stigma? An example from women with chronic mental health problems. *Social Science & Medicine, 55,* 823–834.

Cogan, J. C. (1998). The consumer as expert: Women with serious mental illness and their relationship-based needs. *Psychiatric Rehabilitation Journal, 22*(2), 142–154.

Corrigan, P. W., River, P., Lundin, R. K., Penn, D. L., Wasowski, K. U., Campion, J., et al. (2001). Three strategies for changing attributions about severe mental illness. *Schizophrenia Bulletin, 27,* 187–196.

Corrigan, P. W., Rowan, D., Green, A., Lundin, R., River, P., Uphoff-Wasowski, K., et al. (2002). Challenging two mental illness stigmas: Personal responsibility and dangerousness. *Schizophrenia Bulletin, 28,* 293–309.

Creswell, J. W. (2003). *Research design: Qualitative, quantitative, and mixed methods approaches* (2nd ed.). Thousand Oaks, CA: Sage.

Cronbach, L. J., & Meehl, P. E. (1955). Construct validity in psychological tests. *Psychological Bulletin, 52,* 291–302.

Day, D., & Page, S. (1986). Portrayal of mental illness in Canadian newspapers. *Canadian Journal of Psychiatry, 31,* 813–817.

Desforges, D. M., Lord, C. G., Ramsey, S. L., Mason, J. A., Van Leeuwen, M. D., West, S. C., et al. (1991). Effects of structured cooperative contact on changing negative attitudes toward stigmatized social groups. *Journal of Personality and Social Psychology, 60,* 531–544.

Dougherty, S. J., & Campana, K. A. (1996). Supported education: A qualitative study of the student experience. *Psychiatric Rehabilitation Journal, 19*(3), 59–70.

Dumais, S., Platt, J., Heckerman, D., & Sahami, M. (1998). Inductive learning algorithms and representations for text categorization. *Proceedings of CIKM-98, 7th ACM International Conference on Information and Knowledge Management* (pp. 148–155). New York: ACM Press.

Francis, C., Pirkis, J., Dunt, D., & Blood, R. (2001). Mental health and illness in the media: A review of the literature. *Media Monitoring Project.* Canberra, Australia: Commonwealth Department of Health and Aged Care.

Goffman, E. (1963). *Stigma: Notes on the management of spoiled identity.* Englewood Cliffs, NJ: Prentice Hall.

Henderson-King, E. I., & Nisbett, R. E. (1996). Anti-Black prejudice as a function of exposure to the negative behavior of a single Black person. *Journal of Personality and Social Psychology, 71,* 654–664.

Lawn, S., Pols, R. G., & Barber, J. G. (2002). Smoking and quitting: A qualitative study with community-living psychiatric clients. *Social Science and Medicine, 54*(1), 93–104.

Lin, Z. (1993). An exploratory study of the social judgments of Chinese college students from the perspective of attibutional theory. *Acta Psychologica Sinica, 2,* 155–164.

Link, B. G. (1987). Understanding labeling effects in the area of mental disorders: An assessment of the effects of expectations of rejection. *American Sociological Review, 54,* 96–112.

Link, B. G., Cullen, F. T., Struening, E., Shrought, P. T., & Dohrenwend, B. P. (1989). A modified labeling theory approach to mental disorders: An empirical assessment. *American Sociological Review, 54,* 400–423.

Link, B. G., Phelan, J. C., Bresnahan, M., Stueve, A., & Pescosolido, B. A. (1999). Public conceptions of mental illness: Labels, causes, dangerousness, and social distance. *American Journal of Public Health, 89,* 1328–1333.

Loevinger, J. (1957). Objective tests as instruments of psychological theory. *Psychological Reports, 3,* 635–694.

Markowitz, F. (2001). Modeling processes in recovery from mental illness: Relationships between symptoms, life satisfaction, and self-concept. *Journal of Health and Social Behavior, 42,* 64–79.

Matas, M., el-Guebaly, N., Peterkin, A., Green, M., & Harper, D. (1985). Mental illness and the media: assessment of attitudes and communication. *Canadian Journal of Psychiatry, 30,* 12–17.

Miles, M. B., & Huberman, A. M. (1994). *Qualitative data analysis* (2nd ed.). Thousand Oaks, CA: Sage.

Morgan, D. L. (1988). *Focus groups as qualitative research.* Thousand Oaks, CA: Sage.

Muhlbauer, S. (2002). Experience of stigma by families with mentally ill members. *Journal of the American Psychiatric Nurses Association, 8*(3), 76–83.

Neuendorf, K. (2002). *The Content Analysis Guidebook.* Thousand Oaks, CA: Sage.

Nicholson, J., Sweeney, E. M., & Geller, J. L. (1998a). Mothers with mental illness: I. The competing demands of parenting and living with mental illness. *Psychiatric Services, 49,* 635–642.

Nicholson, J., Sweeney, E. M., & Geller, J. L. (1998b). Mothers with mental illness: II. Family relationships and the context of parenting. *Psychiatric Services, 49,* 643–649.

Onken, S. J. (2002, January). *People with psychiatric impairments define a recovery: Facilitating community: Informing practice through grounded theory development using concept mapping methodology.* Sixth Annual Conference, Society for Social Work and Research. http://sswr.org/papers2002/405.htm

Pescosolido, B. A., Monohan, J., Link, B. G., Stueve, A., & Kikuzawa, S. (1999). Public conceptions of mental illness: Labels, causes, dangerousness, and social distance. *American Journal of Public Health, 89,* 1328–1345.

Philo, G. (Ed.). (1996). *Media and mental distress.* London: Longman.

Piner, K. E., & Kahle, L. R. (1984). Adapting to the stigmatizing label of mental illness: Foregone but not forgotten. *Journal of Personality and Social Psychology, 47,* 805–811.

Rakover, S. S. (1981). Social psychological theory and falsification. *Personality and Social Psychology Bulletin, 7,* 123–130.

Rose, D. (1998). Television, madness, and community care. *Journal of Community and Applied Social Psychology, 8,* 213–228.

Signorielli, N. (1989). The stigma of mental illness on television. *Journal of Broadcasting and Electronic Media, 33,* 325–331.

Smith, E. R. (2000). Research design. In H. T. Reid & C. M. Judd (Eds.), *Handbook of research methods in social and personality psychology* (pp. 17–39). Cambridge, England: Cambridge University Press.

Trochim, W. (1989). An introduction to concept mapping for planning and evaluation. *Evaluation and Program Planning 12*(1), 1–16.

Trochim, W., Cook, J., & Setze, R. (1994). Using concept mapping to develop a conceptual framework of staff's views of a supported employment program for persons with severe mental illness. *Journal of Consulting and Clinical Psychology, 62,* 766–775.

Van Maanen, J. (1988). *Tales of the field: On writing ethnography.* Chicago: University of Chicago Press.

Ward, G. (1997). *Making headlines: Mental health and the national press.* London: Health Education Authority.

Watson, A. (2001). *Mental illness stigma: Ideology, attributions of cause, perceptions of dangerousness and behavioral response.* Unpublished dissertation, University of Chicago School of Social Services Administration.

Weiner, B. W. (1995). *Judgments of responsibility: A foundation for a theory of social conduct.* New York: Guilford Press.

Weiner, B., Perry, R. P., & Magnusson, J. (1988). An attributional analysis of reactions to stigmas. *Journal of Personality and Social Psychology, 55,* 738–748.

Weiner, E. (1999). The meaning of education for university students with psychiatric disability: A grounded theory approach. *Psychiatric Rehabilitation Journal, 22*(4), 403–409.

Williams, M., & Taylor, J. (1995). Mental illness: Media perpetuation of stigma. *Contemporary Nurse 4*(1), 41–46.

Winer, B. (1971). *Statistical principles in experimental design.* New York: McGraw-Hill.

Yang, Y., & Liu, X. (1999). A re-examination of text categorization methods. *Proceedings of SIGIR-99, 22nd ACM International Conference on Research and Development in Information Retrieval* (pp. 42–49). New York: ACM Press.

II
UNDERSTANDING
MENTAL ILLNESS STIGMA

3

FIRST-PERSON ACCOUNTS
OF STIGMA

BETH ANGELL, ANDREA COOKE, AND KELLY KOVAC

I want to have my story written down so I can remember where I've been
and so I don't forget what I've been through. If I have it on paper, I know
it's not a lie, it's something I've been through. If people read our stories,
they know what we've been through. People who haven't been through
what we've been through need to hear our stories so they'd know what
we experience. The system sucks. I've been through the whole nine
yards. The system has to change. One way we can help it to change is by
telling our stories.

—Lalime, 1990, as cited in Deegan, 1997b

As the previous quotation suggests, narratives of illness have the power
to transform both the author and the audience: They serve to both inform the
public about the illness phenomenon and clarify and affirm the experience for
the person who experiences it. In the field of psychiatric research, consumer
narratives are increasingly recognized as an invaluable resource for understanding the perspectives of people who have experienced mental illness first-
hand or in their immediate families and for raising consciousness about
appropriate forms of treatment (Davidson, 1992; Estroff, 1989). Qualitative
analysis of such accounts has been used by others to explicate consumer perspectives on recovery (Jacobson, 2001), social functioning (Davidson &
Stayner, 1997), and coping and adaptation (Hatfield & Lefley, 1993). In this
chapter, we examine themes of stigma in the published narratives of primary
consumers and family members of persons with mental illness.

METHODS OF NARRATIVE SELECTION AND ANALYSIS

We began researching the material for this chapter by reading first-person accounts in the series published regularly by *Schizophrenia Bulletin*, with initial intent of including only primary consumer viewpoints. In reading these accounts, however, it became apparent that family members also experience stigma, and furthermore, their experiences of stigma were both similar to and different from primary consumers. We decided, therefore, to include both types of accounts, but to categorize the experiences separately.

We identified narratives using a combination of strategies. As mentioned earlier, we obtained all first-person accounts published in the *Schizophrenia Bulletin* series; we examined book-length accounts of mental illness written by primary consumers and family members that we identified through book reviews in journals such as *Psychiatric Services*. We also identified a number of primary accounts in an anthology of previously published material related to psychiatric rehabilitation, edited by Spaniol, Gagne, and Kohler (1997). Finally, to locate any published accounts we had missed, we searched the PsycINFO database of literature citations using the key words "first-person account" (through August 2002). Because this search generated primary accounts of various types of experiences, we limited our scope to articles that pertained to serious mental illness. Finally, we used several unpublished accounts obtained from conferences and lectures given by primary consumers. Hence, we have intended for our analysis to treat a wide array of sources, but recognize that there may be accounts that we have omitted. In total, we identified 72 article-length or book-length accounts. Each account was read by at least one of the authors, and screened for stigma related content; then, we categorized the content into themes using basic content analysis procedures.

CONSUMER EXPERIENCES OF STIGMA

Self-Stigma

According to Link and Phelan (2001), stigma may operate through the stigmatized person in addition to operating through discriminatory individuals and social structures. That is, consumers develop stereotypic understandings about mental illness through their socialization and membership in the broader culture, and apply these negative stereotypes to themselves after they are formally labeled. These stereotypes lead consumers to believe that they will be devalued and rejected by others, causing them to withdraw from connections and opportunities, to behave defensively, and to experience the loss of self-esteem. Gallo (1994), coining the phrase *self-stigmatization*, describes the effects of internalized stigma on her sense of self:

I perceived myself, quite accurately, unfortunately, as having a serious mental illness and therefore as having been relegated to what I called "the social garbage heap." I tortured myself with the persistent and repetitive thought that people I would encounter, even total strangers, did not like me and wished that mentally ill people like me did not exist. Thus, I would do things such as standing away from others at bus stops and hiding and cringing in the far corners of subway cars. Thinking of myself as garbage, I would even leave the sidewalk in what I thought of as exhibiting the proper deference to those above me in social class. The latter group, of course, included all other human beings. (pp. 407–408)

In turn, these avoidance behaviors and the dampened self-esteem may be perceived by others as socially awkward, leading to a vicious circle of withdrawal and rejection. One of the important aspects of self-stigma, however, is that the consumer may act on the *anticipation* of rejection, even if the rejection never actually occurs. The first-person account literature contains many references to anticipation of rejection by others in the authors' social environments, as illustrated by the following examples:

To [my] friends, I would never disclose that I have schizophrenia. Although my first inclination is to tell them about my mental illness and to gain their understanding and sympathy, this would never happen. People with schizophrenia are seen as insane, dangerous, deadly, and incomprehensible. The stigma attached to mental illness is too great a risk to friendship, and this is why I will now never tell. (Parker, 2001, p. 717)

And even now in 1980, in a professional pharmacy school, it would probably shock many people to know a schizophrenic was in their class, would be a pharmacist, and could do a good job. And knowledge of it could cause loss of many friends and acquaintances. So even now I must write this article anonymously. (Anonymous, 1983a, p. 155)

Aggravating matters more is the painful knowledge that you can't talk to anybody about these things. Not only are these things hard to talk about, but if you admit to having any of these kinds of problems you are likely to get puzzled looks or face immediate or often final rejection. Most people will put you in the category of "crazy" or "looney tunes" or "nutcase" or something similar. (Weingarten, 1994, p. 374)

As illustrated by the previous quotations and supported in empirical studies of stigma, experiences of self-stigma prompt many consumers to withdraw completely from social interaction (Link, Cullen, Streuning, Shrout, & Dohrenwend, 1989) or to limit their contacts to others with serious mental illness (Angell, 2003; Estroff, 1981; Herman, 1993). These responses serve to further isolate and marginalize the consumer from mainstream society, perpetuating the cycle of stigma.

Although self-devaluation is a common response to stigma, Corrigan and Watson (2002) point out an exceptional pattern of responses that they term the *fundamental paradox of self-stigma*. That is, although many consumers respond to stigma through withdrawal and self-derogation, a sizeable minority of persons respond to stigma by instead becoming righteously angry at the mental health system and channeling these feelings into activities such as activism and mutual empowerment to help improve the lives of other mental health consumers. Gallo's (1994) account illustrates the turn of mind entailed in the shift from demoralization to righteous anger:

> What gave me the drive to fight for my own life was how much I hated the rigid restrictions of poverty and other painful aspects of mental illness and the consequent stigmatization. I knew I could not change the collective mind of society, but I vowed to overcome the overwhelmingly negative effects of self-stigmatization, for I was acutely aware of how terribly narrow and limited choices can be when one passively accepts self-stigmatization. (pp. 408–409)

Bassman's (2000) personal account describes his unwillingness to succumb to self-stigma and its impact on his behavior in treatment:

> I knew that if I gave in, [mental health professionals] would rob me of my spirit and I would lose all the power and self-confidence I had recently obtained. The more they challenged my beliefs with extrasensory perception, precognition, or other extraordinary phenomena, the more emotional and belligerent I became. . . . In order not to give in, I became less available to their reason and logic, and grander in my assertions and beliefs. . . . Looking back I see that self-defeating behavior which got me the most radical and potentially damaging treatments as necessary for me to maintain at least some tiny bit of autonomy and self-respect. (p. 1399)

Interestingly, the kinds of behaviors that Bassman describes are ones that mental health professionals would likely label as difficult or non-compliant. Hence, these narratives illustrate the importance of educating mental health professionals to recognize healthy and self-preserving aspects of "resistance" to treatment. Weingarten's (1994) personal account also illustrates how some consumers resist the tendency to become demoralized by mental illness stereotypes and to instead educate others about the erroneous and specious nature of these attitudes:

> Much of my work as a consumer advocate has been to get the "chronically normal" population to see the mentally ill more clearly. I tell them why the commonly held stereotypes (that the mentally ill are violent, dangerous, retarded, unpredictable, evil) are simply not true. I try to explain to them how these stereotypes serve to prop them up so that they will not have to face their own fears of becoming "mentally ill." I explain why the derogatory words I have mentioned are so damaging. And I also explain how the mentally ill are discriminated against in our society. (p. 374)

Public Stigma

In contrast to self-stigmatization, public stigma refers to actual experiences of rejection or discrimination from the general public. In their conceptualization of stigma, Link and Phelan (2001) define public stigma as the process by which the public labels human differences, ascribes meaning to these differences through stereotypes, and denies life opportunities to those labeled through the exertion of power. Hence, public stigma is most noxious when it leads to the denial of opportunities—both formal and informal—to work, make a home, recreate, and form relationships with others.

Stigma and Employment

Several consumer narratives have focused on the impediments to employment caused by stigma. In some cases consumers describe experiences of out-and-out rejection on the basis of their illness. For example, one consumer author wrote:

> After a suicidal action I ended up hospitalized on a psychiatric unit. I now not only had to deal with this trauma but upon release the stress of losing my job. The stress I was under led me—perhaps foolishly—to "confide" in my employer. I was at work only a few days when I was politely fired but "assured" that I would receive good references. (Anonymous, 1981b, p. 736)

Although legal reforms such as the ADA have made outright discrimination much more difficult for employers, consumers nonetheless perceive the need to be highly selective about with whom and in what way they disclose their illnesses in the workplace so as not to contaminate hiring, retention, and interpersonal interactions at work. For example, some consumers who perceive that disclosing their illness to potential employers may impede them from being hired may creatively construct a work history that conceals gaps in their employment record. The anonymous author quoted previously (1981b) relates that after he or she was fired following a psychiatric hospitalization, the author "eventually did gain employment but only through fixing up my work history on the application. I learned that honesty is not always the best policy" (p. 736).

Anonymous (1983b) describes the importance of keeping a lid on his or her diagnosis for fear that it might damage his or her chances for a pharmacy career—a task that can be quite challenging, for example, when one is confronted with a client with serious mental illness. This narrative relates the author's dilemma when a frightened young client presenting for pharmacy services described his perceptions that he sees danger all around him:

> This young man and I are related in a way I cannot share with him, with my fellow students, or with faculty. Yes, I am a pharmacy student. But

yes, I have been diagnosed as schizophrenic and have been hospitalized on three occasions when I could not function. . . . Realization of this fact makes my role as a pharmacy student seem artificial—almost as if I must pretend and cover up to get by and pass as "normal"—and then there is always the danger that under stress or pressure my schizophrenia will get out of control and I will be found out. (p. 152)

Although many consumers find it advantageous to keep their illness secret from coworkers and supervisors, the deception can be a double-edged sword. For example, lack of disclosure can create difficulties with supervisors when a worsening of symptoms necessitates time off from work. In addition, consumers may become uncomfortable with coworkers because they may worry that their coworkers will discover the truth, and thus expend a great deal of effort managing their presentation of self. Because of these worries, consumers may forgo social activities outside work hours and withdraw from social interactions on the job, contributing to increased marginalization from the workplace environment (Angell, 2003).

Social Relationships

Stigma can also have a tremendous impact on consumers' attempts to form and maintain friendships and romantic relationships. Many consumers have described the painful experience of coming home from their first hospitalization to experiences of rejection from former friends:

One girlfriend refused to see me after I got out of the hospital. She said she saw no potential in me and that I had no future. I was deeply ashamed, but also half believed her. Now I'm selective in whom I tell about my illness. It's got to be pertinent to the conversation or I have to feel that I can trust the person I am talking to. (Weingarten, 1997, p. 127)

As the previous quotation illustrates, and as Herman's (1993) ethnographic work has shown, consumers who experience rejection may develop strategies of selectively sharing information about their illness to prevent such rejection from happening again. Weingarten (1994) wrote of such experiences:

So to avoid [rejection] you are forced to hide or conceal your thoughts and feelings from others, and then ultimately from yourself, which only serves to worsen your situation. This is why persons with mental disorders are often passive, withdrawn, and avoid human contact. (p. 374)

Goffman's seminal work on stigma (1963) makes similar observations about persons with different types of stigmatizing conditions, pointing out that people with invisible conditions such as mental illness may "pass" for normal in certain contexts. Weingarten (1997) describes, for example, the need to normalize one's job identity to pass as a non-mentally ill person in mainstream social interactions:

. . . when I became ill and was unemployed, I knew I needed another vocational identity to satisfy the curiosity of the people living around me. I told people I was a freelance writer. I enjoyed having this identity, having worked as a journalist, and it fit well with my long-term aspirations to become a writer. It also explained why I was not working conventional hours. At job interviews, it helped explain away the gaps in my employment record. (p. 127)

Media Influences

Consumers also point out that the public attitudes that cause them difficulty in everyday interactions are rooted in the very pervasive public problem of media stereotyping. As Wahl's (1995) analyses of media content suggest, the preponderance of media treatments of mental illness focus on stereotypes of violence (see chap. 7, this volume, for an analysis of the dangerousness stereotype). Consumer authors comment that these stereotypes are both unfair and damaging in social interactions:

> The media has not helped in this matter. . . . Hardly a month goes by that we do not read a lurid news story of "man goes berserk and kills neighbor" or "former mental patient kills wife." Those headlines are remembered. We do not remember or pay attention [however] . . . to the fact that thousands of individuals who have undergone treatment, are undergoing counseling, or are stabilized on medication are able to go about their daily lives without harming or frightening others. (Anonymous, 1981b, p. 462)
>
> All I knew were the stereotypes I had seen on television or in the movies. To me, mental illness meant Dr. Jekyll and Mr. Hyde, psychopathic serial killers, loony bins, morons, schizos, fruitcakes, nuts, straight jackets, and raving lunatics. They were all I knew about mental illness, and what terrified me was that professionals were saying I was one of them. (Deegan, 1997a, p. 371)

Stigma From Mental Health Professionals

Professionals who work with mental health consumers generally have benevolent intentions toward their clients and thus do not stigmatize them in the ways that do members of the naive public. Consumer narratives, however, point out that in the course of doing "good," many professionals may hold pejorative attitudes toward consumers that are enacted in paternalistic and coercive treatment strategies. Narratives describing abuses in the mental health system have a long history, beginning with the ex-patients' movement in the 1970s by organizations such as the Mental Patients Liberation Front. Chamberlain (1978), for example, related how her treatment in a hospital setting contributed to self-devaluation and anticipation of rejection by others:

Eleven years ago, I spent about five months as a patient in six mental hospitals. The experience totally demoralized me. I had never thought of myself as a particularly strong person, but after hospitalization, I was convinced of my own worthlessness. I had been told that I could not exist outside an institution. I was terrified that people would find out that I was an ex-patient and look down on me as much as I looked down on myself. (pp. 6–7)

In general, early narratives such as Chamberlain's highlighted the pivotal role of hospitalization in conveying messages of helplessness and despair, and have been associated with rejection of professionally run services and advocacy of services that were completely consumer-run. Even accounts written by consumers who embrace professional services, however, point out several ways that professionals espouse and deliver stigmatizing messages in the course of treatment. These damaging attitudes can be categorized as dehumanization, infantilization, and lowered expectations for improvement.

Dehumanization

Consumer authors frequently describe a sense of dehumanization from mental health professionals on the basis of perceptions that professionals view persons with mental illness as being devoid of feelings, sensitivities, and basic rights. One writer argues that this dehumanization may come from the trend toward viewing mental illness as a disease of the brain: "My humanity has been sacrificed to a computer printout . . . the researchers have dissected me without realizing that I'm still alive. I'm not certain or safe in all their certain uncertainties—I feel they're losing me, the person, more and more" (McGrath, 1984, pp. 638–639).

Dehumanization is implied in narratives that describe experiences of lacking a voice in mental health treatment. Blaska (unpublished), referring to the tendency to refer to people with mental illness as being "chronically mentally ill," or "CMI," relates that one gets the message that one knows that one is a "CMI" when "you spend the entire hour having the two shrinks talk to each other, not to you, but about you, in front of you." Leete (1993) points out that the fact that persons have a mental illness may cause professionals to regard their thoughts and assertions with suspicion:

I can talk, but I may not be heard. I can make suggestions, but they may not be taken seriously. I can voice my thoughts, but they may be seen as delusions. I can recite experiences, but they may be interpreted as fantasies. To be a patient or even an ex-client is to be discounted. Our label is a reality that never leaves us; it gradually shapes an identity that is hard to shed . . . too many times our efforts to cope go unnoticed or are seen as symptoms themselves. (p. 127)

Dehumanization is also present in the use of derogatory labels to describe and typify persons with serious mental illness. Gallo (1994) narrates that hearing herself referred to as a CMI during her first inpatient admission "had an almost totally catastrophic effect upon me!" (p. 407). Frese (2000) revealed that staff on the inpatient unit where he worked as a psychologist would commonly abbreviate the diagnosis of "schizophrenia, chronic undifferentiated type," as "S.C.U.T." Frese noted that staff "would refer to these patients in conversation as "scuts." Several authors describe the humiliation of the label of and concomitant stereotypes associated with borderline personality disorder. As they point out, individuals diagnosed with borderline personality disorder are often derided by professionals because professionals assume that the consumer's efforts to seek help and attention from professionals are calculated and manipulative. Williams (1998), for example, states that "some people believe people with borderline personality disorder 'enjoy' it and don't want to get well" (p. 173). Granat-Goldstein (2001) points out that typification of her behavior as manipulative impeded her from the kind of self-examination that might have permitted her to find more adaptive coping strategies:

> The most difficult behavior for me and for my therapists to manage has always been that of manipulation. Appropriate manipulation of our environment is necessary for everyone's growth and survival. My use of manipulative behavior has always been driven by a sense of urgency . . . at those times, my behavior may have been uninformed, misdirected, or poorly expressed. However, whenever my behavior was simply labeled and rejected as "manipulative," therapists were able to avoid their responsibility to examine their own behavior and the ways in which it blocked my progress. The label also allowed them to avoid understanding what I really needed and was not getting. . . . Although my attempts were not always appropriate, I clung to this tactic because I knew no other way to achieve my goals. The stigma of this label haunted me whenever I sought treatment and effectively prevented me from examining the utility of this behavior. (p. 770)

Others highlight the fact that mental health professionals fail to see them as human beings with the same needs and wants as other human beings, such as the desire to be a worker, parent, or romantic partner. Fox (1999) relates a story in which she was pressured by professionals or family members to give up custody of her children:

> I wanted to keep my family together and was devastated by the loss, but people saw my despair as part of the illness. No one, professionals or family members, thought it was possible for me to maintain my family while coping with bipolar disorder. The message was that I was a hopeless case. . . . No one made an effort to support me in caring for my children. Either I had the children and was totally responsible for their care, or I didn't have them. There was no in-between, and no effort to develop an alternative plan that would help me negotiate the demands of my mental illness and motherhood. (p. 193)

Infantilization

Consumers also report that professionals see them as childlike and in need of caretaking, a common stereotype applied to mental disorders (Corrigan, 2000). Professionals may convey the attitude that consumers require others to parent or make decisions for them when they use force in treatment. Lynch (2000) relates such an experience:

> I felt lonely, disconnected, in the public mental health system. I was forcibly injected, tied down. It felt like the rape I experienced as a child. To have no choice, no voice in treatment, no choice of therapist. It replicated the powerlessness of childhood. To have decisions made for you, not with you, as an adult, was a violation. (p. 1429)

The expression of attitudes about the childlike nature of consumers also permeates the language professionals use when talking about them. Leete (1993) writes:

> Professionals continue to measure our progress with concepts like "consent" and "cooperate" and "comply" instead of "choose," insinuating that we have no control over our illnesses. This is completely erroneous. We can and should be an active agent in managing our own illnesses, as well as partners in the design and implementation of our treatment. (p. 122)

At other times, consumers report that professionals perceive failures to improve as the sole responsibility of the consumer and indicative of moral failure. Granat-Goldstein (2001) related that early in her illness "my treatment teams agreed that I had to 'hit bottom.' I was 'resistant' to treatment. I had the audacity or perversity to fail to get better; my basic character was flawed and I was responsible for my own misery" (p. 769).

Lowered Expectations

One of the key sources of stigma consumers report receiving from professionals is the message that their illnesses will be lifelong and will entail ongoing disability. As Harding, Zubin, and Strauss (1992) and others have shown, research showing moderate levels of functional recovery decades following the onset of schizophrenia challenges professional assumptions that mental illness follows a progressive, debilitating course. Many consumers have written narratives about being given these pessimistic messages during treatment, with initial hospitalizations having played an especially pivotal role:

> I would later learn that during this first hospitalization the doctors had decided that because of the long history of problems and the results of the testing, I had a poor prognosis. My first diagnosis would be chronic schizophrenia. Although I had just turned 19, the professionals expected me to be a back ward patient, and advised my parents to find facilities that were custodial in nature. (Lovejoy, 1982, p. 606)

I was told that I had a disease that was like diabetes, and if I continued to take neuroleptic medications for the rest of my life and avoided stress, I might be able to cope . . . it felt as if my whole teenage world—in which I aspired to dreams of being a valued person in valued roles . . . began to crumble and shatter. It felt as if these parts of my identity were being stripped from me. I was beginning to undergo that radically dehumanizing and devaluing transformation from being a person to being an illness. (Deegan, 1997a, p. 370)

In addition to communicating the irreversibility of the illness, professionals may also suggest that consumers should expect very little accomplishment in various life domains, especially in the area of employment, as evidenced by the following examples:

[My psychiatrist] was emphatic in alerting all of us to the chronic lifelong course of my disease and explained how I would have to learn to live with my limitations. If I did become able to work, future employment would have to be in a low-pressure, low-stress job. (Bassman 2000, p. 1401)

On the negative side, I wish some of my doctors would have shown more faith in me. One doctor told me the only job I could do was that of a dishwasher. (Weingarten, 1997, p. 126)

Once, as I was being discharged from a hospital, my social worker told me, "Face the facts. You'll only be a store clerk a few months out of each year. As you get older, you'll have more and more hospitalizations. You're just not being realistic, Donna, if you expect anything more than that." (Orrin, 1997, p. 141)

These attitudes also get transmitted into how systems work. Despite great progress in vocational rehabilitation technology, many mental health service systems offer a limited range of vocational options, such as sheltered work, which communicates to consumers that they are not capable of doing "real work" (Chamberlain & Rogers, 1990).

Although in many cases professionals act with good intentions in imparting this kind of information, consumer authors argue that these comments are potentially damaging because they function as a kind of death sentence, destroying the consumer's sense of hope. Orrin (1997) states that "a lack of hope has the danger of almost paralyzing a person, or preventing them from going after their dreams" (p. 141).

Deegan (1997c) writes that these messages of low expectation may lead the consumer to develop a "hardened heart," wherein they close themselves off from caring or feeling. Professionals, failing to recognize the effects of their own negative prognostication, may interpret the seemingly apathetic stance of the consumer as being indicative of a "negative syndrome" and dismiss further the consumer's prospects for improvement. Bassman (2000), in addition, argues that the low expectations of professionals can lead to a kind of fundamental attribution area because their assumptions blind them to the successes that exist apart from the mental illness. He states:

Clinicians and policy-makers need to consider other possibilities. What they see and define as behavior stemming from poor functioning can be recast as arising from a social structure that deprives certain people of the opportunity and resources to allow their real competencies to manifest themselves. An episodic crisis can be reflective of developmental issues and may contain the potential for growth when evaluated within the whole and unique context of that individual's life. Can we be so sure that we know a person's limits? (p. 1406)

FAMILY EXPERIENCES OF STIGMA

Like the consumer with mental illness, family members may have existing stereotypes about mental illness that become personally relevant when their ill family member becomes officially labeled. The strains and tensions that result from the difficult behaviors associated with the mental illness multiply as families struggle to manage their own negative attitudes and those of other family members, friends, and the general public. Lefley (1989) distinguished between two types of family stigma. One type is the public stigma that generalizes from the person with mental illness to the family. As Lefley puts it, "The behaviors of persons with psychotic disorders may further isolate the family, diminish its reputation, and jeopardize relationships with friends and neighbors" (p. 557). Public stigma can also be experienced vicariously, as the sense of stigma families experience when others reject or mistreat their mentally ill family members.

The second type of stigma is a self-stigma that Lefley characterizes as iatrogenic, in which the family absorbs messages of culpability from professionals and from society in general and, as a consequence, may experience self-blame and guilt regarding their family member's illness. Attitudes about culpability are conveyed to the immediate family members (primarily parents) of the consumer by both professionals (professional stigma) and by other family members (intrafamily stigma).

Public Stigma

Many families report that acquaintances and friends reacted in negative ways in response to the mental illness of their family member. Individuals who grow up with a mentally ill parent or sibling often recall embarrassing episodes that resulted in painful isolation from peer groups. A participant in Dunn's (1997) study of family members related the following painful story:

> I remember being embarrassed because my mother would use words to describe things that I found out later were not what things were. I remember Show and Tell in school, and bringing something that was normal in my house, and the kids really laughed—they thought that it

was really funny. Kids would laugh; teachers would whisper. I thought that it was me—that there was something wrong with me. (p. 328)

Another participant reflected on the painful recognition that the "neighborhood witch" her peers would joke about turned out to be her own mother (Dunn, 1997).

Parents of people with serious mental illness appear to be especially vulnerable to the stigma of being blamed for the onset of the mental illness. For example, friends and acquaintances may endorse the belief, long held by many mental health professionals, that the mental illness was caused by problematic family dynamics. Clea Simon (1997), in her account of growing up with two older siblings with mental illness, related a story about how a high school friend had responded to her brother Daniel's illness:

> [He] defended Daniel as a sensitive soul with a highly creative mind who had been tragically misunderstood by all of us. He recalled how even back in high school, Daniel had told him of the persecution he faced from his family. And he'd known the pressure had gotten worse, our family was more rejecting, as Daniel had dropped out of college—his father's college, this man pointed out accusingly—to follow his own star. Even I, then an eight year old child, had supposedly taken part in the effort to squelch Daniel's original fire. Nothing was ever "wrong" with Daniel, this man asserted. We simply never understood him. (p. 37)

Such responses compound the shame experienced by family members, prompting many to keep the mental illness a secret as much as possible. Moorman (2002), who has written a memoir about her family's experience with her sibling Sally, recalls that her mother admonished Margaret, then a child, to keep Sally's mental illness a secret from the neighbors. As she notes, "In those days, even divorce carried a crushing stigma among the people we knew; mental illness was unthinkable" (p. 68). Moorman recalls an incident in which her mother had gone to great pains to hide from visitors a magazine whose address label betrayed Sally's presence at the Sheppard Pratt psychiatric hospital. She relates the story:

> As [the guests] walked out of the hall, she grabbed the magazine, glared at me, and shoved it into the drawer with the phone books. After the guests left, she screamed at me: How could I leave the magazine out, with the hospital's address showing? Did I want everyone to know where Sally was? How could I be so careless? (p. 69)

These types of responses serve to propagate stigma within families. As Moorman notes, "This incident, for me, was the beginning of my feelings of shame, for Sally's illness, for my family, and for myself" (p. 69).

Keeping the mental illness shrouded in secrecy can cause family members to feel alienated from others even when they are not socially isolated in an objective sense. In a qualitative study of children raised by adults with mental illness, Dunn (1997) reported that study participants "described a sense of alienation from the community and their peers. Although most reached out to others at some time, whether it was to a friend, a friend's family, or a teacher, they described feeling different from these other, 'normal' people, almost as if they had two lives, each with its own reality" (p. 327).

Some family members report that the stigma of mental illness is so pernicious that family members and acquaintances were unable to acknowledge that the person's behavior could possibly be a mental illness. One spouse of a man with schizophrenia related:

> One of the things that most unsettled me was that no one seemed to acknowledge that something was wrong with my husband. Jon himself claimed that he was perfectly well except for his insomnia, his parents preferred to put down any strange behavior to my nefarious influence, and the doctors just avoided the issue. When acquaintances asked me why Jon didn't have a job or why he didn't participate in social or cultural events, I tried to tell them, but their reactions were discouraging. Either they overreacted ("How do you dare to live with him? He could become violent!") or they looked disbelieving ("You must be imagining things. He looks perfectly normal to me"). So I was alone with this painful knowledge that something was wrong. Sometimes I was on the brink of believing I myself must be hallucinating. (Anonymous, 1994, p. 228)

Vicarious Stigma From the General Public

In addition to the shame experienced from others, family members also experience stigma vicariously through the rejection their relatives with mental illness receive by the general public. Although families may find the appearance and behavior of their relatives repulsive or inappropriate at times, they have a biographical sense of the person that makes them tolerant and sympathetic. They find, however, that the general public is often far less accepting. Kagigebi (1995) relates such a story about her son Burt:

> I have had to force myself to get to know the mentally ill Burt. As you can see, it is hard. Sometimes he's OK and we can do things together, but it still isn't the same. Sometimes his hair is dirty and his clothes look like he slept in them. On one occasion, we were standing in line at a fast food place. The lady standing behind Burt looked at his dirty hair and the rest of his appearance and stepped back from him and whispered something about Burt to her companion. I fought back tears because they really hurt me. To think that someone thought my son was too gross to even stand behind. (p. 159)

As much as they grieve for the loss of relationship with the person with mental illness, families additionally experience sadness over limited opportunities for their relative to participate in valued social roles such as spouse or partner. Betty Hyland reflects on how a woman who she imagines might once have been attracted to her son Ted coldly rejects his social overtures:

Ted [frequents] a booth in a chicken takeout where he develops a crush on a waitress. She looks like a girl he once knew and most likely would have married if it hadn't developed that he had such a faulty blueprint . . . the waitress' training does not include dealing with people like Ted. Soon he's showing up too often and staying too long. The day he tries to explain why he drinks that milk, she says, "Get lost, yo-yo," and the manager tells him to "move it out, Charlie." Ted flees, hurt and perplexed. (p. 542)

Finally, family members experience a sense of indignation when mental health professionals fail to acknowledge and consider the humanity of the person with mental illness in the family. Neugeboren (1997b) eloquently relates such feelings regarding the inpatient treatment of his brother Robert:

But meanwhile, back on the ward, Robert has to sneak out of his room to telephone me . . . meanwhile important messages don't get through . . . meanwhile, back on the ward, the major activities are TV and card games, the staff is outnumbered and overworked, the refrigerator is pad-locked, and the only time patients can get snacks is when an aide unlocks it twice a day at "refrigerator time." . . . In the world Robert too often lives in, ordinary habits and idiosyncrasies (sloppiness about clothing, loud talking) become psychological deficits for which one receives demerits, and worse. . . . [M]odel patients are not very different from model prisoners. (p. 316)

Family Stigma From Mental Health Professionals

The long-standing tension between mental health providers and families of persons with mental illness, much of it emanating from the families' perception of being blamed by professionals for causing the illness of their relative, has been well documented in the family literature (Terkelsen, 1990). The first-person account literature written by parents and siblings in particular contains many examples of these problematic interactions. In her memoir of growing up with mentally ill siblings, Clea Simon (1998) recalls her parents attending family therapy sessions from the late 1960s that focused on the role of problematic family dynamics:

During one of these trips, I learned later, my parents participated in family therapy with other McLean patients, their parents, and a social worker to facilitate discussion. . . . "Why are you putting such high expectations on your son?" she asked my mother, accusing her by implication. "Can't you see what such a high stress environment has done to him?" Nobody told my mother that her son's deterioration wasn't her fault. (pp. 34–35)

Although much of the causal responsibility for the etiology of the illness has been focused on parents of the ill person, other family members may also experience stigmatizing attitudes from professionals who suggest that the responsibility for preventing relapse or further deterioration rests in the family's hands. Dunn (1997), who interviewed a sample of adults who were parented by a person with mental illness, described several examples of professional advice to be "more understanding" and even overt pressure to stay and care for an abusive parent. Others, such as Moorman (2002), relate stories of professionals who eschewed family input on major treatment decisions, disparaging them as meddling and intrusive toward their relative. She recalls, for example, a situation in which her mother had accepted her sister Sally back into the family home when she had no other place to live:

> It was a move that every doctor and social worker who had ever seen Sally inveighed against. They seemed to give Mother no credit for the immense amount of genuine help she offered. Instead, they told her repeatedly that Sally would "never grow up" if she kept "meddling." They made her feel that she was poison for her eldest daughter. (p. 101)

Family members who write from the dual perspective of family members and professionals take issue with interventions that are predicated on the expressed emotion (EE) concept, viewing families as key components of a stressful environment. As Hatfield, Spaniol, and Zipple (1987) wrote,

> Placing families in dichotomous categories of high EE and low EE amounts to stereotyping; such an approach does little to help professionals in understanding the complexities of family life with a mentally ill relative. High EE is seen as a factor that maintains mental illness in a relative. Once more, families feel hurt and alienated. Once more, families feel negatively labeled, but not empathically understood. (p. 221)

In addition to perceptions of blame by professionals, many family members who authored primary accounts report insensitive treatment by professionals that undermined their ability to cope with stigma. One problem reported is that mental health professionals may fail to make themselves available to families: Mittleman (1985) comments that "it takes days before you get to speak to a social worker or doctor. They are busy people and have heavy work loads" (p. 2). Another reported problem is the nature of the assistance offered to families. As one wife of a mentally ill man stated, "When I showed undue anxiety or distress, they only offered me pills to calm me down" (Anonymous, 1994, p. 1).

Intrafamily Stigma

A key source of stigma toward parents is the attribution that they are responsible for the onset of their child's mental illness. Although historically it has been most common for service providers to hold these attitudes (Johnson, 1990), attitudes about the role of families in causing the illness are also pervasive in the wider culture, and thus may be absorbed by the family. In a survey of family members of persons with serious mental illness in New York, for example, half of the sample endorsed the belief that most people blame parents for the mental illness of their children (Streuning et al., 2001). When the stigma of blame comes from within the family, it can be especially painful for the immediate family of the ill person. Wasow (1995), who studied a sample of nonparental family members of persons with mental illness, reported that extended family members would make comments such as "His illness was caused by bad parenting," or "My sister didn't know how to raise him" (p. 120). In another personal account, a brother of a woman with schizophrenia stated, "I thought Lori's illness was a result of the way my parents treated her. I began to feel that [my father] thought the same thing I did—that he had caused Lori's illness, and that he was afraid of causing it in me" (Schiller & Bennett, 1994, p. 56).

Being blamed for the illness by professionals and other family members is very distressing to the family. Families report, for example, feelings of guilt (from being perceived as responsible for the illness) and shame. As Mittleman (1985) put it,

> You get the feeling that no one understands what you and your family are going through, and you can't share it with many people because of the shame. You know somewhere deep down that people are wondering if you were somehow the cause of it all. Even your friends tell you not to talk about it too much because people don't understand. (p. 302)

Because "nurture" theories of child psychopathology are so pervasive in popular culture, families (particularly parents) may actually absorb these stereotypes and blame themselves for their child's illness. Marvin Schiller, who authored sections of his daughter's personal account of mental illness, described his initial assumptions of self-blame after the onset of his daughter's illness:

> Back when I studied psychology in the 1950s, there was only one cause for all mental illnesses, even the most severe: a faulty upbringing. Everything was tied to the way you were raised. . . . A patient with serious mental problems had been subject at an early age to unacceptable pressures, to confusing messages, or to some destructive behavior on the part of the parents. If Lori were really sick, my training told me, then I was to blame. (Schiller & Bennett, 1994, p. 45)

Another author described her painful soul search to determine what she had done to "cause" her son's schizophrenia:

> I blamed myself. It had to be someone's fault. Maybe I shouldn't have smoked when I was pregnant. Then, I remembered I had quit at the time. Maybe I should have never married my ex-husband because he was an alcoholic and verbally abusive. Maybe I shouldn't have been watching my weight when I was pregnant. I was driving myself crazy. (Kagigebi, 1995, p. 157)

When families feel ashamed of their relative's illness, blamed by professionals and friends for the illness, and alone in their experience, they often withdraw from their social networks, resulting in extreme social isolation. As Mittleman (1985) stated, "You no longer open your home as freely. You don't want people to know the extent of tension, suffering, and anguish you are going through. Who wants to be with someone who is so unhappy?" (p. 2). Other families point to the strain placed on the marital dyad, as exemplified by this quote from Mittleman (1985): "When the ill person has to live at home, as often happens, many marriages fail. Even when the ill person lives away, there is always the question of who was responsible. Which mate caused it? What did I do to contribute? The tension takes all that is good out of life and marriage" (p. 302).

HELPING CONSUMERS AND FAMILIES COPE WITH STIGMA

Despite the frequent experience of mistreatment in the mental health system, consumers and families also report positive experiences with mental health professionals. Consumer authors report that professional treatment is most helpful and least noxious when treaters exemplify several personal qualities. First, some reported that it was important that their therapists broke down the traditional professional boundaries of detachment and authority. Treaters who are able to do this must humble themselves to such a degree that they recognize their own shortcomings and frailties, argues Deegan (1988):

> If a rehabilitation program is to be a dynamic setting that promotes and nurtures the recovery process, then the rigid walls separating the "world of the disabled" and the "world of the normal" must be torn down. Staff members must be helped to recognize the ways in which they, too, are deeply wounded. . . . To embrace and accept our own woundedness and vulnerability is the first step toward understanding the experience of persons with disabilities. In so doing we discover that we share a common humanity with them and that we are not worlds apart. (p. 18)

Similarly, Granat-Goldstein (2001) argues: "The kinds of change that I continue to seek are accomplished with the assistance of therapists who understand and accept their personal and professional limitations" (p. 770).

Second, it is important, consumer authors say, for providers to truly believe in the potential for recovery. Unlike the conveyance of low expectations, giving messages of the possibility of recovery helps consumers retain a sense of hope even in the midst of struggle. Lovejoy (1984) describes such a message as the catalyst for change in her own recovery:

> The psychiatrist who saw me in the hospital talked with me at length and then said something I will long remember. He said he had never seen anyone as sick as I was who could express her symptoms as well as I could.

He said he did not want to believe that I could not recover. . . . This was a major turning point for me. (p. 810)

Another author wrote:

The human connection I have developed with the therapist has helped me to reject the idea that I will never be able to relate to people or fit into society like a "normal" person . . . I got a lot of much needed encouragement which has allowed me to have some hope for the future rather than to feel that my life is over. (Anonymous, 1989b, p. 345)

Weingarten (1994) likewise stresses the need for professionals to convey possibility rather than creating a ceiling of expectations:

My report is directed particularly to future mental health professionals: Much of your effectiveness as a professional will depend on how you view the person you are dealing with and how much hope you can communicate to them. These things are largely intangible and can't be taught. They've got to come from inside you. Perhaps the best advice that I can give you is for you to treat the person you're working with like a good teacher treats all of her students. When she expects great things from them, they will usually reward her by performing to her expectations. When given the opportunity, your clients will live up to your expectations. (p. 375)

The importance consumers ascribe to having a close relationship with a therapist calls into question the frequently invoked dictum that persons with mental illness cannot benefit from psychotherapy. McGrath (1984) laments the message that psychotherapy is "useless" for people like herself: "How could he even suggest that without knowing me, the one over here in this corner, who finds a lot of support, understanding, and acceptance with my therapist?" (p. 639).

Leete (1993) argues that it is important not only for individual providers to believe in and promote recovery, but also for treatment environments to embody this philosophy. Describing her experience in a nonauthoritarian treatment environment, she wrote:

There was a strong orientation toward success, and an expectation from the beginning that we would all leave and become independent through the continuing process of building on our individual strengths. To help us with this, treatment focused on our healthy and adaptive aspects rather than our deficits. . . . The residential treatment team considered me a partner in the recovery process rather than a less knowledgeable inferior. . . . The staff did not approach my treatment with a negatively biased view of what I could accomplish. (p. 121)

Family members likewise point out the benefits of working with professionals who understand mental illness and its effects on the family. One child of an adult with serious mental illness attested to the power of being able to name the problem when she stated, "That was one of the greatest days, when someone said, 'Your mother [has paranoid schizophrenia].' They gave it a name, they explained it to me, and I said, 'Thank you! Now I know.' That just meant the world to me. It's so much easier to deal with something concrete" (Dunn, 1997, p. 331). Many family members believe that the most desirable quality in providers is to have made the paradigm shift, viewing the families as victims (as opposed to blaming them) and regarding them as allies in treatment (rather than targets of change [Bernheim, 1990; Lefley, 1989]).

Programs and Stigma

Consumer-run services are increasingly recognized as legitimate and beneficial alternatives to the traditional mental health system. Chamberlain (1997), describing the history and structure of the ex-patient movement, notes that advocacy and self help are the two key components of consumer run services. With respect to challenging the stigma of mental illness, consumer authors report that both facets are critical. Many consumers, for example, highlight the importance of mutual help in reinstating a sense of humanity and empowerment that, for many, eroded in response to mistreatment from the mental health system:

> A peer-run support group can help us understand our disease, and we can learn to function in spite of it by successfully compensating for our disabilities. A support group can given us the personal strength and commitment to overcome the stigma, prejudice, discrimination, and rejection we have experienced, and to reclaim our personal validity, our dignity as individuals, and our autonomy. Here each member is accepted and affirmed, valued and validated. (Leete, 1993, pp. 126–127)

As Chamberlain and Rogers (1990) point out, self-help also benefits consumers by giving them a chance to reciprocate help, which is important when individuals become passive, helpless, and demoralized. They wrote:

> Such user-run programs as drop-in centers and peer case management provide people with a feeling that they can give, as well as receive, which builds self-esteem. At drop-in centers people can find friends and a sense of belonging, maybe for the first time in their lives. They also meet role models—other consumers who are making it in the community. (p. 1243)

The role modeling function highlighted in the previous quotation also figures prominently in consumer narratives regarding self help. Lynch (2000) wrote of the ways that self help participation enabled her to better identify her own personal stressors that led to symptom exacerbation:

> My friends from the Unity Club, a peer support group for people labeled with manic depression, provided love and concern both during the night and the day. Friends helped me recognize patterns in my life that con-

tributed to my episodes of mania and depression and shared tips on how to get through. (p. 1430)

As noted earlier, advocacy is an equally important aspect of consumer-run services. Whereas self-help provides consumers opportunities to learn coping strategies and to derive a sense of self-worth from helping others, advocacy empowers consumers through the process of changing the system that, for many of them, contributed to their former feelings of demoralization. As Deegan (1997a) put it:

> My real hope for rehumanizing the human services rests with people with disabilities as we begin learning that we can organize, that we have power in our numbers, and that we can overcome oppression through expression. (p. 355)

Others point out the benefits of belonging to something larger than oneself, providing a sense of community:

> When I found the c/s/x [consumer/survivor/ex-patient] movement, I found something that made sense. The values that the movement promotes concerning choice, trust, and personal responsibility far outweighed the mantra I had been hearing my entire life—that I was sick. I was finally able to accept the loss of being dependent on the mental health system. At a recent conference I asked one of my peers what being involved in the movement was like for him. He said, "It's like never having to be alone again." I knew exactly what he meant. (Tenney, 2000, p. 1442)

Family Self-Help

For an overwhelming number of family members who have detailed their experiences in personal accounts, participation in advocacy organizations such as NAMI has proven beneficial in managing and combating stigma. Family members report that one of the key advantages of belonging to NAMI at the local and national levels is that it provided them with education about mental illness and assistance with problem solving that they had not been able to get from professionals. Willis (1982) describes the benefit she received from participating in a local support group for families:

> In our problem-sharing get-togethers we find that, although each person's situation is unique, there are many common problems, ranging from those which seem trivial (but which can be difficult to contend with), such as lack of personal care and poor grooming, sleeping and eating too much or not enough, to more serious problems, such as lack of motivation, inability to handle money . . . refusal to take medication, bizarre behavior, delusional thinking, paranoia, occasional violence, and suicide attempts. (p. 618)

In addition to direct assistance in problem solving, family advocacy organizations provide an important message to families about their lack of culpability for causing the mental illness of their family member. Citing public educational media distributed by the advocacy organizations that clearly define mental disorders as no-fault conditions, Neugeboren (1997a) points out:

> Surely, thinking that biology causes it (in the same way it causes cancer, diabetes, or heart disease, illnesses to which it is frequently compared), and that nobody's to blame . . . does enormous good: it reduces anxiety, stigma, and guilt; it inspires hope; it allows for increased coverage under (some) insurance plans; it provides . . . forums and practical assistance for families; enables useful legislation and research and so on. (p. 315)

DISCUSSION

The personal accounts presented here buttress the notion that stigma is a real phenomenon for persons with mental illness and their families, providing vivid illustrations of the picture provided by a recent survey of public attitudes in which respondents strongly endorsed perceptions of dangerousness and personal responsibility regarding persons with serious mental illness (Pescosolido, Monahan, Link, Stueve, & Kilkuzawa, 1999). In this section, we highlight several themes that are pertinent to mental health services and stigma change efforts.

The narratives presented here demonstrate that stigma takes many forms and emanates from numerous sources, such as the general public, extended family, friends, and mental health professionals. This diversity of stereotypes and sources suggests that stigma change efforts must use targeted strategies to be effective (see Watson & Corrigan, chap. 13, this volume, for a discussion of targeted approaches to stigma change). For example, interventions that supply exposure to a person with mental illness who is functioning moderately well may help to counter perceptions of dangerousness among the general public, but this would be a less appropriate strategy for changing the attitudes of mental health professionals because it is likely their extensive exposure to acutely ill populations propagates the assumption that mental illness has a progressive downhill course with little hope for recovery (Harding, Zubin, & Strauss, 1987). Hence, a contact intervention might be more appropriately tailored to professionals if it, for example, involved contact with mental health consumers who would report stories of how maltreatment in the mental health system had affected their progress and recovery.

Some of the most powerful effects of stigma, as Link and Phelan (2001) have suggested, are set into motion far in advance of opportunities for public stigma and discrimination. Prevailing stereotypes of dangerousness and incompetence are absorbed by consumers and family members before the onset of illness, and become relevant when the consumer begins to experience the symptoms of mental illness. For families, embarrassment, shame, and denial about the possibility that their family member may have a mental illness generates a web of secrecy, shame, and ultimately isolation as the family works to keep the mental illness a secret from extended family and friends. Consequently, they may delay getting treatment for their family member or critical social support for themselves. For consumers, hospitalization frequently serves as a critical juncture in the process of self-stigma, as this may be the initial labeling event, and indeed, activates and makes personally relevant stereotypes about the deviance of mental illness and the need to sequester mentally ill people from the rest of society. As Lally's (1989) work has shown, the first hospitalization can shift a consumer's identity to that of a "mental patient," prompting consumers to relinquish hopes and dreams for the future and become demoralized. Similarly, many of the consumer authors whose accounts are presented here depict initial hospitalizations as defining moments that prompted them to view themselves as social outcasts. Because many such negative experiences derive from formal mental health services such as hospitals and clinics, self-help programs may provide alternative or complementary supports to counteract pessimistic messages, as described in the accounts reviewed here. Watson and River (chap. 6, this volume) likewise describe various avenues to empowerment for consumers who experience self-stigma. In progress studies such as the Consumer Operated Services Program Multi-Site Study, funded by the Center for Mental Health Services will evaluate effectiveness of self-help interventions in bolstering empowerment and hope among consumers. With the development of an evidence base for consumer operated services, such services may be more widely disseminated and more comprehensively financed through public insurance.

Although the addition of self-help programs may help to counteract stigma, it is still important for the field to address stereotypes and problematic behaviors among mental health professionals, as these accounts suggest that psychiatrists, psychologists, social workers, and other professionals directly influence the process by which consumers and family members develop internalized stigma. Many consumers, for example, wrote of having to work to overcome the demoralization of messages from professionals that they should expect a long, difficult course of illness and that their prospects for employment would be sharply curtailed. Several also described incidents in which professionals used coercive or paternalistic strategies to get them to use services, or made decisions on their behalf without asking for their input. These professional attitudes and behavior are ripe for further examination and may likewise benefit from stigma change programs specially tailored to target problematic stereotypes and assumptions characteristic of mental health providers and to imbue providers with a sense of the possibilities of consumer recovery and growth. Weinstein (2000), who identified necessary practitioner competencies in psychiatric rehabilitation in collaboration with a task group, argues that a belief in recovery is critical if providers are to help consumers establish and work toward normative community integration and a sense of personal fulfillment. Determining what types of staff training approaches effectively encourage providers to internalize principles of individuality, dignity, and hope should be a focus of future study. With regard to professional attitudes toward family, a longer history exists of advocacy by families to change professional attitudes; however, organizational barriers such as a lack of attention to confidentiality procedures to encourage family-professional collaboration (Marshall & Solomon, 2000) constitute fruitful areas for intervention.

Several of the accounts presented here highlight a tension between consumer and family perspectives regarding the types of information that are helpful in lessening stigma. Family members experience stigma when they perceive that professionals hold them responsible for their ill relative's illness, and thus derive a sense of relief when professionals espouse biologically based models of mental illness that depict mental illness as a disease process or "no-fault brain disorder" that follows a characteristically lifelong course. Consumers, on the other hand, may perceive the message that mental illness is a "brain disorder" as precluding the possibility for recovery and improvement. Hence, it is important, when educating families and consumers about mental illness, to include information about the positive prospects for recovery of function in addition to information about the probable genetic and biochemical basis for the mental illness.

Finally, it is important to note that although consumer and family narratives provide an invaluable and relatively untapped resource for understanding the experiences of these individuals, they do not constitute a representative sample of these experiences. Hence, studies that inquire into the experiences of a broader range of consumers and family members should be conducted regarding consumer and family experiences of stigma.

REFERENCES

Angell, B. (2003). Contexts of social relationship development among assertive community treatment clients. *Mental Health Services Research, 5,* 13–25.

Anonymous. (1981a). First person account: Problems of living with schizophrenia. *Schizophrenia Bulletin, 7,* 196–197.

Anonymous. (1981b). The quiet discrimination. *Schizophrenia Bulletin, 7,* 736–738.

Anonymous. (1983a). First person account: A father's thoughts. *Schizophrenia Bulletin, 9,* 439–442.

Anonymous. (1983b). Schizophrenia: A pharmacy student's view. *Schizophrenia Bulletin, 9,* 153–155.

Anonymous. (1989a). First person account: A delicate balance. *Schizophrenia Bulletin, 15*, 345–346.

Anonymous. (1989b). How I've managed chronic mental illness. *Schizophrenia Bulletin, 15*, 635–640.

Anonymous. (1990). Behind the mask: A functional schizophrenic copes. *Schizophrenia Bulletin, 16*, 547–549.

Anonymous. (1992). First person account: Portrait of a schizophrenic. *Schizophrenia Bulletin, 18*, 333–336.

Anonymous. (1994). First person account: Life with a mentally ill spouse. *Schizophrenia Bulletin, 20*, 227–229.

Bassman, R. (2000). Agents, not objects: Our fights to be. *Journal of Clinical Psychology/In Session, 56*, 1395–1411.

Bernheim, K. F. (1990). Family-provider relationships: Charting a new course. In H. P. Lefley & D. L. Johnson (Eds.), *Families as allies in treatment of the mentally ill: New directions for mental health professionals* (pp. 99–113). Washington, DC: American Psychiatric Press.

Blaska, B. (1990a). The myriad medication mistakes in psychiatry: A consumer's view. *Hospital and Community Psychiatry, 41*, 993–998.

Blaska, B. (1990b). *What it's like to be treated like a CMI.* Unpublished manuscript, Madison, WI.

Bockes, Z. (1985). First person account: "Freedom" means knowing you have a choice. *Schizophrenia Bulletin, 11*, 487–489.

Bowden, W. D. (1993). First person account: The onset of paranoia. *Schizophrenia Bulletin, 19*, 165–167.

Brodoff, A. S. (1988). Schizophrenia through a sister's eyes: The burden of invisible baggage. *Schizophrenia Bulletin, 14*, 113–116.

Caldwell-Smith, G. (1990). A mother's view. *Schizophrenia Bulletin, 16*, 687–690.

Chamberlain, J. (1978). *On our own: Patient-controlled alternatives to the mental health system.* New York: McGraw-Hill.

Chamberlain, J. (1995). Rehabilitating ourselves: The psychiatric survivor movement. *International Journal of Mental Health, 24*, 39–46.

Chamberlain, J. (1997). The ex-patients' movement: Where we've been and where we're going. In L. Spaniol, C. Gagne, & M. Koehler (Eds.), *Psychological and social aspects of psychiatric disability* (pp. 541–551). Boston: Center for Psychiatric Rehabilitation. (Reprinted from *Journal of Mind and Behavior, 11*, 323–336)

Chamberlain, J., & Rogers, J. A. (1990). Planning a community-based mental health system: Perspective of service recipients. *American Psychologist, 45*, 1241–1244.

Corrigan, P. W. (2000). Mental health stigma as social attribution: Implications for research methods and attitude change. *Clinical Psychology: Science and Practice, 7*, 48–67.

Corrigan, P. W., & Watson, A. S. (2002). The paradox of self-stigma and mental illness. *Clinical Psychology: Science and Practice, 9*, 35–53.

Davidson, L. (1992). Developing an empirical-phenomenological approach to schizophrenia research. *Journal of Phenomenological Psychology, 23*, 3–15.

Davidson, L., & Stayner, D. (1997). Loss, loneliness, and the desire for love: Perspectives on the social lives of people with schizophrenia. *Psychiatric Rehabilitation Journal, 20*, 3–12.

Deegan, P. E. (1988). Recovery: The lived experience of rehabilitation. *Psychosocial Rehabilitation Journal, 11*, 11–19.

Deegan, P. E. (1992). The independent living movement and people with psychiatric disabilities: Taking back control over our own lives. *Psychosocial Rehabilitation Journal, 15*, 3–19.

Deegan, P. E. (1997a). Recovering our sense of value after being labeled. In L. Spaniol, C. Gagne, & M. Koehler (Eds.), *Psychological and social aspects of psychiatric disability* (pp. 370–376). Boston: Center for Psychiatric Rehabilitation. (Reprinted from *Journal of Psychosocial Nursing, 31*, pp. 7–11, 33–34)

Deegan, P. E. (1997b). Recovery as a journey of the heart. In L. Spaniol, C. Gagne, & M. Koehler (Eds.), *Psychological and social aspects of psychiatric disability* (pp. 74–83). Boston: Center for Psychiatric Rehabilitation. (Reprinted from *Psychiatric Rehabilitation Journal, 19*, 91–97, 1996)

Deegan, P. E. (1997c). Spirit breaking: When helping professions hurt. In L. Spaniol, C. Gagne, & M. Koehler (Eds.), *Psychological and social aspects of psychiatric disability* (pp. 348–357). Boston: Center for Psychiatric Rehabilitation. (Reprinted from *Humanistic Psychologist, 18*(3), pp. 301–313, 1990)

Dunn, B. (1997). Growing up with a psychotic mother: A retrospective study. In L. Spaniol, C. Gagne, & M. Koehler (Eds.), *Psychological and social aspects of psychiatric disability* (pp. 323–332). Boston: Center for Psychiatric Rehabilitation. (Reprinted from *American Journal of Orthopsychiatry, 63*, 177–189)

Du Val, M. (1979). Giving love . . . and schizophrenia. *Schizophrenia Bulletin, 5*, 631–636.

Estroff, S. E. (1981). *Making it crazy: An ethnography of psychiatric clients in an American community.* Berkeley: University of California.

Estroff, S. E. (1989). Self, identity, and subjective experiences of schizophrenia: In search of the subject. *Schizophrenia Bulletin, 15*, 189–196.

Fortner, R., & Steele, C. (1988). The history and outcome of my encounter with schizophrenia. *Schizophrenia Bulletin, 14*, 701–706.

Fox, L. (1999). Personal accounts: Missing out on motherhood. *Psychiatric Services, 50*, 193–194.

Frese, F. J. (1993). Cruising the cosmos, part three: Psychosis and hospitalization: A consumer's personal recollection. In A. B. Hatfield & H. P. Lefley (Eds.), *Surviving mental illness: Coping and adaptation* (pp. 67–76). New York: Guilford Press.

Frese, F. J. (1997). Twelve aspects of coping for persons with serious and persistent mental illness. In L. Spaniol, C. Gagne, & M. Koehler (Eds.), *Psychological and social aspects of psychiatric disability* (pp. 145–155). Boston: Center for Psychiatric Rehabilitation. (Reprinted from *Innovations and Research, 2*, 39–46, 1993)

Frese, F. J. (2000). Psychology practitioners and schizophrenia: A view from both sides. *Journal of Clinical Psychology, In Session, 56,* 1413–1426.

Fuchs, L. (1986). First person account: Three generations of schizophrenia. *Schizophrenia Bulletin, 12,* 744–747.

Gallo, K. M. (1994). First person account: Self-stigmatization. *Schizophrenia Bulletin, 20,* 407–410.

Ganim, A. R. (1987). First person account: The delusion girl—diary of a schizophrenic. *Schizophrenia Bulletin, 13,* 737–739.

Garrett, B., & Posey, R. (1993). Involuntary commitment: A consumer perspective. *Innovations and Research, 2*(1), 39–41.

Goffman, E. (1963). *Stigma: Notes on the management of spoiled identity.* Englewood Cliffs, NJ: Prentice Hall.

Granat-Goldstein, J. (2001). Personal accounts: Color within the lines . . . Think outside the box. *Psychiatric Services, 52,* 769–770.

Harding, C. M., Zubin, J., & Strauss, J. S. (1987). Chronicity in schizophrenia: Fact, partial fact, or artifact? *Hospital and Community Psychiatry, 38,* 477–486.

Harding, C. M., Zubin, J., & Strauss, J. S. (1992). Chronicity in schizophrenia: Revisited. *British Journal of Psychiatry, 161,* 27–37.

Hatfield, A. B., & Lefley, H. P. (1993). *Surviving mental illness: Coping and adaptation.* New York: Guilford Press.

Hatfield, A. B., Spaniol, L., & Zipple, A. M. (1987). Expressed emotion: A family perspective. *Schizophrenia Bulletin, 13,* 221–226.

Herman, N. J. (1993). Return to sender: Reintegrative stigma-management strategies of ex-psychiatric patients. *Journal of Contemporary Ethnography, 22,* 295–330.

Houghton, J. F. (1982). First person account: Maintaining mental health in a turbulent world. *Schizophrenia Bulletin, 8,* 548–552.

Hyland, B. (1991). A thousand cloudy days. *Schizophrenia Bulletin, 17,* 539–545.

Jacobson, N. (2001). Experiencing recovery: A dimensional analysis of recovery narratives. *Psychiatric Rehabilitation Journal, 24,* 248–256.

Johnson, D. L. (1990). The family's experience of living with mental illness. In H. P. Lefley & D. L. Johnson (Eds.), *Families as allies in treatment of the mentally ill: New directions for mental health professionals* (pp. 31–63). Washington, DC: American Psychiatric Association.

Jordan, J. C. (1995). First person account: Schizophrenia—Adrift in an anchorless reality. *Schizophrenia Bulletin, 21,* 501–503.

Kagigebi, A. (1995). First person account: Living in a nightmare. *Schizophrenia Bulletin, 21,* 155–159.

Lally, S. J. (1989). Does being here mean there is something wrong with me? *Schizophrenia Bulletin, 15,* 253–265.

Lanquetot, R. (1984). First person account: Confessions of the daughter of a schizophrenic. *Schizophrenia Bulletin, 10,* 467–471.

Lefley, H. P. (1989). Family burden and family stigma in major mental illness. *American Psychologist, 44,* 556–560.

Leete, E. (1987). The treatment of schizophrenia: A patient's perspective. *Hospital and Community Psychiatry, 38,* 486–491.

Leete, E. (1988). A consumer perspective on psychosocial treatment. *Psychosocial Rehabilitation Journal, 12,* 45–52.

Leete, E. (1989). How I perceive and manage my illness. *Schizophrenia Bulletin, 15,* 197–200.

Leete, E. (1993). The interpersonal environment: A consumer's personal recollection. In A. B. Hatfield & H. P. Lefley (Eds.), *Surviving mental illness: Stress, coping, and adaptation* (pp. 114–128). New York: Guilford Press.

Link, B. G., Cullen, F. T., Streuning, E., Shrout, P., & Dohrenwend, B. P. (1989). A modified labeling theory approach in the area of mental disorders: An empirical assessment. *American Sociological Review, 54,* 400–423.

Link, B. G., & Phelan, J. C. (2001). Conceptualizing stigma. *Annual Review of Sociology, 27,* 363–385.

Lovejoy, M. (1982). Expectations and the recovery process. *Schizophrenia Bulletin, 6,* 605–609.

Lovejoy, M. (1984). Recovery from schizophrenia: A personal odyssey. *Hospital and Community Psychiatry, 35,* 809–812.

Lyden, J. (1997). *Daughter of the Queen of Sheba.* New York: Penguin.

Lynch, K. (2000). The long road back. *Journal of Clinical Psychology, In Session, 56,* 1427–1432.

Marshall, T. B., & Solomon, P. (2000). Releasing information to families of persons with serious mental illness: A survey of NAMI members. *Psychiatric Services, 51,* 1006–1011.

McGrath, M. E. (1984). Where did I go? *Schizophrenia Bulletin, 10,* 638–690.

Mittleman, G. (1985). First person account: The role of parenthood of the mentally ill. *Schizophrenia Bulletin, 11,* 300–303.

Moorman, M. (2002). *My sister's keeper: Learning to cope with a sibling's mental illness.* New York: Norton.

Neugeboren, J. (1997a). *Imagining Robert: My brother, madness, and survival.* New York: Holt.

Neugeboren, J. (1997b). Meanwhile, back on the ward . . . In L. Spaniol, C. Gagne, & M. Koehler (Eds.), *Psychological and social aspects of psychiatric disability* (pp. 308–316). Boston: Center for Psychiatric Rehabilitation.

O'Neal, J. (1984). Finding myself and loving it. *Schizophrenia Bulletin, 10,* 109–110.

Orrin, D. (1997). Past the struggles of mental illness: Toward the development of quality lives. In L. Spaniol, C. Gagne, & M. Koehler (Eds.), *Psychological and social aspects of psychiatric disability* (pp. 138–144). Boston: Center for Psychiatric Rehabilitation. (Reprinted from *Innovations and Research, 3,* 41–45, 1994)

Parker, C. (2001). First person account: Landing a Mars lander. *Schizophrenia Bulletin, 27,* 717–718.

Payne, R. L. (1992). My schizophrenia. *Schizophrenia Bulletin, 18,* 725–728.

Payne, R. L. (1992). My schizophrenia. *Schizophrenia Bulletin, 18,* 725–728.

Pescosolido, B. A., Monahan, J., Link, B. G., Stueve, A., & Kikuzawa, S. (1999). The public's view of the competence, dangerousness, and need for legal coercion of persons with mental health problems. *American Journal of Public Health, 89,* 1339–1345.

Piercey, B. P. (1985). First person account: Making the best of it. *Schizophrenia Bulletin, 11,* 155–157.

Ruocchio, P. J. (1989). First person account: Fighting the fight—The schizophrenic's nightmare. *Schizophrenia Bulletin, 15,* 163–166.

Ruocchio, P. J. (1991). The schizophrenic inside. *Schizophrenia Bulletin, 17,* 357–359.

Schiller, L., & Bennett, A. (1994). *The quiet room: A journey out of the torment of madness.* New York: Time Warner.

Simon, C. (1998). *Mad house: Growing up in the shadow of mentally ill siblings.* New York: Penguin.

Slater, E. (1986). First person account: A parent's view on enforcing medication. *Schizophrenia Bulletin, 12,* 291–292.

Smith, E. (1991). First person account: Living with schizophrenia. *Schizophrenia Bulletin, 17,* 689–691.

Spaniol, L., Gagne, C., & Koehler, M. (Eds.). (1997). *Psychological and social aspects of psychiatric disability.* Boston: Center for Psychiatric Rehabilitation.

Stainsby, J. (1992). Schizophrenia: Some issues. *Schizophrenia Bulletin, 18,* 543–546.

Streuning, E. L., Perlick, D. A., Link, B. G., Hallman, F., Herman, D., & Sirey, J. (2001). The extent to which caregivers believe most people devalue consumers and their families. *Psychiatric Services, 52,* 1633–1638.

Tenney, L. J. (2000). It has to be about choice. *Journal of Clinical Psychology, In Session, 56,* 1433–1445.

Terkelsen, K. G. (1990). A historical perspective on family-provider relationships. In H. P. Lefley & D. L. Johnson (Eds.), *Families as allies in treatment of the mentally ill: New directions for mental health professionals* (pp. 3–21). Washington, DC: American Psychiatric Press.

Wahl, O. (1995). *Media madness: Public images of mental illness.* New Brunswick, NJ: Rutgers University Press.

Wasow, M. (1995). *The skipping stone: Ripple effects of mental illness on the family.* Palo Alto, CA: Science & Behavior Books.

Weingarten, R. (1994). The ongoing processes of recovery. *Psychiatry, 57,* 369–375.

Weingarten, R. (1997). How I've managed chronic mental illness. In L. Spaniol, C. Gagne, & M. Koehler (Eds.), *Psychological and social aspects of psychiatric disability* (pp. 123–129). Boston: Center for Psychiatric Rehabilitation. (Reprinted from *Schizophrenia Bulletin, 15,* 635–640, 1989)

Weinstein, D. (2000). Practitioner competencies. In R. Hughes & D. Weinstein (Eds.), *Best practices in psychosocial rehabilitation* (pp. 113–143). Columbia, MD: International Association of Psychosocial Rehabilitation Services.

Williams, L. (1998). Personal accounts: A "classic" case of borderline personality disorder. *Psychiatric Services, 49,* 173–174.

Willis, M. J. (1982). The impact of schizophrenia on families: One mother's point of view. *Schizophrenia Bulletin, 8,* 617–619.

Zelt, D. (1981). First person account: The messiah quest. *Schizophrenia Bulletin, 7,* 527–531.

4

SOCIAL PSYCHOLOGICAL MODELS OF MENTAL ILLNESS STIGMA

VICTOR OTTATI, GALEN V. BODENHAUSEN, AND LEONARD S. NEWMAN

If there is anything that resembles a "holy trinity" within psychology, it is perhaps that most psychological phenomena possess a cognitive, affective, and behavioral component (McGuire, 1985). The same is true when adopting a social psychological approach to understanding mental illness stigma. Social psychologists make a distinction between stereotyping, prejudice, and discrimination (Fiske, 1998). A *stereotype* of people with mental illness can be defined as a cognitive representation of this group that is stored in memory. This cognitive representation, which is often a socially shared one, depicts individuals with mental illness as possessing certain traits (e.g., "bizarre") or engaging in certain behaviors (e.g., talking to oneself). In contrast, *prejudice* against persons with mental illness refers to a negative affective reaction, evaluation, or attitude toward this group of people. Completing the trinity, *discrimination* refers to negative behaviors or actions

This paper was made possible, in part, by NIMH grant MH58876 to L. S. Newman. Please address correspondence concerning this manuscript to Victor Ottati, Department of Psychology, Loyola University Chicago, 6525 N. Sheridan Rd., Chicago, IL, 60626; phone 773-508-3024; fax 773-508-8713; vottati@luc.edu.

directed toward people with mental illness (e.g., refusing to hire a person with mental illness). Stereotyping, prejudice, and discrimination are often causally related. For example, an individual who believes that persons with mental illness are incompetent (stereotype) might consequently evaluate an individual with mental illness in a negative fashion (prejudice), and therefore refuse to hire that person (discrimination). Effects of this nature have important implications for mental health workers (e.g., psychologists, psychiatrists, social workers). Namely, efforts to alleviate problems associated with mental illness should include social interventions that are designed to reduce unwarranted discrimination against these individuals.

THE NATURE OF MENTAL ILLNESS STIGMA

In western culture, stereotypes of people with mental illness often suggest that they are dangerous, incompetent, unable to care for themselves, and childlike (Brockington, Hall, Levings, & Murphy, 1993; Corrigan, 1998; Phelan, Link, Stueve, & Pescosolido, 2000; Taylor & Dear, 1981; Wahl, 1992). These stereotypic beliefs are widely shared, at least in the United States (Link, 1987; Rabkin, 1974; Roman & Floyd, 1981) and Europe (Bhugra, 1989; Hamre, Dahl, & Malt, 1994; Madianos, Madianou, Vlachonikolis, & Stefanis, 1987). Some have suggested that these beliefs are, at least in part, accurate (Gove, 1970, 1975). This viewpoint can be derived from the "kernel of truth" hypothesis, an approach that suggests group stereotypes can reflect real group differences (Allport, 1954/1979; Campbell, 1967; McCauley, 1995; McCauley & Rozin, 1989; Ottati & Lee, 1995; Triandis & Vassiliou, 1967; Vinacke, 1949). A considerable amount of research, however, suggests that stereotypes of persons with mental illness are often inaccurate or exaggerated. For example, although psychotic people are stereotyped as dangerous (Link, Cullen, Frank, & Wozniak, 1987; Link, Monohan, Stueve, & Cullen, 1999; Link, Phelan, Bresnahan, Stueve, & Pescosolido, 1999), mental illness fails to be associated with a substantial increase in violence when focusing on individuals who are free of substance abuse (Steadman et al., 1998). In a related vein, stereotypic portrayals of persons with mental illness often underestimate the degree to which this group of individuals varies along a given trait dimension (Harding & Zahniser, 1994).

Stereotypic beliefs can elicit an overall prejudiced attitude toward people with mental illness. However, these stereotypic beliefs may also be associated with more specific emotional reactions. For example, an individual might be afraid of a person with mental illness because he or she believes people with mental illness are dangerous (Devine, 1995; Hilton & Hippel, 1996; Krueger, 1996). Alternatively, anger toward individuals with mental illness might be triggered by the belief that these individuals are personally responsible for their illness. However, as will be discussed presently, some emotional reactions to people with mental illness may arise for reasons that have little to do with such cognitive considerations.

Discrimination against people with mental illness undoubtedly occurs in many different forms. Some people may behave in an overtly hostile or aggressive manner toward persons with mental illness, whereas others may exhibit more subtle forms of discrimination. As mentioned in chapter 1, these more subtle forms of discrimination include failing to hire a person with mental illness (Bordieri & Diemer, 1986; Farina & Felner, 1973; Link, 1987; Olshansky, Grob, & Ekdahle, 1960), refusing to rent an apartment to a person with mental illness (Page, 1995), or pressing false criminal charges against a person with mental illness.

From a social psychological perspective, the study of mental illness stigma constitutes a specific application of stereotyping, prejudice, and discrimination research. Social psychological approaches to understanding these phenomena more generally are therefore directly relevant to understanding mental illness stigma more specifically. These approaches can be divided into three basic categories: those that emphasize the role of affect, motivation, or cognition. We begin by discussing approaches that fall within these three categories and then move on to consider the role of ambivalence, suppression, and projection as they relate to mental illness stigma.

AFFECTIVELY-DRIVEN APPROACHES

The affectively-driven approaches share the assumption that prejudice originates as a negative emotional response. The root of the problem, according to this view, resides within human emotion. Negative stereotyping and discriminatory behavior are derived on the basis of this prior emotional root. A compelling demonstration of the affectively-driven approach might involve showing that emotional responses determine global attitudes toward persons with mental illness independently of beliefs or stereotypes of this group. Effects of this nature have been obtained in a variety of domains. For example, the frequency with which voters experience positive and negative emotional reactions to a political candidate predicts voting preference independently of beliefs about the candidate (Abelson, Kinder, Peters, & Fiske, 1982; Ottati, Steenbergen, & Riggle, 1992). This sort of evidence is open to a variety of interpretations and criticisms, however (Ottati, 1996, 2001). This is because theoretical conceptualizations regarding the initial emotion-eliciting process differ in the degree to which they emphasize the mediating role of cognition (see Isbell & Ottati, 2002, for a related discussion in the political domain).

Cognitive appraisal theory suggests that emotional reactions to a person with mental illness are elicited by a prior process of cognitive appraisal (Arnold, 1960; Lazarus, 1984; Ortony, Clore, & Collins, 1988). This approach suggests that emotional reactions to a person with mental illness (e.g., "He makes me nervous.") are determined by stereotype-based cognitive appraisals (e.g., "Because he is mentally ill, he is dangerous."). If this is true, the emotion and underlying belief appraisal should contain redundant evaluative information when predicting global attitudes toward a person with mental illness. Other models of the emotion-eliciting process, however, generate an opposite prediction. One such model suggests that affect and cognition function as partially independent systems (Murphy, Monahan, & Zajonc, 1995; Zajonc, 1980). This implies that emotional responses to a stimulus can arise without any prior process of cognitive appraisal. For example, the facial expression of a person with mental illness might directly elicit an emotional reaction in an observer in the absence of any conscious, cognitive mediation. Because this emotional reaction is directly elicited, it might predict the observer's global attitude toward this person independently of beliefs about that person.

Unfortunately, the degree to which emotions and beliefs serve as unique predictors of global attitudes is not particularly meaningful. This is because prejudice and discrimination can be "affectively-driven" even when emotions and beliefs function as redundant predictors of global attitudes toward a person with mental illness. This might occur when (a) a directly elicited emotional response triggers a belief inference that subsequently influences the observer's global attitude toward a person with mental illness, or (b) a direct effect of the emotional response on global attitude is justified by a belief (see Isbell & Ottati, 2002; Ottati, 1997, 2001). In these cases, beliefs about people with mental illness arise as a consequence (not antecedent) of emotional reactions to these individuals. These possibilities serve as reminder of the limitations associated with taking a purely correlational approach when investigating questions of this nature.

Fortunately, experimental approaches have enabled social psychologists to identify a number of processes that are truly affectively-driven. Three of these approaches are directly relevant to understanding mental illness stigma. These are the classical conditioning, misattribution, and displaced aggression approaches.

Classical Conditioning

According to the classical conditioning model, prejudice against a social group is shaped by socialization experiences that repeatedly pair an aversive stimulus with the social group. For example, a child might observe its parent grimace whenever a policeman is present. The parent's grimace is an aversive unconditioned stimulus that elicits discomfort in the child. Repeated pairing of this unconditioned stimulus with policemen (conditioned stimulus) will eventually result in a classically conditioned emotional response. That is, policemen will elicit discomfort in the child even when the parent is absent. Classical conditioning effects can emerge even when the conditioned stimulus is paired with a subliminal unconditioned stimulus during learning (Krosnick, Betz, Jussim, & Lynn, 1992). Moreover, the effect on attitude toward the conditioned stimulus is evident even when one assesses unconscious attitudes toward the conditioned stimulus (Olson & Fazio, 2002). Apparently, effects of this nature do not require any conscious, cognitive mediation.

The classical conditioning effect might play an important role in determining people's reactions to persons with mental illness. Parents might grimace, frown, or otherwise convey discomfort in the presence of people with mental illness. In doing so, their own discomfort regarding this social group might be passed on to their children. In addition, individuals may often encounter homeless individuals that they label as mentally ill in an unpleasant context (e.g., a dirty alley). Moreover, media portrayals of people with mental illness commonly present them within a seedy, dangerous, or otherwise aversive context (Wahl, 1992). Negative emotional responses to the aversive context might thereby become classically conditioned to persons with mental illness. Thus, both personal experience and media exposure might serve to elicit classical conditioning effects that foster prejudice against people with mental illness.

Misattribution

Related to the classical conditioning approach is the mood misattribution model, which emphasizes that individuals are often unaware of the actual source of their affective state. As a consequence, affect elicited by an aversive contextual stimulus can be misattributed to a target stimulus (Ottati & Isbell, 1996; Ottati & Wyer, 1993; Schwarz & Clore, 1983, 1996). This theoretical approach offers an alternative interpretation of the examples provided previously. In this alternative formulation, the mother's frown serves as the actual source of the child's discomfort. The child misattributes this negative affect to the actions of a person with mental illness. An analogous interpretation would be applied to the media effect described earlier. Namely, the aversive context in which the person appears would serve as the actual source of the observer's discomfort. However, the observer might misattribute this negative affect to a person with mental illness who is perceived within this aversive context.

The classical conditioning and mood misattribution approach both suggest that affect elicited by an aversive contextual stimulus can produce negative attitudes toward persons with mental illness. The difference between these approaches is twofold. First, unlike the mood misattribution effect, the classical conditioning effect often requires repeated pairing of an aversive stimulus with the target stimulus. Thus, the classical conditioning model is primarily relevant to long-term socialization experiences that involve repeated pairing of negative stimuli with exposure to people labeled as mentally ill. Second, unlike the classical conditioning effect, mood misattribution effects should only emerge when the observer cognitively misattributes the contextually-induced affect. This means that, should the observer be reminded of the actual source of their affective response, the misattribution effect should fail to emerge (Isbell & Clore, 1994; Schwarz & Clore, 1983). This latter prediction, which is solely characteristic of the misattribution approach, has an interesting implication. To reduce stigmatization of persons with mental illness, one should remind the public that their affective reaction to these people often reflects their reaction to the context in which these individuals are encountered, not the individuals themselves.

Displaced Aggression

Although many textbooks on aggression consider displaced aggression to be a conceptually obsolete phenomenon, a recent meta-analysis suggests that the construct is alive and well (Marcus-Newall, Pederson, Carlson, & Miller, 2000). Not unlike the mood misattribution hypothesis, the displaced aggression model suggests that anger elicited by one stimulus can increase anger and aggression toward a subsequently encountered stimulus. Effects of this nature occur when aggression toward the initial provoking agent is impossible or likely to elicit retaliation. Displaced aggression is most likely to occur when the initial provocation of anger is followed by a low intensity, ambiguous cue that "triggers" aggression toward some other person, or when the subsequent target person is encountered in an unpleasant setting (Pederson, Gonzales, & Miller, 2000). Thus, an employee who has been mistreated by his or her boss might return home and yell at a family member who displays only a minor form of impoliteness. Displaced aggression toward the subsequent target violates the tit-for-tat rule of social exchange (Axelrod, 1984). Namely, the aggression that is directed toward the subsequent target exceeds that which is justified by that person's level of provocation.

A disturbing example of the displaced aggression effect involves the link between economic conditions and racial violence (Hepworth & West, 1988). Hovland and Sears (1940) specifically focused on the relation between economic conditions and the lynching of Black people in the United States. They found that from 1882 to 1930, the number of lynchings rose when economic conditions declined. It appears that membership in a social out-group increases the likelihood that a minor social infraction will be sufficient to trigger an overwhelming and deadly form of displaced aggression (Marcus-Newall et al., 2000). As a consequence, frustration regarding economic conditions resulted in the displacement of aggression toward Black people during this particular historical time period.

Recent conceptualizations of the displaced aggression hypothesis suggest that this effect is often cognitively mediated. From this perspective, the initial anger-provoking event primes negative thoughts that produce selective attention to negative information and a negative interpretation of ambiguous actions performed by a subsequently encountered target person. These cognitive biases increase the likelihood that a subsequently encountered target will be viewed as hostile or threatening, and thereby increase the likelihood of an aggressive response (Berkowitz, 1990, 1993; Pederson et al., 2000; see Martin & Tesser, 1989, for a related conceptualization).

It is possible that displaced aggression contributes to discrimination against individuals with mental illness. For the mainstream population, individuals labeled mentally ill constitute an out-group. In addition, mental illness may be associated with a tendency to exhibit minor norm violations that are misinterpreted as hostile or threatening. Moreover, individuals with mental illness may often be encountered within negative settings. As just noted, these are precisely the conditions that promote the displacement of aggression.

MOTIVATIONAL APPROACHES

The motivational approaches share the assumption that prejudice serves some emotional need. Among the most relevant approaches that fall within this category are the just world hypothesis, authoritarian and social dominance approaches, and the social identity theory approach.

Just World Hypothesis

The motivation to perceive justice in the world is a powerful force that can influence reactions to individuals in a wide range of unfortunate circumstances, including persons with serious mental illnesses (e.g., Ross & Miller, 2002). The belief in a just world fundamentally revolves around the assumption that people get what they deserve: Good people obtain positive outcomes, whereas bad things only happen to bad people (Lerner, 1980). If a seemingly good person suffers a negative outcome, this threatens our sense of justice, and we may be motivated to reinterpret the situation, potentially convincing ourselves that the person must really have deserved what happened to him or her. Blaming the victim, and withholding help, thus can be an unfortunate consequence of the need to perceive the world as fair and just. The roots of this motivation lie at least partially in a desire to feel safe and secure—"If I am a good and prudent person, I need not worry about calamity striking me." When we observe others experiencing illness, accident, or victimization, it tends to elicit defensive attributions of responsibility that emphasize the victim's own role in creating his or her circumstances, thereby reducing our feelings of vulnerability to capricious misfortune (e.g., Thornton, 1984). The more severe the misfortune, the greater the need to convince ourselves that victims are personally responsible for their fates (e.g., Chaikin & Darley, 1973), implying that people have the capacity to control their vulnerability to such events; therefore, we need not fear a similar fate ourselves.

Of course, not all victims are blamed in all circumstances (see Weiner, 1995), and sometimes it is crystal clear that a victim has done nothing to precipitate negative outcomes. Nevertheless, in a number of circumstances, individuals who strongly endorse just world beliefs show a greater tendency to blame victims and withhold help. For example, DePalma, Madey, Tillman, and Wheeler (1999) demonstrated that persons who strongly endorse just-world beliefs were less likely to help a medical patient who was perceived as responsible for his medical condition. To the extent that persons with serious mental illness are commonly viewed as responsible for their condition, prejudice and discrimination against such persons may arise in substantial part because of concerns about justice and personal vulnerability to misfortune.

Lerner (1998) has recently argued that just-world beliefs need not necessarily operate at a conscious, explicit level. When asked to state their reactions to victims of misfortune, people may consciously realize that it is inappropriate to make victim-blaming statements, yet their more implicit and automatic reactions may nevertheless reflect the influence of justice beliefs. In support of this proposition, Hafer (2000) provided evidence that the need to perceive the world as fair and just does indeed influence automatic mental reactions. Consistent with this finding, other research indicates that victim blaming is especially prevalent under conditions of high cognitive load (Goldinger, Kleider, Azuma, & Beike, 2003). More research is needed specifically addressing the role of just-world beliefs in the stigmatization of persons with serious mental illnesses, but given the substantial array of findings in other domains (e.g., stigmatization of rape victims), there is reason to believe that these motives can play a role in prejudice directed at this population.

Authoritarian and Social Dominance Approaches

In examining the determinants of prejudice, personality theorists originally focused on the role of authoritarianism (Adorno, Frenkel-Brunswik, Levinson, & Sanford, 1950). The authoritarian personality is marked by submission to authority, strict adherence to middle class norms, rigid thinking, and aggression toward individuals who differ from the mainstream (Adorno et al., 1950). It was originally suggested that authoritarians harbor prejudice because they rely on ego-defensive mechanisms to protect themselves from unacceptable impulses (Adorno et al., 1950; Katz, McClintock, & Sarnoff, 1957; Katz, Sarnoff, & McClintock, 1956). For example, when experiencing unacceptable aggressive impulses toward their parents, authoritarians might displace their aggression toward minority group members. Alternatively, authoritarians might project their unacceptable impulses onto minority group members, and thereby transform them into suitable targets for prejudice and discrimination. Empirical evidence, however, provides limited support for the claim that ego-defensive mechanisms account for the relation between authoritarianism and prejudice (see Eagly & Chaiken, 1993). Nevertheless, many studies report that authoritarianism is correlated with prejudice, even if the psychological basis for this association is unclear (Altemeyer, 1996; Duckitt, 1993; Haddock, Zanna, & Esses, 1993; McFarland & Adelson, 1996; Peterson, Doty, & Winter, 1993).

A related approach suggests that individual differences in "social dominance orientation" underlie prejudice and discrimination (Pratto & Cathey, 2001). Individuals who possess this orientation emphasize competitiveness and status. They prefer a hierarchical social structure that maintains power differences between different groups. They endorse social practices that enable the more privileged segments of society to maintain a position of social dominance. This fundamental social dominance orientation is what fosters the development of prejudice and discrimination.

The authoritarian and social dominance approaches emphasize that deeply ingrained and chronic motivational orientations play an important role in determining more specific forms of prejudice and discrimination. In both cases, it is assumed that prejudice and discrimination will be directed primarily toward minority groups occupying a position of low social status. Persons with mental illness, of course, constitute a social group that fits this profile. Thus, one would anticipate that both authoritarianism and social dominance orientation would be associated with a tendency to stigmatize the mentally ill.

Social Identity Theory

Individuals possess not only an individual or personal identity, but also a social identity (Tajfel, 1981). Indeed, a substantial body of work suggests that personal and social identity function as separate concepts when individuals represent information that is relevant to the self (Bettencourt & Hume, 1999; Brewer & Gardner, 1996; Hogg & Abrams, 1988; Jetten, Branscombe, & Spears, 2002; Kessler, Mummendey, & Leisse, 2000; Trafimow, Triandis, & Goto, 1991; Turner, 1987). Moreover, just as individuals are motivated to maintain high levels of self-esteem, they are motivated to maintain a positive sense of social identity (Tajfel, 1981; Tajfel & Turner, 1986). The motive to maintain a positive sense of social identity influences the way in which individuals evaluate and perceive both in-group and out-group members. Most important, it fosters a tendency for individuals to harbor less favorable attitudes toward out-group members than in-group members. Cognitive processing of information pertaining to in-group and out-group members is biased so as to maintain this difference in inter-group evaluation. For example, we tend to attribute desirable behaviors by members of our in-group to stable, internal causes; but to attribute desirable behaviors by members of out-groups to transitory or external causes (Hewstone, Bond, & Wan, 1983). This attributional tendency enables individuals to ascribe positive traits in greater measure to in-group than out-group members (Boski, 1988).

From the perspective of the nonclinical population, individuals labeled mentally ill are members of an out-group. Thus, to maintain a positive sense of social identity, the nonclinical population is motivated to evaluate individuals with mental illness less favorably than "normal" people. This form of intergroup prejudice might also be expected to elicit the attributional biases identified earlier. Cognitive biases of this sort will, of course, foster the development of negative stereotypes of the mentally ill.

Although social identity theory emphasizes the motive to maintain a positive sense of social identity, it also points to the central role of cognition. It is the cognitive act of categorization that initially serves to distinguish the in-group from the out-group, and a variety of cognitive biases are presumed to function in the service of maintaining a more favorable view of the in-group. Thus, our discussion of social identity theory leads directly to a consideration of the cognitive approaches to mental illness stigma.

COGNITIVE APPROACHES

The cornerstone of the cognitive approach to understanding prejudice and stereotypes is the concept of categorization (e.g., Allport, 1954/1979; Tajfel, 1969). Humans routinely and reflexively categorize the objects and events that we encounter (e.g., "dog" or "car" or "thunderstorm") without giving any thought to the nature and consequences of these category assignments. The complexity of the physical world requires that we establish ways of grouping stimuli together into meaningful categories, to form reasonable expectations about (and to generate appropriate reactions to) the multitude of objects and events that we might encounter. This necessity is no less evident in the social world than in the physical world. The diversity of kinds of people we encounter (e.g., lawyers, Cubans, and lesbians) leads us to seek general principles that characterize each kind of person, thereby imparting a much-needed sense of predictability and control over social situations. This process of extracting (and applying) a generic view of a group of people is referred to as stereotyping.

The process of clinical diagnosis represents an interesting analog of the stereotyping process. When clinicians assign a client to a diagnostic category, they are glossing over individual peculiarities and focusing on a resemblance between the client and a particular symptom profile that defines membership in a particular group (e.g., people with bipolar disorder). Subsequent interactions with the client, including therapeutic strategies, may be substantially based on generalizations about the group as a whole, rather than the idiosyncratic characteristics of the individual client. Even though there is good reason to believe that the clinician's diagnostic categories represent a generally accurate and useful set of generalizations, nevertheless a danger exists that reliance on these categories can lead to the overuse of preconceptions and a corresponding insensitivity to the unique individuality of each client. Still more problematic are the generalizations of the lay public about various groups of persons with serious mental illness. As previously noted, the relevant stereotypes include both a patronizing attribution of incompetence and a fear of dangerousness and unpredictability (Link, Phelan, Bresnahan, Stueve, & Pescosolido, 1999). When people with schizophrenia, for example, are reduced to this kind of caricature, the full dimension of their humanity is lost in the process. Thus, although categorization is a necessary and highly functional process, it can sometimes have highly undesirable consequences, as the widespread stigmatization of persons with mental illness demonstrates.

The accuracy of stereotypes is an important but thorny matter (Judd & Park, 1993; Lee & Jussim, 1995; Ottati & Lee, 1995). If people are correct in thinking that persons with serious mental illnesses are dangerous and incompetent, then it might be quite defensible to deny them employment, housing, etc. Unfortunately, the cognitive processes involved in stereotyping are often self-validating, potentially leading to exaggerated and inaccurate generalizations. Dozens of studies have shown, for example, that people are most likely to associate negative characteristics with minority groups (e.g., Stroessner & Plaks, 2001). One explanation for this phenomenon lies in our sensitivity to distinctive information. Because minority groups, such as people with serious mental illnesses, are by definition relatively uncommon, it is more noteworthy when we encounter them. In addition, negative behavior is much more salient and distinctive than positive behavior (Fiske, 1980). Thus, if a person with a mental illness were to behave in a threatening way, this would be a doubly distinctive event. Research on illusory correlation (e.g., Hamilton & Gifford, 1976) confirms that even when no actual overall association between a minority group and the tendency to perform negative behaviors appears, and even if there are no preconceptions about the group at all, people nevertheless tend to associate the group with the negative characteristic, given the distinctiveness of the conjunction.

Of course, when it comes to mental illnesses, people do have lots of preconceptions. Once an expectancy forms in the mind of the perceiver, many expectancy-confirming biases are likely to be initiated. One of the most famous demonstrations of the power of expectancies to shape perceptions was a study conducted by Langer and Abelson (1974). In their study, traditional (analytic) psychotherapists were shown a videotape of a young man being interviewed. Half of the therapists were told that the man was a "job applicant," and the rest were told that he was a "patient." The therapists then rated the psychological adjustment of the man in the video. Although they all saw the same video, the therapists who had labeled the man as a patient viewed his behavior as more disturbed than those who had labeled the man as a job candidate. Thus, category labels can affect what the perceiver sees in ways that are independent of the actual data at hand.

How do such biased perceptions arise? Researchers have documented that group-based expectations can orient the mind in pervasive ways that bias attention, interpretation, memory, and action directed toward group members. For example, Bodenhausen (1988) showed that mock jurors were more likely to attend to and use incriminating evidence consistent with their preconceptions about the likely guilt of stereotypic defendants (e.g., a young Hispanic man accused of criminal assault); the very same evidence, when applied to a nonstereotypic defendant, was less attention-grabbing. In the realm of mental illness stigma, this bias implies that prospective employers, landlords, and indeed the general public may be especially likely to notice behaviors and characteristics that fit with their negative image of persons with serious mental illnesses, while failing to notice many other features that fail to jibe with preconceptions.

A general tendency also exists to interpret the meaning of ambiguous behavior in a way that is consistent with stereotypic generalizations. For instance, Sagar and Schofield (1980) showed that the very same ambiguous behavior (e.g., poking someone with a pencil) was perceived as hostile when performed by an African American actor but was perceived as playful when performed by a European American actor. People experiencing mental health problems may sometimes behave in distinctive or unusual ways, leaving uncertainty about the person's motives, abilities, or behavioral tendencies that many perceivers will resolve by applying their stereotypes about the group. However, even commonplace, otherwise positive behaviors can be interpreted negatively in light of stereotypic expectations. If people with serious mental illnesses are expected to be dangerous, then relatively mundane actions on their part may be misconstrued as threatening. Even something as normatively positive as a smile could be viewed ominously ("trying to trick me into letting my guard down"), given the fundamental mistrust associated with mental illness stigma. In a particularly well-known demonstration, Rosenhan (1973) had himself and several colleagues admitted to a psychiatric ward under the initial diagnosis of schizophrenia. Despite subsequently behaving in a normal and symptom-free manner, the staff assimilated their behavior to their expectations for patients with schizophrenia, discounting the competence they demonstrated and continuing to view them as disturbed. Thus, what we perceive in others is far from an objective record of them; rather, it is a subjective construal that, to varying degrees, is informed by preconceptions as well as by the "facts" at hand.

Another important consequence of stereotypic expectations is their power to alter the behavior of members of the relevant group. This phenomenon, known as the self-fulfilling prophecy, has been documented in many domains. Once perceivers have clear expectations about a target, they are likely to behave in ways that elicit the expected behavior. For example, if African American schoolchildren are stereotypically expected by their teacher to be intellectually inferior, the teacher may treat them in systematically different ways—ways that in fact undermine their academic performance (e.g., less attention, less corrective feedback, etc.; see Rubovits & Maehr, 1973). The negative expectancies that often accompany psychiatric labels can have similar effects (e.g., Szasz, 1961). For example, by assuming that a person with a serious mental illness is incapable of basic self-management, a caregiver may communicate a sense of incompetence to the person, undermining the levels of motivation and effort that are then expended in taking care of basic life tasks. The ensuing lack of success is taken, in turn, as confirmatory evidence that the initial low expectations were warranted. Self-fulfilling prophecies thus constitute another important mechanism whereby stereotypes are capable of generating an illusory database that seems to validate their accuracy and relevance. Because these biases are largely automatic ones that happen outside of conscious awareness, we are generally unaware of the extent to which this evidentiary base is comprised of stereotypic supposition rather than accurate or objective data.

Once people develop a group stereotype of persons with mental illnesses, the important issue becomes understanding the conditions under which this stereotype will influence perceptions of, and reactions to, specific group members. As just noted, relying on stereotypes to judge others represents a rapid, largely automatic, and largely effortless process. Stereotyped group members become relatively interchangeable, each being judged in terms of generic preconceptions about the group. In contrast, getting to know a person in terms of his or her unique individuality requires some effort and the generation of new knowledge. Thus, one of the functional advantages of stereotypes is their efficiency (Lippmann, 1922). A great deal of research has confirmed the implication of this view that stereotypes are most likely to be applied in judging a particular individual when efficiency of response is either highly desirable or necessary (for a review, see Bodenhausen, Macrae, & Sherman, 1999). When motivation for accuracy is high, perceivers will undertake the extra measure of effort required to really get to know the individual. However, in many everyday life contexts in which persons with serious mental illnesses are encountered, people may lack the motivation to really know them. Given the apprehensiveness that people feel about mental disorders, they may often be motivated to terminate social interactions with group members quickly, rather than taking time to become fully acquainted. The rapid, automatic activation of stereotypes (e.g., of potential dangerousness) may in this case directly undermine the motivation that is necessary to devote more effort to knowing the unique individual by triggering a desire for greater social distance (see Link, Cullen, Frank, & Wozniak, 1987).

Stereotypic efficiency is also called for whenever the social perceiver is busy, distracted, or otherwise attentionally taxed (Sherman, Macrae, & Bodenhausen, 2000). Working in an environment in which multiple goals must be pursued simultaneously is one circumstance that promotes greater reliance on stereotypes. This finding may help to explain why even experienced health-care providers can sometimes respond stereotypically to consumers of mental health services (Ryan, Robinson, & Hausmann, 2002). Under the pressure of multiple job-related demands, the free attention available for responding to each consumer uniquely may be notably constrained. Anxiety is another factor that tends to reduce attentional capacity (e.g., Darke, 1988). Thus, stereotypes are more likely to influence judgments and behavior when perceivers are feeling anxious (see Bodenhausen, Mussweiler, Gabriel, & Moreno, 2001). For example, Baron, Inman, Kao, and Logan (1992) showed that anxious dental patients (awaiting treatment from a novice dentist) were more likely to respond stereotypically than were nonanxious patients. To the extent that the apprehension about dangerousness is rapidly and automatically associated with mental illness, anxiety may be aroused that actually impedes the process of forming a more effortful, individuated impression of persons diagnosed with a mental illness. Preoccupied by thoughts about potential dangers, the perceiver has fewer mental resources to devote to other tasks. Thus, even in conditions in which people are in fact motivated to respond thoughtfully, automatically activated stereotypes may work against the prospects for actually doing so successfully. It seems clear that, just as in other domains of prejudice, an understanding of mental illness stigma requires the identification and examination of the cognitive processes that determine when and how biased perceptions and discriminatory actions will arise.

Ambivalence and Stereotype Suppression

Our review of the cognitive approaches has focused on the antecedents and consequences of beliefs about persons with mental illness. But attitudes derived from these beliefs are not the only attitudes that can play a role in others' interactions with them. It is clear that many people are committed to egalitarianism and have genuine concerns about acting in a prejudiced way toward others (Bodenhausen & Macrae, 1998). In fact, reliable and valid measures have been developed to assess desires to be fair and unprejudiced (Dunton & Fazio, 1997; Plant & Devine, 1998). People with internalized nonprejudiced values will be motivated not to apply stereotypes mindlessly when forming impressions of others. At the same time, they will be well aware of societal stereotypes, or even grudgingly accept them as being somewhat valid. Even if they do not, they might not always be able to control the extent to which stereotypes affect how they process information about other people (Banaji & Hardin, 1996; Devine, 1989). Thus, many people may feel conflicted when judging the characteristics and qualifications of people with mental illness. Imagine, for example, well-intentioned employers presented with a job applicant who was once diagnosed with schizophrenia and hospitalized. On the one hand, they will be motivated not to jump to any conclusions about the applicant's traits and abilities, and they will not want to make any assumptions about his or her likely job performance without any concrete evidence. On the other hand, their stereotypes will provide them with a ready-made tool for sizing up the applicant. As a result, they might find it hard not to avoid suspecting that he or she is someone who will antagonize coworkers or fail to complete assignments in a competent manner.

Ambivalence

An implication of the previous discussion is that evaluative reactions to those with psychiatric disabilities—and other stigmas— might often be characterized by ambivalence (Crocker, Major, & Steele, 1998). People could have strong yet conflicting feelings about how they should judge and behave toward people who have been labeled as mentally ill, who may be seen as deviant, but also as disadvantaged (Katz, Hass, & Bailey, 1988). Although researchers generally treat attitudes as bipolar constructs (ranging from very negative to very positive), it has long been recognized that attitudes toward a given object, issue, or behavior can be more complex than that (Kaplan, 1972). Attitudes can consist of both strong positive and negative feelings, and the resulting state of ambivalence can be reliably measured (Cacioppo, Gardner, & Bernstein, 1997; Priester & Petty, 1996; Thompson, Zanna, & Griffin, 1995).

People considering whether or not to, for example, hire someone with psychiatric disabilities or rent an apartment to him or her could well find themselves grappling with ambivalent feelings. Renting to or hiring such people might be perceived to involve risks, but at the same time, many (if not most) people would like to see themselves as fair and open-minded people who give everyone a "fair shake." Ambivalence in this context would have at least two important implications. First of all, it has been found that when people feel ambivalence toward members of stigmatized groups, their reactions toward the stigmatized others often end up being quite extreme, a phenomenon sometimes called response amplification. For example, Haas, Katz, Rizzo, Bailey, and Eisenstadt (1991) had White students participate in a task with White or Black confederates who were clearly responsible for the group's success or failure at the task. The students—especially those who were ambivalent about Black people, as assessed by a questionnaire—subsequently reported polarized impressions of the Black confederate. They felt more positively about him than about the White confederate when he facilitated success, and more negatively about him than about the White confederate when he let the group down. According to Haas et al. (1991), activation of people's ambivalence creates psychological discomfort (see Haas, Katz, Rizzo, Bailey, & Moore, 1992), and an extreme evaluation reduces that discomfort by "defending a self-image as a humane yet discerning individual" (p. 84). In other words, ambivalent people are motivated to convince themselves that a stigmatized person being judged or treated negatively really deserves that kind of a response, and that a stigmatized person being judged or treated positively is truly praiseworthy (Bell & Esses, 2002). The implication of this line of research is that mentally ill people will often be on the receiving end of extreme responses from other people. And paradoxically, those extreme responses will more than likely come from precisely those people who are reluctant to behave with prejudice toward the mentally ill.

But simply having conflicting criteria for evaluating attitude objects does not guarantee that one will subjectively experience ambivalent feelings when confronted with that object. Having reasons for evaluating someone or something both positively and negatively means only that one has the *potential* to feel ambivalent (Newby-Clark, McGregor, & Zanna, 2002). Some contexts, however, can selectively prime only the positive or negative standards of evaluation (Newman & Chamberlin, 2002). For example, people often report potential ambivalence about high calorie but tasty foods like cake and ice cream (Bargh, Chaiken, Govender, & Pratto, 1992). But if an ice cream sundae is encountered at a birthday party it will probably trigger a very different affective response than if it is encountered on the way to a workout at the gym. Similarly, reactions to and behavior toward people with mental illness could vary quite a bit across different situations. People's feelings about the mentally ill and how they should be treated are unlikely to be represented by simple bipolar attitudes that will be retrieved from memory and expressed regardless of the context. In some contexts, the relevance of values like fairness and egalitarianism will be highly salient; in others, risk-aversion might be primed. Thus, a second implication of the potentially ambivalent feelings people have about how they should treat people with mental illness is that their behavior toward them might be highly inconsistent and context-dependent.

In sum, although unflattering stereotypes of persons with mental illness are not hard to document, the negative attitudes derived from those stereotypes interact in complicated ways with people's other values and beliefs. Thus, predicting how a member of a stigmatized group will be treated in any given context is far from straightforward.

Stereotype Suppression

A great deal of time, effort, and money has been devoted to the goal of educating the general public about mental illnesses and, in particular, in reducing the stigmas that are attached to them. Once these attempts at consciousness-raising take root, individuals are confronted with new dilemmas. Given the previously documented automaticity with which stereotypic reactions come to mind and color our perceptions, how can motivated individuals successfully counteract their initial tendency to respond negatively to persons with serious mental illnesses? More specifically, if an egalitarian person wanted to resolve the ambivalence he or she was feeling toward a person with mental illness by simply suppressing prejudiced thoughts, how easy would it be to do that?

The effortful suppression of unwanted thoughts has been a subject of intensive recent investigation (e.g., Wenzlaff & Wegner, 2000). The lesson emerging from this research is that, although people are able to successfully ward off unwanted thoughts while focally motivated to do so (provided that they have ample free attention), the act of suppressing a thought often is accompanied by a subsequent "rebound" period in which the undesirable thought returns with even greater urgency than if it had never been suppressed. Wegner (1994) explained this phenomenon by postulating that the task of suppressing a thought ironically requires the thought to be activated, albeit at low levels, so that one can remember what it is one is trying not to think about. A *monitoring* process checks to see whether the unwanted thought has come into consciousness, and it can only perform this check if a representation of the unwanted thought is activated to serve as a criterion for the search. So long as an *operating* process is in place to direct attention away from the unwanted thought, the thought can be successfully avoided. However, the operating process requires effort and attention, and if these mental resources should be constrained, the stage is set for an ironic rebound.

These processes were investigated in the specific domain of stereotype suppression by Macrae, Bodenhausen, Milne, and Jetten (1994). Confirming the basic claims of Wegner's model, they found that focal efforts at stereotype suppression were generally successful, but once the motivation for suppression lapsed, rebound effects were observed. One study specifically confirmed that the goal of suppressing stereotypes actually resulted in their "hyperaccessibility," or heightened readiness to spring into consciousness. Subsequent findings on stereotype suppression (summarized by Monteith, Sherman, & Devine, 1998) showed that suppression can be successful and rebound effects can be avoided in the long run, but individuals who lack a consistent motivation for egalitarian responses may be particularly vulnerable to the pattern of short-term success followed by the rebounding of stereotypes. Although most studies have examined stereotype suppression in domains other than mental illness, one recent study by Penn and Corrigan (2002) examined reactions to a person with schizophrenia as a function of instructions to suppress stereotypes. In contrast to the earlier research, they failed to find evidence of a post-suppression rebound effect. More research will be needed before we can determine just how easily the stereotypes surrounding mental illness can be suppressed.

PROJECTION AND MENTAL ILLNESS STIGMA

Understanding the nature and function of stereotypes—and how easily they can be suppressed—is important because stereotypes play a role in determining how people construe the behavior of individuals labeled as mentally ill. That is, once perceivers categorize other people, the societal stereotypes associated with those categories influence how those people are perceived and treated. In short, a theme of this chapter has been that stereotypes relating to mental illness can cause bias in social inferences.

However, stereotypes are not the only cognitive structures that are capable of eliciting biased social inferences. Social inferences are also biased by idiosyncratic knowledge structures specific to the individual perceiver. For example, Newman, Duff, and Baumeister (1997) argued that people are often quick to see in others personality traits that they themselves are motivated to deny. This phenomenon will, of course, be recognizable to most readers as *defensive projection*. Most readers will also know that defensive projection is most closely associated with the psychoanalytic tradition (Freud, 1936). For that reason, perhaps, experimental psychologists have often expressed skepticism about the reality of the phenomenon (see Holmes, 1968, 1978, 1981).

Newman et al. (1997) developed a model of defensive projection on the basis of empirically supported social cognitive processes. According to the model, people have cognitive representations of their "unwanted selves" (cf. Higgins, 1987; Ogilvie, 1987)—that is, people are highly motivated not to possess or appear to possess specific personal characteristics. Given the relative ambiguity of much human behavior, people will inevitably say, think, or do things that could be taken as evidence for those unwanted traits. There are many ways for a person to react to the possibility that he or she might actually have an undesired trait. One strategy might involve simply trying not to think about it (Wegner & Zanakos, 1994). Unfortunately, as just noted, thought suppression is likely to backfire: Trying *not* to think about something (such as an undesired personality trait) can lead the unwanted thought to actually become more cognitively accessible than it was previously (Macrae et al., 1994; Wegner, 1992). In the long run, then, suppressing thoughts about an unwanted trait can lead the trait concept to become chronically accessible, and chronically accessible trait concepts are very likely to be used by perceivers to interpret other people's behavior (Higgins & King, 1981).

Overall, then, defensive projection is a consequence of attempts to avoid unwanted knowledge about the self. Research based on the Newman et al. (1997) model has shown that (a) when people are instructed to suppress thoughts about an unwanted trait, they subsequently project the trait on other people (Caldwell, Newman, Griffin, & Chamberlin, 2001; Newman et al., 1997; Smart & Wegner, 1999) and (b) people who are dispositionally inclined to suppress thoughts are more likely than other people to project their unwanted traits (Mikulincer & Horesh, 1999; Newman et al., 1997).

Whether or not certain kinds of people are more prone to be targets of projection than others has not yet been explored. Instead, the focus has been on the ambiguity of behavior: When the meaning of a behavior is uncertain, it is open to many different interpretations, including those based on cognitively accessible unwanted traits. In previous research, ambiguity has usually been operationalized by means of specific behaviors that could be interpreted in different ways. It is also possible, though, that behaviors will be ambiguous by virtue of the fact that specific *people* engage in them. A person's behavior is ambiguous if a perceiver is unsure of that person's goals, intentions, knowledge, beliefs, or affective reactions. It is possible that learning that someone has had a serious mental illness increases that uncertainty.

Of course, when people are able to label others and determine their group memberships, they typically use that information to *dis*ambiguate their behavior. Stereotypes associated with different groups allow perceivers to make default assumptions about the attributes of people in those groups. Identifying someone as a person with a psychiatric disability such as schizophrenia, however, could have the opposite effect: It could make that person seem even more unfathomable and difficult to predict. People might be hesitant to apply their default assumptions about internal states when they encounter people with schizophrenia, because they could be biased to assume that those states differ dramatically from those of "normal" people. If so, then the behavior of people with schizophrenia will seem to be more ambiguous in general than other people's behavior. As a consequence, people with mental illness might be even more prone to be labeled in terms of other people's chronically accessible traits, and might be especially likely to be targets of projection.

In sum, people with a history of mental illness might not only be prone to be labeled with those traits that are part of the general societal stereotypes associated with mental illness (e.g., dangerous, childlike, irresponsible), but might also be prone to be labeled with *any* unfavorable traits that for idiosyncratic reasons are cognitively accessible for a given perceiver. Furthermore, such trait inferences could play a particularly insidious role in social interaction. As noted earlier, a fair-minded person not wanting to be prejudiced might make an attempt to correct for the biased perceptions that could result from well-known stereotypes about the mentally ill. And as discussed previously, there is as yet little direct evidence that suppressing stereotypes related to mental illness cannot be done successfully. The biases caused by defensive projection, in contrast, are likely to occur without awareness (Newman et al., 1997). People will not be able to adjust their trait impressions unless they are aware of the possibility that they might have been biased (Strack & Hannover, 1996; Wilson & Brekke, 1994). Defensive projection can thus further complicate the stigmatization experienced by people with mental illnesses.

CONCLUSION AND FUTURE DIRECTIONS

This chapter has identified a number of social psychological models of prejudice and applied them toward understanding the nature of mental illness stigma and its causes. Our discussion initially summarized the implications of theoretical models falling within three broad categories of research. These were the affectively driven, motivational, and cognitively oriented approaches. This was followed by a consideration of how ambivalence, suppression, and projection might relate to mental illness stigma. Thus, the primary strategy of this chapter has been to identify relevant social psychological models of prejudice and consider their implications when specifically focusing on prejudice against persons with mental illness. We regard this strategy to be an extremely useful one and encourage social psychologists and clinically oriented researchers to continue to engage in collaborative efforts designed to further our understanding of mental illness stigma.

It should be noted, however, that the implementation of this strategy is yet to be completed. In almost every case, the models described in this chapter have yet to be empirically tested when specifically focusing on the mentally ill as the target group. On the contrary, most of the models described in this chapter have been tested using artificially constructed groups within the laboratory, or by investigating stereotyping and prejudice against members of racial or ethnic groups.

The need for conceptual replication using persons with mental illness as the target group pervades all of the categories of research summarized in this chapter. Within the affectively-driven category, neither the misattribution or displaced aggression approaches have been examined using individuals with mental illness as the target group. An untested implication of the misattribution model, for example, is that negative reactions to people with mental illness will decrease if individuals are reminded that their negative reactions to these people are often elicited by the context in which they are encountered. An untested implication of the displaced aggression hypothesis is that discrimination against persons with mental illness is especially likely to emerge when people have recently experienced an anger-provoking situation that they are unable to respond to directly.

Analogous forms of conceptual replication are needed when considering the motivational models. According to the just world hypothesis, for example, individuals who adhere to the just-world philosophy should show a greater propensity to stigmatize individuals diagnosed with a mental illness. In a similar fashion, individuals scoring high on authoritarianism or social dominance orientation should be especially likely to stigmatize the mentally ill. The cognitively oriented approaches are also in need of replication using persons with mental illness as the target group. We are unaware of any studies, for example, that specifically isolate the process of illusory correlation, selective attention, or selective retrieval as it occurs when individuals are provided with information pertaining to a person labeled as mentally ill.

A comprehensive approach to understanding mental illness stigma might also benefit by considering approaches that fall outside the boundaries of traditional social psychology. Advances within the area of evolutionary psychology, for example, might provide some insight into the ultimate evolutionary causes of mental illness stigma. In a recent discussion of this approach, it is argued that natural selection has provided humans with inborn adaptations for social exclusion. These adaptations serve the function of excluding poor social exchange partners, exploiting subordinate groups, and decreasing parasitic infection. From this perspective, individuals with mental illness are avoided (or even aggressed against) because they possess qualities that signal they are poor social exchange partners or that signal they are relatively more likely to carry infectious disease (Kurzban & Leary, 2001). Of course, evolutionary approaches to understanding human behavior are not without criticism. Because social psychologists are trained to focus on the current situational determinants of human behavior, they are often skeptical of the evolutionary approach. Nevertheless, advances within the area of evolutionary psychology remind us that social psychology is not the sole source of theoretical approaches that are relevant to understanding mental illness stigma.

REFERENCES

Abelson, R. P., Kinder, D. R., Peters, M. D., & Fiske, S. T. (1982). Affective and semantic components in political person perception. *Journal of Personality and Social Psychology, 42,* 619–630.

Adorno, T., Frenkel-Brunswik, E., Levinson, D., & Sanford, R. (1950). *The authoritarian personality.* New York: Harper & Row.

Allport, G. W. (1979). *The nature of prejudice.* New York: Doubleday. (Original work published 1954)

Altemeyer, B. (1996). *The authoritarian specter.* Cambridge, MA: Harvard University Press.

Anderson, C. A. (1997). Effects of violent movies and trait hostility on hostile feelings and aggressive thoughts. *Aggressive Behavior, 23,* 161–178.

Arnold, M. B. (1960). *Emotions and personality* (Vols. I and II). New York: Columbia University Press.

Ashmore, R., & McConahay, J. (1975). *Psychology and America's urban dilemmas.* New York: McGraw-Hill.

Axelrod, R. (1984). *The evolution of cooperation.* New York: Basic Books.

Banaji, M. R., & Hardin, C. D. (1996). Automatic stereotyping. *Psychological Science, 7,* 136–141.

Bargh, J. A., Chaiken, S., Govender, R., & Pratto, F. (1992). The generality of the automatic attitude activation effect. *Journal of Personality and Social Psychology, 62*, 893–912.

Baron, R. S., Inman, M. L., Kao, C. F., & Logan, H. (1992). Negative emotion and superficial social processing. *Motivation and Emotion, 16*, 323–346.

Bell, D. W., & Esses, V. M. (2002). Ambivalence and response amplification: A motivational perspective. *Personality and Social Psychology Bulletin, 28*, 1143–1152.

Berkowitz, L. (1989). Frustration-aggression hypothesis: Examination and reformulation. *Psychological Bulletin, 106*, 59–73.

Berkowitz, L. (1990). On the formation and regulation of anger and aggression: A cognitive-neoassociationistic analysis. *American Psychologist, 45*, 494–503.

Berkowitz, L. (1993). Perspectives on anger and emotion. In R. S. Wyer & T. K. Srull (Eds.), *Advances in social cognition* (Vol. 10, pp. 83–94). Mahwah, NJ: Erlbaum.

Bettencourt, B. A., & Hume, D. (1999). The cognitive contents of social-group identity: Values, emotions, and relationships. *European Journal of Social Psychology, 29*, 113–121.

Bhugra, D. (1989). Attitudes towards mental illness: A review of the literature. *Acta Psychiatrica Scandinavica, 80*, 1–12.

Bobo, L. (1983). Whites' opposition to busing: Symbolic racism or realistic group conflict? *Journal of Personality and Social Psychology, 45*, 1196–1210.

Bodenhausen, G. V. (1988). Stereotypic biases in social decision making and memory: Testing process models of stereotype use. *Journal of Personality and Social Psychology, 55*, 726–737.

Bodenhausen, G. V., & Macrae, C. N. (1998). Stereotype activation and inhibition. In R. S. Wyer, Jr. (Ed.), *Advances in social cognition* (Vol. 11, pp. 1–52). Mahwah, NJ: Erlbaum.

Bodenhausen, G. V., Macrae, C. N., & Sherman, J. W. (1999). On the dialectics of discrimination: Dual processes in social stereotyping. In S. Chaiken & Y. Trope (Eds.), *Dual process theories in social psychology* (pp. 271–290). New York: Guilford Press.

Bodenhausen, G. V., Mussweiler, T., Gabriel, S., & Moreno, K. N. (2001). Affective influences on stereotyping and intergroup relations. In J. P. Forgas (Ed.), *Handbook of affect and social cognition* (pp. 319–343). Mahwah, NJ: Erlbaum.

Bordieri, J., & Diemer, D. (1986). Hiring decisions for disabled workers: Looking at the cause. *Journal of Applied Social Psychology, 16*, 197–208.

Boski, P. (1988). Cross-cultural studies of person perceptions: Effects of ingroup/outgroup membership and ethnic Schemata. *Journal of Cross-Cultural Psychology, 19*, 287–328.

Brewer, M. B., & Gardner, W. (1996). Who is this "We"? Levels of collective identity and self representations. *Journal of Personality and Social Psychology, 71*, 83–93.

Brockington, I., Hall, P., Levings, J., & Murphy, C. (1993). The community's tolerance of the mentally ill. *British Journal of Psychiatry, 162*, 93–99.

Cacioppo, J. T., Gardner, W. L., & Berntson, G. G. (1997). Beyond bipolar conceptualizations and measures: The case of attitudes and evaluative space. *Personality and Social Psychology Review, 1*, 3–25.

Caldwell, T., Newman, L. S., Griffin, T. D., & Chamberlin, B. W. (2001, June). *Thought suppression, projection, and the development of stereotypes.* Paper presented at the annual meeting of the American Psychological Society, Toronto, Canada.

Campbell, D. (1967). Stereotypes and the perception of group differences. *American Psychologist, 22*, 817–829.

Chaikin, A. L., & Darley, J. M. (1973). Victim or perpetrator? Defensive attribution of responsibility and the need for order and justice. *Journal of Personality and Social Psychology, 25*, 268–275.

Corrigan, P. W. (1998). The impact of stigma on severe mental illness. *Cognitive and Behavioral Practice, 5*, 201–222.

Crocker, J., Major, B., & Steele, C. (1998). Social Stigma. In D. T. Gilbert, S. T. Fiske, & G. Lindzey (Eds.), *Handbook of social psychology* (4th ed., Vol. 2, pp. 504–553). New York: McGraw-Hill.

Darke, S. (1988). Anxiety and working memory capacity. *Cognition & Emotion, 2*, 145–154.

DePalma, M. T., Madey, S. F., Tillman, T. C., & Wheeler, J. (1999). Perceived patient responsibility and belief in a just world affect helping. *Basic and Applied Social Psychology, 21*, 131–137.

Devine, P. (1989). Stereotypes and prejudice: Their autonomic and controlled components. *Journal of Personality and Social Psychology, 56*, 5–18.

Devine, P. (1995). Getting hooked on research in social psychology. Examples from eyewitness identification and prejudice. In G. G. Brannigan & M. R. Merrens (Eds.), *The social psychologists: Research adventures.* New York: McGraw-Hill.

Dollard, J., Doob, L., Miller, N., Mowerer, O. H., & Sears, R. R. (1939). *Frustration and aggression.* New Haven, CT: Yale University Press.

Duckitt, J. (1993). Right-wing authoritarianism among White South African students: Its measurement and correlates. *Journal of Social Psychology, 133*, 553–563.

Dunton, B. C., & Fazio, R. H. (1997). An individual difference measure of motivation to control prejudiced reactions. *Personality and Social Psychology Bulletin, 23*, 316–326.

Eagly, A. H., & Chaiken, S. (1993). *The psychology of attitudes.* New York: Harcourt.

Farina, A., & Felner, R. (1973). Employment interviewer reactions to former mental patients. *Journal of Abnormal Psychology, 82*, 268–272.

Fiske, S. (1980). Attention and weight in person perception: The impact of negative and extreme behavior. *Journal of Personality and Social Psychology, 38*, 889–906.

Fiske, S. (1998). Stereotypes, prejudice, and discrimination. In D. Gilbert, S. Fiske, & G. Lindzey (Eds.), *Handbook of social psychology* (4th ed, pp. 357–411). Oxford, England: Oxford University Press.

Freud, A. (1936). *The ego and the mechanisms of defence*. London: Hogarth Press.

Goldinger, S. D., Kleider, H. M., Azuma, T., & Beike, D. R. (2003). "Blaming the victim" under memory load. *Psychological Science, 14*, 81–85.

Gove, W. (1970). Who is hospitalized: A critical review of some sociological studies of mental illness. *Journal of Health and Social Behavior, 11*, 294–303.

Gove, W. (Ed.). (1975). *The labeling of deviance: Evaluating a perspective*. New York: Wiley.

Haddock, G., Zanna, M. P., & Esses, V. M. (1993). Assessing the structure of prejudicial attitudes: The case of attitudes toward homosexuals. *Journal of Personality and Social Psychology, 65*, 1105–1118.

Hafer, C. L. (2000). Do innocent victims threaten the belief in a just world? Evidence from a modified Stroop task. *Journal of Personality and Social Psychology, 79*, 165–173.

Hamilton, D. L., & Gifford, R. K. (1976). Illusory correlation in interpersonal perception: A cognitive basis for stereotypic judgments. *Journal of Experimental Social Psychology, 12*, 392–407.

Hamre, P., Dahl, A., & Malt, U. (1994). Public attitudes to the quality of psychiatric treatment, psychiatric patients, and prevalence of mental disorders. *Norwegian Journal of Psychiatry, 4*, 275–281.

Harding, C., & Zahniser, J. (1994). Empirical correction of seven myths about schizophrenia with implications for treatment. *Acta Psychiatrica Scandinavica, Supplementum, 90*, 140–146.

Hass, R., Katz, I., Rizzo, N., Bailey, J., & Eisenstadt, D. (1991). Cross-racial appraisal as related to attitude ambivalence and cognitive complexity. *Personality and Social Psychology Bulletin, 17*, 83–92.

Hass, R., Katz, I., Rizzo, N., Bailey, J., & Moore, L. (1992). When racial ambivalence evokes negative affect, using a disguised measure of mood. *Personality and Social Psychology Bulletin, 17*, 786–797.

Hepworth, J. T., & West, S. G. (1988). Lynchings and the economy: A time-series reanalysis of Hovland and Sears (1940). *Journal of Personality and Social Psychology, 55*, 239–247.

Hewstone, M., Bond, M. H., & Wan, K. C. (1983). Social factors and social attributions: The explanation of inter-group differences in Hong Kong. *Social Cognition, 2*, 142–157.

Higgins, E. T. (1987). Self-discrepancy: A theory relating self and affect. *Psychological Review, 94*, 319–340.

Higgins, E. T., & King, G. A. (1981). Accessibility of social constructs: Information processing consequences of individual and contextual variability. In N. Cantor & J. Kihlstrom (Eds.), *Personality, cognition, and social interaction* (pp. 69–121). Hillsdale, NJ: Erlbaum.

Hilton, J., & von Hippel, W. (1996). Stereotypes. *Annual Review of Psychology, 47,* 237–271.

Hogg, M. A., & Abrams, D. (1988). *Social identifications.* London: Routledge.

Holmes, D. S. (1968). Dimensions of projection. *Psychological Bulletin, 69,* 248–268.

Holmes, D. S. (1978). Projection as a defense mechanism. *Psychological Bulletin, 85,* 677–688.

Holmes, D. S. (1981). Existence of classical projection and the stress-reducing function of attributive projection: A reply to Sherwood. *Psychological Bulletin, 90,* 460–466.

Hovland, C. I., & Sears, R. R. (1940). Minor studies in aggression: VI. Correlation of lynchings with economic indices. *Journal of Psychology, 9,* 301–310.

Isbell, L. M., & Clore, G. L. (1994). [The effects of odor on political judgment]. Unpublished data.

Isbell, L. M., & Ottati, V. (2002). The emotional voter: Effects of episodic affective reactions on candidate evaluation. In V. Ottati, R. S. Tindale, J. Edwards, F. B. Bryant, L. Heath, D. C. O'Connell, et al. (Eds.), *The social psychology of politics. Social psychological application to social issues* (Vol. 5, pp. 55–74). New York: Kluwer Academic/Plenum Publishers.

Jetten, J., Branscombe, N. R., & Spears, R. (2002). On being peripheral: Effects of identity insecurity on personal and collective self-esteem. *European Journal of Social Psychology, 32,* 105–123.

Judd, C. M., & Park, B. (1993). Definition and assessment of accuracy in social stereotypes. *Psychological Review, 100,* 109–128.

Kaplan, K. (1972). On the ambivalence-indifference problem in attitude theory and measurement: A suggested modification of the semantic differential technique. *Psychological Bulletin, 77,* 361–372.

Katz, D., McClintock, C., & Sarnoff, I. (1957). The measurement of ego-defense as related to attitude change. *Journal of Personality, 25,* 465–474.

Katz, D., Sarnoff, D., & McClintock, C. (1956). Ego-defense and attitude change. *Human Relations, 9,* 27–45.

Katz, I., Hass, R., & Bailey, J. (1988). Attitudinal ambivalence and behavior toward people with disabilities. In H. Yuker (Ed.), *Attitudes toward persons with disabilities* (pp. 47–57). New York: Springer Publishing.

Kessler, T., Mummendey, A., & Leisse, U. K. (2000). The personal-group discrepancy: Is there a common information base for personal and group judgment? *Journal of Personality and Social Psychology, 79,* 95–109

Krosnick, J. A., Betz, A. L., Jussim, L. J., & Lynn, A. R. (1992). Subliminal conditioning of attitudes. *Personality and Social Psychology Bulletin, 18,* 152–162.

Krueger, J. (1996). Personal beliefs and cultural stereotypes about racial characteristics. *Journal of Personality and Social Psychology, 71,* 536–548.

Kurzban, R., & Leary, M. R. (2001). Evolutionary origins of stigmatization: The function of social exclusion. *Psychological Bulletin, 127*, 187–208.

Langer, E. J., & Abelson, R. P. (1974). A patient by any other name . . . : Clinician group differences in labeling bias. *Journal of Consulting and Clinical Psychology, 42*, 4–9.

Lazarus, R. S. (1984). On the primacy of cognition. *American Psychologist, 39*, 124–129.

Lee, Y.-T., & Jussim, L. (Eds.) (1995). *Stereotype accuracy: Toward appreciating group differences*. Washington, DC: American Psychological Association.

Lerner, M. J. (1980). *The belief in a just world: A fundamental delusion*. New York: Plenum Press.

Lerner, M. J. (1998). The two forms of belief in a just world: Some thoughts on why and how people care about justice. In L. Montada & M. J. Lerner (Eds.), *Responses to victimization and belief in a just world: Critical issues in social justice* (pp. 247–269). New York: Plenum Press.

Link, B. G. (1987). Understanding labeling effects in the area of mental disorders: An assessment of the effects of expectations of rejection. *American Sociological Review, 52*, 96–112.

Link, B. G., Cullen, F. T., Frank, J., & Wozniak, J. F. (1987). The social rejection of former mental patients: Understanding why labels matter. *American Journal of Sociology, 92*, 1461–1500.

Link, B. G., Monahan, J., Stueve, A., & Cullen, F. (1999). Real in their consequences: A sociological approach to understanding the association between psychotic symptoms and violence. *American Sociological Review, 64*, 316–332.

Link, B. G., Phelan, J. C., Bresnahan, M., Stueve, A., & Pescosolido, B. A. (1999). Public conceptions of mental illness: Labels, causes, dangerousness, and social distance. *American Journal of Public Health, 89*, 1328–1333.

Lippmann, W. (1922). *Public opinion*. New York: Harcourt Brace.

Macrae, C. N., Bodenhausen, G. V., Milne, A. B., & Jetten, J. (1994). Out of mind but back in sight: Stereotypes on the rebound. *Journal of Personality and Social Psychology, 67*, 808–817.

Madianos, M. G, Madianou, D., Vlachonikolis, J., & Stefanis, C. N. (1987). Attitudes towards mental illness in the Athens area: Implications for community mental health intervention. *Acta Psychiatrica Scandinavica, 75*, 158–165.

Marcus-Newall, A., Pederson, W. C., Carlson, M., & Miller, N. (2000). Displace aggression is alive and well: A meta-analytic review. *Journal of Personality and Social Psychology, 78*, 670–689.

Martin, L. L., & Tesser, A. (1989). Toward a motivational and structural theory of ruminative thought. In J. S. Uleman & J. A. Bargh (Eds.), *Unintended thought* (pp. 306–326). New York: Guilford Press.

McCauley, C. (1995). Are stereotypes exaggerated? A sampling of racial, gender, academic, occupational, and political stereotypes. In Y. Lee, L. Jussim, &

C. McCauley (Eds.), *Stereotype accuracy: Toward appreciating group differences* (pp. 215–243). Washington, DC: American Psychological Association.

McCauley, C., & Rozin, P. (1989, April). *Mutual stereotyping of business and liberal arts students: A study of stereotype accuracy.* Paper presented at the annual meeting of the Eastern Psychological Association, Washington, DC.

McFarland, S. G., & Adelson, S. (1996). *An omnibus study of personality, values and prejudices.* Paper presented at the Annual Convention of the International Society for Political Psychology, Vancouver, British Columbia.

McGuire, W. J. (1985). Attitudes and attitude change. In G. Lindzey & E. Aronson (Eds.), *Handbook of social psychology* (3rd ed., Vol. 2, pp. 233–346). New York: Random House.

Mikulincer, M., & Horesh, N. (1999). Adult attachment style and the perception of others: The role of projective mechanisms. *Journal of Personality and Social Psychology, 76,* 1022–1034.

Monteith, M. J., Sherman, J. W., & Devine, P. G. (1998). Suppression as a stereotype control strategy. *Personality and Social Psychology Review, 2,* 63–82.

Murphy, S. T., Monahan, J. L., & Zajonc, R. B. (1995). Additivity of nonconscious affect: Combined effects of priming and exposure. *Journal of Personality and Social Psychology, 69,* 589–602.

Newby-Clark, I. R., McGregor, I., & Zanna, M. P. (2002). Thinking and caring about cognitive inconsistency: When and for whom does attitudinal ambivalence feel uncomfortable? *Journal of Personality and Social Psychology, 82,* 157–166.

Newman, L. S., & Chamberlin, B. W. (2002, February). *On cigarettes, ice cream, and dentists: The role of ambivalence and context in automatic evaluation.* Paper presented at the annual meeting of the Society for Personality and Social Psychology, Savannah, GA.

Newman, L. S., Duff, K. J., & Baumeister, R. F. (1997). A new look at defensive projection: Thought suppression, accessibility, and biased person perception. *Journal of Personality and Social Psychology, 72,* 980–1001.

Ogilvie, D. M. (1987). The undesired self: A neglected variable in personality research. *Journal of Personality and Social Psychology, 52,* 379–385.

Olshansky, S., Grob, S., & Ekdahl, M. (1960). Survey of employment experience of patients discharged from three mental hospitals during the period 1951–1953. *Mental Hygiene, 44,* 510–521.

Olson, M. A., & Fazio, R. H. (2002). Implicit acquisition and manifestation of classically conditioned attitudes. *Social Cognition, 20,* 89–103.

Ortony, A., Clore, G., & Collins, A. (1988). *The cognitive structure of emotion.* Cambridge, England: Cambridge University Press.

Ottati, V. (1996). When the survey question directs retrieval: Implications for assessing the cognitive and affective predictors of global evaluation. *European Journal of Social Psychology, 26,* 1–21.

Ottati, V. (2001). The psychological determinants of political judgment. In A. Tesser & N. Schwarz (Eds.), *Blackwell handbook of social psychology: Intraindividual processes* (pp. 615–634). Oxford, England: Blackwell.

Ottati, V., & Isbell, L. (1996). Effects of mood during exposure to target information on subsequently reported judgments: An on-line model of misattribution and correction. *Journal of Personality and Social Psychology, 71,* 39–53.

Ottati, V., & Lee, Y. (1995). Accuracy: A neglected component of stereotype research. In Y. Lee, L. Jussim, & C. McCauley (Eds.), *Stereotype accuracy: Toward appreciating group differences* (pp. 29–59.) Washington, DC: American Psychological Association.

Ottati, V., Steenbergen, M., & Riggle, E. (1992). The cognitive and affective components of political attitudes: Measuring the determinants of candidate evaluations. *Political Behavior, 14,* 423–442.

Ottati, V., & Wyer, R. S., Jr. (1993). Affect and political judgment. In S. Iyengar and J. McGuire (Eds.), *Explorations in political psychology* (pp. 296–320). Durham, NC: Duke University Press.

Page, S. (1995). Effects of the mental illness label in 1993: Acceptance and rejection in the community. *Journal of Health and Social Policy, 7,* 61–68.

Pederson, W. C., Gonzales, C., & Miller, N. (2000). The moderating effect of trivial triggering provocation on aggression. *Journal of Personality and Social Psychology, 78,* 913–927.

Penn, D. L., & Corrigan, P. W. (2002). The effects of stereotype suppression on psychiatric stigma. *Schizophrenia Research, 55,* 269–276.

Peterson, B. E., Doty, R. M., & Winter, D. G. (1993). Authoritarianism and attitudes towards contemporary social issues. *Personality and Social Psychology Bulletin, 19,* 174–184.

Phelan, J., Link, B., Stueve, A., & Pescosolido, B. (2000). Public conceptions of mental illness in 1950 and 1996: What is mental illness and is it to be feared? *Journal of Health and Social Behavior, 41,* 188–207.

Plant, E. A., & Devine, P. G. (1998). Internal and external motivation to respond without prejudice. *Journal of Personality and Social Psychology, 75,* 811–832.

Pratto, F., & Cathey, C. (2001). The role of social ideologies in legitimizing political attitudes and public policy. In V. Ottati, R. S. Tindale, J. Edwards, F. B. Bryant, L. Heath, D. C. O'Connell, et al. (Eds.), *The social psychology of politics. Social psychological application to social issues* (Vol. 5, pp. 135–156). New York: Kluwer Academic/Plenum Publishers.

Priester, J. R., & Petty, R. E. (1996). The gradual threshold model of ambivalence: Relating the positive and negative bases of attitudes to subjective ambivalence. *Journal of Personality and Social Psychology, 71,* 431–449.

Rabkin, J. (1974). Public attitudes toward mental illness: A review of the literature. *Psychological Bulletin, 10,* 9–33.

Roman, P., & Floyd, H. (1981). Social acceptance of psychiatric illness and psychiatric treatment. *Social Psychiatry, 16,* 16–21.

Rosenhan, D. L. (1973). On being sane in insane places. *Science, 179,* 250–258.

Ross, M., & Miller, D. T. (Eds.). (2002). *The justice motive in everyday life*. Cambridge, England: Cambridge University Press.

Rubovits, P. C., & Maehr, M. L. (1973). Pygmalion Black and White. *Journal of Personality and Social Psychology, 25*, 210–218.

Ryan, C. S., Robinson, D. R., & Hausmann, L. R. (2002). Stereotyping among providers and consumers of public mental health services: The role of perceived group variability. *Behavior Modification, 25*, 406–442.

Sagar, H. A., & Schofield, J. W. (1980). Racial and behavioral cues in Black and White children's perceptions of ambiguously aggressive acts. *Journal of Personality and Social Psychology, 39*, 590–598.

Schwarz, N., & Clore, G. L. (1983). Mood, misattribution, and judgments of well-being: Informative and directive functions of affective states. *Journal of Personality and Social Psychology, 45*, 513–523.

Schwarz, N., & Clore, G. L. (1996). Feelings and phenomenal experiences. In E.T. Higgins & A. W. Kruglanski (Eds.), *Social psychology handbook of principles* (pp. 433–465). New York: Guilford Press.

Sherif, M., Harvey, D. J., White, B. J., Hood, W. R., & Sherif, C. W. (1961). *The Robber's Cave experiment*. Norman, OK: Institute of Group Relations.

Sherman, J. W., Macrae, C. N., & Bodenhausen, G. V. (2000). Attention and stereotyping: Cognitive constraints on the construction of meaningful social impressions. *European Review of Social Psychology, 11*, 145–175.

Smart, L., & Wegner, D. M. (1999). Covering up what can't be seen: Concealable stigma and mental control. *Journal of Personality and Social Psychology, 77*, 474–486.

Steadman, H. (1981). Critically reassessing the accuracy of public perceptions of the dangerousness of the mentally ill. *Journal of Health and Social Behavior, 22*, 310–316.

Steadman, H., Mulvey, E., Monahan, J., Robbins, P., Appelbaum, P., Grisso, T., et al. (1998). Violence by people discharged from acute psychiatric inpatient facilities and by others in the same neighborhoods. *Archives of General Psychiatry, 55*, 393–401.

Strack, F., & Hannover, B. (1996). Awareness of influence as a precondition for implementing correctional goals. In P. M. Gollwitzer & J. A. Bargh (Eds.), *The psychology of action: Linking cognition and motivation to behavior* (pp. 579–596). New York: Guilford Press.

Stroessner, S. J., & Plaks, J. E. (2001). Illusory correlation and stereotype formation: Tracing the arc of research over a quarter century. In G. Moskowitz (Ed.), *Cognitive social psychology* (pp. 247–259). Mahwah, NJ: Erlbaum.

Szasz, T. (1961). *The myth of mental illness*. New York: Harper & Row.

Tajfel, H. (1969). Cognitive aspects of prejudice. *Journal of Social Issues, 25*, 79–97.

Tajfel, H. (1981). *Human groups and social categories*. Cambridge, England: Cambridge University Press.

Tajfel, H., & Turner, J. C. (1986). The social identity theory of intergroup behavior. In S. Worchel & W. Austin (Eds.), *Psychology of intergroup relations*. Chicago: Nelson-Hall.

Taylor, S. M., & Dear, M. J. (1981). Scaling community attitudes towards the mentally ill. *Schizophrenia Bulletin, 7*, 225–240.

Thompson, M. M., Zanna, M. P., & Griffin, D. W. (1995). Let's not be indifferent about (attitudinal) ambivalence. In R. E. Petty & J. A. Krosnick (Eds.), *Attitude strength: Antecedents and consequences* (pp. 361–386). Hillsdale, NJ: Erlbaum.

Thornton, B. (1984). Defensive attribution of responsibility: Evidence for an arousal-based motivational bias. *Journal of Personality and Social Psychology, 46*, 721–734.

Trafimow, D., Triandis, H. C., & Goto, S. G. (1991). Some tests of the distinction between the private self and the collective self. *Journal of Personality and Social Psychology, 60*, 649–655.

Triandis, H., & Vassiliou, V. (1967). Frequency of contact and stereotyping. *Journal of Personality and Social Psychology, 7*, 316–328.

Turner, J. C. (1987). *Rediscovering the social group: A self-categorization theory*. Oxford, England: Blackwell.

Vinacke, W. (1949). Stereotyping among national-racial groups in Hawaii: A study in ethnocentrism. *Journal of Social Psychology, 30*, 265–291.

Wahl, O. (1992). Mass media images of mental illness: A review of the literature. *Journal of Community Psychology, 20*, 343–352.

Webster's seventh new collegiate dictionary. (1972). Springfield, MA: Merriam-Webster.

Wegner, D. M. (1992). You can't always think what you want: Problems in the suppression of unwanted thoughts. In M. Zanna (Ed.), *Advances in experimental social psychology* (Vol. 25, pp. 193–225). San Diego, CA: Academic Press.

Wegner, D. M. (1994). Ironic processes of mental control. *Psychological Review, 101*, 34–52.

Wegner, D. M., & Zanakos, S. (1994). Chronic thought suppression. *Journal of Personality, 62*, 615–640.

Weiner, B. (1995). *Judgments of responsibility: A foundation for a theory of social conduct*. New York: Guilford.

Wenzlaff, R. M., & Wegner, D. M. (2000). Thought suppression. *Annual Review of Psychology, 51*, 59–91.

White, R. K. (1977). Misperception in the Arab-Israeli Conflict. *Journal of Social Issues, 33*, 190–221.

Wilson, T. D., & Brekke, N. (1994). Mental contamination and mental correction: Unwanted influences on judgments and evaluations. *Psychological Bulletin, 116*, 117–142.

Zajonc, R. B. (1980). Feeling and thinking: Preferences need no inferences. *American Psychologist, 35*, 151–175.

5

SOCIOLOGICAL MODELS OF MENTAL ILLNESS STIGMA: PROGRESS AND PROSPECTS

FRED E. MARKOWITZ

Although much of the sociology of mental illness is concerned with how *social statuses*—positions in the social structure—such as social class, age, race, and gender contribute to the occurrence of mental disorder, there has been a great deal of research concerning the stigmatizing consequences of mental illness as a social status. This research is largely driven by the collection of ideas known as labeling theory. In this chapter, I review theoretical and empirical developments in the sociological understanding of the stigma associated with mental illness. I begin with a brief overview of the classic conceptions of stigma as formulated by Goffman and others. Next, I trace how sociologists have contributed to our understanding of public conceptions of mental illness and public reactions to mental illness. Finally, I discuss progress and prospects in research on the effects of stigma on persons with mental illness.

Although *stigma* is a somewhat nebulous concept, most sociologists proceed on the classic definition provided by Goffman—" . . . an attribute that is deeply discrediting . . ." that reduces the bearer " . . . from a whole and usual person to a tainted, discounted one" (1963, p. 3). Thus, stigma has also come to refer to the adverse cognitive and behavioral consequences associated with devalued statuses. Link and Phelan (2001) elaborate on the concept of stigma, defining it as a *process* by which persons with salient social differences become labeled, triggering certain stereotypes that result in discrimination, loss of socioeconomic status, and diminished life chances. Mental illness is perhaps one of the most discrediting attributes. It is linked to an array of negative stereotypical traits (e.g., dangerousness, weakness, incompetence), it is widely misunderstood by the general public, and is often inaccurately and negatively portrayed in the media (Corrigan & Lundin, 2001; Wahl, 1995).

Labeling theory is the explanatory framework that has been developed by sociologists to account for the stigmatization associated with devalued statuses, such as "delinquent," "criminal," or "mentally ill" (Becker, 1963; Lemert, 1951, 1967; Scheff, 1984). The theory is rooted in the symbolic interactionist tradition within sociology. The basic premise of symbolic interactionism is that the meanings of social objects (persons and actions) are *socially constructed* (Blumer, 1969; Mead, 1934). From this perspective, the meaning of behavior is not inherent, but rather, through the use of language and symbols, it is subject to processes of interpretation and definition. Responses in social interaction are based on assigned meanings ("definitions of the situation"), which are drawn from shared cultural knowledge. Thus, Becker (1963) argued that deviance is not a quality of actions, but rather results from others' definitions of those acts. Some social groups (e.g., legislators and psychiatrists) have the power to set and impose definitions of what constitutes deviant behavior. These definitions are imposed in ways to preserve the interests of more powerful social groups. Social actors at a power disadvantage (of lower social standing) are less able to resist application of deviant labels. Their behavior is thus more likely to be labeled as deviant. For Becker, a deviant is "one to whom the label has been successfully applied" (Becker, 1963, p. 9).

Within the symbolic interactionist framework, self-conceptions result from perceptions of how others view the self. This is known as the *reflected appraisals process*. On the basis of others' responses to the self as a social object, we 'come to see ourselves as others see us' (Cooley, 1902). Self-conceptions that are linked to occupied social positions are *role-identities* (Stryker, 1980). When acting in accord with our role-identities, we fulfill the expectations that others have of us. Persons normally occupy many roles (e.g., teacher, parent, spouse) with accompanying behavioral expectations. According to labeling theory, the role of "mentally ill" is one that persons may be cast in.

Early versions of labeling theory specified the processes by which deviant labels are applied and persons' self-conceptions and social opportunities are altered. Scheff (1984) argued that many behaviors violating social norms are easily categorized, such as criminal acts that have specific legal definitions. However, numerous acts are not easily categorized and constitute "residual" forms of deviance, such as social withdrawal, talking to oneself, displaying inappropriate affect—the kinds of behaviors that treatment professionals (and many lay persons) are likely to consider indicative of mental illness. When individuals generally regarded as "normal" engage in these types of behavior, it is often dismissed by others and has limited significance for a person's identity. Lemert (1951) referred to these types of behaviors as *primary deviance*. Primary deviance is treated by others as transitory in nature and not seen as characteristic of the person. This type of behavior arises from diverse sources, such as stress, intentional defiance, childhood socialization, as well as organic causes. Scheff argued that most residual rule-breaking is explained away, unrecorded, transitory, and generally insignificant, hence the rate of residual rule-breaking is probably far greater than that which is identified and treated as "mental illness."

According to Scheff, stereotyped conceptions of mental illness are learned early in childhood and are continually reaffirmed in ordinary social interaction and mass media. We thus learn to recognize and define "crazy" behavior (Scheff, 1984). When a person's behavior continually violates social norms and is highly visible (e.g., in "crisis" situations), it is regarded by others as more serious, and may then come to be viewed as evidence of mental illness, a property of the person. Scheff argued that psychiatrists, as a result of professional socialization, financial incentives, and ideological commitment to the medical model of illness, operate with a presumption of illness, and are thus inclined toward making diagnoses and recommendations for treatment despite uncertainty in many cases.

Once residual rule-breaking is labeled as mental illness, Scheff suggests that labeled deviants may be rewarded for playing the stereotyped role. Because it is so highly discrediting, one's status as patient may emerge as a "master status" (Becker, 1963) or what Schur (1971) termed an "engulfing role," overriding other status characteristics, becoming a potent influence in social interaction. Because of the devalued status of mental patient and the attendant stigmatization, rejection by "normal individuals," isolation from normative networks, restricted social opportunities, and changes in the self-concept (including lowered self-esteem) are likely outcomes (Goffman, 1961). For example, persons labeled as mentally ill may be rejected in both subtle and direct ways when they attempt to return to normal social roles (e.g., as friends, employees, or tenants). The theory further predicts that persons labeled as mentally ill may "drift" away from normative groups and conform to their changed role expectations, leading to future deviance (in the case of mental illness—non-normative, symptomatic behavior), what

Lemert called *secondary deviance*. The strongest proposition offered by Scheff is that "among residual rule-breakers, labeling is among the most important causes of careers of residual deviance" (1984, p. 69). In this early version of labeling theory, it is through these mechanisms that treatment can lead to continued symptoms. This view places greater emphasis on labeling and social reaction as causes of sustained disturbing behavior, and minimizes the assumption that those who are labeled as mentally ill are experiencing true, underlying disorders. A summary of these processes is shown in Figure 5.1A. Although this version of the theory denies the reality of mental illness and downplays its possible biogenetic underpinnings, it does provide a framework

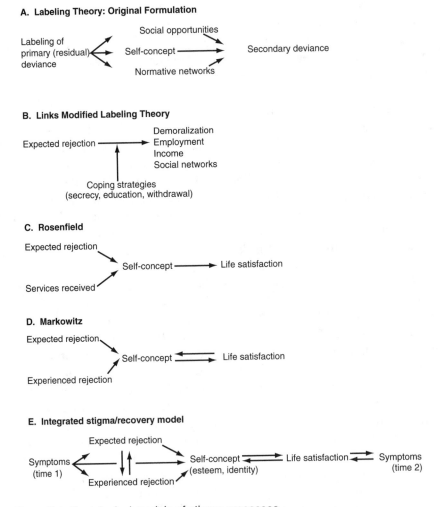

Figure 5.1. Sociological models of stigma processes.

for understanding some of the adverse consequences of treatment for mental illness.

Alternatively, critics of labeling theory argued, from what came to be termed the "psychiatric" perspective, that the actual illness and related behavior are what affects social outcomes and continued illness (Gove, 1979, 1982; Gove & Fain, 1973; Gove & Howell, 1974; Weinstein, 1979, 1983). They countered the labeling argument along several key lines. First, they argued that little evidence exists to suggest a "psychiatric victimization" or tendency to diagnose without thorough screening. Second, from the standpoint of primary relations (e.g., family members), mental illness is often denied as an explanation for abnormal behavior and only accepted as a last resort. Thus, behavior must become quite severe before it is no longer tolerated and treatment is pursued. Third, people with fewer resources are not any more likely to enter the role of mentally ill. In fact, those with greater resources may be more likely to identify behaviors as indicative of mental illness and seek treatment voluntarily. Fourth, they argued that psychiatric treatment, including hospitalization, does not entail the negative consequences suggested by the secondary deviance hypothesis. In fact, critics argued that ample evidence exists to suggest treatment generally improves psychiatric conditions. The heart of their critique is that deviant labels are *consequences* of inherent mental conditions rather than the primary *cause* of deviant careers. Thus, the central empirical issue surrounding the labeling approach to mental illness is whether social rejection is because of the stigmatizing consequences of the label of "mentally ill" or whether it is resulting from disturbing, symptomatic behavior that results from illness.

Labeling theory was somewhat on the ropes until a landmark 1982 study by Link. Using a community sample, he examined the effects of both the symptoms of mental illness and being labeled mentally ill (through treatment) on employment and income. He found that, controlling for other variables that affect employment and income (marital status, education, age, and occupation), patient status had twice as large an effect on income and employment than psychiatric symptoms did. This study led to a more recent, "modified" version of labeling theory (Link, Cullen, Frank, & Wozniak, 1987; Link, Cullen, Struening, Shrout, & Dohrenwend, 1989). In this version, the strong claim that labeling causes "careers in residual deviance" is replaced by a more subtle approach to how stigmatization affects the course of illness. According to the modified theory, generally held stereotypical attitudes about the mentally ill, (e.g., as incompetent and dangerous) become personally relevant to an individual when diagnosed with a mental illness. Because of these attitudes, persons treated and labeled as mentally ill expect to be devalued and discriminated against. These beliefs act as self-fulfilling prophecies. To avoid rejection, persons who are labeled engage in various coping strategies, such as secrecy, disclosure, or social withdrawal, which may enhance the effects of expected stigma by constricting social networks, leading to unemployment and lowered income. Moreover, those labeled as mentally ill are predicted to experience lowered self-esteem and feelings of demoralization. Drawing on the stress-process model and research (one of the dominant sociological approaches to mental illness), the theory further predicts that a low sense of self combined with reduced social and material resources increases stress, placing persons at greater risk for continued symptoms (Pearlin, Menaghan, Lieberman, & Mullan, 1981; Turner 1981). Thus, labeling and stigmatization indirectly leads to sustained illness by affecting the self-concept and social outcomes.

Following from these theoretical developments are important lines of sociological research that center around three questions. First, how much does the public know about mental illness? Second, how are they likely to react to those with mental illness? Third, what are the social and psychological consequences for those labeled as mentally ill? Research on each of these questions is reviewed in this chapter.

PUBLIC CONCEPTIONS OF MENTAL ILLNESS

Sociological research on public conceptions of mental illness has yielded some good news and some bad news. First, the good news is that the public seems to have a better understanding of the nature of mental illness than it had in previous decades. Early research in the 1950s based on nationally representative surveys showed that Americans had a very narrow view of mental illness (Star, 1952, 1955). In 1950, respondents were asked an open-ended question: "When you hear someone say that a person is 'mentally ill,' what does that mean to you?" A substantial portion (about 41%) gave responses reflecting psychosis (e.g., "person's not in touch with reality," "lives in his own world") or they used colloquial terms such as "nuts," "deranged," or "out of his mind." About 49% of those surveyed gave responses reflecting anxiety or depression (e.g., "appears worried or anxious all the time," "emotional ups and downs"). Comparatively fewer respondents thought of mental illness in terms that would be considered personality disorders, substance abuse disorders, or cognitive impairment. In 1996, the same question was asked again in a nationally representative survey (Pescosolido, Monahan, Link, Steuve, & Kikuzawa, 1999; Phelan, Link, Stueve, & Pescosolido, 2000). This time, fewer persons gave answers reflecting psychosis (35%) and anxiety/depression (34%), and more gave responses indicating other disorders such as personality disorders, substance abuse disorders, or cognitive impairment. This suggests that the public's conceptions of mental illness has broadened beyond stereotypical conceptions associated with psychotic disorders and now may be considered as something less alien and extreme.

Other recent research, using data from the same survey, included vignettes that describe persons who fit the criteria for major mental illnesses, including schizophrenia, major depression, and drug and alcohol dependence (Phelan et al., 2000). When respondents were asked whether they "thought the person was likely to have mental illness," about 88% said yes when a person with schizophrenia was described and about 69% said yes when a person with major depression was described. When asked specifically whether they thought the person was "likely to have depression," 95% said yes. This suggests less of a gulf exists between lay and professional conceptions of mental illness. Also, recent studies show Americans are more likely to attribute the causes of mental disorders such as schizophrenia and depression to "chemical imbalances," "genetic factors," and "stressful life circumstances," rather than to "bad character," "the way the person was raised," or "God's will," suggesting that public understanding of the causes of mental illness is somewhat sophisticated and consistent with professionals' views.

Public Reactions to Persons With Mental Illness

Unfortunately, concurrent with the favorable developments discussed previously, there has been an increase in the proportion of persons who associate mental illness with perceptions of dangerousness, violence, and unpredictability. When asked what "mental illness" means to them, about 7% mentioned violent manifestations/symptoms in 1950 compared to 12% in 1996 (Phelan et al., 2000; Star 1952, 1955). Moreover, those who think of mental illness in terms of psychosis are more likely to associate mental illness with dangerousness. They are also are less willing to live near, socialize, or work with people with psychiatric disorders, to have a group home for the mentally ill nearby, or to have someone with mental illness marry into their family. They want to have what sociologists call greater *social distance*.

Early research incorporated the critical issue surrounding labeling theory —to what extent does social distance or rejection result from the degree of stigmatizing psychiatric labels or from disturbing, symptomatic behavior? In an innovative study using a sample of small-town residents, Phillips (1963) had participants read case abstracts of a person having one of five psychiatric states (paranoid schizophrenia, simple schizophrenia, depressed neurosis, phobic-compulsive disorder, and normal) and one of five sources of help, indicating the degree of labeling (none, clergy, physician, psychiatrist, and mental hospital) as independent variables. An additive measure of social rejection (willingness to have the person marry your children, rent them a room, work with them, join an organization of yours, have the person as a neighbor) was the dependent variable. Although he found that rejection scores increased with both the severity of illness and level of involvement in professional help (labeling), level of symptoms was found to have a greater effect.

Other studies have followed designs similar to Phillips', such as Link et al. (1987), where they considered the relative importance of labeling and disturbing behavior as determinants of social distance. In that study, they administered a series of vignettes to a random sample of participants in a 3×2 factorial design with three levels of behavior (no objectionable behavior, mildly disturbing, and severely disturbing) and two levels of labeling (mental hospitalization or hospitalization for back problems). They also included measures of perceived dangerousness of "mental patients" in general. There were two main findings. One was that disturbing behavior had a significant effect on social rejection whereas the label did not. However, they also found that labeling interacts with perceived dangerousness in its effect on social rejection; that is, when persons are labeled as mentally ill (in this case via hospitalization), the perceived dangerousness of "mental patients" has a significant effect on social distance. The findings from this study suggest that psychiatric labels may trigger generalized beliefs about the dangerousness of persons with mental illness, which then lead to social rejection.

More recently, research has turned to public support for coercive treatment and segregation of persons with mental illness. Using data from the nationally representative General Social Survey (GSS), this research shows that the general public may support coercive treatment for those with mental illness who are believed to be dangerous (Pescosolido et al., 1999). Also, more than 40% of the respondents agreed that persons with schizophrenia should be forced to enter the hospital, take medication, and visit outpatient clinics (Pescosolido et al., 1999). Although dangerousness was the primary predictor of support for coercive treatment, consistent with attribution theory, Martin, Pescosolido, and Tuch (2000) also found that internal attributions for mental illness (e.g., "bad character") led to increased social distance, whereas external attributions (e.g., stress) reduce social distance. Similarly, a vignette-type study by Corrigan and colleagues (2003) showed that internal attributions for the cause of mental illness and perceptions of dangerousness increased anger and fear. These feelings, in turn, were related to increased support for coercive treatment and reduced likelihood of willingness to help.

So, paradoxically, public understanding of mental illness has apparently increased, yet the perception of persons with psychotic disorders as being dangerous has also increased (also see chap. 7). This pattern of findings has led some to conclude that disorders such as depression may be seen as something that can happen to "us," but schizophrenia is something that happens to "them" (Phelan et al., 2000). In addition, the tendency toward social rejection and support for coercion/segregation of persons with mental illness remains high. Public perceptions of dangerousness are not entirely irrational, given studies that show persons who are experiencing certain untreated psychotic symptoms are at an increased risk of violence. However, the risk is comparable to certain demographic characteristics, such as being male, younger, non-White, and less educated (Link, Andrews, & Cullen, 1992; Link, Monahan, Stueve, & Cullen, 1999). Media images and high publicity surrounding certain violent events may have created misperception of the actual risk of violence (Wahl, 1995).

The Effects of Stigma on Persons With Mental Illness

A third area of sociological research deals with how stigma affects the well-being of persons with mental illness. This research, most of which is based on the modified version of labeling theory, takes a balanced approach. Its basic premise is that although labels may not "cause" sustained mental illness, the stigma associated with treatment for mental disorder affects the course of illness by lowering a person's self-esteem, constricting their interpersonal networks, and reducing their chances for employment and income, all of which increase stress. These stressors, in turn, place persons at risk for increased symptoms.

In a series of studies, Link and colleagues developed and tested modified labeling theory using combined community and treatment samples (1987, 1989, 1991). In these studies, stigma is operationalized using the Devaluation-Discrimination (DD) scale, a 12-item index that measures the extent of *expected rejection*—beliefs that persons treated for mental illness will be rejected as friends, teachers, employees, dating partners (e.g., "Most people would willingly accept a former mental patient as a close friend," "Most employers would not hire a person who has been hospitalized for mental illness," "Most people believe that former mental patients cannot be trusted"). These studies first show that persons with a mental disorder who are either treated (i.e., labeled) or not, and persons without a mental disorder all believe that those who are labeled will experience a degree of devaluation and discrimination, supporting the notion of generalized expectations of rejection of the mentally ill. Second, these studies show that, among persons in treatment, expectations of rejection have an adverse effect on "demoralization," income, employment, and social support networks. Third, these individuals not only hold expectations of devaluation and discrimination; but they also endorse certain strategies for coping with stigma, including secrecy, education (telling others), and social withdrawal. However, these strategies appear to produce more harm than good—they interact with DD in constricting social networks and diminishing economic outcomes (see Figure 5.1B).

In an influential study, Rosenfield (1997) addressed the issue of how labeling via treatment can have both beneficial and detrimental effects on subjective quality of life (see Figure 5.1C). Using a sample of clients in a model treatment program, she showed that certain aspects of services (vocational rehabilitation, financial support, perception of empowerment, MICA [mental illness/chemical abuse] group, leisure activities) had positive effects on quality of life, but, controlling for staff-reported symptoms, stigma (operationalized using the DD scale) had negative effects on quality of life. She also found that much of the effects of stigma and services on quality of life were mediated by self-esteem and self-efficacy.

Most of the studies testing modified labeling theory are based on cross-sectional data. However, some recent studies build on this research by using longitudinal data. The use of longitudinal data, although certainly not without limitations, does offer certain methodological advantages. By controlling for baseline (lagged) measures of outcomes, researchers can estimate the effects of stigma on changes in outcome variables, controlling for unmeasured causes, allowing for more stringent tests of causality (see Finkel, 1995; Kessler & Greenberg, 1981). Also, these more recent studies examine the effects of both anticipated and experienced rejection, asking respondents about discriminatory treatment. In one study, Link, Struening, Rahav, Phelan, and Nuttbrock (1997) surveyed 84 men with dual diagnosis of mental illness and substance abuse at two points in time (upon entering a treatment program and one year later). They found that even though symptoms declined and functioning improved at follow-up, expected and experienced stigma and endorsement of socially isolating coping strategies remained at the same levels. The study also showed how stigma had an adverse effect on the change in depressive symptoms. Significantly, by including baseline symptoms, they controlled for the relationship between initial symptoms and stigma.

In a related study, Markowitz (1998), using two-wave data (two surveys, 18 months apart) from 600 persons with mental illness sampled from outpatient and self-help groups, examined the effect of both expected and experienced rejection on self-concept (self-esteem, efficacy) and life-satisfaction (economic and interpersonal). His findings indicated adverse effects of stigma on all of these outcomes. However, he found that much of the effects of anticipated rejection diminished when discriminatory experiences were controlled. This finding suggests that part of the effects of anticipated rejection may be because of rejection experiences. It still leaves unresolved the causal relationship between anticipated and experienced rejection. The results of that study also indicated that stigmatization is related to depressive-anxiety types of symptoms, but not psychotic-types of symptoms. Although the findings showed that the negative effect of stigma on life satisfaction is partly mediated by self-concept, reciprocal effects models indicated that the relationship between self-concept and life satisfaction is bidirectional—self-concept not only influences interpersonal and economic outcomes, but is influenced by them as well (see Figure 5.1D). Another longitudinal study used three-wave data (participants surveyed three times) from 88 formerly institutionalized persons with mental illness to show how stigmatizing experiences negatively impacted self-esteem and self-efficacy (Wright et al., 2000).

All of these recent studies suggest several ways in which stigma processes need to be explored in greater detail, in particular, by examining causal relationships over time, by estimating the effects of both anticipated and experienced social rejection, and by considering the reciprocal effects among variables. One important limitation of these studies however, is that they focus exclusively on treated or self-identified cases, thus eliminating variability in labeling.

CONCLUSIONS: DIRECTIONS FOR FUTURE RESEARCH

Although all of the research reviewed previously provides a more detailed understanding of the effects of stigma, still more exists to be done. What is needed is an integration of stigma into our overall understanding of the recovery process—the dynamics between symptoms of mental illness, self-concept, and social outcomes (Anthony, 1991, 1993; Markowitz, 2001). Several avenues of research could be pursued toward this goal (see Figure 5.1E). First, there needs to be a more direct examination of the relative impact of symptomatic behavior (including medication side effects) on self-concept and social outcomes"—is it the stigma associated with the label of "mentally ill" or the behavior?

Second, the need exists to further examine how stigmatizing expectations affect stigmatizing experiences and vice versa. Although existing research suggests that persons who expect rejection may act in ways to fulfill those expectations, the reverse effect could be operating as well. To the extent that persons experience social rejection, they may come to expect it.

A third line of research could focus on how stigma both affects and how it is affected by psychological and social wellbeing. Most of the research on the effects of stigma has focused on how anticipated and experienced social rejection impacts symptoms of illness as well as social and economic wellbeing, yet neglects how social and psychological wellbeing impacts the likelihood of anticipated and experienced stigma. Although the longitudinal research that includes lagged measures of outcomes helps isolate the effects of stigma, it is not clear how much outcomes affect stigma. Significantly, if the bidirectionality of these relationships is ignored, and only cross-sectional models are estimated, researchers run the risk of overestimating the impact of stigma.

A fourth set of questions concerns the extent to which persons reveal or conceal their mental illness (both in terms of symptoms and treatment), whether it is apparent to others, and with what effects. Research to date has not fully examined how such knowledge affects stigmatization and well-being among persons with mental illness. Moreover, degree of concealment may both affect and be affected by anticipated and experienced stigma.

Fifth, the role of self-concept in stigma processes has long been of theoretical concern. Although much research has examined how stigma affects the *evaluative* dimension of the self-concept of persons with mental illness (e.g., self-esteem, self-efficacy), it has not examined the identity dimension of self. For example, how does being diagnosed with mental illness affect self-conceptions in terms of being "deviant," "abnormal," or, in Goffman's terms, as having a "spoiled identity?" Moreover, how do the perceptions and reflected appraisals of "significant others" (e.g., family, friends, service providers) of persons with mental illness affect identity formation? In turn, how does identity affect the recovery process? Matsueda (1992) provided a seminal test of these processes in the area of juvenile delinquency. Using data from a large scale, multiwave, nationally representative sample of youth, he found that parental and self (reflected) appraisals of youths as "rule violators" and "troublemakers" are more likely (net of delinquency) to be applied to non-Whites and urban dwellers. He also found that parents' and teachers' appraisals affect delinquency through youths' reflected appraisals. A similar study could be conducted with persons with mental illness and their significant others. Toward this goal, measures of identity formation variables centered around the salience of mental illness need to be developed.

An additional area of research might concern how social demographic variables play a role in stigma and recovery processes. Does having other devalued identities (e.g., racial minority, criminal history) interact with the stigma of mental illness in its impact on recovery? In other words, is there a "double stigma" that is associated with certain status characteristics? Also, what is the role of neighborhood context in recovery from mental illness? How does the stigma of living in economically disadvantaged neighborhoods affect the course of illness? Some research with general population samples has shown that neighborhood context affects physical health and psychological distress (Ross & Mirowsky, 2001; Ross, Reynolds, & Geis, 2000). How do these effects generalize to persons with serious mental illness and to what extent are they because of stigma?

Finally, much of the research on stigma has been based on cross-sectional data, precluding the ability to establish causal relationships, model reciprocal effects, and determine how long it takes for stigma to impact well-being. Although there has been some limited research using longitudinal (mostly two-wave) data, these designs do not allow for the estimation of both cross-lagged (over time) and simultaneous (concurrent) reciprocal effects. Studies are needed that make use of longer longitudinal designs (e.g., four-wave, multiyear), enabling the estimation of such effects and for experimentation with various time order specifications in stigma and recovery process models.

Ideally, such studies would involve general population samples with a sufficient number of respondents having psychiatric symptoms and variability in treatment contact. However, the rather large number of persons required to obtain a sufficient number of persons experiencing symptoms of psychotic disorders may prohibit such studies. Thus, whereas some of the initial studies based on modified labeling theory involved community samples and have greater generalizability, the more recent research examining stigma processes in greater detail have an important limitation—only those who have already been treated (labeled) are included, eliminating a key variable. It may be more feasible to examine stigma processes associated with common types of disorders (e.g., depression) in general population samples, yet difficult to include those who meet diagnostic criteria for psychotic disorders.

Extending sociological research based on modified labeling theory can lead to educational programs and treatment strategies that will help improve the lives of persons with serious mental illness in several ways. Although many of the stigma change programs that have been developed to date address stigmatizing attitudes among members of the general public, studies that include consumers, service providers, and family members will contribute information that will enable the development of targeted stigma change efforts. First, by understanding how discriminatory experiences affect consumers' attitudes that lead to self-defeating behaviors, strategies can be developed that minimize the impact of those experiences, such as specialized skill training modules for managing stigma and discrimination. Second, by understanding how the likelihood of anticipated and experienced stigma is affected by social and clinical variables, we can better target efforts to reduce the experience of stigma and discrimination. Third, understanding the ways in which the attitudes of significant others impact consumers will highlight the need to target stigma-reduction strategies toward families and service providers, to strengthen client-provider relationships, and promote greater involvement of families in treatment programs. For example, if pessimism regarding recovery is transmitted to clients from family members and professionals, educational interventions to raise family and provider awareness about the heterogeneity of mental illness outcomes and the possibilities for recovery and improvement could be developed.

In conclusion, sociologists have been at the forefront of theory and research on the stigma associated with mental illness. Early on, some influential sociologists questioned the reality of mental illness. In doing so, they provided a foundation for understanding how diagnosis and treatment for mental illness may be highly stigmatizing, affecting the well-being of those treated. More recently, although most sociologists have come to accept the "reality" of mental illness and the efficacy of treatment, many assign a more prominent causal role to social, rather than biological factors in the onset and course of illness (see Horowitz, 2002; Link & Phelan, 1995). With continued theoretical and methodological refinement, even further progress can be made in detailing the ways in which stigmatization—an eminently social process—affects the course of mental illness.

REFERENCES

Anthony, W. A. (1991). Recovery from mental illness: The new vision of services researchers. *Innovations in Research, 1,* 13–14.

Anthony, W. A. (1993). Recovery from mental illness: The guiding vision of the mental health service system in the 1990s. *Psychosocial Rehabilitation Journal, 16,* 11–23.

Becker, H. S. (1963). *Outsiders: Studies in the sociology of deviance*. New York: Free Press.

Blumer, H. (1969). *Symbolic interactionism: Perspective and method*. Englewood Cliffs, NJ: Prentice-Hall.

Cooley, C. H. (1902). *Human nature and the social order*. New York: Scribner.

Corrigan, P., & Lundin, R. (2001). *Don't call me nuts: Coping with the stigma of mental illness*. Chicago: Recovery Press.

Corrigan, P., Markowitz, F. E., Watson, A., Rowan, D., & Kubiak, M. A. (2003). An attribution model of public discrimination toward persons with mental illness. *Journal of Health and Social Behavior, 44*, 1–69.

Finkel, S. (1995). *Causal analysis with panel data*. Thousand Oaks, CA: Sage.

Goffman, E. (1961). *Asylums*. Garden City, NJ: Anchor Books.

Goffman, E. (1963). *Stigma: Notes on the management of spoiled identity*. Englewood Cliffs, NJ: Prentice-Hall.

Gove, W. R. (1979). The labeling versus psychiatric explanation for mental illness: A debate that has become substantively irrelevant. *Journal of Health and Social Behavior, 20*, 301–304.

Gove, W. R. (1980). Labeling mental illness: A critique. In W. R. Gove (Ed.), *Labeling deviance behavior* (pp. 53–109). Beverly Hills, CA: Sage.

Gove, W. R. (1982). The current status of the labeling theory of mental illness. In W. R. Gove (Ed.), *Deviance and mental illness* (pp. 273–300). Beverly Hills, CA: Sage.

Gove, W. R., & Fain, T. (1973). The stigma of mental hospitalization: An attempt to evaluate its consequences. *Archives of General Psychiatry, 29*, 494–500.

Gove, W. R., & Howell, P. (1974). Individual resources and mental hosptialization: A comparison and evaluation of the societal reaction and psychiatric perspectives. *American Sociological Review, 39*, 86–100.

Horwitz, A. (2002). *Creating mental illness*. Chicago: University of Chicago Press.

Kessler, R. C., & Greenberg, D. F. (1981). *Linear panel analysis: Models of quantitative change*. New York: Academic Press.

Lemert, E. (1951). *Social pathology*. New York: McGraw-Hill.

Lemert, E. (1967). *Human deviance, social problems, and social control*. Englewood Cliffs, NJ: Prentice-Hall.

Link, B. G. (1982). Mental patient status, work, and income: An examination of the effects of a psychiatric label. *American Sociological Review, 47*, 202–215.

Link, B. G. (1987). Understanding labeling effects in the area of mental disorders: An empirical assessment of the effects of expectations of rejection. *American Sociological Review, 52*, 96–112.

Link, B. G., Andrews, H., & Cullen, F. T. (1992). The violent and illegal behavior of mental patients reconsidered. *American Sociological Review, 52*, 96–112.

Link, B. G., Cullen, F. T., Frank, J., & Wozniak, J. F. (1987). The social rejection of former mental patients: Understanding why labels matter. *American Journal of Sociology, 92*, 1461–1500.

Link, B. G., Cullen, F. T., Struening, E., Shrout, P. E., & Dohrenwend, B. P. (1989). A modified labeling theory approach to mental disorders: An empirical assessment. *American Sociological Review, 54*, 400–423.

Link, B. G., Mirotznik, J., & Cullen, F. T. (1991). The effectiveness of stigma coping orientations: Can negative consequences of mental illness labeling be avoided? *Journal of Health and Social Behavior, 32*, 302–320.

Link, B. G., Monahan, J., Stueve, A., & Cullen F. T. (1999). Real in their consequences: A sociological approach to understanding the association between psychotic symptoms and violence. *American Sociological Review, 64*, 316–332.

Link, B. G., & Phelan, J. C. (1995). Social conditions as fundamental causes of disease. *Journal of Health and Social Behavior*, (Extra Issue), 80–94.

Link, B. G., & Phelan, J. C. (2001). Conceptualizing stigma. *Annual Review of Sociology, 27*, 363–385.

Link, B. G., Struening, E., Rahav, M., Phelan, J. C., & Nuttbrock, L. (1997). On stigma and its consequences: Evidence from a longitudinal study of men with dual diagnoses of mental illness and substance abuse. *Journal of Health and Social Behavior, 38*, 177–190.

Markowitz, F. E. (1998). The effects of stigma on the psychological well-being and life satisfaction of persons with mental illness. *Journal of Health and Social Behavior, 39*, 335–348.

Markowitz, F. E. (2001). Modeling processes in recovery from mental illness: Relationships between symptoms, life satisfaction, and self-concept. *Journal of Health and Social Behavior, 42*, 64–79.

Martin, J. K., Pescosolido, B. A., & Tuch, S. A. (2000). Of fear and loathing: The role of "disturbing behavior," labels, and causal attributions in shaping public attitudes toward persons with mental illness. *Journal of Health and Social Behavior, 41*, 208–223.

Matsueda, R. L. (1992). Reflected appraisals, parental labeling, and delinquency: Specifying a symbolic interactionist theory. *American Journal of Sociology, 97*, 1577–1611.

Mead, G. H. (1934). *Mind, self, and society*. Chicago: University of Chicago Press.

Pearlin, L. I., Menaghan, E. G., Lieberman, M. A., & Mullan J. T. (1981). The stress process. *Journal of Health and Social Behavior, 22*, 337–356.

Pescosolido, B. A., Monahan, J., Link, B. G., Steuve, A., & Kikuzawa, S. (1999). The public's view of the competence, dangerousness, and need for legal coercion of persons with mental health problems. *American Journal of Public Health, 89*, 1339–1345.

Phelan, J. C., Link, B. G., Steuve, A., & Pescosolido, B. A. (2000). Public conceptions of mental illness in 1950 and 1996: What is mental illness and is it to be feared? *Journal of Health and Social Behavior, 41*, 188–207.

Phillips, D. (1963). Rejection: A possible consequence of seeking help for mental disorders. *American Sociological Review, 28*, 963–972.

Rosenfield, S. (1997). Labeling mental illness: The effects of services vs. stigma. *American Sociological Review, 62*, 660–672.

Ross, C. E., & Mirowsky, J. (2001). Neighborhood disadvantage, disorder, and health. *Journal of Health and Social Behavior, 42,* 258–276.

Ross, C. E., Reynolds, J. R., & Geis, K. J. (2000). The contingent meaning of neighborhood stability for residents' psychological well-being. *American Sociological Review, 65,* 581–597.

Scheff, T. J. (1984). *Being mentally ill: A sociological theory* (2nd ed.). Chicago: Aldine.

Schur, E. (1971). *Labeling deviant behavior.* New York: Harper/Collins.

Star, S. A. (1952). *What the public thinks about mental health and mental illness.* Paper presented at the annual meeting of the National Association of Mental Health, Indianapolis, IN.

Star, S. A. (1955). *The public's ideas about mental illness.* Unpublished report presented at the National Opinion Research Center, Chicago.

Stryker, S. (1980). *Symbolic interactionism: A social structural version.* Menlo Park, CA: Benjamin Cummings.

Turner, R. J. (1981). Social support as a contingency in psychological well-being. *Journal of Health and Social Behavior, 22,* 357–367.

Wahl, O. F. (1995). *Media madness: Public images of mental illness.* New Brunswick, NJ: Rutgers University Press.

Weinstein, R. M. (1979). Patient attitudes toward mental hospitalization: A review of quantitative research. *Journal of Health and Social Behavior, 20,* 237–258.

Weinstein, R. M. (1983). Labeling theory and the attitudes of mental patients: A review. *Journal of Health and Social Behavior, 24,* 70–84.

Wright, E. R., & Gronfein, W. P. (2000). Deinstitutionalization, social rejection, and the self-esteem of former mental patients. *Journal of Health and Social Behavior, 41,* 68–90.

6

A SOCIAL–COGNITIVE MODEL OF PERSONAL RESPONSES TO STIGMA

AMY C. WATSON AND L. PHILIP RIVER

A SOCIAL–COGNITIVE MODEL OF SELF-STIGMA

It seems logical to conclude that individuals with a psychiatric disability, living in a society that widely endorses stigmatizing ideas about mental illness, would consider such ideas self-relevant and believe that they are less valuable because of their disorder. Self-esteem is affected, as is confidence in one's future (Corrigan, 1998; Holmes & River, 1998). However, not everyone with a mental illness experiences a loss of self-esteem because of stigma. Some people react to stigma by becoming energized and empowered, whereas others remain relatively indifferent and unaffected (Chamberlin, 1978; Corrigan & Watson, 2002; Deegan, 1990). Current theories fail to adequately explain these different reactions to mental illness stigma. We propose a social–cognitive model and argue that the response of an individual with mental illness to stigma may be diminished self-esteem and self-efficacy, righteous anger and empowerment, or relative indifference, depending on the parameters of the situation. Expanding on sociological research on perceived stigma, we present evidence of alternative responses to stigma, outline a social–cognitive model of self-stigma that explains these differing reactions, and review supporting theories and empirical studies from social psychology. The chapter concludes with further consideration of self-stigma's opposite—empowerment. The role of empowerment in recovery will be discussed.

PERCEIVED STIGMA

Sociological research suggests that perceived stigma results in a loss of self-esteem and self-efficacy and limits prospects for recovery (Link, Mirotznik, & Cullen, 1991; Link, Struening, Neese-Todd, Asmussen, & Phelan, 2001; Link, Cullen, Frank, & Wozniak, 1987; Link, Cullen, Struening, Shrout, et al., 1989; Markowitz, 1998; Perlick et al., 2001; Rosenfield, 1997; Sirey et al., 2001; Wright & Gronfein, 1996). From a labeling theory perspective, these studies assume that prior to being labeled as "mentally ill," individuals have internalized cultural stereotypes about the group. With the onset of a mental illness, these stereotypes become relevant to the self, causing self-esteem to be affected. This perspective also suggests that individuals constrict their social networks and opportunities in anticipation of rejection because of stigma, which leads to isolation, unemployment and lowered income. These "failures" result in self-esteem and self-efficacy decrements (Link et al., 1987; Markowitz, 1998). Although what is most often measured in studies of this phenomenon is perceived devaluation and discrimination, it is assumed that the loss of self-esteem and self-efficacy results from experiencing or anticipating discrimination *and* internalization of stereotypes.

Our model of self-stigma expands on the labeling perspective on perceived stigma in several ways by considering alternative responses to stigma that do not result in lowered self-esteem or self-efficacy. Additionally, our model allows for variations in how an individual responds to stigma on the basis of situational factors. In this chapter, we elaborate our model of self-stigma. First, however, we define self-stigma.

A SOCIAL–COGNITIVE DEFINITION OF SELF-STIGMA

Given the breadth of the impact of stigma on persons with mental illness, it is important to define the parameters of self-stigma. Such a definition has to differentiate between experiences that would be included under the rubric of self stigma, and those better understood as reactions to anticipated and perceived discrimination. Self-stigma can be understood using the same concepts that comprise public stigma-stereotypes, prejudice, and discrimination (described in detail in chap. 1).

Many persons with mental illness are aware of the stereotypes that exist about their group. Dominant among these is the belief that persons with mental illness are incompetent or immoral (Hayward & Bright, 1997). Note, however, that awareness of stigma is not synonymous with internalizing it

(Crocker & Major, 1989). Many persons with mental illness report being aware of the negative stereotypes about persons with their condition (Bowden, Schoenfeld, & Adams, 1980; Kahn, Obstfeld, & Heiman, 1979; Shurka, 1983; Wright, Gronfein, & Owens, 2000) but do not necessarily agree with these stereotypes (Hayward & Bright, 1997).

Like public stigma, self-stigma also includes prejudice and its two components. Prejudice requires that the person concur with the stereotype, believing, for example, that people with mental illness are too incompetent or lazy to hold responsible jobs. To constitute self-stigma, the person must agree with and apply the stereotype to the self (e.g., "I have a mental illness so I must be too incompetent to work."). Thus, self-stigma leads to negative emotional reactions. Prominent among these are low self-esteem and self-efficacy. Finally, self-stigma may lead to behavioral responses (e.g., discrimination). Low self-efficacy and demoralization have been shown to be associated with failing to pursue work or independent living opportunities at which an individual might otherwise succeed (Link 1982, 1987). Obviously, this kind of self-stereotype, self-prejudice, and self-discrimination will significantly interfere with a person's ability to pursue life goals and with his or her quality of life. Long-standing theories have assumed that this response is the automatic result of being a member of a stigmatized group (Allport, 1954/1979; Erikson, 1956; Jones et al., 1984). However, more recent research has failed to support self-stigma as the universal response to occupying a devalued status. Before reviewing our model of variations in reactions to stigma, we briefly review evidence of two alternative responses: indifference and righteous anger.

Indifference and Righteous Anger as Alternative Responses to Stigma

According to traditional theories of self-stigma, African American individuals, women, and persons with physical disabilities, because they belong to stigmatized groups, should have lower self-esteem compared to the majority (Allport, 1979; Erikson, 1956; Jones et al., 1984). However, studies of self-esteem in people of color and other ethnic minorities (Hoelter, 1983; Jensen, White, & Gelleher, 1982; Porter & Washington, 1979; Verkuyten, 1994, 1995; Wylie, 1979) and women (Maccoby & Jacklin, 1974; Wylie, 1979) have not found minority group members to have lower self-esteem than members of the majority group. More specific to the focus of this chapter, researchers have not found lower self-esteem among persons with disabilities than in the general public. Groups studied in this research include people with learning disabilities (Johnson, Johnson, & Rynders, 1981), mental retardation (Gibbons, 1985; Stager, Chassin, & Young, 1983; Willy & McCandless, 1973), physical handicaps (Burden & Parish, 1983), and disfiguring conditions such as cleft lip and palate (Clifford & Clifford, 1986).

Similar results have been found in studies of persons with mental illness. Whereas persons with mental illness are aware of the negative stereotypes about them, several studies have been unable to find a sharp decline in self-esteem in this group (see Hayward & Bright, 1997, for a review). This suggests the self-esteem of some members of stigmatized groups may be relatively unaffected by or indifferent to stigma.

Self-stigma and indifference still do not tell the entire story in terms of responses to stigma. Crocker and colleagues (Crocker & Lawrence, 1999; Crocker & Major, 1989) highlight a third and perhaps counterintuitive trend in stigma and self-esteem. Members of stigmatized groups may respond to stigma with *higher* self-esteem than the majority. Studies have supported this assertion for persons of color (Hoelter, 1983; Jensen et al., 1982; Porter & Washington, 1979) and people with disabilities (Fine & Caldwell, 1967; Willy & McCandless, 1973). For these individuals, it seems that being stigmatized somehow stimulates psychological reactance (Brehm, 1966). Instead of accepting the pervasively negative image, these individuals become energized and empowered to embrace positive self-perceptions and reject stigma and discrimination.

Righteous anger arises against those who have unjustly labeled them. Research on groups of African Americans suggests that anger is a healthy response to stigma. Anger and depression were inversely related in a group of Black adolescents coping with racism (Stevenson, Reed, Bodison, & Bishop, 1997). Anger seems to be associated with responding to the stigmatizing behaviors of the majority through collective and affirming actions (Wright, 1997), such as advocating for better services and opportunities.

A SITUATIONAL MODEL OF THE PERSONAL RESPONSE TO STIGMA

These divergent reactions to stigma have been discussed as part of a continuum, with loss of self-esteem and righteous anger occupying opposite poles and indifference falling in the middle (Corrigan & Watson, 2002; Rappaport, 1987; Zimmerman & Rappaport, 1988). These responses to stigma might seem to be traits of the person that remain constant over the course of the illness. However, research on self-esteem suggests that self-reactions to stigma can vary within the person as well as between individuals. Crocker and Wolfe (2001) discuss self-esteem as "global," referring to overall judgments of self-worth, or as "domain-specific," referring to evaluations of specific aspects of the self. "Global" and "domain-specific" levels of self-esteem may be either a "trait" (one's typical level of self-esteem), or a "state" (how one feels about one's self at the moment). Thus, people have typical global and domain-specific levels of self-esteem around which momentary judgments fluctuate.

In self-esteem terms, reactions to stigma represent "state" responses that vary across time and situation around a "trait" level of self-esteem (Crocker, 1999; Crocker & Lawrence, 1999; Crocker & Wolfe, 2001). In some situations, a person with a serious mental illness may report a loss of self-esteem because of stigma, whereas in others the same person might respond with indignation. Figure 6.1 outlines our model of the *personal response* to stigma. The strength of the effect of a negative event on self-esteem depends on its relevancy to the individual's contingencies of self-worth, the domains on which the person has based his or her self-esteem (Crocker & Wolfe, 2001). These domains may be competencies, approval from others, moral–ethical standards, or faith in God's love. People tend to hold multiple contingencies of self-worth that vary in intensity. Negative events in domains relevant to a person's contingencies have particularly strong effects on self-esteem. Attempts to cope with these threats may result in adaptive or problematic behaviors.

According to our model, the nature of the effect of circumstances such as stigma and discrimination because of mental illness depends on both personal factors and perceptions that are shaped by the situation. How persons

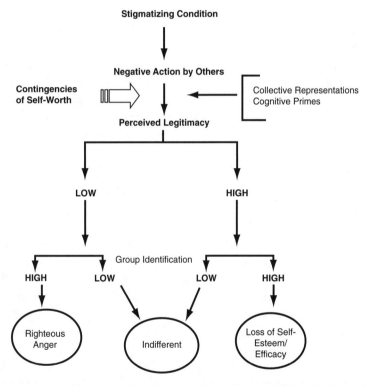

Figure 6.1. A path diagram explains the personal response to stigma by the self. People who perceive negative treatment of others as legitimate will have diminished self-esteem. Those who do not believe this treatment is justified will have intact self-esteem. Individuals who identify with the stigmatized group will become angry, whereas those who do not will appear unaware of self-stigma or complacent. Adapted from "The Paradox of Self-Stigma and Mental Illness," by P. W. Corrigan and A. C. Watson, 2002, *Clinical Psychology: Science and Practice, 9*(1), p. 40. Copyright 2002 by the Oxford University Press. Adapted with permission.

with a stigmatizing condition like serious mental illness respond to the label and the negative reactions of others in a specific situation (e.g., landlords refusing to show an apartment or employers failing to offer job interviews) depends on their perceptions of legitimacy and degree of group identification. Collective representations and cognitive primes influence appraisal of the legitimacy of the stigma and discrimination experienced. As shown in Figure 6.1, persons confronted with stigma might have one of three subsequent reactions. Those who closely identify with the stigmatized group but consider stigma to be illegitimate ("I have a mental illness and I'm not ashamed") will experience righteous anger ("I won't allow others to treat me unfairly"). These individuals are likely to be active in group advocacy and empowerment efforts. Conversely, people who do not seem to identify with the group will appear relatively indifferent to self-stigma, regardless of their perceptions of its legitimacy. Individuals who self stigmatize, however, identify with the stigmatized group but view the negative stereotypes and resulting discrimination as legitimate, experiencing further injury to their self-esteem. The intensity to which a person is affected by stigma is mediated by how contingent his or her self-esteem is on the domain in question (e.g., honesty, work ethic, attractiveness).

In the next section, we will review evidence that supports the individual components of Figure 6.1: (a) how collective representations and cognitive primes influence the situational appraisal of stigma; (b) how low and high perceived legitimacy leaves self-esteem intact or undermines one's self image, respectively; and (c) how low and high group identification yields indifference or righteous anger.

Collective Representations and Cognitive Priming Lead to Situational Effects

Crocker (1999) identified three components of collective representations relevant to the perception of self-stigma: cultural stereotypes, perceived place of the group in the social hierarchy, and sociopolitical ideology. We discussed cultural stereotypes related to mental illness earlier in this chapter (e.g., persons with mental illness are dangerous and unable to competently care for themselves). The point here is to remember that cultural stereotypes are important mediators of situational experiences with self-stigma.

Perceptions about the social hierarchy also have important effects on state experiences of self-stigma. Individuals who believe that stigma about their group arises from unjust social pressures will deflect negative attitudes from themselves (thereby protecting their sense of self-esteem) to the social hierarchy. Research has illustrated this point among African Americans. Black people are more likely than White people to believe that they have personally been discriminated against and that this discrimination is rooted in the American system of government (Crocker & Blanton, in press;

Crocker, Luhtanen, Broadnax, & Blaine, 1999). This kind of system blame seems to moderate the effect of stigma on self-esteem. Those African Americans who attribute more systemic prejudice to "American society" show higher self-esteem.

Some advocates with mental illness mirror this concern, arguing that systemic prejudice exists against persons with psychiatric disabilities (Chamberlin, 1998; Deegan, 1990). Hence, we would hypothesize that persons with mental illness who recognize system-based prejudice (e.g., the economic system sets up structural barriers that prevent people with psychiatric disabilities from being successful at white-collar jobs) would report higher self-esteem than a comparison group of people with mental illness who do not attribute difficulties to structural discrimination.

The third variable that seems to affect self-stigmatizing states is socio-political ideology, the Protestant ethic in particular. Individualism as embodied in the Protestant ethic has been viewed as the dominant socio-political ideology of the Western world (Katz & Haas, 1988; Weber, 1930/1958). The Protestant ethic holds that an individual's hard work is the foundation of success; lack of success indicates the person's self-indulgence and poor self-discipline. The Protestant ethic is associated with intolerance and dislike of members of stigmatized groups (Biernat, Vescio, & Theno, 1996; Furnham, 1985; Weber, 1930/1958). Instead of viewing the stigmatized as victims of systemic prejudice, proponents of the Protestant ethic view the lost opportunities of the stigmatized as the rightful consequence of self-indulgence (Quinn & Crocker, 1999). Hence, persons who endorse the Protestant ethic are more likely to stigmatize various minority groups.

A recent study has examined the impact of the Protestant ethic on self-stigma. Quinn and Crocker (1999) found that the self-esteem and psychological well-being of overweight women were inversely associated to their agreement with the Protestant work ethic; overweight women who endorsed the Protestant ethic reported lower self-esteem, whereas no such association was found for women with "normal" weight. The study's authors implied that this relationship might be specific to groups stigmatized for weight and not other minority groups. They believed that obesity is stigmatized in Western culture because it is viewed as controllable (Crandall, 1994) and is frequently the target of humor in the media. Mental illness is also viewed as controllable by the public (Corrigan, 2000) and is often singled out for disrespectful treatment (Wahl, 1995). Hence, we hypothesize that future research would show an inverse relationship between endorsement of the Protestant work ethic and self-esteem because of self-stigma in persons with mental illness.

The Effects of Primes on Collective Representations

Cultural stereotypes and other collective representations are activated by information that emerges from the individual situation (Crocker, 1999). For example, the cultural stereotypes of overweight women were manipulated in one study when research participants were asked to read a "report" from the Surgeon General (Amato & Crocker, 1995). In fact, half the group read a statement that said weight is controllable via diet and exercise, whereas the second report stated that weight is a function of genetics and difficult to control through external means. Those reading the diet and exercise report (thereby priming the collective notion that weight-gain is controllable) reported significantly lower self-esteem than the group that received the genetics report. Quinn and Crocker (1999) found a similar result in their study of overweight women and the Protestant ethic. Overweight women who read a paragraph from a political speech touting the Protestant work ethic (thereby activating this collective representation) showed significantly lower psychological well-being than a similar group who read a relatively neutral speech. We would expect this research design to yield similar results in research on mental illness. Namely, we hypothesize that situations that prime the cultural stereotypes and Protestant ideology of persons with mental illness will lead to greater sensitivity to stigmatizing stimuli.

How Perceived Legitimacy Affects Self-Esteem

The effects of cognitive primes and collective representations on self-esteem and self-efficacy are mediated by perceived legitimacy. In some situations members of stigmatized groups believe negative outcomes that result from stigma are just, whereas other times they believe these outcomes are not (Finchilescu & de la Rey, 1991; Jetten, Spears, Hogg, & Manstead, 2000; Miller, Jackson, Mueller, & Schersching, 1987). Crocker and Major (1994) explained the effects of justification or legitimacy in terms of equity theory. Namely, a negative outcome (e.g., not hiring someone because they are labeled mentally ill) is perceived as legitimate if a stigmatizing expectation (i.e., persons with mental illness are incompetent and will do poorly at work) is *perceived as accurate*. Applying equity theory to the self, we would expect that persons who view the negative responses of others to them as justified because of stigma would experience diminished self-esteem (Janoff-Bulman, 1979).

Crocker and colleagues (Crocker & Major, 1989; Crocker & Major, 1994; Crocker & Wolfe, 2001) identified various mechanisms that protect an individual's sense of self from stigma. These factors may also account for a rebound effect in which people become energized and react righteously to stigmatizing images about their groups. Hence, these factors may be candidates for mediators of perceived legitimacy. Three of these mechanisms and their specific relevance to the experience of mental illness stigma are reviewed here.

External Versus Internal Attribution of Negative Feedback

Research has generally shown that internal attribution of negative feedback ("My incompetence and laziness are the reason why I can't hold a job.") and external attribution of positive feedback ("The only reason I was able to keep my job is because of the job coach's hard work") lead to low self-esteem (Crocker, Alloy, & Kayne, 1988; Weiner, 1995). In fact, the first of these two processes—internal attribution of negative feedback—may be an explanatory mechanism for stigma and diminished self-esteem. Hence, the contrary mechanism may be a self-protective factor against stigma: attributing negative feedback to external causes ("I can't get a job because employers are prejudiced!"). Persons who attribute negative feedback (e.g., not getting a job) to prejudice against their group are less likely to experience lowered self-esteem (Crocker, Voekl, Cornwell, & Major, 1989; Testa, Crocker, & Major, 1988).

What variables mediate this process? According to Kelley's (Kelley, 1967) model of causal attribution, people attribute causality based on the covariance of events. Persons with mental illness who perceive their group as receiving negative feedback whereas other groups do not are likely to attribute stigmatizing images to the prejudice experienced by their group (Crocker & Major, 1989). This kind of experience can lead to indignation if individuals are particularly sensitive to negative feedback for the domain in question and identify strongly with their group.

Selectivity of Values as Self-Protection

A person's self-esteem may be affected because of affiliation with a group that reflects characteristics that are devalued by the majority. For example, the majority values industry and productivity as exhibited in the Protestant work ethic; persons with mental illness are stigmatized as not able to meet the demands of this cultural norm. Individuals can protect themselves from this kind of stigma by simply devaluing those domains on which stigma is based or by not basing their self-esteem on those domains (Crocker & Wolfe, 2001; Nieva & Gutek, 1981; Taylor, 1983). Hence, persons with mental illness who are unable to work (because of disability or discrimination) experience little harm to their self-esteem if their self esteem is not contingent on the values that form the basis of the stigma about them. Turning one's back on the values of the majority is consistent with the kind of righteous anger that some survivors of the mental health system tout (Chamberlin, 1978; Deegan, 1990).

Steele (1997) described a negative consequence of this kind of devaluation. He argued that negative stereotypes undermine a person's identification with a specific domain (e.g., school, work, social interactions) and lessen the person's motivation to achieve in that domain. He coined the phenomenon that causes this cascade "stereotype threat;" that is, the social-psychological threat that occurs when members of a stereotyped out-group (e.g., African Americans, women, persons with serious mental illness) find themselves in a situation specific to a domain for which a negative stereotype applies. For example, a negative stereotype about African Americans suggests they are intellectually inferior and not likely to do well scholastically (Herstein & Murray, 1994). Therefore, African Americans experiencing stereotype threat may feel anxious when faced with an achievement exam in school.

Persons who occasionally experience the emotional distress that results from stereotype threat may *disengage* from the situations in which this stress occurs (Crocker, Major, & Steele, 1998; Major, Spencer, Schmader, Wolfe, & Crocker, 1998). African Americans, for example, may report that the kind of scholastic ability required in a specific situation that elicits stereotype threat is not important. This kind of disengagement seems to protect minority group members from the low self-esteem that might otherwise arise in these stigmatizing situations (Major et al., 1998).

Alternatively, people who experience stereotype threat and emotional distress over a prolonged time may *disidentify* with the domain and task altogether (Steele, 1997). Minority group members who may have once believed that cognitive performance in a specific domain was an important part of their identity ("Doing well in school is essential for my success") may no longer recognize performance in this domain as part of their self-evaluative framework. Disengaging from and disidentifying with performance domains undermines achievement motivation for tasks in that domain and interferes with cognitive performance. This kind of process has been demonstrated in several groups in addition to ethnic minorities. These groups include women (Brown & Josephs, 1999; Shih, Pittinsky, & Ambady, 1999; Spencer, Steele, & Quinn, 1999), the elderly (Levy, 1996), and persons with low socioeconomic status (Croizet & Claire, 1998).

Corrigan and colleagues have speculated elsewhere that a similar process of disengagement may account for the poor cognitive processes that disable the social functions of many persons with mental illness (Corrigan & Calabrese, 2003; Corrigan & Holzman, 2001). Recognizing that the majority views persons with mental illness as "crazy" and "out of touch with reality," persons with psychiatric disabilities devalue careful cognition and may seem disoriented or confused in social interactions. They may disengage from the perceptual and comprehension mechanisms that are needed to understand the rules and roles that define interpersonal situations. This is an especially provocative point, given that current research primarily attributes cognitive deficits to neurobiological processes (Green, 1999) rather than self-protection from stigma. Future research is needed to determine whether this kind of devaluation process might secondarily lead to, or otherwise exacerbate, diminished social cognitive processes.

High Group Identification Leads to Righteous Anger

According to Figure 6.1, persons with intact self-esteem might turn their reactions to stigma into righteous anger or might be personally indifferent to prejudice. *Identification* with the broader "group" of persons with mental illness is a key variable that influences whether the person is indignant or indifferent (Frable, Wortman, & Joseph, 1997). On one hand, individuals who belong to stigmatized groups may internalize the negative statements aimed at that group. Of equal interest, however, are persons who develop a positive identity via their interactions with peers from the stigmatized group (e.g., despite the negative cultural views about homosexuality, gays have much to be proud of). As a result, they develop more positive self-perceptions (Porter & Washington, 1993; Tajfel, 1978). This assertion has been supported in research on several stigmatized groups.

In a study of more than 800 gay and bisexual men, Frable and colleagues (1997) found that positive gay identity (i.e., believing that group membership is important to the individual) was positively associated with self-esteem and well-being. Additionally, having gay friends and attending gay social events were indirectly related to high self-esteem, high well-being, and low distress through their effect on positive gay identity. In another approach to group identity, Phinney and Alipuria (1990) examined commitment to ethnic identity and self-esteem among college students. Their analysis suggests that levels of identity search and ethnic commitment are positively related to self-esteem for persons of color. Similarly, Munford (1994) found racial identification to be positively related to self-esteem in a sample of students and members of the general population.

This pattern also seems to apply to group identity and gender. Ossana, Helms, and Leonard (1992) found that a highly developed gender identity was associated with higher self-esteem in women. Increased self-esteem may be the result of women coming to terms with their identity as women and internalizing positive feelings about themselves. The authors also speculate that some women with less developed gender identities may benefit from joining women's support groups.

Thus, the evidence suggests that high group identification helps individuals shield themselves from the deleterious effects of stigma and maintain their self-esteem. Regarding themselves positively, members of stigmatized groups may become righteously indignant about the negative social identity and discrimination bestowed on them by society. Expanding these findings to mental illness, we would expect that persons with psychiatric stigma who identify with peers would show a higher sense of empowerment. Consistent with previous factor analyses on empowerment, this increment would correspond with increased self-esteem and righteous anger (Corrigan, Faber, Rashid, & Leary, 1999; Rogers, Chamberlin, Ellison, & Crean, 1997).

The concept of empowerment has been discussed as the polar opposite of self-stigma (Corrigan & Watson, 2002; Rappaport, 1987; Zimmerman & Rappaport, 1988) and is given a prominent place in the consumer recovery literature (e.g., Jacobson & Greenley, 2001; Ralph, 2000). Anthony (1993, 2000) and Jacobson and Greenley (2001) suggest that a high level of empowerment is associated with greater recovery.

The term "consumer empowerment" refers to a specific ideology, one that has arisen partly in reaction to perceived inequities in the mental health system (Dickerson, 1998). Mainstream mental health care is unique among social programs in its sanctioned use of potentially coercive interventions such as physical restraint, involuntary hospital commitment, and psychotropic medication. Empowerment ideology is a response on the part of consumers of mental health services to the dominant role that mental health professionals play in individual treatment decisions as well as in mental health policy formulation.

Thus, empowerment has significance both for individuals with mental illness and the larger groups to which they belong. For the individual, empowerment is thought to require the general qualities of self-determination (encompassing a sense of personal agency), personal competence (including acceptance of illness and positive self-esteem), and social engagement (which includes social advocacy for self and others [Dickerson, 1998]). Politically, empowerment represents an effort on the part of consumers as a disenfranchised group to play a larger role in mental health care policy development and service delivery.

Contemporary examples of consumer empowerment include consumer-directed research, consumer mental healthcare policy lobbying, and consumer-run clubhouse programs (Dickerson, 1998). Such initiatives may be empowering whether they are met with support or resistance on the part of mental health care providers and policy makers. In contrast to a paternalistic system in which power is granted by a ruling elite, individual consumers and consumer groups are thought to be empowered by the very process of asserting themselves or their agenda in the interpersonal or political arena.

Chapter 11 by Corrigan and Calabrese later in this book describes strategies for fostering empowerment. This kind of effort frequently coincides with a shift from a relatively passive to a more active struggle. This kind of change, when it occurs, represents the very essence of personal empowerment, a renewed sense of purpose, and a more active self-orientation manifesting itself in new individual behaviors. Such changes may bring with them an increasing ability to cope, both with psychiatric symptoms and with the life stressors that can precipitate them (Bradshaw & Brekke, 1999). Although the path of recovery that follows is often arduous, recovering individuals may remain motivated in part by a desire to reclaim a place for themselves in their community (Anthony, 1993; Deegan, 1988).

CONCLUSION

Self-stigma is considered by many to be a significant obstacle to recovery from severe mental illness. The good news is that some people with mental illness do not self-stigmatize and experience loss of self-esteem and self-efficacy. We have presented a social–cognitive model that accounts for variations in individual responses to negative social stereotypes. This model provides a framework for investigating processes by which individuals with mental illness respond to public stigma and the development of methods for supporting empowerment and recovery. Such methods should not solely focus on changing how persons with mental illness respond to stigma. They must also challenge they ways in which clinicians view their role in working with consumers of mental health services.

REFERENCES

Allport, G. W. (1979). *The nature of prejudice.* New York: Doubleday. (Original work published 1954)

Amato, M., & Crocker, J. (1995, August). *Perceived controllability of weight and women's reactions to rejection.* Paper presented at the American Psychological Association, New York.

Anthony, W. A. (1993). Recovery from mental illness: The guiding vision of the mental health service system in the 1990s. *Psychosocial Rehabilitation Journal, 16*(4), 11–23.

Anthony, W. A. (2000). A recovery-oriented service system: Setting some system level standards. *Psychiatric Rehabilitation Journal, 24,* 159–168.

Biernat, M., Vescio, T. K., & Theno, S. A. (1996). Violating American values: A "value congruence" approach to understanding outgroup attitudes. *Journal of Experimental Social Psychology, 32,* 387–410.

Bordieri, J. E., & Drehmer, D. E. (1986). Hiring decisions for disabled workers: Looking at the cause. *Journal of Applied Social Psychology, 16,* 197–208.

Bowden, C. L., Schoenfeld, L. S., & Adams, R. L. (1980). Mental health attitudes and treatment expectations as treatment variables. *Journal of Clinical Psychology, 36,* 653–657.

Bradshaw, W., & Brekke, J. S. (1999). Subjective experience in schizophrenia: Factors influencing self-esteem, satisfaction with life, and subjective distress. *American Journal of Orthopsychiatry, 69,* 254–260.

Brehm, J. W. (1966). *A theory of psychological reactance.* San Diego, CA: Academic Press.

Brockington, I. F., Hall, P., Levings, J., & Murphy, C. (1993). The community's tolerance of the mentally ill. *British Journal of Psychiatry, 162,* 93–99.

Brown, R. P., & Josephs, R. A. (1999). A burden of proofs: Stereotype relevance and gender differences in math performance. *Journal of Personality and Social Psychology, 76,* 246–257.

Burden, P. R., & Parish, T. S. (1983). Exceptional and normal children's descriptions of themselves. *Education, 104*, 204–205.

Chamberlin, J. (1978). *On our own: Patient-controlled alternatives to the mental health system.* New York: McGraw-Hill.

Chamberlin, J. (1997, Fall/Winter). Confessions of a non-compliant patient. *National Empowerment Center Newsletter.*

Chamberlin, J. (1998). Citizenship rights and psychiatric disability. *Psychiatric Rehabilitation Journal, 21*, 405–408.

Clifford, E., & Clifford, M. (1986). Social and psychological problems associated with clefts: Motivations for cleft palate treatment. *International Dental Journal, 36*, 115–119.

Corrigan, P. W. (1998). The impact of stigma on severe mental illness. *Cognitive and Behavioral Practice, 5*(2), 201–222.

Corrigan, P. W. (2000). Mental health stigma as social attribution: Implications for research methods and attitude change. *Clinical Psychology: Science and Practice, 7*(1), 48–67.

Corrigan, P. W., & Calabrese, J. D. (2003). Cognitive therapy and schizophrenia. In M. A. Reinecke & D. A. Clark (Eds.), *Cognitive therapy across the lifespan: Theory, research and practice* (pp. 315–333). Cambridge, England: Cambridge University Press.

Corrigan, P. W., Faber, D., Rashid, F., & Leary, M. (1999). The construct validity of empowerment among consumers of mental health services. *Schizophrenia Research, 38*(1), 77–84.

Corrigan, P. W., & Holzman, K. L. (2001). Do stereotype threats influence social cognitive deficits in schizophrenia? In P. W. Corrigan & D. Penn (Eds.), *Social cognition and schizophrenia.* Washington, DC: American Psychological Association.

Corrigan, P. W., & Watson, A. C. (2002). The paradox of self-stigma and mental illness. *Clinical Psychology: Science and Practice, 9*(1), 35–53.

Crandall, C. S. (1994). Prejudice against fat people: Ideology and self interest. *Journal of Personality and Social Psychology, 66*, 882–894.

Crocker, J. (1999). Social stigma and self-esteem: Situational construction of self-worth. *Journal of Experimental Social Psychology, 35*, 89–107.

Crocker, J., Alloy, L. B., & Kayne, N. T. (1988). Attributional style, depression, and perceptions of consensus for events. *Journal of Personality and Social Psychology, 54*, 840–846.

Crocker, J., & Blanton, H. (in press). Social stigma: Vulnerabilities for low self-esteem. In T. Tyler, R. Kramer, & O. John (Eds.), *The social self.* Hillsdale, NJ: Erlbaum.

Crocker, J., & Lawrence, J. S. (1999). Social stigma and self-esteem: The role of contingencies. In D. A. Prentice, D. T. Miller, et al. (Eds.), *Cultural divides: Understanding and overcoming group conflict* (pp. 364–392). New York: Russell Sage Foundation.

Crocker, J., Luhtanen, R., Broadnax, S., & Blaine, B. E. (1999). Belief in US government conspiracies against blacks among black and white college students: Powerlessness or system blame? *Personality and Social Psychology Bulletin, 25,* 945–953.

Crocker, J., & Major, B. (1989). Social stigma and self-esteem: The self-protective properties of stigma. *Psychological Review, 96,* 608–630.

Crocker, J., & Major, B. (1994). Reactions to stigma: The moderating roles of justifications. In M. P. Zanna & J. M. Olson (Eds.), *The psychology of prejudice: The Ontario Symposium: Vol. 7. Ontario symposium on personality and social psychology* (pp. 149–169). Hillsdale, NJ: Erlbaum.

Crocker, J., Major, B., & Steele, C. (1998). Social stigma. In T. D. Gilbert, S. T. Fiske, et al. (Eds.), *The handbook of social psychology* (Vol. 2, 4th ed., pp. 504–553). New York: McGraw-Hill.

Crocker, J., Voekl, K., Cornwell, B., & Major, B. (1989). *Effects on self-esteem of attributing interpersonal feedback to prejudice.* Unpublished manuscript, State University of New York at Buffalo.

Crocker, J., & Wolfe, C. T. (2001). Contingencies of self-worth. *Psychological Review, 108,* 593–623.

Croizet, J., & Claire, T. (1998). Extending the concept of stereotype and threat to social class: The intellectual underperformance of students from low socioeconomic backgrounds. *Personality and Social Psychology Bulletin, 24,* 588–594.

Davidson, L., & Strauss, J. S. (1995). Beyond the psychosocial model: Integrating disorder, health, and recovery. *Psychiatry, 58,* 44–56.

Deegan, P. E. (1988). Recovery: The lived experience of rehabilitation. *Psychosocial Rehabilitation Journal, 11,* 11–19.

Deegan, P. E. (1990). Spirit breaking: When the helping professions hurt. *Humanistic Psychologist, 18,* 301–313.

Dickerson, F. B. (1998). Strategies that foster empowerment. *Cognitive and Behavioral Practice, 5,* 255–275.

Erikson, E. (1956). The problem of ego identity. *Journal of the American Psychoanalytic Association, 4,* 56–121.

Estroff, S. (1989). Self, identity, and subjective experiences of schizophrenia: In search of the subject. *Schizophrenia Bulletin, 15,* 189–196.

Farina, A. (1998). Stigma. In K. T. Mueser & N. Tarrier (Eds.), *Handbook of social functioning in schizophrenia* (pp. 247–279). Needham Heights, MA: Allyn & Bacon.

Finchilescu, G., & de la Rey, C. (1991). Understanding intra-group variations in prejudice: The role of perceived legitimacy and stability. *South African Journal of Psychology, 21,* 225–232.

Fine, M. J., & Caldwell, T. E. (1967). Self evaluation of school related behavior of educable mentally retarded children: A preliminary report. *Exceptional Children, 33,* 324.

Frable, D. E., Wortman, C., & Joseph, J. (1997). Predicting self-esteem, well-being, and distress in a cohort of gay men: The importance of cultural stigma, personal visibility, community networks, and positive identity. *Journal of Personality, 65,* 599–624.

Furnham, A. (1985). The determinants of attitudes toward Social Security recipients. *British Journal of Social Psychology, 24,* 19–27.

Gabbard, G. O., & Gabbard, K. (1992). Cinematic stereotypes contributing to the stigmatization of psychiatrists. In P. J. Fink & A. Tasman (Eds.), *Stigma and mental illness* (pp. 113–126). Washington, DC: American Psychiatric Publishing.

Gibbons, F. X. (1985). The social psychology of mental retardation: What's in a label? In S. S. Brehm, S. M. Kassin, & F. X. Gibbons (Eds.), *Development and social psychology* (pp. 249–270). New York: Oxford University Press.

Green, M. F. (1999). Interventions for neurocognitive deficits. *Schizophrenia Bulletin, 25,* 197–200.

Hayward, P., & Bright, J. A. (1997). Stigma and mental illness: A review and critique. *Journal of Mental Health, 6,* 345–354.

Herstein, R. A., & Murray, C. (1994). *The bell curve.* New York: Grove Press.

Hoelter, J. W. (1983). Factorial invariance and self-esteem: Reassessing race and sex differences. *Social Forces, 61,* 834–846.

Holmes, P., & River, L. P. (1998). Individual strategies for coping with the stigma of severe mental illness. *Cognitive and Behavioral Practice, 5,* 231–239.

Hyler, S. E., Gabbard, G. O., & Schneider, I. (1991). Homicidal maniacs and narcissistic parasites: Stigmatization of mentally ill persons in the movies. *Hospital and Community Psychiatry, 42,* 1044–1048.

Jacobson, N., & Greenley, D. (2001). What is recovery? A conceptual model and explication. *Psychiatric Services, 52,* 482–485.

Janoff-Bulman, R. (1979). Characterological versus behavioral self-blame: Inquiries into depression and rape. *Journal of Personality and Social Psychology, 37,* 1798–1809.

Jensen, G. F., White, C. S., & Gelleher, J. M. (1982). Ethnic status and adolescent self-evaluations: An extension of research on minority self-esteem. *Social Problems, 30,* 226–239.

Jetten, J., Spears, R., Hogg, M., & Manstead, A. S. R. (2000). Discrimination constrained and justified: Variable effects of group variability and in-group identification. *Journal of Experimental Social Psychology, 36,* 329–356.

Johnson, R. T., Johnson, D. W., & Rynders, J. (1981). Effect of cooperative, competitive, and individualistic experiences on self-esteem of handicapped and nonhandicapped students. *The Journal of Psychology, 108,* 31–33.

Jones, E. E., Farina, A., Hastorf, A. H., Markus, H., Miller, D. T., & Scott, R. A. (1984). *Social stigma: The psychology of marked relationships.* New York: Freeman.

Kahn, M. W., Obstfeld, L., & Heiman, E. (1979). Staff conceptions of patients' attitudes toward mental disorder and hospitalization as compared to patients' and staff's actual attitudes. *Journal of Clinical Psychology, 35,* 415–420.

Katz, I., & Haas, R. G. (1988). Racial ambivalence and American value conflict: Correlational and priming studies of dual cognitive structures. *Journal of Personality and Social Psychology, 55,* 893–905.

Keane, M. (1990). Contemporary beliefs about mental illness among medical students: Implications for education and practice. *Academic Psychiatry, 14,* 172–177.

Kelley, H. (1967). Attribution theory in social psychology. In D. Levine (Ed.), *Nebraska Symposium on Motivation* (Vol. 15, pp. 192–240). Lincoln: University of Nebraska Press.

Lehman, A. F., Slaughter, J. G., & Myers, C. P. (1992). Quality of life experiences of the chronically mentally ill. *Evaluation and Program Planning, 15,* 7–12.

Levy, B. (1996). Improving memory in old age through implicit self-stereotyping. *Journal of Personality and Social Psychology, 71,* 1092–1107.

Link, B. G. (1982). Mental patient status, work and income: An examination of the effects of a psychiatric label. *American Sociological Review, 47,* 202–215.

Link, B. G. (1987). Understanding labeling effects in the area of mental disorders: An assessment of the effects of expectations of rejection. *American Sociological Review, 52*(1), 96–112.

Link, B. G., Cullen, F. T., Frank, J., & Wozniak, J. F. (1987). The social rejection of former mental patients: Understanding why labels matter. *American Journal of Sociology, 92,* 1461–1500.

Link, B. G., Cullen, F. T., Struening, E. L., Shrout, P. E., & Dohrenwend, B. P. (1989). A modified labeling theory approach to mental disorders: An empirical assessment. *American Sociological Review, 54,* 400–423.

Link, B., Mirotznik, J., & Cullen, F. (1991). The effectiveness of stigma coping orientations: Can negative consequences of mental illness labeling be avoided? *Journal of Health and Social Behavior, 32,* 302–320.

Link, B., Struening, E., Neese-Todd, S., Asmussen, S., & Phelan, J. (2001). Stigma as a barrier to recovery: The consequences of stigma for the self-esteem of people with mental illnesses. *Psychiatric Services, 52,* 1621–1626.

Lyons, M., & Ziviani, J. (1995). Stereotypes, stigma, and mental illness: Learning from fieldwork experiences. *American Journal of Occupational Therapy, 49,* 1002–1008.

Maccoby, E., & Jacklin, C. N. (1974). Myth, reality and shades of gray: What we know and don't know about sex differences. *Psychology Today, 8,* 109–112.

Major, B., Spencer, S., Schmader, T., Wolfe, C., & Crocker, J. (1998). Coping with negative stereotypes about intellectual performance: The role of psychological disengagement. *Personality and Social Psychology Bulletin, 24,* 77–78.

Markowitz, F. E. (1998). The effects of stigma on the psychological well-being and life satisfaction of persons with mental illness. *Journal of Health and Social Behavior, 39,* 335–347.

Mayer, A., & Barry, D. D. (1992). Working with the media to destigmatize mental illness. *Hospital and Community Psychiatry, 43*(1), 77–78.

Miller, C. E., Jackson, P., Mueller, J., & Schersching, C. (1987). Some social psychological effects of group decision rules. *Journal of Personality and Social Psychology, 52*, 325–332.

Mirabi, M., Weinman, M. L., Magnetti, S. M., & Keppler, K. N. (1985). Professional attitudes toward the chronic mentally ill. *Hospital and Community Psychiatry, 36*, 404–405.

Monahan, J. (1992). Mental disorder and violent behavior: Perceptions and evidence. *American Psychologist, 47*, 511–521.

Munford, M. B. (1994). Relationship of gender, self-esteem, social class, and racial identity to depression in Blacks. *Journal of Black Psychology, 20*, 157–174.

Nieva, V. F., & Gutek, B. A. (1981). *Women and work: A psychological perspective.* New York: Praeger Publishers.

Ossana, S. M., Helms, J. E., & Leonard, M. M. (1992). Do "womanist" identity attitudes influence college women's self-esteem and perceptions of environmental bias? *Journal of Counseling and Development, 70*, 402–408.

Page, S. (1977). Effects of the mental illness label in attempts to obtain accommodation. *Canadian Journal of Behavioural Science, 9*(2), 85–90.

Page, S. (1980). Social responsiveness toward mental patients: The general public and others. *Canadian Journal of Psychiatry, 25*, 242–246.

Page, S. (1983). Psychiatric stigma: Two studies of behaviour when the chips are down. *Canadian Journal of Community Mental Health, 2*(1), 13–19.

Page, S. (1995). Effects of the mental illness label in 1993: Acceptance and rejection in the community. *Journal of Health and Social Policy, 7*, 61–68.

Perlick, D., Rosenheck, R., Clarkin, J., Sirey, J., Salahi, J., Struening, E., et al. (2001). Stigma as a barrier to recovery: Adverse effects of perceived stigma on social adaptation of persons diagnosed with bipolar affective disorder. *Psychiatric Services, 52*, 1627–1632.

Phinney, J. S., & Alipuria, L. L. (1990). Ethnic identity in college students from four ethnic groups. *Journal of Adolescence, 13*, 171–183.

Porter, J. R., & Washington, R. E. (1979). Black identity and self-esteem: A review of studies of black self-concept, 1968–1978. *Annual Review of Sociology, 5*, 53–74.

Porter, J. R., & Washington, R. E. (1993). Minority identity and self-esteem. *Annual Review of Sociology, 19*, 139–161.

Quinn, D. M., & Crocker, J. (1999). When ideology hurts: Effects of belief in the Protestant Ethic and feeling overweight on the psychological well-being of women. *Journal of Personality and Social Psychology, 77*, 402–414.

Ralph, R. (2000). Recovery. *Psychiatric Rehabilitation Skills, 4*, 480–517.

Rappaport, J. (1987). Terms of empowerment/exemplars of prevention: Toward a theory for community psychology. *American Journal of Community Psychology, 15*, 121–148.

Rogers, E. S., Chamberlin, J., Ellison, M. L., & Crean, T. (1997). A consumer-constructed scale to measure empowerment among users of mental health services. *Psychiatric Services, 48,* 1042–1047.

Rosenfield, S. (1997). Labeling mental illness: The effects of received services and perceived stigma on life satisfaction. *American Sociological Review, 62,* 660–672.

Scott, D., & Philip, A. (1985). Attitudes of psychiatric nurses to treatment and patients. *British Journal of Medical Psychology, 58*(2), 169–173.

Shih, M., Pittinsky, T. L., & Ambady, N. (1999). Stereotype susceptibility: Identity salience and shifts in quantitative performance. *Psychological Science, 10,* 80–83.

Shurka, E. (1983). The evaluation of ex-mental patients by other ex-mental patients. *International Journal of Social Psychology, 29,* 286–291.

Sirey, J. A., Bruce, M. L., Alexopoulos, G. S., Perlick, D. A., Friedman, S. J., & Meyers, B. S. (2001). Stigma as a barrier to recovery: Perceived stigma and patient-rated severity of illness as predictors of antidepressant drug adherence. *Psychiatric Services, 52,* 1615–1620.

Spencer, S., Steele, C. M., & Quinn, D. M. (1999). Stereotype threat and women's math performance. *Journal of Experimental Social Psychology, 35,* 4–28.

Stager, S. F., Chassin, L., & Young, R. D. (1983). Determinants of self-esteem among labeled adolescents. *Social Psychology Quarterly, 46,* 3–10.

Steele, C. M. (1997). A threat in the air: How stereotypes shape intellectual identity and performance. *American Psychologist, 52,* 613–629.

Stevenson, H. C., Reed, J., Bodison, P., & Bishop, A. (1997). Racism stress management: Racial social beliefs and the experience of depression and anger in African American youth. *Youth & Society, 29,* 197–222.

Strauss, J. S., Hafez, H., Lieberman, P., & Harding, C. M. (1985). The course of psychiatric disorder: III. Longitudinal principles. *American Journal of Psychiatry, 142,* 289–296.

Tajfel, H. (Ed.). (1978). *Differentiation between social groups: Studies in the social psychology of intergroup relations.* New York: Academic Press.

Taylor, S. (1980). Scaling community attitudes toward the mentally ill. *Schizophrenia Bulletin, 7,* 225–240.

Taylor, S. E. (1983). Adjustment to threatening events: A theory of cognitive adaptation. *American Psychologist, 38,* 1161–1173.

Testa, M., Crocker, J., & Major, B. (1988, May). *The self protective function of prejudice: Effects of negative feedback and evaluator prejudice on mood and self-esteem.* Paper presented at the Midwestern Psychological Association, Chicago.

Verkuyten, M. (1994). Self-esteem among ethnic minority youth in western countries. *Social Indicators Research, 32,* 21–47.

Verkuyten, M. (1995). Self-esteem, self-concept stability, and aspects of ethnic identity among minority and majority youth in the Netherlands. *Journal of Youth and Adolescence, 24,* 155–175.

Wahl, O. F. (1995). *Media madness: Public images of mental illness.* New Brunswick, NJ: Rutgers University Press.

Weber, M. (1958). *The Protestant ethic and the spirit of capitalism.* New York: Scribner. (Original work published 1930)

Weiner, B. (1995). *Judgments of responsibility: A foundation for a theory of social conduct.* New York: Guilford Press.

Willy, N. R., & McCandless, B. R. (1973). Social stereotypes for normal educable mentally retarded, and orthopedically handicapped children. *Journal of Special Education, 7,* 283–288.

Wright, E. R., & Gronfein, W. P. (1996, August). *Deinstitutionalization, social rejection, and the self-esteem of former mental patients.* Paper presented at the American Sociological Association, 92nd Annual Meeting, New York.

Wright, E. R., Gronfein, W. P., & Owens, T. J. (2000). Deinstitutionalization, social rejection, and the self-esteem of former mental patients. *Journal of Health Social Behavior, 41,* 68–90.

Wright, S. C. (1997). Ambiguity, social influence, and collective action: Generating collective protest in response to tokenism. *Personality and Social Psychology Bulletin, 23,* 1277–1290.

Wylie, R. (1979). *The self-concept* (Vol. 2). Lincoln: University of Nebraska Press.

Zimmerman, M., & Rappaport, J. (1988). Citizen participation, perceived control, and psychological empowerment. *American Journal of Community Psychology, 16,* 725–750.

7

MENTAL ILLNESS AND DANGEROUSNESS: FACT OR MISPERCEPTION, AND IMPLICATIONS FOR STIGMA

PATRICK W. CORRIGAN AND AMY E. COOPER

Regardless of where someone stands on the issue of mental illness and dangerousness, both sides agree that it is a major source of prejudice and discrimination against people with mental illness. Results of a nationwide probability survey showed that as much as 75% of the public view people with mental illness as dangerous (Link, Phelan, Bresnahan, Stueve, & Pescosolido, 1999; Pescosolido, Monahan, Link, Stueve, & Kikuzawa, 1999). A recent study found that twice as many Americans view people with mental illness as dangerous as they did 40 years ago (Phelan, Link, Stueve, & Pescosolido, 2000). Why do so many members of the general public think mental illness is strongly linked to a potential for violence? Some believe this link represents facts, whereas others argue it is stigma.

Those who believe that mental illness is, in fact, strongly associated with dangerousness view rising public concern in this area as an accurate reflection of increased violence by people with mental illness that is a result of diminished care (especially institutional care [Torrey, 1994]). Others argue that titillating media portrayals of people with mental illness as violent, especially in the entertainment industry, contribute to the widespread misperception that mental illness and dangerousness go hand in hand (Wahl, 1995). Advocates for these contrary perspectives on mental illness and dangerousness interpret a large amount of research examining violence in people with mental illness to support each of their claims. In this chapter we review the relevant data to sort out the disagreement over the link between mental illness and dangerousness. We briefly review the research literature on the level of dangerousness of people with mental illness as compared to the rest of the population. We also examine public perceptions of the association between mental illness and violence, and how these perceptions shape the lives of people with psychiatric disorders. Finally, we discuss the social and political implications of framing mental illness largely in terms of potential dangerousness.

The Stigma Is Based on Fact: Mental Illness Is Strongly Related to Dangerousness

Advocates and scholars from the Treatment Advocacy Center (TAC) and the Health Policies section of the American Enterprise Institute (AEI) have cited several bodies of evidence that seem to support the assertion that mental illness is strongly associated with a potential for violence. The TAC, for example, estimates that persons with serious mental illness commit approximately 1,000 homicides per year in the United States (TAC, 2002a). They base this estimate on findings from three studies.

- In a 1988 review of 2,655 homicides committed in a representative sample of 33 large U.S. counties, Dawson and Langan (1994) reported that 4.3% of assailants had a history of mental illness. The TAC used this statistic to infer that of the 20,680 homicides occurring nationwide in 1988, 889 were committed by people with mental illness.
- A comprehensive review of *The Washington Post's* published news stories in 1992 showed that people with serious mental illness committed 13 homicides in the Washington, DC, metropolitan area (Torrey, 1994). The TAC reasoned that the news stories provided a comprehensive annual report of homicides in a metropolitan area of 3 million people. On the basis of this assumption, the TAC estimated that in a national population of 225 million people, individuals with serious mental illness committed 1,105 homicides that year.

- Analyses of data from the National Comorbidity Survey suggest that people with serious and persistent mental illness account for about 3% of violent crime, an estimate that increases three- to five-fold when the person also abuses alcohol and other substances (Harwood et al., 1992). The TAC extrapolated these numbers to 1998 national homicide rates (N = 16,910), to suggest that 9% to 15% of murders in America were committed by people with mental illness who also abuse drugs and alcohol (N = 1,522 to 2,537).

Satel (1998) of the AEI draws similar conclusions in a *National Review* article, citing one research finding that three hundred inpatients of California's State Hospital in 1975 committed violent crimes at a rate that was ten times higher than the general population, and another finding, from the 1994 British Camberwell study, showing a rate of violent crime for people with mental illness that was four to five times higher than the general population.

The findings presented by the TAC and AEI are echoed by other research. A 1979 review of patient case records found arrest ratios to vary from as low as 1.16 to as high as 15 (Rabkin, 1979). Rabkin's summary was mirrored by subsequent studies in which people with mental illness were consistently more likely to be arrested for violent crimes compared to non-psychiatric samples (Harry & Steadman, 1988; Holcolm & Ahr, 1988; McFarland, Falkner, Bloom, Hallaux, & Bray, 1989; Shore, Filson, & Rae, 1980). In summing up these trends, Steadman (1981) said, "it no longer seems defensible for mental health professionals or social scientists to attend a neighborhood meeting to assuage prospective neighbors of a hostel by assuring them that mental patients are less dangerous statistically than their present neighbors" (p. 314).

A body of practice-based evidence also seems to provide empirical support for the perception of a strong link between mental illness and dangerousness. Reviews of admission records for inpatient units have found that between 18% and 41% of people with mental illness had been violent prior to admission (Humphreys, Johnstone, MacMillan, & Taylor, 1992; Johnstone, Crow, Johnson, & MacMillan, 1986; Lagos, Perlmutter, & Saexinger, 1977). This research reflects the *clinical* practice perspective that many mental health providers come to believe because of their direct experience (Wessely, 1997). Some people have complained that the mental health profession has turned its back on clinical practice evidence, which has led to complacency and a reduction in the perceived level of risk of people with mental illness (Noble, 1997) Proponents of the clinical practice perspective believe that the news media's focus on the dangerousness of people with mental illness accurately reflects reality. They argue that news stories will shift focus away from dangerousness only when the actual level of violence by people with mental illness diminishes (Treatment Advocacy Center, 2002b; Torrey, 1994, 2002).

Critical Examination of These Arguments

Several research groups have criticized these interpretations (Bonovitz & Bonovitz, 1981; Link, Andrews, & Cullen, 1992; Link, Monahan Stueve, & Cullen, 1999; Monahan, 2002; Steadman, Cocozza, & Melick, 1978; Teplin, 1983, 1984; Wahl, 1995). Three particular rejoinders are common.

- General versus specific effects in research on mental illness stigma appear that need to be distinguished in this research summary. The public seems to generally stigmatize all people labeled mentally ill and then specifically stigmatize those with more serious mental illnesses like psychoses beyond the baseline label (Corrigan et al., 1999). Yet, the TAC, for example, suggests that *all* people with a mental illness diagnosis are potentially dangerous. The TAC fails to identify specific symptoms or disabilities resulting from mental illness that cause violence.
- Some advocates forward the relatively simplistic assertion that untreated mental illness leads to murder. However, the relationship between mental illness and violence is quite complex, and could be partially explained by other relationships. Consider, for example, that the mental illness label is associated with demographic characteristics that have a stronger demonstrated tie to violence, that people committing violent crimes are viewed more frequently as mentally ill because of the psychiatrization of criminal behavior (Abram & Teplin, 1991; Monahan, 1973), and that people with mental illness are more likely to be arrested for offending behaviors than are people without mental illness who commit these behaviors (Klassen & O'Connor, 1988; Teplin, 1984).
- Generalization from samples of people with mental illness who are in crises (either acutely ill and requiring hospitalization, or police-involved because of a violent act) to the entire population of people with mental illness is also problematic. Extrapolating statistics from criminal records to estimate dangerousness in the population of people with mental illness is not a valid generalization technique. Doing so is parallel to determining the dangerousness of ethnic groups by means of court records rather than probability samples of the population. As Monahan (2002) suggests, a less biased approach would involve comparing violent behavior in representative samples of people with

mental illness with violence rates in probability samples drawn from the general population.

Probability Samples of Dangerousness and Mental Illness

Several studies have been completed that avoid some of these concerns by using probability samples; that is, groups of people with mental illness that were randomly selected from geographic areas in stratified formats so key demographics relevant to crime and violence are appropriately distributed. Comparison groups were also drawn from the general population and are representative of all key variables. This line of research has produced two important findings. First, evidence suggests that people with mental illness *are* more likely to commit violent crimes than are comparable samples of people without mental illness in the general population. Research of this kind completed in the United States show a two- to six-fold increase in the rate of violence in samples of people with mental illness compared to samples of people without mental illness drawn from the general population (Corrigan & Watson, 2003; Link et al., 1992; Steadman et al., 1998; Stueve & Link, 1997; Swanson, Holzer, Ganju, & Jono, 1990). Moreover, rate of crime in people with mental illness increases dramatically when that person has a co-morbid history of substance abuse; in fact, analysis from one study suggested higher violence rates because of mental illness may actually be attributable to co-morbid substance abuse (Steadman et al., 1998). These findings were replicated in the United Kingdom; depending on demographics, results of the Camberwell study suggest people with schizophrenia might be twice as likely as comparison groups to commit violent crimes (Wessely, 1997).

We need to put these findings in perspective by transferring the ratios into percentages of the population. For example, the report by Swanson and colleagues (1990) using the ECA data showed that 12% of those in the study who were diagnosed with schizophrenia admitted to having been violent in the previous year and 2% of ECA participants with no such diagnoses admitted to violence. Hence, the six-fold increase in rates of violence found in the ECA analysis translates to about one tenth of people with schizophrenia.

Note that these relationships are correlational and do not clearly demonstrate that the symptoms or disabilities related to mental illness lead to violence and crime. A second set of studies has found that a cluster of psychotic symptoms are unique and robust predictors of violence in people with mental illness (Link et al., 1999; Link & Stueve, 1995; Swanson et al., 1996), though one study failed to find this relationship (Appelbaum, Robbins, & Monahan, 2000). Link and Stueve (1995) called the cluster "threat control-override symptoms;" individual items of the cluster include, "(1) How often have you felt that your mind was dominated by forces beyond your control?; (2) How often have you felt that thoughts were put into your head that were not your own?; and (3) How often have you felt that there were people who wished to do you harm?" (p. 175). Further analyses showed that the relationship between mental illness and violence disappeared when threat control-override symptoms were co-varied out of the analyses (Link et al., 1999). If this finding is replicated in future research, it will significantly improve our understanding of the relationship between mental illness and dangerousness. Such a finding suggests that violence is not the result of mental illness in general; hence, there would be no evidence that people with such disorders as nonpsychotic major depression, generalized anxiety disorders, or phobias are more violent than the rest of the population. Moreover, replication of these data would provide strong evidence that violence does not arise from psychosis per se but from a specific cluster of delusional symptoms.

Critical Reply to These Studies

Conclusions drawn from population-based studies have their detractors, too (Satel, 1998; Torrey, 1994). Prominent among these critiques include the following:

- Probability samples of the general population exclude important groups of potentially violent persons by not sampling from jails, forensic hospitals, or long-term-care facilities.

- The comparison group included in these studies was not representative of the general population but instead tended to be violence-prone (e.g., residents of poor, chaotic, drug-ridden sections of urban areas). As a result, a comparison of violence rates in the samples of people with mental illness and the general population yielded deflated ratios because of the inordinately high rate of dangerousness in the surveyed regions.

On the Size of the Problem

Like the jury at a criminal hearing, the reader of this chapter is left to sift through contradictory evidence about whether or not people with mental illness are guilty of being more violent than the rest of the population. Advocates of the dangerousness-as-fact perspective cite many studies that support this point of view. Detractors provide epidemiological findings that people with mental illness are more dangerous than the rest of the population, but argue that this relationship is neither large nor important. They prefer to change the question from "Is there a causal relationship between mental illness and dangerousness?" (the answer seems to be yes), to "How strong is this relationship?" Or more to the point, "How much of an association is needed to justify stereotypic attitudes (e.g., "People with mental illness are potentially violent!") and discriminatory behaviors (e.g., "People with mental illness should be avoided.")?"

Swanson and colleagues (1990) took a major step in answering this question by analyzing data from the ECA study; see Table 7.1. As a baseline, they found that only 2.05% of people in the study with no psychiatric disorders reported violent behavior in the past year. That compared to almost 5% of people with diagnosed with phobias and about 11% to 13% for each of the following disorders: obsessive compulsive disorder, panic disorder, major depression, bipolar disorder, and the schizophrenias. This suggests that violence is about six times greater in these various mental disorders compared to the non-disordered population. But this ratio does not clearly suggest the *size* of the problem because it negates base rates of various groups. One way to appreciate the size of the relationship is to use the ECA data to conduct the following thought experiment. The task in this exercise is to protect an American community of one million by identifying those among the community who are potentially dangerous using existing diagnostic and demographic predictors. How does mental illness compare to various demographics that have been shown to also be significantly related to violence and crime?

The second column of Table 7.1 lists the point prevalence rates for the various diagnoses also gleaned from the ECA data (Regier & Burke, 1995). The third column represents the number of people in the community of one million who would be identified as potentially violent on the basis of their diagnosis (determined as the product of the precent violent rate, the percent of general population, and the total community population [N = 1,000,000]). The sum of correct identifications across the six groups is 8,899, though this number is slightly inflated because some ECA respondents met criteria for more than one disorder thereby increasing the index representing percentage

TABLE 7.1

Rates of Violent Behavior in Diagnostic Groups and Two Key Demographics

	% violent in ECA data	% of general population	Correct identifications	False positives
Phobia	4.97	6.2[1]	3038	58962
OCD	10.66	1.3	1378	11622
Panic Disorder	11.56	.05	580	4420
Major Depression	11.68	2.2	2574	19426
Bipolar Disorder	11.02	.04	440	3560
Schizophrenias	12.69	.07	889	6111
		subtotal	8899	104101
Age (18–29)	7.34	13.9[2]	10203	
Male	5.29	49.1	25974	

[1]Diagnoses represent one month point prevalence rates from the ECA.

[2] Demographic data determined from the 2000 U.S. Census.

violent. This number suggests .9% of one million would be potentially violent because of mental illness.

How does this finding compare to numbers of potentially dangerous people identified by two key demographics: gender and age? Let's consider ECA findings once again (Swanson et al., 1990); analyses suggest the violence rate for young people (age 18 to 29 years) was 7.34%, lower than most of the psychiatric diagnostic groups. However, the 2000 U.S. Census shows that this age group makes up 13.9% of the American population. Using these ratios, 10,203 young adults would be correctly identified as violent. This sample would be 115% larger than the group identified through psychiatric diagnoses. ECA data also showed that 5.29% of men reported violent behavior in the past year. With U.S. Census data showing the population to be 49.1% male, gender would lead to the identification of 25,974 individuals in the million as violent, a sample that is 292% larger than the mental illness criterion. Clearly, if the goal is to identify potentially violent people, age is a slightly better predictor than diagnosis and gender can increase the net of potentially dangerous people by almost threefold.

The last column of Table 7.1 lists the false positive rates; people who might be potentially identified as violent because of mental illness but are not. Note that 104,101 people would fall in this category, more than 10% of the million person community! Hence, not only are there better predictors of violence than mental illness, psychiatric diagnosis will inaccurately identify vast numbers of potentially violent people. These analyses suggest the size of the problem is indeed small and that stressing the violence angle to mental illness represents stigma and not fact.

Humans Are Bad at Understanding the Base Rates

The previous thought experiment suggests that humans tend to view the threat of dangerousness from people with mental illness to be much higher than it actually is. It is unlikely, however, that raising awareness of base rates like these will be enough to change perceptions of mental illness and dangerousness because decision research has shown that humans are not rational number crunchers. Several biases in judgment heuristics undermine the accurate perception of social phenomena (Kahneman & Tversky, 1996; see also Woll, 2002, for a recent and comprehensive review of this topic). The availability heuristic illustrates the nature of this bias in terms of mental illness and dangerousness (Tversky & Kahneman, 1973, 1974). The availability heuristic operates when a person makes estimates about the frequency of an event based on the ease with which related associations are brought to mind. Salient events are most likely to be accessible in our thoughts, so the news media's sensational coverage of mental illness and violence is likely to make this association vivid and available. As a result, the public is likely to view people with mental illness as more dangerous then they are.

Perceptions of out-group homogeneity represent another well-studied social cognitive bias that may contribute to the belief that people with mental illness are more dangerous than facts would suggest. Social psychological research has revealed that outgroups are viewed as homogeneous members of a collective (Simon & Brown, 1987). Hence, stereotypes about salient members of an out-group are likely to generalize to all members of the group. People assume that media portrayals of dangerousness and mental illness accurately reflect the level of violence committed by all people with mental illness. Replacing perceptions of homogeneous groups with information about the heterogeneity of group members and the fluidity of group boundaries may be a useful way to reduce stigma (Brewer, 2000; Dovidio, Kawakami, & Gaertner, 2002).

Consensus Statement

The epidemiological research described earlier provides compelling evidence for a link between mental illness and dangerousness. In recognition of this body of evidence, the National Stigma Clearinghouse partnered with the MacArthur Research Network on Mental Health and the Law to develop a consensus statement that honestly reflects the empirical research findings and seeks to contextualize them socially and politically (Monahan & Arnold, 1996). The 41 researchers, service providers, and consumer advocates who signed the consensus statement agreed on three points:

- Results of several large-scale studies suggest that mental illness is *weakly* associated with violence.
- In spite of these findings, the public perceives a *strong* link to exist between mental illness and dangerousness; as a result, individuals with mental illness and their families experience high levels of stigma.
- Resolving this injustice requires eliminating the stigma and discrimination as well as providing quality treatments to individuals with mental illness.

HOW DO PERCEPTIONS ABOUT MENTAL ILLNESS AND DANGEROUSNESS AFFECT THE MENTAL HEALTH AGENDA?

In some ways, the argument over what the facts say about people with mental illness and dangerous are irrelevant to the issue of stigma. As previously discussed, the public is relatively insensitive to base rates of violence committed by people with mental illness. Instead, their judgments are biased by perceptions of salient events and out-group homogeneity that do not correspond with reality. According to Link, Monohan, et al. (1999), the very act of *perceiving* people with mental illness as dangerous translates to *fact* regardless of contrary epidemiological data because situations that are defined as real "are real in their consequences," regardless of what evidence might say about them. If this is the case, then it is important to consider the issue of mental illness and dangerousness in a different light: What is the impact of public beliefs that many individuals with mental illness are dangerous? What effect does this belief have on the life opportunities of people with mental illness and on the mental health system that provides these people with services?

Highlighting Dangerousness May Increase Resources for the Mental Health System

Some advocates believe that highlighting the relationship between violence and mental illness may be a significant wake up call for state legislators who have traditionally ignored sufficient and equitable funding for mental health programs (Torrey, 2002). D. J. Jaffe (1999), board member of the TAC, succinctly made this point: "Laws change for a single reason, in reaction to highly publicized incidences of violence. People care about public safety. I am not saying it is right. I am saying this is the reality. . . . So if you're changing your laws in your state, you have to understand that. . . . It means that you have to take the debate out of the mental health arena and put it in the criminal justice–public safety arena." Sally Satel (1998) of the AEI asserts that political correctness has prevented policymakers from publicly acknowledging the dangerousness of many people with mental illness which, in turn, has limited the amount of resources that mental health programs need to treat these people.

Concerns about developing treatment programs to deal with the problem of dangerousness among people with mental illness has led to a call for more mandated service programs that range in coerciveness from relatively benign advanced directives to more intrusive measures like outpatient commitment. Advocates of involuntary treatment programs believe that a comprehensive mental health system that includes mandated care will reduce mental illness stigma by actually reducing the level of violence committed by individuals with mental illness (Torrey & Zdanowicz, 2001).

Public Perceptions of Dangerousness May Rob People of Life Opportunities

Despite hypothesized benefits, highlighting the dangerousness of people with mental illness will likely exacerbate prejudice and discrimination toward people with mental illness. Research by members of CCSR has shown that people who endorse beliefs that individuals with mental illness are dangerous are more likely to report fear and avoidance of them (i.e., not want to work with or near people with mental illness [Corrigan et al., 2002]). In addition, perceptions of dangerousness and fear make people less willing to help those with mental illness and more likely to endorse segregation and coercive treatment (Corrigan, Markowitz, Watson, Rowan, & Kubiak, 2003). Raising awareness of the link between mental illness and violence will likely increase stigma, social isolation, and loss of opportunities for people with mental illness.

Our present research directly tests this hypothesis by means of a public education paradigm (Corrigan, Watson, Warpinski & Gracia, in press). In the study, members of the general public are randomly assigned to one of three education programs. The first program is based on information provided by the TAC and highlights the violence of people with mental illness and the need for treatment programs to address that violence. The second program is based on prior anti-stigma research and contrasts common myths about mental illness with corresponding facts (Corrigan et al., 2001). The third was a control group. Results show that participation in the TAC program led to significantly greater endorsement of attitudes that people with mental illness are dangerous, should be feared, and must be segregated, compared with the control group. Stigmatizing attitudes of people in the education group actually diminished compared with the control group during this trial.

In addition to measuring changes in attitudes about mental illness, our study examines how education programs might influence government spending for various mental health programs. Research participants were asked to rate the importance of more resources for two sets of mental health programs: those consistent with mandated care versus rehabilitation. Findings failed to support the TAC assertion that this kind of campaign will yield more resources for any kind of mental health program. In fact, nonsignificant trends suggested highlighting aggression might actually lead to fewer resources for rehabilitation programs.

SUMMARY

Although the evidence is complex, researchers and advocates seem to agree that a significant relationship between mental illness and dangerousness exists. The two perspectives are now at odds over whether this relationship is sufficiently important to drive policy decisions over the allocation of funds for mental health services. We believe that framing mental illness mainly in terms of dangerousness perpetuates stigmatizing attitudes and discriminatory behaviors against a population of individuals whose majority are by no means dangerous. Focusing attention on a small subgroup of dangerous individuals with mental illness and attributing this potential for violence to all people with mental illness strengthens and reproduces stereotypes, prejudice, and discrimination because it exacerbates the already prominent public misconception that people with mental illness are dangerous. Continuing to focus on the exaggerated link between dangerousness and mental illness will perpetuate this kind of injustice for people with mental illness.

We also question whether focusing on dangerousness will positively affect the political agenda and lead to more funds for mental health services. We admit that this is an empirical question for which no data yet exists in support of either perspective. However, we believe the findings from our research will show that this kind of education program will lead to greater support for coercive treatments to the exclusion of evidence-based programs that support rehabilitative goals for persons with mental illness.

REFERENCES

Abram, K. M., & Teplin, L. A. (1991). Co-occurring disorders among mentally ill jail detainees: Implications for public policy. *American Psychologist, 46,* 1036–1045.

Appelbaum, P. S., Robbins, P. C., & Monahan, J. (2000). Violence and delusions: Data from the MacArthur Violence Risk Assessment Study. *American Journal of Psychiatry, 157,* 566–572.

Bonovitz, J. C., & Bonovitz, J. S. (1981). Diversion of the mentally ill into the criminal justice system: The police intervention perspective. *American Journal of Psychiatry, 138,* 973–976.

Brewer, M. (2000). Reducing prejudice through cross-categorizaton: Effects of multiple self-identities. In S. Oskamp (Ed.), *Reducing prejudice and discrimination, The Claremont Symposium on Applied Social Psychology.* Mahwah, NJ: Erlbaum.

Corrigan, P. W., Markowitz, F. E., Watson, A., Rowan, D., & Kubiak, M. A. (2003). An attribution model of public discrimination towards persons with mental illness. *Journal of Health and Social Behavior, 44,* 162–179.

Corrigan, P. W., River, L. P., Lundin, R. K., Penn, D. L., Uphoff-Wasowski, K., Campion, J., et al. (2001). Three strategies for changing attributions about severe mental illness. *Schizophrenia Bulletin, 27,* 187–195.

Corrigan, P. W., River, L. P., Lundin, R. K., Wasowski, K. U., Campion, J., Mathisen, J., et al. (1999). Predictors of participation in campaigns against mental illness stigma. *Journal of Nervous and Mental Disease, 187,* 378–380.

Corrigan, P. W., Rowan, D., Green, A., Lundin, R., River, P., Uphoff-Wasowski, K., et al. (2002). Challenging two mental illness stigmas: Personal responsibility and dangerousness. *Schizophrenia Bulletin, 28,* 293–309.

Corrigan, P. W., & Watson, A. C. (2005). Findings from the National Comorbidity Survey on the frequency of violent behavior in individuals with psychiatric disorders. Manuscript submitted to *American Journal of Psychiatry.*

Corrigan, P. W., Watson, A. C., Warpinski, A. C., & Gracia, G. (in press). Mental Illness, violence, and stigma: Implications for educating the public. *Psychiatric Services*.

Dawson, J. M., & Langan, P. A. (1994). *Murder in families*. Washington, DC: U.S. Department of Justice.

Dovidio, J. F., Kawakami, K., & Gaertner, S. L. (2002). Implicit and explicit prejudice and interracial interaction. *Journal of Personality and Social Psychology, 82*, 62–68.

Harry, B., & Steadman, H. J. (1988). Arrest rates of patients treated at a community mental health center. *Hospital and Community Psychiatry, 39*, 862–866.

Harwood, H., Ameen, A., Denmead, G., Englert, E., Fountain, D., & Livermore, G. (2000). *The economic costs of mental illness*. Rockville, MD: National Institute for Mental Health.

Holcomb, W. R., & Ahr, P. R. (1988). Arrest rates among young adult psychiatric patients treated in inpatient and outpatient settings. *Hospital and Community Psychiatry, 39*, 52–57.

Humphreys, M. S., Johnstone, E. C., MacMillan, J. F., & Taylor, P. J. (1992). Dangerous behavior preceding first admissions for schizophrenia. *British Journal of Psychiatry, 161*, 501–505.

Jaffe. D. J. (1999, June 30–July 3). *Remarks on assisted outpatient treatment*. Presentation given at the Annual Meeting of the National Alliance for the Mentally Ill, Chicago.

Johnstone, E. C., Crow, T. J., Johnson, A. L., & MacMillan, J. F. (1986). The Northwick Park Study of first episodes of schizophrenia: I. Presentation of the illness and problems relating to admission. *British Journal of Psychiatry, 148*, 115–120.

Kahneman, D., & Tversky, A. (1996). On the reality of cognitive illusions. *Psychological Review, 103*, 582–591.

Keith, S., Regier, D., Rae, D., & Matthews, S. (1992). The prevalence of schizophrenia: Analysis of demographic features, symptom patterns, and course. In A. Z. Schwartzberg & A. H. Esman. (Eds.), *International Annals of Adolescent Psychiatry, Vol. 2* (pp. 260–284). Chicago: University of Chicago Press.

Klassen, D., & O'Connor, W. A. (1988). Predicting violence in schizophrenic and non-schizophrenic patients: A prospective study. *Journal of Community Psychology, 16*, 217–227.

Lagos, J. M., Perlmutter, K., & Saexinger, H. (1977). Fear of the mentally ill: Empirical support for the common man's response. *American Journal of Psychiatry, 134*, 1134–1137.

Link, B. G., Andrews, H., & Cullen, F. T. (1992). The violent and illegal behavior of mental patients reconsidered. *American Sociological Review, 57*, 275–292.

Link, B. G., Monahan, J., Stueve, A., & Cullen, F. T. (1999). Real in their consequences: A sociological approach to understanding the association between psychotic symptoms and violence. *American Sociological Review, 64*, 316–332.

Link, B. G., Phelan, J. C., Bresnahan, M., Stueve, A., & Pescosolido, B. A. (1999). Public conceptions of mental illness: Labels, causes, dangerousness, and social distance. *American Journal of Public Health, 89,* 1328–1333.

Link, B. G., & Stueve, A. (1995). Evidence bearing on mental illness as a possible cause of violent behavior. *Epidemiologic Review, 17,* 172–181.

McFarland, B. H., Faulkner, L. R., Bloom, J. D., Hallaux, R., & Bray, J. D. (1989). Chronic mental illness and the criminal justice system. *Hospital and Community Psychiatry, 40,* 718–723.

Monahan, J. (1973). Psychiatrization of criminal behavior: Reply. *Hospital and Community Psychiatry, 24,* 105–107.

Monahan, J. (2002). The scientific status of research on clinical and actuarial predictions of violence. In D. Faigman, D. Kaye, M. Saks, & J. Sanders (Eds.), *Modern scientific evidence: The law and science of expert testimony* (2nd ed., Vol. 1, pp. 423–445). St Paul, MN: West Publishing Company.

Monahan, J., & Arnold, J. (1996). Violence by people with mental illness: A consensus statement by advocates and researchers. *Psychiatric Rehabilitation Journal, 19,* 67–70.

Noble, P. (1997). Violence in psychiatric inpatients: Review and clinical implications. *International Review of Psychiatry, 9,* 207–216.

Pescosolido, B. A., Monahan, J., Link, B. G., Stueve, A., & Kikuzawa, S. (1999). The public's view of the competence, dangerousness, and need for legal coercion of persons with mental health problems. *American Journal of Public Health, 89,* 1339–1345.

Phelan, J. C., Link, B. G., Stueve, A., & Pescosolido, B. A. (2000). Public conceptions of mental illness in 1950 and 1996: What is mental illness and is it to be feared? *Journal of Health and Social Behavior, 41,* 188–207.

Rabkin, J. G. (1979). Criminal behavior of discharged mental patients: Critical appraisal of the research. *Psychological Bulletin, 86,* 1–27.

Regier, D., & Burke, J. D. (1995). Epidemiology. In H. I. Kaplan & B. J. Sadock (Eds.), *Comprehensive textbook of psychiatry* (6th ed., Vol. 1, pp. 377–396). New York: Williams & Wilkins.

Satel, S. L. (1998). Violent fantasies: Mentally ill more prone to violence. *National Review,* July 20, 1998: 36–37.

Shore, D., Filson, C. R., & Rae, D. S. (1990). Violent crime arrest rates of White House case subjects and matched control subjects. *American Journal of Psychiatry, 147,* 746–750.

Simon, B., & Brown, R. (1987). Perceived intragroup homogeneity in minority-majority contexts. *Journal of Personality and Social Psychology, 53,* 703–711.

Sosowsky, L. (1978). Crime and violence among mental patients reconsidered in view of the new legal relationship between the state and the mentally ill. *American Journal of Psychiatry, 135,* 33–42.

Steadman, H. J. (1981). Critically reassessing the accuracy of public perceptions of the dangerousness of the mentally ill. *Journal of Health and Social Behavior, 22,* 310–316.

Steadman, H. J., Cocozza, J. J., & Melick, M. E. (1978). Explaining increased arrest rate among mental patients: Changing clientele of state hospitals. *American Journal of Psychiatry, 135*, 816–820.

Steadman, H. J., Mulvey, E. P., Monahan, J., Robbins, P. C., Appelbaum, P. S., Grisso, T., et al. (1998). Violence by people discharged from acute psychiatric inpatient facilities and by others in the same neighborhoods. *Archives of General Psychiatry, 55*, 393–401.

Stueve, A., & Link, B. G. (1997). Violence and psychiatric disorders: Results from an epidemiological study of young adults in Israel. *Psychiatric Quarterly, 68*, 327–342.

Swanson, J. W., Borum, R., Swartz, M. S., & Monahan, J. (1996). Psychotic symptoms and disorders and the risk of violent behaviour in the community. *Criminal Behaviour and Mental Health, 6*(4), 309–329.

Swanson, J. W., Holzer, C. E., Ganju, V. K., & Jono, R. T. (1990). Violence and psychiatric disorder in the community: Evidence from the Epidemiologic Catchment Area surveys. *Hospital and Community Psychiatry, 41*, 761–770.

Teplin, L. A. (1983). The criminalization of the mentally ill: Speculation in search of data. *Psychological Bulletin, 94*, 54–67.

Teplin, L. A. (1984). Criminalizing mental disorder: The comparative arrest rate of the mentally ill. *American Psychologist, 39*, 794–803.

Torrey, E. F. (1994). Violent behavior by individuals with serious mental illness. *Hospital and Community Psychiatry, 45*, 653–662.

Torrey, E. F. (2002). Stigma and violence. *Psychiatric Services, 53*, 1179.

Torrey, E. F., & Zdanowicz, M. (2001). Outpatient commitment: What, why, and for whom. *Psychiatric Services, 52*, 337–341.

Treatment Advocacy Center. (2002a). *Approximately 1,000 homicides per year in the United States are committed by individuals with severe mental illnesses. Where does this number come from?* Briefing paper retrieved June 17, 2004, from http://www.psychlaws.org/BriefingPapers/BP11.htm

Treatment Advocacy Center. (2002b). *Stigma and violence.* Briefing paper retrieved June 17, 2004, from http://www.psychlaws.org/BriefingPapers/BP9.htm

Tverksy, A., & Kahneman, D. (1973). Availability heuristic for judging frequency and probability. *Cognitive Psychology, 5*, 207–232.

Tversky, A., & Kahneman, D. (1974). Judgment under uncertainty: Heuristics and biases. *Science, 185*, 1124–1131.

Wahl, O. F. (1995). *Media madness: Public images of mental illness.* New Brunswick, NJ: Rutgers University Press.

Wessely, S. (1997). The epidemiology of crime, violence and schizophrenia. *British Journal of Psychiatry, 170*, 8–11.

Woll, S. (2002). *Everyday thinking: Memory, reasoning, and judgment in the real world.* Mahwah, NJ: Erlbaum.

8

SENSELESS CRIMES: SIN OR SICKNESS? IMPLICATIONS FOR MENTAL ILLNESS STIGMA

PATRICK W. CORRIGAN AND AMY C. WATSON

Over the course of 10 days in March 1999, the Chicago area news focused on a series of senseless and horrible acts. Marilyn Lemak, a nurse and mother from a wealthy western suburb, was arrested for drugging, and then suffocating, her three young children. Andrew Kokoraleis was put to death for raping, torturing, and murdering up to seventeen women; in some of these cases, he cut the breasts off his victims and used them in religious ceremonies. Joseph and Carmen Grad were imprisoned for keeping their 6-year-old son locked in a bathroom closet for months. During that time, they chained him, bound him in chicken wire, urinated on him, rubbed feces in his face, and went days without feeding him. Egregious acts like these boggle the mind for explanations.

Perhaps as frightening as these specific acts is the frequency in which they seem to occur. On a daily basis, we are barraged with news stories that relay examples of senseless pain and terror inflicted on others (Kelleher,

1998). One might want to believe that these crimes are the actions of a unique, depraved, and easily identifiable few. However, perpetrators are our neighbors, coworkers, and friends; they are rich and poor, young and old, urban and rural, educated and naive. Often, news outlets show us sound bites from a neighbor or childhood friend indicating the perpetrator was a nice and quiet person: "I just can't believe he would do something like this!"

The omnipresent quality of such mind-boggling horror leads us to frequently ask: Are these acts the result of sin or the effect of sickness? News reports suggest Marilyn Lemak had a history of depression and neurological disorder. Did mental illness cause her to kill her children? The jury did not think so and rejected her insanity plea (Coen & Barnum, 2002). The lawyers of Andrew Kokoraleis never claimed innocence because of insanity; was his crime an act of evil? No one died in the Grad family, but the cruel torture of an innocent child is so disturbing we assume the parents must be either sick or evil. The question of sin or sickness is tackled in daily news reports, from the Sunday pulpit, among debating legislators, within behavioral health clinics, and by social scientists. Hoping for quick answers, people look to mental illness as a cause; is this reality or stigma? Senseless crimes offer a different challenge to understanding mental illness and stigma from the argument about violence in the previous chapter. The purpose of this chapter is to deconstruct the idea of senseless crime, and examine its relationship to the public's desire to know why these offenses occur.

In this chapter, we do not attempt to apply psychological methods to *answer* the question of sin or sickness. Definitive solutions to a question like this exceed the limitations of a single discipline. Nor, for that matter, are the social sciences particularly adept at addressing the moral aspect of questions about sin. Rather, the focus of this paper is on the *function* of the question itself. What purpose is served by answering whether a crime represents sin or sickness? Does the result lead to stigma or reflect veracity? Solutions to the question, in part, depend on the reasons why it was posed. However, before addressing these various reasons, we provide a definition of senseless crime that is suitable to the behavioral sciences.

WHAT IS A SENSELESS CRIME?

The notion of senseless crime is not a legal concept; no federal statutes or common law agreements exist that define the concept. Nor does the idea of senseless crime readily fit the view of behavioral science. According to notions of psychological determinism, all human behaviors (including crimes) have some cause for their event (Robinson, 1976; Skinner, 1953). "Senseless" suggests the crime was committed with no reason, an inconceivable event.[1] Senseless, therefore, reflects the perceptions of an observer rather than an objective estimation of the event's causes. This phenomenological perspective is consistent with attribution theory, a model of human motivation and emotion on the basis of the assumption that individuals search for causal understanding of everyday events (Weiner, 1980b, 1983, 1993, 1995).

Several factors influence the individual's perspective about the causes of crime and what makes it senseless. American jurisprudence defines a crime in terms of *actus reus* (an unlawful *act* occurred) and *mens rea* (this act was based on criminal *intent*).[2] A crime is perceived to be senseless when its intent either fails to rest on one of the normative motivators of crime or lacks legal justification. Social scientists have identified several normative motivators for crime, or common reasons why unlawful acts occur. These reasons include greed, retribution, economic need, affiliation and peer group pressure (e.g., crimes committed by youth gangs), passion (e.g., crimes committed in rage), and protection from prosecution (e.g., pejury or witness tampering [Hannon & Defronzo, 1998; Ray & Briar, 1988; Swaffer & Hollen, 1995; Wright & Rossi, 1986]). None of these factors seemed to motivate Andrew Kokoraleis to rape, torture, and kill his victims.

In terms of justification, the legal system recognizes several conditions related to intent that mitigate responsibility for a criminal act. These include accident (where harm occurred through no effort of the person, such as a car crash on slippery pavement); recklessness (unintended harm occurred as the result of risk-taking behavior such as a drunk driver killing a pedestrian); compulsion (where another person bodily compelled or otherwise required the perpetrator to commit the act); defense of self, others, and property; entrapment (where a crime is committed in response to police enticements); and infancy (young children may not be accountable for some criminal acts [Robinson, 1984]). The facts known about Marilyn Lemak failed to prove to the jury that any of these conditions mitigated the intent of her crime.

Crimes are senseless when justification or normative motivation is absent. Yet senseless, as a conclusion, stymies the person motivated to find the causes of acts like heinous crimes. What other alternatives might explain these events? Sin and sickness are two conclusions that may settle the question of why a senseless act occurred. Mental illness may be a factor that motivates persons to commit a crime; for example, a person acting on a paranoid

---

[1]Proponents of chaos theory (Gleick, 1987; Warren, Franklin, & Streeter, 1998) may disagree with notions of psychological determinism. However, the motivation to find causes to compelling events suggests that the general population believes behaviors are determined and reasons for their occurrence are comprehensible.

[2]In the examples of this paper, we assume that the criminal act occurred by the identified perpetrator. Hence, questions of guilt or innocence, due to facts of the crime, are not meant to be disputed.

delusion might murder another for no apparent reason. Thus, psychiatric illness is a mitigator for justification in many courts; the not guilty by reason of insanity defense is one example. Sin is the default category. In the absence of justice, motivation, and sickness, the act is a sin and the perpetrator is guilty of evil. For some observers, sin may also be the default for when the crime exceeds some subjective level of horror, regardless of evidence of mental illness or other mitigators. For these people, perhaps attributing the crime to sickness somehow seems like condoning it (Miller, Gordon, & Buddie, 1999). Marilyn Lemak's defense team argued that her crime was the result of sickness—depression and psychosis made her believe she had to kill her children to protect them and reunite with them in a better place. The prosecution argued it was the result of sin—the desire to harm her husband for abandoning her (Coen & Barnum, 2002).

According to attribution theory, people are motivated to determine why events occur (Weiner, 1995). In terms of brutal crimes, if the perpetrator has a diagnosable mental disorder, he or she may not be held responsible for the crime. Sin is the default category for acts society does not have the ability to understand. For example, behaviors now understood as symptoms of psychosis were once considered manifestations of demonic possession (Pilgrim & Rogers, 1999). Over time, as knowledge about brain and behavior increased, the default category of sin narrowed.

A DEFINITION OF SIN

Psychologists have been reasonably successful at tackling the concept of sickness; medical, cognitive–behavioral, and disability models have yielded pragmatic approaches to describing mental illness that have held up to empirical tests (Corrigan & Penn, 1997). Sin, on the other hand, is a more cumbersome concept for social scientists; thus they tend to avoid it. For example, in a review of 2,348 articles published in four major psychiatric journals between 1978 and 1982, only 59 assessed a variable related to religion; only 3 studies examined a hypothesis that primarily involved religious behavior (Larson, Pattison, Blazer, Omran, & Kaplan, 1986). Moreover, empirical definitions may corrupt what moral philosophers consider better representations of sin (Downing, 1991; Watson, Hood, Morris, & Hall, 1985).

Despite the distance between social science and philosophical approaches, some overlap appears in concepts about sin that serve the purpose of this paper (i.e., constructs relevant to sin that are approachable by the theories and methods of psychology). Moral philosophers and theologians believe sin is evident as both an act (the behavior related to a heinous crime) and a condition (the perpetrator is in a state of sin that accounts for this act [Wiley, 1952]). Psychologists and moralists can bring their respective methodologies to explain a sinful act as well as personal conditions relevant to that act. Moreover, consequences of the evinced sin lead to personal blameworthiness. Responsibility and controllability have been well-studied by social psychologists (Weiner, 1995). Anchoring issues of sin to concepts of responsibility and blame bypasses many of the ontological and epistemological conundra posed by trying to bridge the concept of sin and the concerns of social science. For example, these concepts sidestep the tension between free will (a frequent element in moral theories of sin) and psychological determinism (Rychlak & Rychlak, 1990; Skinner, 1971).

A FUNCTIONAL ANALYSIS OF "SIN OR SICKNESS"

For decades, psychologists have used functional analysis to answer the "why" of social behavior (Katz, 1960; Smith, Bruner, & White, 1956). Why are persons attracted to certain groups? What purpose does conforming to authority serve? Why do people commit heinous crimes? Functional analysis addresses the reasons and purposes that explain social phenomena, the needs and goals they serve, and the plans and motives that underlie them (Leigland, 1995; Mace, 1994; Snyder, 1994; Snyder & Cantor, 1998). In this paper, functional analysis concerns itself with motives underlying the question of whether a criminal act and its perpetrator represent sin or sickness and the function of drawing one or the other conclusions. This is sometimes labeled a "hot" approach toward explaining social psychological phenomena and is distinguished from "cool" paradigms with explanations on the basis of form and processes that comprise the cognitive apparatus (Miller & Porter, 1998). Although hot models have their foundations in psychodynamic theory, they have more recently gained significant support through empirical evidence gathered by social psychologists.

Functional analysis returns questions of sin or sickness from the abstract and limited realm of philosophers and theologians to the everyday concerns shared by us all. All citizens are motivated to know whether a senseless crime covered on the evening news is the product of illness or the incarnation of evil. Functional analysis searches for the reason behind the common question. Contrary to naive perspectives, not one motive definitively explains a behavioral event; not a single reason exists for questioning "sin" or "sickness." Therefore, no one can answer the question of whether a senseless crime resulted from sin or sickness. Functional analyses provide a paradigm for discerning the multiple motives underlying the "why" question that is evoked by abominable acts.

Social psychologists have distinguished two levels of functional analysis: individual and societal (Brewer, 1994; Snyder & Cantor, 1998). Individuals ask whether a senseless crime represents sin or sickness to address immediate concerns (e.g., "Should I vote guilty on this murder trial?"). Societies develop stereotypes to comprehend designated out-groups (e.g., criminals and persons

TABLE 8.1
Some Reasons Why Persons Ask Questions About "Sin or Sickness"

	Individual level of analysis	Societal level of analysis
Products		
Cognitive Understanding	• Comprehension through causal attributions	• Stereotypes and stigma
Decisions/Actions	• Jury decisions • Avoidance of sinners and sick	• Treatment/legal policy • Anti-stigma campaigns

with mental illness). Functional analyses at the personal and societal level yield two products: cognitive *understanding* and *action* on the basis of this understanding. Individuals and groups are motivated psychologically because they wish to make sense out of the experience and then act on these interpretations. Hence, the various functions related to an analysis of a social-behavioral phenomenon are described by a two-by-two matrix in Table 8.1. Specific examples of functions related to the question about sin or sickness are also listed. This list is not meant to be exhaustive but rather exemplary of the individual and societal level functions of asking whether a deplorable act represents sin or sickness. In this paper, we discuss only individual level analyses describing their impact on understanding senseless crimes and responding to perpetrators. We leave to a subsequent paper the implications of social level analyses to questions of sin or sickness.

PERSONAL UNDERSTANDING OF SENSELESS CRIMES

A variety of social cognitive models are relevant to understanding the function of questions on sin or sickness for the individual. These include research on self-esteem and downward comparison (supporting one's self-esteem by contrast with persons who are lower in social status, like perpetrators of crime [Krueger, 1998; Wills, 1991]), self-identity through distinctive group membership (supporting a positive identity by belonging to groups that are clearly distinct from the class of crime perpetrators [Lindeman, 1997; Verkuyten, 1997]), and causal attribution models (Weiner, 1995). Attribution models are consistent with phenomenological approaches to behavior and have developed the notion of intent and controllability. These models are also promising because they provide a broad theoretical base and rigorous research methodology for understanding a person's perceptions about senseless crimes.

Weiner (1993) believed the answer to "sin or sickness?" rested on controllability attributions. Persons who are deemed to be in control of an event are blamed for the outcomes more than individuals considered to lack control of the situation. Controllability refers to the amount of perceived volitional influence an individual exerts over a cause (Weiner, 1993, 1995). As discussed previously, a judge is less likely to hold a mother responsible for killing a child when clear mitigating circumstances suggest she was not in control of the situation. This implies that a key aspect to research on attribution theory is identification of these mitigating circumstances. Sickness, in particular, is an often-studied source of factors that affect the uncontrollability of a situation.

One might think that physical health factors, mental illness, and substance abuse are all possible sickness variables that moderate a perpetrator's actions. However, research suggests that persons with physical illness are judged to be in less control of their disability, and related situations, than psychiatric and substance abuse disorders (Corrigan et al., 2000; Weiner, Perry, & Magnusson, 1988). Note, however, that although mental illnesses are judged more harshly than physical illnesses, psychiatric disorders are still viewed as largely uncontrollable (Corrigan et al., 2000). Persons with substance abuse disorders, however, are considered to be in control of their actions and hence more responsible for events. This distinction is consistent with criminal law in most states (Galan & Leiebelt, 1997). Intoxication because of substance use is rarely sufficient for an insanity defense.

Weiner's theory suggests that controllability and responsibility attributions produce emotional responses. Persons who are viewed to be in control of a negative event such as a crime are more likely to be held responsible and reacted to angrily (Dooley, 1995; Graham, Weiner, & Zucker, 1997; Reisenzein, 1986; Rush, 1998; Schmidt & Weiner, 1988; Weiner, Graham, & Chandler, 1982; Weiner et al., 1988). Conversely, individuals who are not believed to be in control of a negative event may be pitied by others (Dooley, 1995; Reisenzein, 1986; Schmidt & Weiner, 1988; Weiner et al., 1982, 1988). A mother who smothered her children with no obvious mitigators is likely to be judged harshly and receive the wrath of her community. The Chicago community, through its newspaper and electronic media, castigated Marilyn Lemak upon her arrest. In the months that followed, story headlines and letters to the editor varied between evil and mental illness, with the jury casting the final vote by rejecting her insanity defense. The judge ordered psychiatric treatment for Lemak so she could "always maintain the capacity to understand the horror of your crime" (Coen & Barnum, 2002). Conversely, a mother whose children are killed when her car slides out of control in bad weather is likely to receive the pity of neighbors. Some may question if she was using enough caution given road conditions, but for the most part, the event will be viewed as an uncontrollable accident.

Controllability attributions are affected by the perceived stability of causal factors (Weiner, 1995). Some factors remain potent over time, whereas others wax and wane. Research suggests that attributions about the stability of a cause do not affect the type of emotional or behavioral responses as much as the strength of those responses (Barnes, Ickes, & Kidd, 1979; Weiner, 1995; Weiner et al., 1982). Causal attributions are given more weight when viewed as stable and unchanging rather than unstable and fluctuating. Hence, Marilyn Lemak's murder of her children may be judged more mildly if viewed as a transitory event; this is consistent with the notion of temporary insanity (Sadoff, 1992). Serial murderer Andrew Kokoraleis reportedly raped, tortured, and killed women over a several month period. This ongoing pattern of behavior likely contributed to the harshness with which he was judged.

ACTING ON ONE'S PERCEPTION ABOUT SIN OR SICKNESS

Although attribution theory is fundamentally a phenomenological model—explaining a person's perception of causation—the model's use is not limited to cognitive explanations. Weiner's theory on controllability attributions suggests that inferences about cause and responsibility lead to behavioral decisions and consequent action; see this path at the top of Figure 8.1. Graham and colleagues (1997) illustrated this point in a survey of 177 persons in the week following the murder of Nicole Brown Simpson. Research

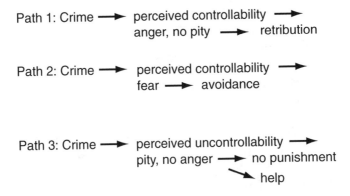

Figure 8.1. Three causal pathways implied by attribution theory. Path 1 illustrates the relationship between crimes, anger, controllability attribution, and retribution. Path 2 shows how controllability attributions about a crime lead to feelings of fear or anger and avoidance behaviors. Path 3 suggests that uncontrollability attributions actually lead to helping behavior. From Weiner (1995) and Graham, Weiner, and Zucker (1997).

participants were asked if O. J. Simpson were guilty of the crime and responsible for his actions. Results suggest that individuals who thought Simpson was responsible endorsed the behavioral decision that he should be punished; punishment varied from mandatory rehabilitation to retribution and experiencing the consequences of his crimes. An independent study reported by Graham and colleagues (1997) showed that vignettes of a murder case in which the crime was described as a stable and controllable act yielded greater calls for retribution. These results show a similar link between cognitive understanding of the situation and behavioral decision to act.

Unfortunately, these findings do not suggest how a person might really act; no assurance exists that someone's statement about a behavioral decision will correlate with their subsequent action. Other research on attribution theory has shown a link between controllability attributions and actual behavior, suggesting that attitudes about a person's responsibility may lead to related behavior (Barnes et al., 1979; Corrigan, Markowitz, Watson, Rowan, & Kubiak, in press; Corrigan et al., 2002). These findings, although not directly testing Path 1 in Figure 8.1, support the notion that controllability attributions about a crime lead to anger and a call for retribution. In what ways might this demand for requital appear behaviorally?

Jury Decisions

Citizens are called to act on their perceptions of sin and sickness when they fulfill their jury duty. Juries may need to decide the guilt or innocence of a person on the basis of the insanity defense. In some states, this decision is affected by the M'Naghten Rule, based on English common law from the 1800s; namely, persons are not accountable for their acts if, because of mental disease or defect, they are incapable of knowing that act was wrong. The American Law Institute (ALI) expanded on this rule in 1954; in addition to disease or defect, persons who lack *substantial capacity* to appreciate the wrongfulness of an act or comply their behavior according to the law are considered insane. A recent survey found 26 states used the M'Naghten rule and 21 states adhered to all criteria in making decisions about guilt and insanity (Blau, 1998).

Research with mock juries shows their decision making about insanity pleas is affected by causal attributions. Juror attributions about guilt and responsibility are positively associated with decisions about punishment (Poulson, 1990; Poulson, Braithwaite, Brondino, & Wuensch, 1997). What is equally interesting to discover is that disapproving reactions to the notion of an insanity defense also influence decisions about guilt. Mock jurors who believe the insanity defense leads to unnecessary judicial leniency (e.g., "Guilty perpetrators are able to escape conviction by feigning mental illness") are more likely to attribute responsibility to a defendant in a trial that involves an insanity defense (Poulson, Brondino, Brown, & Braithwaite, 1988; Poulson, Wuensch, Brown, & Braithwaite, 1997). Moreover, citizens are concerned that judicial leniency occurs too frequently (Low, Jeffries, & Bonnie, 1986). This concern does not reflect actual practice, however; a review of more than 950,000 felony dockets across seven states showed only 7,299 pleas of insanity; 2,220 of these pleas actually were supported after trial (Cirincione, 1996).

Note that the decisions of the jury about sin or sickness are relatively simple compared to the moral and social science dilemmas discussed earlier. Either the defendant is sick and remanded to the mental health system for care, or sinful and sentenced to prison. Moreover, the reactions of the population to those who are judged sick or sinner vary beyond the jury room. Let us consider some other behavioral responses.

Avoiding the Criminal or Helping the Sick

The second and third paths in Figure 8.1 suggest two other courses of actions that may result from a person's answer to the question of sin or sickness. Path 2 implies that viewing a person as responsible for violent crimes leads not only to anger but also fear (Corrigan & Penn, 1999; Johson-Dalzine, Dalzine, & Martin-Stanly, 1996). The combined reaction produces a set of avoidance behaviors; these could take the form of landlords not renting apartments to or employers not hiring persons with known criminal histories. Citizens do not seem to limit their avoidance to the perpetrator. Research on courtesy stigma suggests family, friends, and other known associates of felons are also likely to be the object of this kind of discrimination (Goffman, 1963).

The relationship between crime, controllability attribution, and avoidance makes sense. What is of greater surprise may be Path 3: attributions of crime uncontrollability lead to pity! Pity generates two responses: no punishment and help. This finding is supported by the substantial research showing that an unfortunate event and an uncontrollability attribution leads to pity and helping behavior; for example, parents need solace because their child drowned at summer camp (Meyer & Mulherin, 1980; Reisenzein, 1986; Schmidt & Weiner, 1988; Weiner, 1980a, 1980b). There may be some parallel in criminal activities. For example, letters to the editor about the Lemak case that supported her claim of mental illness expressed pity and also demanded that she receive help in the mental health system. Those who considered Lemak's crime an act of premedititated evil demanded the death penalty or life in prison. However, no controlled research exists on the relationship between crime, irresponsibility, pity, and help.

The pattern outlined in Path 2 (crime → controllability [sin] → anger → retribution–avoidance) not only suggests persons guilty of crimes are shunned, but also that persons found not guilty of crimes may avoid this opprobrium. Hence, one might think that perpetrators who point to mitigating factors (e.g., mental illness) would avoid the stigma and discrimination experienced by criminals. However, research suggests persons with mental illness are likely to be blamed and stigmatized as much as those "sinners" who are guilty of the crime (Albrecht, Walker, & Levy, 1982; Brand & Claiborn, 1976; Skinner, Berry, Griffith, & Byers, 1995). Moreover, citizens are less likely to hire persons who are labeled mentally ill (Bordieri & Drehmer, 1986; Farina & Felner, 1973; Link, 1982, 1987; Link, Cullen, Frank, & Wozniak, 1987; Olshansky, Grob, & Ekdahl, 1960; Webber & Orcutt, 1984) and less likely to lease them apartments (Farina, Thaw, Lovern, & Mangone, 1974; Lefley, 1992; Page, 1977, 1983, 1995). Families also report lowered self-esteem and strained relationships with others because of their association with relatives with mental illness (Lefley, 1992; Wahl & Harmon, 1989).

This finding seems to challenge the dichotomy implied by questions of sin or sickness. If not guilty of the crime, the person should escape retribution. This contradiction may, in part, arise from limiting the answer to an individual level of analysis. Understanding functions of the question in terms of societal levels may resolve the puzzling relationship between crime, mental illness, irresponsibility, and failure to escape retribution.

Another explanation for the contradiction may be fear. Recent survey research suggests that the public is more fearful of individuals with mental illness than it was 50 years ago (Phelan, Link, Stueve, & Pescosolido, 2000). A defendant may not be held personally responsible for a crime because of "sickness," but because of that "sickness" he or she is also perceived as dangerous and unpredictable. Hence, others prefer to distance themselves by not hiring, not renting to, and not associating with the "sick" individual out of self-protection motives. They may, however, endorse help in the form of treatment for the person.

SOCIETAL FUNCTIONS OF SIN OR SICKNESS

As suggested in Table 8.1, societal understanding of events (like senseless crimes) often manifests itself as stereotypes (Crocker, Major, & Steele, 1998; Fiske, 1998). Hence, one function of questions about sin or sickness may be to reinforce existing stereotypes. These stereotypes, in turn, lead to behavior responses. Formally, societal attitudes about mental illness may affect policy toward persons with mental illness (Corrigan & Penn, 1999) and legal approaches toward the insanity defense (Callahan, Mayer, & Steadman, 1987). Hence, a complete analysis of the function of questions about senseless crimes must include both individual and societal levels.

SUMMARY

To make sense of the horrible crimes that repeatedly confront us, we ask whether these acts represent sin or sickness. Although psychology is not particularly adept at answering questions that are moral in nature, our discipline can come to some understanding about the question by examining its functions. Functional analysis is useful because it provides a rigorous method for examining phenomena of interest that are epistemologically and ontologically distant to psychology (Leigland, 1995). For example, research strategies from social cognition and attribution theory are useful for examining how persons understand sin versus sickness as related to senseless crimes. These strategies are also useful for examining the relationship between individual understanding and behavioral responses. The individual level of analysis is augmented by understanding societal representations. Research methods on social attitudes and stereotypes examine the relationship between stigma and reactions to the question of sin or sickness. Moreover, it may suggest how society reacts to these stereotypes, in terms of informal discriminatory responses and governmental policies. Multiple levels of analysis provide the best descriptions of the functions related to questions of sin or sickness.

REFERENCES

Albrecht, G., Walker, V. G., & Levy, J. A. (1982). Social distance from the stigmatized: A test of two theories. *Social Science Medicine, 16*, 1319–1327.

Barnes, R. D., Ickes, W., & Kidd, R. F. (1979). Effects of the perceived intentionality and stability of another's dependency on helping behavior. *Personality and Social Psychology Bulletin, 5*, 367–372.

Blau, T. H. (1998). *The psychologist as expert witness* (2nd ed.). New York: Wiley.

Bordieri, J. E., & Drehmer, D. E. (1986). Hiring decisions for disabled workers: Looking at the cause. *Journal of Applied Social Psychology, 16*, 197–208.

Brand, R. C., & Claiborn, W. L. (1976). Two studies of comparatative stigma: Employer attitudes and practices toward rehabilitated convicts, mental and tuberculosis patients. *Community Mental Health Journal, 12*, 168–175.

Brewer, M. B. (1994). *Social psychology.* Minneapolis: West Publishing.

Callahan, L., Mayer, C., & Steadman, H. J. (1987). Insanity defense reform in the United States: Post-Hinckley. *Mental and Physical Disability Law Reporter, 11*, 54–59.

Cirincione, C. (1996). Revisiting the insanity defense: Contested or concensus? *Bulletin of the American Academy of Psychiatry and the Law, 24*, 165–176.

Coen, J., & Barnum, A. (2002, April 9). Lemak gets life term for killing her 3 kids. *Chicago Tribune*, p. 1.

Corrigan, P. W., Markowitz, F. E., Watson, A. C., Rowan, D., & Kubiak, M. A. (2003). An attribution model of public discrimination towards persons with mental illness. *Journal of Health and Social Behavior, 44,* 162–179.

Corrigan, P. W., & Penn, D. (1997). Disease and discrimination: Two paradigms that describe severe mental illness. *Journal of Mental Health, 6,* 355–366.

Corrigan, P. W., & Penn, D. L. (1999). Lessons from social psychology on discrediting psychiatric stigma. *American Psychologist, 54,* 765–776.

Corrigan, P. W., River, L., Lundin, R. K., Uphoff-Wasowski, K., Campion, J., Mathisen, J., et al. (2000). Stigmatizing attributions about mental illness. *Journal of Community Psychology, 28,* 91–102.

Corrigan, P. W., Rowan, D., Green, A., Lundin, R., River, L., Uphoff-Wasowski, K., et al. (2002). Challenging two mental illness stigmas: Personal responsibility and dangerousness. *Schizophrenia Bulletin, 28,* 293–310.

Crocker, J., Major, B., & Steele, C. (1998). Social stigma. In D. T. Gilbert & S. T. Fiske (Eds.), *The handbook of social psychology* (4th ed., Vol. 2, pp. 504–553) New York: McGraw-Hill.

Dooley, P. A. (1995). Perceptions of the onset controllability of AIDS and helping judgments: An attributional analysis. *Journal of Applied Social Psychology, 25,* 858–869.

Downing, D. S. (1991). A public philosophy of psychiatry: A view from theology. In D. S. Browning & I. S. Evison (Eds.), *Does psychiatry need a public philosophy?* Chicago: Nelson-Hall.

Farina, A., & Felner, R. D. (1973). Employment interviewer reactions to former mental patients. *Journal of Abnormal Psychology, 8,* 368–372.

Farina, A., Thaw, J., Lovern, J. D., & Mangone, D. (1974). People's reactions to a former mental patient moving to their neighborhood. *Journal of Community Psychology, 2,* 108–112.

Fiske, S. T. (1998). Stereotyping, prejudice, and discrimination. In D. T. Gilbert & S. T. Fiske (Eds.), *The handbook of social psychology* (4th ed., Vol. 2, pp. 357–411). New York: McGraw-Hill.

Galan, P. A., & Leiebelt, R. A. (1997). Involuntary treatment of substance abuse disorders. In M. R. Munetz (Ed.), *Can mandatory treatments be therapeutic?* (Vol. 75, pp. 35–48). San Francisco: Jossey-Bass.

Gleick, J. (1987). *Chaos: Making new science.* New York: Penguin.

Goffman, E. (1963). *Stigma: Notes on the management of spoiled identity.* Englewood Cliffs, NJ: Prentice-Hall.

Graham, S., Weiner, B., & Zucker, G. S. (1997). An attributional analysis of punishment goals and public reactions to O. J. Simpson. *Personality and Social Psychology Bulletin, 23,* 331–346.

Hannon, L., & Defronzo, J. (1998). The truly disadvantaged, public assistance, and crime. *Social Problems, 45,* 383–392.

Johson-Dalzine, P., Dalzine, L., & Martin-Stanly, C. (1996). Fear of criminal violence and the African American elderly: An assessment of a crime prevention strategy. *Journal of Negro Education, 65,* 462–469.

Katz, D. (1960). The functional approach to the study of attitudes. *Public Opinion Quarterly, 24,* 163–204.

Kelleher, M. D. (1998). *When good kids kill.* Westport, CO: Praeger Publishers.

Krueger, J. (1998). Enhancement bias in descriptions of self and others. *Personality and Social Psychology Bulletin, 24,* 505–516.

Larson, D. B., Pattison, E. M., Blazer, D. G., Omran, A. R., & Kaplan, B. H. (1986). Systematic analysis of research on religious variables in four major psychiatric journals, 1978–1982. *American Journal of Psychiatry, 143,* 329–334.

Lefley, H. P. (1992). The stigmatized family. In P. J. Fink & A. Tasman (Eds.), *Stigma and mental illness* (pp. 127–138). Washington, DC: American Psychiatric Press.

Leigland, S. (1995). The functional analysis of psychologocal terms: In defense of a research program. *Analysis of Verbal Behavior, 13,* 105–122.

Lindeman, M. (1997). In-group bias, self enhancement and group identification. *European Journal of Social Psychology, 27,* 337–355.

Link, B. G. (1982). Mental patient status, work and income: An examination of the effects of a psychiatric label. *American Sociological Review, 47,* 202–215.

Link, B. G. (1987). Understanding labeling effects in the area of mental disorders: An assessment of the effects of expectations of rejection. *American Sociological Review, 52,* 96–112.

Link, B. G., Cullen, F. T., Frank, J., & Wozniak, J. F. (1987). The social rejection of former mental patients: Understanding why labels matter. *American Journal of Sociology, 92,* 1461–1500.

Low, P. W., Jeffries, J. C., & Bonnie, R. J. (1986). *The trial of John W. Hinckley Jr.: A case study in the insanity defense.* Mineola, NY: Foundation Press.

Mace, F. C. (1994). The significance and future of functional analysis methodologies. *Journal of Applied Behavior Analysis, 27,* 385–392.

Meyer, J. P., & Mulherin, A. (1980). From attribution to helping: An analysis of the mediating effects of affect on expectancy. *Journal of Personality and Social Psychology, 39,* 201–210.

Miller, A. G., Gordon, A. K., & Buddie, A. M. (1999). Accounting for Evil and Cruelty: Is it to Explain or Condone? *Personality and Social Psychology Review, 3,* 254–268.

Miller, D. T., & Porter, C. A. (1998). Errors in biases in the attribution process. In L.Y. Abramson (Ed.), *Social cognition and clinical psychology: A synthesis* (pp. 3–30). New York: Guilford Press.

Olshansky, S., Grob, S., & Ekdahl, M. (1960). Survey of employment experience of patients discharged from three mental hospitals during the period 1951–1953. *Mental Hygiene, 44,* 510–521.

Page, S. (1977). Effects of the mental illness label in attempts to obtain accommodation. *Canadian Journal of Behavioral Science, 9,* 85–90.

Page, S. (1983). Psychiatric stigma: Two studies of behavior when the chips are down. *Canadian Journal of Community Mental Health, 2,* 13–19.

Page, S. (1995). Effects of the mental illness label in 1993: Acceptance and rejection in the community. *Journal of Health and Social Policy, 7,* 61–68.

Phelan, J. C., Link, B. G., Stueve, A., & Pescosolido, B. A. (2000). Public conceptions of mental illness in 1950 and 1996: What is mental illness and is it to be feared? *Journal of Health & Social Behavior, 41,* 188–207.

Pilgrim, D., & Rogers, A. (1999). *A Sociology of Mental Health and Illness* (2nd ed.). Buckingham, UK: Open University Press.

Poulson, R. L. (1990). Mock juror attribution of criminal responsibility: Effects of race and the Guilty But Mentally Ill (GBMI) verdict option. *Journal of Applied Social Psychology, 2,* 1596–1611.

Poulson, R. L., Braithwaite, R. L., Brondino, M. J., & Wuensch, K. L. (1997). Mock jurors' insanity defense verdict selections: The role of evidence, attitudes, and verdict options. *Journal of Social Behavior and Personality, 12,* 743–758.

Poulson, R. L., Brondino, M. J., Brown, H., & Braithwaite, R. L. (1988). Relations among mock jurors' attitudes, trial evidence, and their selections of an insanity defense verdict: A path analytic approach. *Psychological Reports, 82,* 3–16.

Poulson, R. L., Wuensch, K. L., Brown, M. B., & Braithwaite, R. L. (1997). Mock jurors' evaluations of insanity defense verdict selection: The role of death penalty attitudes. *Journal of Social Behavior and Personality, 12,* 1065–1078.

Ray, J., & Briar, K. H. (1988). Economic motivators for shoplifting. *Journal of Sociology and Social Welfare, 15,* 177–189.

Reisenzein, R. (1986). A structural equation analysis of Weiner's attribution–affect model of helping behavior. *Journal of Personality and Social Psychology, 50,* 1123–1133.

Robinson, P. H. (1984). *Criminal law defenses* (Vol. 2). St. Paul, MN: West Publishers.

Robinson, P. W. (1976). *Fundamentals of experimental psychology: A comparative approach.* Englewood Cliffs, NJ: Prentice-Hall.

Rush, L. (1998). Affective reactions to multiple social stigmas. *Journal of Social Psychology, 138,* 421–430.

Rychlak, J. F., & Rychlak, R. J. (1990). The insanity defense and the question of human agency. *New Ideas in Psychology, 8,* 3–24.

Sadoff, R. L. (1992). In defense of the insanity defense. *Psychiatric Annals, 22,* 556–560.

Schmidt, G., & Weiner, B. (1988). An attribution-affect-action theory of behavior: Replications of judgments of help-giving. *Personality and Social Psychology Bulletin, 14,* 610–621.

Skinner, B. F. (1953). *Science and human behavior.* New York: MacMillan.

Skinner, B. F. (1971). *Beyond freedom and dignity* (1st ed.). New York: Knopf.

Skinner, L., Berry, K. K., Griffith, S. E., & Byers, B. (1995). Generalizability and specificity of the stigma associated with the mental illness label: A reconsideration twenty-five years later. *Journal of Community Psychology, 23,* 3–17.

Smith, M. B., Bruner, J. S., & White, R. W. (1956). *Opinions and personality.* New York: Wiley.

Snyder, M. (1994). Traits and motives in the psychology of personality. *Psychological Inquiry, 5*, 162–166.

Snyder, M., & Cantor, N. (1998). Understanding personality and social behavior: A functionalist strategy. In D. T. Gilbert & S. Fiske (Eds.), *The handbook of social psychology* (Vol. 2, 4th ed., pp. 635–679). Boston: McGraw-Hill.

Swaffer, T., & Hollen, C. R. (1995). Adolescent fire setting: Why do they say they do it? *Journal of Adolescence, 18*, 619–623.

Verkuyten, M. (1997). Intergroup evaluation and self-esteem motivations: Self-enhancement and self-protection. *European Journal of Social Psychology, 21*, 115–119.

Wahl, O. F., & Harmon, C. R. (1989). Family views of stigma. *Schizophrenia Bulletin, 15*, 131–139.

Warren, K., Franklin, C., & Streeter, C. L. (1998). New directions in systems theory: Chaos and complexity. *Social Work, 43*, 357–372.

Watson, P. J., Hood, R. W., Morris, R. J., & Hall, J. R. (1985). Religiosity, sin and self-esteem. *Journal of Psychology and Theology, 13*, 116–128.

Webber, A., & Orcutt, J. D. (1984). Employer's reactions to racial and psychiatric stigmata: A field experiment. *Deviant Behavior, 5*, 327–336.

Weiner, B. (1980a). A cognitive (attribution)-emotion-action model of motivated behavior: An analysis of judgments of help-giving. *Journal of Personality and Social Psychology, 39*, 186–200.

Weiner, B. (1980b). May I borrow your class notes? An attributional analysis of judgments of help giving in an achievement-related context. *Journal of Educational Psychology, 72*, 676–681.

Weiner, B. (1983). Some methodological pitfalls in attributional research. *Journal of Educational Psychology, 75*, 530–543.

Weiner, B. (1993). On sin versus sickness: A theory of perceived responsibility and social motivation. *American Psychologist, 48*, 957–965.

Weiner, B. (1995). *Judgments of responsibility: A foundation for a theory of social conduct.* New York, NY: Guilford Press.

Weiner, B., Graham, S., & Chandler, C. (1982). Pity, anger, and guilt: An attributional analysis. *Personality and Social Psychology Bulletin, 8*(2), 226–232.

Weiner, B., Perry, R. P., & Magnusson, J. (1988). An attributional analysis of reactions to stigmas. *Journal of Personality and Social Psychology, 55*, 738–748.

Wiley, M. L. (1952). *The subtle knot: Creative skepticism in seventeenth century England.* Cambridge, MA: Harvard University Press.

Wills, T. A. (1991). Similarity and self-esteem in downward comparison. In J. Sulls & T. A. Wills (Eds.), *Social comparison: Contemporary theory and research* (pp. 51–78). Hillsdale, NJ: Erlbaum.

Wright, J. D., & Rossi, P. H. (1986). *Armed and considered dangerous.* Hawthorne, NY: Aldine de Gruyter.

9

STIGMA AND THE POLICE

AMY C. WATSON, VICTOR OTTATI, ARTHUR LURIGIO,
AND MARK HEYRMAN

The number of individuals with mental illness involved with the criminal justice system has increased over the past 40 years. Several factors have influenced this growth, including the deinstitutionalization movement, changes in commitment laws, tougher drug control laws (Lurigio, 2001), and general attitudes of "lock 'em up" (Lamb & Weinberger, 1998; Teplin, 1983). Regardless of the reason, the criminal justice system is dealing with more and more individuals with mental illness. According to recent studies, 2.7% to 5.9% of individuals considered suspects by police (Engel & Silver, 2001; Teplin & Pruett, 1992), 7% of all police contacts (Borum, Deane, Steadman, & Morrisey, 1998; Deane, Steadman, Borum, Veysey, & Morrisey, 1999), and between 6% and 15% of the prison and jail populations in the United States have a serious mental illness (Ditton, 1999; Lamb & Weinberger, 1998; Teplin, Abram, & McClelland, 1996, 1997).

Police officers are usually the first point of contact with the criminal justice system, and as a result have become the gatekeepers of the both the criminal justice and mental health systems. Although the majority strive to be impartial in their dealings with all segments of the population, they may be prone to negative stereotypes and prejudices about individuals with mental illness. Given that police officers make daily decisions that affect the liberty, freedom, and well-being of others, it is important to understand to what extent they endorse negative stereotypes about persons with mental illness and how these attitudes influence the decisions they make and actions they take in the course of their work.

Little direct research has examined the attitudes of police officers toward persons with mental illness. However, social psychological research on stereotypes and prejudice provides a basis for understanding officer attitudes and behavior in relation to individuals with mental illness. After discussing the growing numbers of persons with mental illness coming in contact with the police, we summarize relevant social psychological research as it applies to law enforcement personnel. We then examine the existing literature on police decision making as it relates to persons with mental illness and how stigma can affect these decisions and the consequent behaviors. We conclude by discussing additional stigmatized statuses that may be occupied by persons with mental illness who come in contact with the police.

INVOLVEMENT OF PERSONS WITH MENTAL ILLNESS IN THE CRIMINAL JUSTICE SYSTEM

Studies of the prevalence of people with serious mental illness in jails across the country have found rates between 6% and 15% (Ditton, 1999; Lamb & Weinberger, 1998; Teplin, Abram, & McClelland, 1996, 1997). According to one account, these numbers represent a 154% increase in the proportion of persons with mental illness in jail between 1980 and 1992 (Travis, 1997). Some evidence suggests that the large and disproportionate numbers of individuals with mental illness in our jails and prisons is attributable to the criminalization of mental illness (Teplin, 1984). Criminalization refers to the movement of persons who would have been treated previously in mental health programs into the criminal justice system for reasons other than increased criminality (Lamb & Grant, 1982; Teplin, 1984). Some research suggests that people exhibiting symptoms and signs of serious mental illness are more likely than others to be arrested by police (Teplin, 1984), and, if taken to jail, to spend more time than people without serious mental illnesses (Steadman, McCarty, & Morrisey, 1989). A number of causes for the increase in arrest rates have been cited. Changes in mental health laws have made civil commitment criteria more stringent and strengthened the right to refuse treatment, making mandated treatment more difficult to impose (Lamb & Weinberger, 1998). Hence, many individuals who previously would have been hospitalized and treated against their wishes may now choose to remain untreated in the community and may come to the attention of the police. At the same time, the number of available public hospital beds has been dramatically reduced and access to services in the community is limited (Belcher,

1988; Jemelka, Trupin, & Chiles, 1989; Lamb, Weinberger, & Gross, 1999; Steadman, Morris, & Dennis, 1995). Thus, even individuals who would prefer treatment have difficulty accessing services. Added to the shortage of services is the increasing public fear of individuals with mental illness (Martin, Pescosolido, & Tuch, 2000) and growing intolerance of offenders that has led to harsher laws and has hampered effective treatment planning for offenders with mental illness (Jemelka et al., 1989; Lamb & Weinberger, 1998). Drug laws, in particular, may be responsible for much of the increase, given the high rate of comorbid substance abuse disorders among individuals with mental illness (Lurigio, 2001).

Police Contact

Recent studies of law enforcement indicate that 2.7% to 5.9% of individuals considered suspects by police have a serious mental illness (Engel & Silver, 2001; Teplin & Pruett, 1992). Including contacts with persons with mental illness in other roles, medium and large police departments estimate that 7% of their contacts with the public involve persons with mental illness (Borum et al., 1998; Deane et al., 1999).

When officers encounter persons with mental illness, they have discretion regarding the appropriate disposition of the contact. They may choose formal actions such as arrest or transport to the hospital for psychiatric evaluation, or informal action such as a verbal warning or referral to services. In effect, police officers have become the gatekeepers of the criminal justice and mental health systems. Their perceptions and actions have important implications in terms of whether individuals receive treatment, remain in their current situation, or face the problems inherent in a criminal justice system ill prepared to their needs (Bittner, 1967; National Counsel of State Governments, 2002; Pogrebin, 1987; Teplin & Pruett, 1992; Wachholz & Mullaly, 1993). Therefore, it is crucial that we understand how police officers' attitudes and beliefs shape these decisions. Social psychological research on prejudice and discrimination provides a useful lens for examining these issues.

IMPLICATIONS OF SOCIAL PSYCHOLOGICAL RESEARCH

Although rarely addressing mental illness stigma, social psychological research regarding stereotyping and prejudice is vast and comprehensive (Fiske, 1998; Hamilton & Sherman, 1994). To examine how this literature is relevant to the topic at hand, we distinguish between the formation of group stereotypes and the application of a group stereotypes when judging an individual group member. In this context, the first topic concerns the process whereby police officers form prejudicial stereotypes of persons with mental illness as a *social group*. The second topic concerns the process whereby these group stereotypes elicit prejudice and discrimination against an *individual* with mental illness. Hence, we summarize relevant social psychological research in these domains and consider the implications for understanding mental illness stigma among police officers.

The Formation of Group Stereotypes and Prejudice

Research has considered the motivational and cognitive determinants of group stereotypes and prejudice. The motivational models relevant to our concerns have adopted an *individual difference* or *personality* approach. These approaches assume that individuals vary considerably in their propensities to exhibit prejudice or discrimination. Traditional work in this area emphasized the role of *authoritarianism*, a personality trait marked by submission to authority, strict adherence to middle class norms, rigid thinking, and aggression toward nonconventional persons (Adorno, Frenkel-Brunswik, Levinson, & Stanford, 1950). The authoritarian personality is presumed to arise out of childhood socialization experiences that are shaped by a strict, punitive, and dominant parent who demands absolute obedience, conformity, and submissiveness in the child. The child, unable to acknowledge or express any anger toward the parent, displaces aggression toward minority groups who deviate from the powerful majority. Right-wing authoritarianism is correlated with anti-Black prejudice, homophobia, and anti-immigration prejudice (Altemeyer, 1996; Duckitt, 1993; Haddock, Zanna, & Esses, 1993; McFarland & Adelson, 1996; Peterson, Doty, & Winter, 1993; Whitley, 1999; Zick & Pretzel, 1999).

More recent work suggests that individual differences in "social dominance orientation" also underlie prejudice and racism (Pratto & Cathey, 2002). According to this perspective, societies are organized as group-based social hierarchies (Lenski, 1984; Murdock, 1956). Subordinate groups and individuals are socialized to be inclusive, empathic, respectful, and to develop a preference for group inclusion and equality. Dominant groups and individuals are socialized to be competitive and status oriented, and to develop a preference for differentiation of groups along a power dimension that allows for group dominance (Pratto, Sidanius, Stallworth, & Malle, 1994). Prejudice against less powerful minorities is derived from this more fundamental social dominance orientation.

Both the authoritarian and social dominance approaches raise concerns about mental illness stigma in the criminal justice system. According to theory, prejudice is most likely to be directed toward members of society who are outside the mainstream or who occupy a relatively low position in the social hierarchy. Clearly, people with mental illness constitute such a group. Moreover, these approaches suggest that individuals who score high on authoritarianism or social dominance orientation will be attracted to social roles and institutions that maintain a clear sense of hierarchy. Law enforcement epitomizes this kind of "hierarchy-enhancing" institution (Pratto, Stallworth, &

Sidanius, 1997; Sidanius & Pratto, 1999). Thus, it is unsurprising that social dominance orientation is relatively high among law enforcement professionals (Pratto et al., 1997; Sidanius & Pratto, 1999; see Allport, 1954/1979 and Ottati, Triandis, & Hui, 1999 for related evidence regarding the military). Given that law enforcement personnel tend to be relatively high in authoritarianism and social dominance orientation, they might be especially likely to stigmatize people with mental illness.

Cognitive Formation of Group Stereotypes

Whereas the research discussed previously emphasizes deeply rooted personality motivations, other research has focused on the cognitive determinants of stereotyping and prejudice. These approaches define stereotypes as a natural consequence of categorization, a basic cognitive process that is necessary for survival (Allport, 1954/1979; Taylor & Dear, 1981). Humans are unlikely to perceive each and every instance of a category as a completely unique and distinct event. To do so would plunge the individual into a perpetual state of information overload. To make the onslaught of stimulus information manageable, the human brain is necessarily equipped with a tendency to group similar stimuli into a common group or category. Thus, one perceives all of the chairs in an auditorium as members of a single category, and thereby responds to one chair much like another. This fundamental tendency, which is required for survival, becomes the process of group stereotyping when people are substituted for chairs. Related to the basic categorization perspective is the "kernel of truth" hypothesis. From this perspective, stereotypes are rational categories that are derived from, and therefore accurately reflect, actual group characteristics (Allport, 1954/1979; Campel, 1967). Stereotype accuracy is implicated when (a) multiple groups converge on a common stereotype of a target group, (b) the stereotype of a target group converges with that target group's self-image, or (c) the stereotype of the target group converges with more objective assessments of the target group (Lee & Ottati, 1995). Evidence of these forms of convergence has been reported for gender stereotypes and stereotypes of a variety of occupational and ethnic groups (Lee & Ottati, 1995).

Stereotypes of persons with mental illness appear to grossly exaggerate the degree to which they are bizarre, dangerous, incompetent, and irresponsible (Harding, Zubin, & Strauss, 1992; Link, Phelan, Bresnahan, Stueve, & Pescosolido, 1999; Steadman et al., 1998). Moreover, impressions of persons with mental illness often underestimate the range of variability that characterizes the group (Corrigan, Watson, & Ottati, in press). Inaccurate stereotyping of persons with mental illness is prevalent in the general population and also exists within the mental health professions (Keane, 1990; Lyons & Ziviani, 1995; Page, 1980; Scott & Philip, 1985). It is unlikely that criminal justice professionals will fare any better in terms of their view of persons with mental illness.

If stereotypes of people with mental illness are indeed inaccurate or exaggerated, one might ask how this came to be. The motivational approaches we described earlier provide an affectively driven answer to this question. Negative distortions in perceptions of persons with mental illness serve an emotional need or motive. Moreover, because police officers tend to be high in social dominance orientation, negatively distorted perceptions of persons with mental illness should be quite prevalent in this group of perceivers. However, distorted stereotypes of persons with mental illness can also result from nonmotivational, cognitive biases. It has long been recognized that readily available and accessible information exerts an especially strong impact on social judgments (Tversky & Kahneman, 1973; Wyer & Srull, 1989). This tendency produces distorted stereotypes when accessible information pertaining to a social group is unrepresentative of that group. Many reasons exist why this might be the case for persons with mental illness. Although individuals with mental illness are commonly no more dangerous than the typical teenager (Link et al., 1999), televised programs suggest that the vast majority of individuals with mental illness are dangerous, homicidal maniacs (Wahl & Lefkowits, 1989). In other words, the television viewer is selectively exposed to a biased sample of persons with mental illness, a sample that is considerably more dangerous than the average person with mental illness (see Ottati, Wyer, Deiger, & Houston, 2002, for a discussion of selective exposure). This form of biased, selective exposure increases the availability and accessibility of dangerous examples of individuals with mental illness, which in turn produces a stereotype of persons with mental illness that exaggerates their overall level of dangerousness (Smith, 1992). Little reason exists to believe that police officers would be immune to this media-based process.

Of course, the accessibility of exemplar model that we outlined earlier is not solely applicable to media-induced exposure. Even when attention is directed away from the media, it is possible for individuals to encounter a biased sample of information pertaining to persons with mental illness. For example, certain occupations might predispose one to encounter a biased sample of information pertaining to this group. Indeed, this is one reason why mental health professionals possess an overly pessimistic and negative view of persons with mental illness, a view that has been coined the "clinician's illusion" (Harding & Zahniser, 1994; Harding, Zubin, & Strauss, 1992). Clinicians are most frequently exposed to individuals with mental illness who require extensive clinical attention for psychological disorders that persist for long periods of time. Of course, this sample of persons with mental illness is less functional and more impaired than the average individual with mental illness. Thus, it is not surprising that stereotypes of the persons with mental illness are unrealistically negative among mental health professionals. The same logic should apply to police officers. They are selectively exposed to individuals with mental illness who are in crisis and have committed crimes. This sample is probably more dangerous than the average person with mental illness. Thus, one would expect police officers would exaggerate the risk of dangerousness among persons with mental illness.

Applying the Group Stereotype to a Specific Group Member

Even if a group stereotype has been formed, it is not necessarily applied when a perceiver judges an individual group member. Impressions of the group member can be based on piecemeal processing of the individual's personal attributes (Brewer, 1988; Fiske, 1998). When the perceiver engages in this more careful form of processing, the target person is viewed as an individual, not merely a group member. This piecemeal or personalized mode of processing, however, requires adequate levels of cognitive capacity and motivation (Brewer, 1988; Fiske, 1998). When capacity or motivation is limited, the perceiver is likely to engage in category-based processing. Category-based processing involves categorizing the individual as a group member and simply applying the group stereotype when judging an individual group member. That is, the perceiver judges a group member based on a stereotype of the group average. This is especially likely to occur when a group label is explicitly presented and the group member seems to be typical of the social category.

To what extent are police officers likely to use category-based processing when judging or responding to an individual with mental illness? To answer this question, it is useful to consider how their occupational status might influence their motivation or capacity to engage in piecemeal processing. Police officers may be highly motivated to arrive at accurate and personalized impressions of the individuals with mental illness they encounter. After all, the legal system explicitly outlaws a multitude of discriminatory practices and, as such, police might be especially likely to avoid the use of stereotypes. On the other hand, police may not construe persons with mental illness as being stigmatized to the same degree as other groups (e.g., Blacks, Muslims), and therefore might be less likely to actively suppress stereotyping of individuals with mental illness.

Related research raises additional concerns regarding motivation to suppress stereotyping of minority groups among police. Specifically, it has been demonstrated that individuals in positions of power are more likely to rely on category-based processing than are individuals in subordinate positions (Fiske, 1998). For example, a driver that has been pulled over by an officer would be motivated to note details about the officer (perhaps to determine how to influence the officer not to give a ticket), whereas the officer is less motivated to notice specifics about each driver he stops for a traffic violation. Presumably, this effect emerges because the driver cannot significantly influence the outcomes of the officer, and therefore is unlikely to motivate the officer to arrive at a detailed individualized judgment. Of course, contact between police officers and persons with mental illness commonly occurs in settings in which the officers occupy the position of greater power. This increases the likelihood that a police officer will apply a group stereotype when judging a specific person with mental illness.

As previously noted, limitations in cognitive capacity can induce category-based processing (Fiske, 1998). Information overload, a need to attend to multiple tasks simultaneously, time pressure, or simple distraction can all serve to reduce cognitive resources that might otherwise be allocated to piecemeal processing of information about an individual. Police officers face many of these challenges. They must make snap judgments when pursuing suspects (e.g., "Is that a gun in the suspect's hand?") and be aware of all aspects of their environment. Under these conditions, police officers are likely to rely on the simple application of a group stereotype when judging or responding to a specific person with mental illness.

Even when individuals engage in piecemeal processing, it is possible for an activated stereotype to bias the nature of this processing. A variety of information processing biases can result in judgments of a group member that are assimilated toward the group stereotype. These include selective encoding, biased interpretation or attribution, and biased retrieval (Wyer & Srull, 1989). Selective encoding refers to a process whereby stereotype-consistent information is more likely to be encoded into memory than stereotype-inconsistent information. For example, aggressive behaviors that imply a person with mental illness is dangerous might be more likely to be encoded than other less aggressive behaviors. Biases in attribution might lead the perceiver to attribute aggressive behavior to the dispositional makeup of a person with mental illness. When performed by a "normal" person, the same aggressive behavior might be attributed to situational factors (Crocker, Hannah, & Weber, 1983). Selective retrieval refers to stereotype-consistent information more likely being retrieved (and used for purposes of forming a judgment) than stereotype-inconsistent information. For example, although only 2% of the behaviors of a person with mental illness might be aggressive, 25% of the behaviors retrieved by the perceiver might imply aggressiveness. Selective encoding, biased interpretation, and selective retrieval may all result in judgments of a specific individual that are assimilated toward a stereotype.

These biases might be viewed as a "closed-minded" attempt to maintain a prejudicial attitude toward persons with mental illness. However, even individuals who are motivated to arrive at an accurate assessment of a person can be susceptible to these cognitive biases. This is because all of these biases can be triggered by the activation of a group stereotype. According to this nonmotivational perspective, the mere recognition that an individual is "mentally ill" activates a stereotype that increases the cognitive accessibility of traits commonly associated with this social category (e.g., incompetent, dangerous). When relevant to the task at hand, these accessible traits will guide the encoding, interpretation, and retrieval of information pertaining to a specific individual with mental illness (Wyer & Srull, 1989). This purely cognitive account of biased processing has disturbing implications. Even police officers who are motivated to engage in piecemeal processing might form judgments that are shaped by stereotypes about mental illness.

Changing the Impact of Group Stereotypes

Some individuals might recognize that activation of a group stereotype has produced a biased judgment of a group member. When this awareness is accompanied by the motivation and ability to eliminate this bias, individuals can engage in a process of correction. For example, if officers recognize that their initial assessments of individuals with mental illness are negatively biased, they can reinterpret the behaviors in an alternative manner (Martin, 1986) or attempt to "subtract" out the bias to arrive at revised and uncontaminated judgments (Petty, Wegener, & Fabrigar, 1997). Such persons might underestimate, correctly estimate, or overestimate the degree to which the initial judgments were biased (Petty et al., 1997). If the initial biases are underestimated, correction will be insufficient and the judgment of this group will remain (albeit to a lesser extent) negatively biased. If the initial biases are correctly estimated, correction should eliminate the bias. If the initial biases are over-estimated, over-corrections will lead to biases in the opposite direction. In this case, a person with mental illness might be judged as less dangerous than would an otherwise identical individual who has no "mentally ill" label.

This discussion suggests that elimination of stereotype induced biases requires that the perceiver possess the *conjunction* of the following: (a) awareness that the initial judgment is biased, (b) motivation to correct for the bias, (c) ability or capacity to correct for the bias, and (d) correct estimation of the direction and amount of the initial bias. When any of these conditions are absent, judgments of a individual with mental illness will differ from that of an otherwise identical "normal" person. In the absence of empirical evidence, it would be premature to arrive at conclusions regarding the degree to which police might judge individuals with mental illness in a biased manner. Nevertheless, this model illuminates the multifaceted nature of corrections and the myriad of conditions in which corrections can fail to completely eliminate stereotype-induced bias. Clearly, police officers face a formidable challenge in trying to eliminate prejudice and discrimination when judging and responding to a mentally ill individual.

What does this mean for police officers and persons with mental illness? In the next section, we move beyond theoretical discussions of stereotype formation and application to examine how mental illness stigma can affect the day-to-day decisions and behaviors of police officers.

Issues related to police interactions with persons with mental illness are beginning to gain the attention of policy makers and researchers alike. However, the body of literature remains limited. In this section of the chapter, we review the police literature that is relevant to our concerns and discuss its implications. First, we briefly discuss police culture and personality, concepts that are consistent with the social psychological literature on authoritarianism and social dominance orientation. Then we examine existing studies of factors that influence police decisions pertaining to persons with mental illness and the evidence regarding whether they differentially respond to persons with mental illness. A few studies have directly examined police officer attitudes about persons with mental illness. We examine these studies and discuss the implications of stigma on police decision-making.

Police Personality

Consistent with the previous arguments, the law enforcement literature discusses "police personality" and "police culture" as characterized by conservatism, cynicism, authoritarianism, emotional detachment, secrecy, suspiciousness, social isolation, group loyalty, an "us" versus "them" orientation toward citizens, and aggressive policing style (Manning, 1995; Sparrow, Moore, & Kennedy, 1990; Sykes & Brent, 1980; Tauber, 1970). These are traits that could be especially problematic in interactions with persons with mental illness. Substantial evidence suggests that rather than simply being characteristics of men and women attracted to police work, these qualities result from the occupational stress of the work itself (Crank, 1997; Teahan, 1975). For example, a 1980 study (Teahan, Adams, & Podany), found that officers underwent significant value changes in the first 18 months of service, becoming more emotionally detached, less forgiving of others, and more concerned with achieving inner harmony. A more recent study suggests, however, that instead of a monolithic police "personality," significant variation appears in officer orientation to their role and to the citizenry (Paoline, Myers, & Worden, 2000). The authors suggest that changes in the composition of police personnel in terms of race, education, and gender, and promulgation of community policing approaches is eroding the traditional police culture, if it ever truly existed. Thus, police officer attitudes about citizens in general, and specific lower status groups, may not be as negative as conventional wisdom might suggest. However, given their authority and *de facto* gatekeeping role, any act of bias on a police officer's part can have extremely severe consequences. Therefore, officers must be especially aware of how their personal biases influence interactions with members of stigmatized groups such as persons with mental illness.

Factors Influencing Officer Decisions

What explains the decisions police officers make in situations involving persons with mental illness? Although they did not focus on officer attitudes or stigma, several studies have examined situational and individual factors that influence police officers' decisions to arrest, informally handle, or divert individuals with mental illness. Their findings suggest that police are more likely to arrest individuals with mental illness when evidence of a crime exists; when the individual has a criminal history (Green, 1997); when they feel the individual is unacceptable to the hospital or other care-taking systems; when public encounters exceed the community's tolerance for deviant behavior; and when it is likely the person will continue to cause a problem (Teplin, 1983). Additionally, less experienced officers are more likely to arrest persons with mental illness than their more experienced colleagues (Green, 1997). Officers are more likely to file for commitment when persons with mental illness show extreme behaviors and symptoms or when a person in an instrumental position, such as a doctor or employer, requests commitment (Bittner, 1967), and least likely to take formal action when no evidence of a crime exists and the person is homeless (Green, 1997). More experienced officers are the most likely to take no action: formal or informal (Green, 1997).

Differential Treatment?

The evidence regarding whether officers are more likely to arrest individuals with mental illness than non-mentally ill others is equivocal. In her landmark 1983 study, Teplin found that police were more likely to arrest suspects that had a mental illness than suspects without mental illness. More recent data suggest that police are not more likely to arrest individuals with mental illness (Engel & Silver, 2001). Data from 1996 to 1997 indicate that odds of arrest were reduced by a factor of 2.9 if the suspect had a mental illness. Factors that increased the odds of arrest included being male, under the influence of drugs or alcohol, disrespectful to the officer, noncompliant, known to police, fighting with a citizen or the officer, possessing a weapon, or committing a serious offense. One possible explanation for the contradictory findings is that between the late 1970s, when Teplin collected her data, and 1996–1997, police policies and training became more geared toward diverting individuals with mental illness to services. Different criteria for determining whether individuals were mentally ill may also have contributed to the different findings. Teplin had field interviewers screen participants for signs of mental illness. They identified individuals as having a mental illness whom the officers did not. Engel and Silver only had information regarding whether or not the officer felt the individual had a mental illness.

Findings from studies examining police responses to persons with mental illness as victims are more consistent and suggest that police are less likely to take action on their behalf (Finn & Stalans, 1995; Mastrofski, Snipes, Parks, & Maxwell, 2000; Stalans & Finn, 1995; Watson, Corrigan, & Ottati, 2002). This is particularly disturbing in light of the evidence that persons with mental illness are disproportionately victimized (Chuang, Williams, & Dalby, 1987; Darves-Bornoz, Lemperiere, Degiovanni, & Gaillard, 1995; Hiday, Swartz, Swanson, Borum, & Wagner, 1999; Jacobson, 1989).

Attitudes About Persons With Mental Illness

Since Bittner (1967) described police attitudes toward persons with mental illness as more or less homogeneous, only a few studies have ventured into this area. One recent study (Bolton, 2000) examined officers' perceptions of the dangerousness, credibility, and self-sufficiency of an individual presenting with symptoms of schizophrenia. Officer age, race, and training were related to perceptions of dangerousness, with younger officers, white officers, and officers with less training related to mental illness perceiving more danger. Previous contact with individuals with mental illness was related to increased perceptions of credibility, and departmental focus on community policing was related to increased perceptions of self-sufficiency. Another study of police officers in the Midwest found that officers perceived persons with a mental illness label as more dangerous, less credible, and less responsible for their situation than an identical person without such a label (Watson, Corrigan, & Ottati, 2002).

How Does Mental Illness Stigma Influence Police Decision Making?

On the basis of what is known about mental illness stigma and the existing research on police interactions with individuals with mental illness, we can make some hypotheses about the role that mental illness stigma may play in police decision-making. These hypotheses vary depending on the situation and specific attitude(s) involved (see Exhibit 9.1). Officers who endorse the dangerousness stigma may overestimate the risk of violence associated with mental illness and respond to situations with undue force. Ruiz (1993) suggests that dangerousness is the most prevalent misconception held by police officers about persons with mental illness. He posits that the heightened sense of alert triggered by dispatch codes for mental illness can become a self-fulfilling prophecy. Officers approaching a person with mental illness can inadvertently escalate the situation through threatening body language and speech. Ruiz indicates that a fear of personal injury and a lack of understanding and empathy on behalf of police officers, combined with the difficulty or reluctance to comply with instructions on the part of the person with mental illness, are the leading causes of violent confrontations between the two. Such violent confrontations risk injury to the officer, the individual who is mentally ill, and bystanders.

EXHIBIT 9.1
Implications of Stigma for Police Decisions

	Danger	Responsibility	Credibility
Suspect	Use of force	Arrest vs. services	Willingness to investigate other possible suspects Arrest vs. services
Victim		Willingness to assist or pursue alleged suspect	Willingness to assist or pursue alleged suspect
Person in crisis	Use of force	Willingness to assist Arrest vs. services	Willingness to assist Arrest vs. services
Witness			Source of useful information

Research on helping behavior suggests that officers who believe that individuals are responsible for their illness may be less willing to provide appropriate assistance (Weiner, 1995). Our research on mental illness stigma supports this relationship between responsibility and helping intentions and behaviors (Corrigan et al., 2001; Corrigan, Rowan, Green, Ludin, River, & Uphoff-Wasowski, 2002; Corrigan, Markowitz, Watson, Rowan, & Kubiak, 2003). In terms of police contact with persons with mental illness, this may occur in situations in which an individual needs assistance accessing or referral to mental health or other social services. If an offense has occurred, officers who blame the individual for his or her illness may be more inclined to arrest, even if deferring to mental health services would be more appropriate. Officers may also be less willing to assist individuals with mental illness who are victims of crime, or fulfill their requests to control another citizen (Mastrofski et al., 2000; Watson, Corrigan & Ottati, 2002).

An additional stereotype about mental illness that is relevant to police work relates to credibility. People with mental illness are often viewed as untrustworthy and lacking integrity (Stone & Colella, 1996). Conversely, they may be viewed as incompetent and unable (as opposed to unwilling) to provide reliable information, as suggested in training texts (Harr & Hess, 1998). Several studies have found that perceived credibility of persons with mental illness affects police decisions to arrest or refer to mental health services in domestic violence situations (Finn & Stalans, 1995; Stalans & Finn, 1995). This is particularly important because persons with mental illness are more vulnerable to victimization than members of the general population; however, the crimes committed against them often go unreported (Hiday et al., 1999; Marley & Buila, 1999). Unfortunately, when they do report their crimes, they frequently are viewed as unreliable witnesses and little is done on their behalf (National Counsel of State Governments, 2002). Perceived credibility may also influence the extent to which officers are willing to assist an individual in crisis access appropriate services. If officers dismiss the individual's claims of circumstances requiring aid as not credible, they may be less likely to make an effort to assist. If they do intervene, they may do so in a punitive manner (e.g., coercive treatment, arrest). In the case of a person with mental illness that is a suspect, police may dismiss his or her account of an event and fail to pursue other potential suspects.

Beyond Individual Attitudes: Structural Stigma

The impact of stigma on police decision-making is not limited to the individual attitudes and behaviors of police officers. Some of the previously mentioned research suggests structural factors exist that shape police interactions with individuals with mental illness. Stigma is embedded in many of these social structures. In Teplin's study (1983), for example, police officers reported that time spent working with persons with mental illness was not rewarded within the department. Thus, officers may have an incentive to avoid these situations or dispose of them as quickly as possible in favor of more valued "crime fighting" activity. Formal training and consultation related to mental illness are rarely provided to police officers (Lamb, Shaner, Elliot, DeCuir, & Foltz, 1995). Police officers may arrest persons with mental illness rather than transport them to a hospital or other mental health settings because they lack the experience or training to recognize mental illness.

Even when officers recognize that individuals have a mental illness, they may not divert them to mental health services because they believe these individuals can be served more quickly and efficiently in the criminal justice system. In one recent study, police officers indicated that on average, it takes significantly less time to take offenders with mental illness to jail than to take them to a mental health center or hospital (Falk & Watson, 2001). Police officers reported frustrating experiences with the mental health system, such as unresponsive providers and being refused hospital admissions because of lack of insurance. Police might even take persons with mental illness who have not committed a crime to jail rather than to a community service site if the officer on the scene believes no appropriate community alternatives are available. This practice has been referred to as "mercy booking" (Lamb & Weinberger, 1998).

CONCLUSIONS

Police officers are only the first point of contact with the criminal justice system. Persons with mental illness come in contact with numerous groups of criminal justice professionals as they progress through the system, including jail personnel; judges, prosecutors, defense attorneys and other court personnel; probation and community corrections officers; and prison guards. In each part of the system, decisions are made that influence their opportunities for life and liberty. Thus, the potential for stigma to influence outcomes exists at many points in the process.

As if facing mental illness stigma at each point in the process were not enough of a burden, a large proportion of persons with mental illness who become involved in the criminal justice system face stigma related to substance abuse and dependence. Persons with major psychiatric disorders have high rates of drug abuse and dependence problems (Mueser, Bellack, & Blanchard, 1992; Regier, Narrow, & Rae, 1990). The presence of a co-occurring drug or alcohol use among persons with mental illness probably leads them to be more intensely and perniciously stigmatized. The demonization of drug users as "dope fiends," "potheads," and "junkies" has been pervasive in our country since the beginning of the last century when the federal government began regulating the distribution and sales of narcotics (Hamid, 1998). The President's Commission on Drug Control Policy has furthered this demonization with public service announcements equating drug use with supporting terrorism. Thus, it is unsurprising that recent research suggests that the public blames and fears people with drug and alcohol addictions even more than persons with mental illness (Link et al., 1999).

The disproportionate minority representation in the criminal justice system in this county also suggests that persons with mental illness who become involved may occupy a number of stigmatized statuses related to race, ethnicity, religion, sexual orientation, and socioeconomic status. On the basis of the social psychological model presented earlier, we would expect the attitudes of police officers to be at least as negative as those of the general population. However, the combined effect of multiple stigmas is not known.

REFERENCES

Adorno, T. W., Frenkel-Brunswik, E., Levinson, D. J., & Stanford, R. N. (1950). *The authoritarian personality*. New York: Harper & Row.

Allport, G. W. (1979). *The nature of prejudice*. New York: Doubleday. (Original work published 1954)

Altemeyer, B. (1996). *The authoritarian specter*. Cambridge, MA: Harvard University Press.

Belcher, J. R. (1988). Are jails replacing the mental health system for the homeless mentally ill? *Community Mental Health Journal, 24*(3), 185–195.

Bittner, E. (1967). Police discretion in emergency apprehension of mentally ill persons. *Social Problems, 14*, 278–292.

Bolton, M. J. (2000). *The influence of individual characteristics of police officers and police organizations on perceptions of persons with mental illness.* Unpublished dissertation, Virginia Commonwealth University, Richmond.

Borum, R., Deane, M. W., Steadman, H. J., & Morrisey, J. (1998). Police perspective on responding to mentally ill people in crisis: Perceptions of program effectiveness. *Behavioral Sciences and the Law, 16,* 393–405.

Brewer, M. B. (1988). A dual process model of impression formation. In R. S. Wyer (Ed.), *A dual process model of impression formation. Advances in social cognition.* (Vol. 1, pp. 1–36). Hillsdale, NJ: Erlbaum.

Campel, D. (1967). Stereotypes and the perception of group differences. *American Psychologist, 22,* 817–829.

Chuang, H. T., Williams, R., & Dalby, J. (1987). Criminal behaviour among schizophrenics. *Canadian Journal of Psychiatry, 32,* 255–258.

Corrigan, P. W., Markowitz, F. E., Watson, A. C., Rowan, D., & Kubiak, M. A. (2003). Attribution and dangerousness models of public discrimination towards persons with mental illness. *Journal of Health and Social Behavior, 44,* 162–179

Corrigan, P. W., River, L., Lundin, R. K., Penn, D. L., Uphoff-Wasowski, K., Campion, J., et al. (2001). Three strategies for changing attributions about severe mental illness. *Schizophrenia Bulletin, 27,* 187–195.

Corrigan, P. W., Rowan, D., Green, A., Lundin, R., River, L., Uphoff-Wasowski, K., et al. (2002). Challenging two mental illness stigmas: Personal responsibility and dangerousness. *Schizophrenia Bulletin, 28,* 293–310.

Corrigan, P. W., Watson, A. C., & Ottati, V. (2003). From whence comes mental illness stigma? *International Journal of Social Psychiatry, 49(2),* 142–157.

Crank, J. P. (1997). *Understanding police culture.* Cincinnati, OH: Anderson.

Crocker, J., Hannah, D. B., & Weber, R. (1983). Person memory and causal attributions. *Journal of Personality and Social Psychology, 44,* 55–66.

Darves-Bornoz, J., Lemperiere, T., Degiovanni, A., & Gaillard, P. (1995). Sexual victimization in women with schizophrenia and bipolar disorder. *Social Psychiatry and Psychiatric Epidemiology, 30(2),* 78–84.

Deane, M. W., Steadman, H. J., Borum, R., Veysey, B. M., & Morrisey, J. P. (1999). Emerging partnerships between mental health and law enforcement. *Psychiatric Services, 50,* 99–101.

Ditton, P. M. (1999, July). *Mental health and treatment of inmates and probationers* (Bureau of Justice Assistance Special Report NCJ 174463). Washington, DC: U.S. Department of Justice.

Duckitt, J. (1993). Right-wing authoritarianism among White South African students: Its measurement and correlates. *Journal of Social Psychology, 133,* 553–563.

Engel, R. S., & Silver, E. (2001). Policing mentally disordered suspects: A reexamination of the criminalization hypothesis. *Criminology, 39,* 225–252.

Falk, M. L., & Watson, A. C. (2001). *Police officer perceptions of misdemeanor offenders with mental illness.* Unpublished manuscript.

Finn, M. A., & Stalans, L. J. (1995). Police referrals to shelters and mental health treatment: Examining their decisions in domestic assault cases. *Crime and Delinquency, 41,* 467–480.

Fiske, S. T. (1998). Stereotyping, prejudice, and discrimination. In D. T. Gilbert, S. T. Fiske, & G. Lindzey (Eds.), *The handbook of social psychology* (4th ed., Vol. 2, pp. 357–411). New York: McGraw-Hill.

Green, T. M. (1997). Police as frontline mental health workers: The decision to arrest or refer to mental health agencies. *International Journal of Law and Psychiatry, 20,* 469–486.

Haddock, G., Zanna, M. P., & Esses, V. M. (1993). Assessing the structure of prejudicial attitudes: The case of attitudes toward homosexuals. *Journal of Personality and Social Psychology, 65,* 1105–1118.

Hamid, A. (1998). *Drugs in America: Sociology, economics, and politics.* Gaithersburg, MD: Aspen.

Hamilton, D. L., & Sherman, J. W. (1994). Stereotypes. In R. S. Wyler & T. K. Srull (Eds.), *Handbook of social cognition* (pp. 1–68). Hillsdale, NJ: Erlbaum.

Harding, C. M., & Zahniser, J. H. (1994). Empirical correction of seven myths about schizophrenia with implications for treatment. *Acta Psychiatrica Scandinavica, Supplementum, 90*(384), 140–146.

Harding, C. M., Zubin, J., & Strauss, J. S. (1992). Chronicity in schizophrenia: Revisited. *British Journal of Psychiatry, 16*(Suppl. 18), 27–37.

Harr, J., & Hess, K. (1998). *Constitutional law for criminal justice professionals.* Belmont, CA: West/Wadsworth.

Hiday, V. A., Swartz, M. S., Swanson, J. W., Borum, R., & Wagner, H. (1999). Criminal victimization of persons with severe mental illness. *Psychiatric Services, 50*(1), 62–68.

Jacobson, A. (1989). Physical and sexual assault histories among psychiatric outpatients. *American Journal of Psychiatry, 146,* 755–758.

Jemelka, R., Trupin, E., & Chiles, J. A. (1989). The mentally ill in prisons: A review. *Hospital and Community Psychiatry, 40,* 481–491.

Keane, M. (1990). Contemporary beliefs about mental illness among medical students: Implications for education and practice. *Academic Psychiatry, 14*(3), 172–177.

Lamb, H. R., & Grant, R. W. (1982). The mentally ill in an urban county jail. *Archives of General Psychiatry, 39*(1), 17–22.

Lamb, H. R., Shaner, R., Elliot, D. M., & DeCuir, W., & Fultz, J. T. (1995). Outcome for psychiatric emergency patients seen by an outreach police–mental health team. *Psychiatric Services, 46,* 1267–1271.

Lamb, H. R., & Weinberger, L. E. (1998). Persons with severe mental illness in jails and prisons: A review. *Psychiatric Services, 49,* 483–492.

Lamb, H. R., Weinberger, L. E., & Gross, B. H. (1999). Community treatment of severely mentally ill offenders under the jurisdiction of the criminal justice system: A review. *Psychiatric Services, 50,* 907–913.

Lee, Y.-T., & Ottati, V. (1995). Perceived in-group homogeneity as a function of group membership, salience, and stereotype threat. *Personality and Social Psychology Bulletin, 21*, 610–619.

Lenski, G. E. (1984). *Power and privilege: A theory of social stratification.* Chapel Hill: University of North Carolina Press.

Link, B. G., Phelan, J. C., Bresnahan, M., Stueve, A., & Pescosolido, B. A. (1999). Public conceptions of mental illness: Labels, causes, dangerousness, and social distance. *American Journal of Public Health, 89*, 1328–1333.

Lurigio, A. J. (2001, November). *The mentally ill in the criminal justice system: A review of causes and solutions.* Paper presented at the Chicago Consortium for Stigma Research.

Lyons, M., & Ziviani, J. (1995). Stereotypes, stigma, and mental illness: Learning from fieldwork experiences. *American Journal of Occupational Therapy, 49*, 1002–1008.

Manning, P. K. (1995). Dynamics and tensions in police occupational culture. In W. Baily (Ed.), *The encyclopedia of police science* (pp. 472–475). New York: Garland Publishing.

Marley, J., & Buila, S. (1999). When violence happens to people with mental illness: Disclosing victimization. *American Journal of Orthopsychiatry, 69*, 398–402.

Martin, J. K., Pescosolido, B. A., & Tuch, S. A. (2000). Of fear and loathing: The role of "disturbing behavior," labels, and causal attributions in shaping public attitudes toward people with mental illness. *Journal of Health and Social Behavior, 41*, 208–223.

Martin, L. L. (1986). Set/reset: The use and disuse of concepts in impression formation. *Journal of Personality and Social Psychology, 51*, 493–504.

Mastrofski, S., Snipes, J. B., Parks, R. B., & Maxwell, C. D. (2000). The helping hand of the law: Police control of citizens on request. *Criminology, 38*, 307–342.

McFarland, S. G., & Adelson, S. (1996, July). *An omnibus study of personality, values and prejudices.* Paper presented at the Annual Convention of the International Society for Political Psychology, Vancouver, British Columbia.

Mueser, K. T., Bellack, A. S., & Blanchard, J. J. (1992). Comorbidity of schizophrenia and substance abuse: Implications for treatment. *Journal of Consulting and Clinical Psychology, 60*, 845–856.

Murdock, B. (1956). "Backward" learning in paired associates. *Journal of Experimental Psychology, 51*, 213–215.

National Counsel of State Governments. (2002). *Criminal Justice Mental Health Consensus Project.* Retrieved January 12, 2002, from http://consensusproject.org/

Ottati, V., Triandis, H. C., & Hui, C. (1999). Subjective culture and the workplace: Comparing Hispanic and mainstream naval recruits. In Y.-T. Lee, C. R. McCauley, & J. G. Draguns (Eds.), *Personality and person perception across cultures* (pp. 235–253). Mahwah, NJ: Erlbaum.

Ottati, V., Wyer, R. S., Deiger, M., & Houston, D. (2002). The psychological determinants of candidate evaluation and voting preference. In V. Ottati, R. S. Tindale, D. C. O'Connell, J. Edwards, E. Posavac, Y. Suarez-Balcazar, et al. (Eds.), *The social psychology of politics*. New York: Plenum Press.

Page, S. (1980). Social responsiveness toward mental patients: The general public and others. *Canadian Journal of Psychiatry, 25*, 242–246.

Paoline, E. A., Myers, S. M., & Worden, R. E. (2000). Police culture, individualism, and community policing: Evidence from two police departments. *Justice Quarterly, 17*, 575–605.

Peterson, B. E., Doty, R. M., & Winter, D. G. (1993). Authoritarianism and attitudes toward contemporary social issues. *Personality and Social Psychology Bulletin, 19*, 174–184.

Petty, R. E., Wegener, D. T., & Fabrigar, L. R. (1997). Attitudes and attitude change. *Annual Review of Psychology, 48*, 609–647.

Phelan, J. C., Link, B. G., Stueve, A., & Pescosolido, B. A. (2000). Public conceptions of mental illness in 1950 and 1996: What is mental illness and is it to be feared? *Journal of Health and Social Behavior, 41*, 188–207.

Pogrebin, M. R. (1987). Police responses for mental health assistance. *Psychiatric Quarterly, 58*(1), 66–73.

Pratto, F., & Cathey, C. (2002). The role of social ideologies in legitimizing political attitudes and public policy. In V. C. Ottati, R. S. Tindale, D. C. O'Connell, J. Edmunson, E. Posavac, Y. Suarez-Balcazar, et al. (Eds.), *The social psychology of politics: Social psychological applications to social issues* (pp. 135–155). New York: Plenum Press.

Pratto, F., Sidanius, J., Stallworth, L. M., & Malle, B. F. (1994). Social dominance orientation: A personality variable predicting social and political attitudes. *Journal of Personality and Social Psychology, 67*, 741–763.

Pratto, F., Stallworth, L. M., & Sidanius, J. (1997). The gender gap: Differences in political attitudes and social dominance orientation. *British Journal of Social Psychology, 36*(1), 49–68.

Regier, D. A., Narrow, W. E., & Rae, D. S. (1990). The epidemiology of anxiety disorders: The epidemiological catchment area (ECA) experience. *Journal of Psychiatric Research, 24*(Suppl. 2), 3–14.

Ruiz, J. (1993). An interactive analysis between uniformed law enforcement officers and the mentally ill. *American Journal of Police, 12*(4), 149–177.

Scott, D., & Philip, A. (1985). Attitudes of psychiatric nurses to treatment and patients. *British Journal of Medical Psychology, 58*(2), 169–173.

Sidanius, J., & Pratto, F. (1999). *Social dominance: An intergroup theory of social hierarchy and oppression*. New York: Cambridge University Press.

Smith, E. (1992). The role exemplars in social judgment. In L. L. Martin & A. Tesser (Eds.), *The construction of social judgements*. Hillsdale, NJ: Erlbaum.

Sparrow, M. K., Moore, M. H., & Kennedy, D. M. (1990). *Beyond 911: A new era for policing*. New York: Basic Books.

Stalans, L. J., & Finn, M. A. (1995). How novice and experienced officers interpret wife assaults: Normative and efficiency frames. *Law and Society Review, 29*, 287–321.

Steadman, H. J., McCarty, D. W., & Morrisey, J. P. (1989). *The mentally ill in jail: Planning for essential services*. New York: Guilford Press.

Steadman, H. J., Morris, S. M., & Dennis, D. L. (1995). The diversion of mentally ill persons from jails to community-based services: A profile of programs. *American Journal of Public Health, 85*, 1630–1635.

Steadman, H. J., Mulvey, E. P., Monahan, J., Robbins, P. C., Appelbaum, P. S., Grisso, T., et al. (1998). Violence by people discharged from acute psychiatric inpatient facilities and by others in the same neighborhoods. *Archives of General Psychiatry, 55*, 393–401.

Stone, D., & Colella, A. (1996). A model of factors affecting the treatment of disabled individuals in organizations. *Academy of Management Review, 21*, 352–401.

Sykes, R. E., & Brent, E. E. (1980). The regulation of interaction by police: A systems view of taking charge. *Criminology, 18*(1), 82–97.

Tauber, R. K. (1970). Danger and the police. In M. E. Wolfgang (Ed.), *The sociology of punishment and correction* (pp. 95–104). New York: Wiley.

Taylor, S., & Dear, M. J. (1981). Scaling community attitudes toward the mentally ill. *Schizophrenia Bulletin, 7*, 225–240.

Teahan, J. E. (1975). A longitudinal study of attitude shifts among Black and White police officers. *Journal of Social Issues, 31*(1), 47–56.

Teahan, J. E., Adams, K. M., & Podany, E. C. (1980). A comparison of the value structure of British and U.S. Police. *The International Journal of Social Psychiatry, 26*, 246–254.

Teplin, L. A. (1983). The criminalization of the mentally ill: Speculation in search of data. *Psychological Bulletin, 94*(1), 54–67.

Teplin, L. A. (1984). Criminalizing mental disorder: The comparative arrest rate of the mentally ill. *American Psychologist, 39*, 794–803.

Teplin, L. A., Abram, K. M., & McClelland, G. M. (1996). Prevalence of psychiatric disorders among incarcerated women: Pretrial jail detainees. *Archives of General Psychiatry, 53*, 505–512.

Teplin, L. A., Abram, K. M., & McClelland, G. M. (1997). Mentally disordered women in jail: Who receives services? *American Journal of Public Health, 87*, 604–609.

Teplin, L., & Pruett, N. (1992). Police as streetcorner psychiatrist: Managing the mentally ill. *International Journal of Law and Psychiatry, 15*, 139–156.

Travis, J. (1997, September). *The mentally ill offender: Viewing crime and justice through a different lens*. Speech to the National Association of State Forensic Mental Health Directors, Washington, DC.

Tversky, A., & Kahneman, D. (1973). Availability: A heuristic for judging frequency and probability. *Cognitive Psychology, 5*, 207–232.

Wachholz, S., & Mullaly, R. (1993). Policing the deinstitutionalized mentally ill: Toward an understanding of its function. *Crime, Law and Social Change, 19*, 281–300.

Wahl, O. F., & Lefkowits, J. Y. (1989). Impact of television film on attitudes toward mental illness. *American Journal of Community Psychology, 17*, 521–528.

Watson, A. C., Corrigan, P. W., & Ottati, V. (2002). *Police officer attitudes and decisions regarding persons with mental illness.* Unpublished manuscript.

Weiner, B. (1995). *Judgments of responsibility: A foundation for a theory of social conduct.* New York: Guilford Press.

Whitley, B. E. (1999). Right-wing authoritarianism, social dominance orientation, and prejudice. *Journal of Personality and Social Psychology, 77*(1), 126–134.

Wyer, R. S., & Srull, T. K. (1989). *Memory and cognition in its social context.* Hillsdale, NJ: Erlbaum.

Zick, A., & Pretzel, T. (1999). Authoritarianism, racism, and ideologies about acculturation. *Politics, Groups and the Individual, 8*, 41–64.

10

STIGMA AND SUBSTANCE USE DISORDERS

KENNETH A. RASINSKI, PAMELA WOLL,
AND ANDREA COOKE

In this chapter we investigate the stigma associated with dependence on addictive substances. Although this dependence is considered to be a psychiatric disorder, features of the disorder exist, and social factors are associated with it, that distinguish it from other mental illnesses. These features affect the nature of stigma associated with the disorder—how people with the disorder are viewed and treated and how they view themselves. Moreover, an investigation of these distinguishing features and their relationship to stigma may provide additional elements to the understanding of stigma and mental illness in general.

One distinguishing feature of dependence on addictive substances is that it can occur in the absence or presence of other psychiatric disorders, such as major depression, schizophrenia, or bipolar disorder. In the absence of other disorders, substance dependence may be considered by the public as the most likely of the psychiatric disorders to be outside of the realm of a medical disorder and within the realm of individual choice. According to some theories of stigmatization, this would make the disorder especially likely to be stigmatized by the public (Weiner, 1995, Corrigan et al., 2001). Recent survey data seem to indicate that this is the case. Hypothetical individuals described as substance abusers were rated more negatively than those described as having other psychiatric disorders (Link, Phelan, Stueve, & Pescosolido, 1999).

A complication associated with substance dependence is that it frequently co-occurs with other psychiatric disorders. Surveys of large populations have indicated that a past history of mental disorder more than doubled the risk of alcohol dependence and quadrupled the risk of drug dependence (Regier et al., 1990). The National Comorbidity Survey found about a 50% lifetime co-occurrence rate between substance dependence and mental disorders (Kessler et al., 1994; Ragin, Rasinski, Cerbone, & Johnson, 1999). This has two implications. First, the co-occurrence of two stigmatizing problems, substance dependence and other mental illness, again doubles the chance of stigmatization and magnifies the potential for opportunity loss. Second, the treatment of dual-diagnosis has not been well worked out, leading to a conundrum for persons so afflicted. Treatment providers who are familiar with the substance dependence component may not understand or be trained to deal with other co-occurring psychiatric disorders, and vice versa.

This sets up a difficult situation for both the person with the disorder and the treatment provider that may result, unfortunately, in the expression of stigmatizing attitudes in the provider. Understanding and treatment of dual-diagnosis individuals is a rapidly emerging field in psychiatry. A further difficulty exists. Many people with substance dependence disorders fall afoul of the law. As discussed briefly in the first chapter and again at length in chap. 9, law enforcement officials often do not have the training to deal with the mental illness component of those with dual diagnosis. Thus they are open to the danger of abusive treatment resulting from a system not equipped to cater to their particular needs.

A second distinguishing feature of substance dependence is that it is associated with crime and violence. The procurement of some addictive substances itself is a crime, and public violence and other criminal acts occur more frequently when people are under the influence of drugs or alcohol. This has two implications for stigma. First, any stigmatization associated with illegal acts is potentially carried as baggage by the person with a substance abuse disorder. The dual stigmatization associated with substance dependence, that it is a psychiatric disorder and may involve criminal behavior, makes it more likely that those experiencing the disorder will be affected by the opportunity losses discussed in the first chapter. Second, the widespread perception exists that substance abuse is associated with violent behavior. Thus, fear of harm may be a significant component of public stigmatization of substance dependence.

The preceding discussion indicates the complex nature of stigma associated with substance dependence. To disentangle some of the complexity it is necessary to examine this stigmatization at multiple levels. At one level, societal values exist concerning the use of these substances. These come into play in the public attribution of blame for the disorder. Values are also important in understanding why some addictive substances have been declared illegal, which, of course, has implications for the relationship between substance dependence and the criminal justice system. Second, psychological factors exist related to people's motives and reasons for stigmatizing others. Third, the stigma is internalized by the person with the disorder. All of these interact to define both the phenomenon of stigma and its effect. We begin at the societal level by discussing the relationship between social values and stigma associated with the use of addictive substances, and by exploring briefly some historical factors associated with substance control policies.

PURITANISM AND LIBERTARIANISM AS THE BASES OF STIGMA OF SUBSTANCE DEPENDENCE

The American debate on the legality and use of addictive substances is rooted in value differences (MacCoun & Reuter, 2001). In examining the history of America's relationship with addictive substances, the Puritan ethic (Marsden, 1991) has been associated with early "reform" movements aimed at the use of narcotics and alcohol. For example, according to Musto (1987), the Reverend Brent, an early reformer, took the position that use of illegal substances for purely hedonistic purposes was morally wrong. Because narcotics had neither caloric nor medicinal value, they should be prohibited (Courtwright, 1997; Trebach, 1988).

Not everyone agreed with Brent's view. MacCoun and Reuter (2001) note the Libertarian view that people should be free to do what they want as long as they are not harming others. Modern drug reformers hold the belief that no one has the right to tell others what they can or cannot ingest. If people find pleasure in taking drugs they should be free to engage in this pleasurable behavior as long as no one else is being harmed (see also Weiner, 1981).

Thus, two competing values may be driving the controversy surrounding substance abuse policy in America. The dominant position arises from Puritanism and is associated with policies that restrict access to certain addictive substances. The less common value is Libertarianism, which is subscribed to by modern drug reformers who advocate freedom of choice and who favor the legalization of all drugs. The dominant position seems to be the one most often associated with stigma.

The Origins of Substance Abuse Policy in America

Two historic factors appear to be at the root of substance abuse policy in America: the commercial use of narcotics and fear of immigrant groups with values different from those of the mainstream. Musto (1987) traces the history of addictive substances in the United States to the use of morphine, which is a derivative of opium, by physicians to sedate and ease the pain of wounded soldiers during the Civil War. The addictive properties of morphine were not well known, and physicians of that time had little else to offer their patients for their comfort. However, opium smoking was a common phenomenon in this country even before the Civil War. Veterans who had become addicted to morphine as a result of medical treatment may have helped spread opium use through recruitment of other users, but the medical use of morphine was not the beginning of substance dependence in America (Musto, 1987).

Formal societal responses toward addictive substances began to take hold in response to the wider medical use of narcotics. Formal bureaucratic control over addictive substances arose slowly as a reaction to the social problems caused by physicians' use of "patent medicines," which usually contained narcotics. Opposition to these practices, on the basis of the realization that addiction rates were rising, led to the eventual creation of a set of government regulations about the dispensation of medicines and the labeling of their ingredients. Beginning with the Pure Food and Drug Act of 1906 and culminating in the Harrison Act of 1914, physicians lost control to pharmacists in the dispensation of narcotics through patent medicines. These two acts marked the beginning of government regulation of narcotics.

Historic events and attitudes toward minority groups have also played a role in shaping American attitudes toward illegal substances. Musto (1987) indicates that before and during the Civil War the United States experienced growth in its Chinese population, some of whom smoked opium. This group was viewed with fear and suspicion because some of their values were outside the mainstream. Moreover, they competed for scarce economic resources (jobs), as did other groups (e.g., African Americans, Mexican Americans, Puerto Ricans). Threat to mainstream values and competition formed the basis of beliefs that certain types of drugs caused certain types of undesirable behaviors in these minority groups, leading to repressive enforcement of anti-drug policies (Kassanda & Williams, 1989; Duke, 1990).

MacCoun and Reuter (2001) point out that attitudes and policies about restricting addictive substances are also rooted in societal concerns about personal and social consequences associated with the use of these substances. It is difficult to estimate the health costs related to the use of addictive substances, from nicotine to drugs that are injected, but they are considerable. Heart disease, high blood pressure, cancer, and HIV–AIDS associated with substance abuse impose substantial burdens on our health care system. High social costs are exacted, as well. Drug dealing is associated with violent crime, as is drug use. Drug dealers prey on the poor and help keep them in a state of poverty. Campaigns to "crack down" on drug dealers have swollen the prison population over the past 15 years because of mandatory minimum sentences for drug possession.

Great personal costs also exist. Teenagers become addicted to, die from, or experience permanent brain damage from the use of illicit substances. Intravenous drug users become infected with AIDS or hepatitis C, two deadly diseases for which no cure exists. Other costs to the individuals exist. Recovery from addiction can be an unpleasant and difficult process in many ways, particularly in the early stages of recovery. Alcohol and drug addiction has cost people their jobs, their families, and in some cases their lives.

SOCIAL PSYCHOLOGICAL FACTORS AS THE BASIS OF STIGMA

From a societal view, stigma associated with a substance use disorder may be the result of Puritan elements in our culture, racism, and the desire to reduce harmful consequences associated with the use of certain addictive substances. However, stigma also has roots in individual psychology. As indicated in the introductory chapter of this book, at the psychological level one of the foundations of stigma is the natural tendency of the social perceiver to make category-based judgments (i.e., to engage in stereotyping [Biernat & Dovido, 2000]). That view suggests that stigma, at least in part, is a result of the social perceiver's tendency to judge like things similarly. Stereotyping may aid in processing information, but when it is tinged with negative attitudes, it yields stigma (Corrigan & Penn, 1999).

In addition, social psychologists have argued that people have a natural desire to search for reasons or causes for outcomes (Heider, 1958). According to this view, we stigmatize those with disorders that we can attribute to individual responsibility (Weiner, 1995). This tendency, along with the moralistic Puritan element in our culture, combine to make stigma associated with addictive substances particularly strong.

Note, however, that our natural tendency to categorize and our tendency to attribute outcomes to individual responsibility are not the only reasons we attach stigma to others. When our self-esteem is threatened, we feel better if we have someone to look down on (Crocker & Major, 1989; Wills, 1981). The stereotypical down-and-out alcoholic or drug addict is a perfect target. In addition, when we compete for scarce social resources we may degrade other groups to maintain a position of hegemony for our own group (Jost & Banaji, 1994; Sidanius, 1993). Again, alcoholics and drug addicts become useful targets. As we saw in the discussion of social values, if the undesirable behavior associated with substance use disorders is connected to an ethnic group, and that group poses a threat to resources, then immoderate substance use is one more reason to apply ethnic or racial stigma.

Some scholars argue that the application of a stigma may be a way of marking those individuals who are untrustworthy or unhealthy to associate with, a practice seen as a throwback to early survival skills that required strong group cohesiveness (Kurzban & Leary, 2001). Alcoholics and drug addicts can fit easily into this category because they are often perceived as being irresponsible and untrustworthy. Finally, stigma may be society's attempt to control unwanted social behavior. If certain behavior—for example, the use of cocaine or heroin—has a social stigma attached to it, meaning that those who engage in the behavior are degraded, then it may deter others from engaging in the behavior to avoid the degradation (Braithwaite, 1989).

THE EFFECTS OF STIGMA ON THE PERSON WITH THE SUBSTANCE USE DISORDER

Up to this point we have explored the origins of stigma associated with substance use disorders. Studies have shown that the stigma of those with mental illness is prevalent (Corrigan & Penn, 1999; Link, 1987) and that it affects the quality of life and opportunity structure of the stigmatized person (Alisky & Iczkowski, 1990; Link, 1987; Steadman, 1981). If people with mental illnesses are affected by stigma, we assume that people with substance use disorders are affected even more. Studies have shown that people with substance use disorders are evaluated *more* negatively than those with other mental or physical illnesses (Corrigan et al., 2001; Link, Phelan, Stueve, & Pescosolido, 1999). What little empirical research has been conducted on this topic indicates that the problem is long-standing. Link and his colleagues have shown that stigma associated with drug addiction and mental illness can affect the well-being of those who have been drug free for years (Link, Stuening, Rahav, Phelan, & Nuttbrock, 1997).

Stigma results in discrimination that, in turn, restricts access to resources, even those resources that might help the person with the substance use disorder. Thus, stigma may contribute to inadequate access to treatment facilities (White, 1998). Addiction treatment has suffered, and continues to suffer, severe losses in funding and reimbursement, with resulting losses in treatment availability. For example, most employer-provided health insurance policies are requiring greater cost-sharing, copayments, and deductibles from patients receiving substance-related services, and covering fewer visits or days in treatment, with lower annual and lifetime expenditure limits (Centers for Disease Control and Prevention, 2002a). Managed care policies have decreased the types, length, and intensity of treatment services provided and reduced coverage of essential complementary services, such as psychological counseling and aid with medical, legal, financial, and job-related issues (Centers for Disease Control and Prevention, 2002a). In a survey of people recovering from substance use disorders (Hart Research Associates, 2001), 40% cited the cost of treatment or the lack of insurance as a major obstacle to recovery.

Is this trend toward decreasing coverage simply an essential cost-management policy? The answer to this question seems to be no. A review by the National Council on Alcoholism and Drug Disorders concludes that parity in coverage of addiction treatment would increase insurance premiums by only $5.11 per person per year (Sturm, 1999). Other studies estimate the cost increase at less than $1 per family per month (Milliman & Robertson, 1997), or .2% per year (SAMHSA, 1998). In addition, it is estimated that there would be a potential savings in overall health care costs (an estimated $5 saved for every $1 spent on addiction treatment) and costs related to crime and criminal justice ($7 saved for every $1 spent [National Institute on Drug Abuse, 1999]). Thus, it is difficult to call the trend toward noncoverage of addiction treatment a cost-saving measure. Instead, stigma may be the force that drives this trend.

In his discussion of societal positions on substance use disorders, White (1998) predicted that the availability of substance abuse treatment would continue to decrease over the coming years. That prediction seems to have some support. The SAMHSA national directory of residential treatment centers, which held 25,000 programs in 1998, now holds 8,800 programs ("Treatment Spending Shrinks," n.d.). The Centers for Disease Control and Prevention reports that of the estimated 13 to 16 million people who need substance abuse treatment each year, only 3 million receive it (Centers for Disease Control and Prevention, 2002b); of the estimated 600,000 people with opiate addictions in 1997, less than 20% were receiving methadone treatment (Centers for Disease Control and Prevention, 2002a); and of the estimated 800,000 people in the criminal justice system who need substance abuse treatment, fewer than 150,000 receive it (Centers for Disease Control and Prevention, 2002a).

Unfortunately, stigma has also been observed among human service providers. White (1998) contends that service providers' contempt for people with substance use disorders has had a negative effect on the quality of treatment. This contempt is most pronounced in staff attitudes—even staff of methadone clinics—toward people receiving methadone treatment for opiate addiction. A director of a clinic in Georgia is quoted as saying, "It is no big surprise that methadone is stigmatized. During one of my first contacts with a staff member at another clinic, I was told never to forget that the patients are all liars, cheats, and thieves" ("The Ghost Haunting Methadone," 1996, p. 1).

Such contempt and stigma have a negative effect on treatment regimes. Studies have shown that approximately half of all methadone programs use subtherapeutic doses, which results in premature withdrawal; methadone professionals show substantial ambivalence about methadone treatment; and people become disillusioned with using methadone as a form of treatment when they encounter negative attitudes from program staff (Woods, 2001).

Programs that limit methadone doses and treatment duration have been associated with increased heroin use during treatment, decreased retention, and earlier relapse after discharge (Caplehorn, Irwig, & Saunders, 1996).

In complicated ways, stigma also affects the person with a substance use disorder from within. Symbolic interactionists have maintained that we construct our identity from our situation, place, or role in society and from the way others perceive and treat us (Mead, 1934). If society takes a negative view of the person who has a substance use disorder, that person may view him- or herself negatively. Negative behavioral consequences can result from negative self-expectations (Steele, 1997). Internalized self-stigma may be a natural development for people with substance use disorders who were raised in a society that heavily stigmatizes addiction. In many cases, they may have learned to embrace the prevalent stigmatizing attitudes long before they began to develop symptoms of substance use disorders. Even after the onset of these disorders, people often retain and maintain socially conferred self-stigma (Williams, 1976).

Corrigan and Lundin (2001) named a number of psychological effects of self-stigma in people with mental illnesses. These included low self-esteem, feelings of unworthiness, low levels of confidence, increased numbers of problems and disabilities stemming from their disorders, a questioning of fundamental goals, guilt, loss of hope, and difficulty identifying with specific tasks (e.g., school, work, social interactions). Given the increased sense of personal blame often associated with substance use disorders, one can speculate that feelings of unworthiness and guilt might be even more severe with these disorders.

Factors That Increase Stigma and Its Effects

The stigma associated with substance use disorders takes place in a society that is already segmented, stratified, and complicated by the attachment of stigma to multiple demographic and situational characteristics. A number of factors can increase the impact of stigma and self-stigma on the individual. Among these are socioeconomic status, race, gender, age, the particular drug of use, and the co-occurrence of mental illness.

Those with fewer economic resources are less likely to be able to resist a stigmatizing label or to challenge the organizational body that is applying the label (Substance Abuse Network of Ontario, 1999). History and current events provide ample evidence of the disproportionate application of substance-related stigma to people of color (White, 1998). For example, African Americans make up only 15% of users of illegal drugs, but they are the targets of 37% of drug arrests, 42% of federal drug-related prison terms, and 60% of state felony drug prison terms (White, 2001). Many women with substance use problems are assumed to be sexually promiscuous (Woll & Gorsky, 1995), and so are targets of a double stigma, whether or not promis-

cuity is a factor. Most older adults spent their formative years in social settings in which addiction was stigmatized even more heavily and more rigidly
than it is today, and with less scientific information to counter the stigma
(White, 1998). Many older adults with substance use problems feel the self-
stigma more severely (Substance Abuse and Aging Committee, 2001).

A number of factors often add layers of stigma and self-stigma to the addictive use of a particular drug, including the drug's legal status, its route of entry
(e.g., injection), or its association with poverty and criminal subcultures in public perception (as in the case of crack cocaine or heroin [Woll, 2001]). In cases
of multiple stigmatized conditions, the effects of stigma can be greater than the
sum of its parts. In a study of stigma's effects on men with co-occurring psychiatric and substance use disorders, Link, Struening, Rahav, Phelan, and Nuttbrock (1997) found that 70% of participants reported experiencing four or
more types of rejection and that 65% assumed that most people would look
down on them. Link and colleagues also found that the effects of stigma were
unchanged even after one year's successful treatment for both conditions.

Even successful recovery from substance use disorders does not exempt
people from the psychological effects of stigma and self-stigma. In the survey
of people in recovery, 39% of respondents reported having experienced
shame or embarrassment about being in recovery, and 37% reported that they
had at first been concerned that others might find out they were seeking help
(Hart & Associates, 2001).

Impact on Seeking and Acceptance of Help

Given the multiple negative effects of stigma, one might imagine that
the desire to avoid it would propel large numbers of people into treatment
centers and mutual-help recovery groups. However, evidence suggests that
the result is precisely the opposite; in many cases, both societal and self-
stigma may render people less likely to seek or accept help. In the survey of
people in recovery (Hart & Associates, 2001), 63% asserted that shame and
discrimination hindered their recovery.

Belonging to a stigmatized group does not necessarily mean that one
accepts the stigma or is continually affected by it (Corrigan & Watson, 2002;
Crocker & Quinn, 2000). From the symbolic interactionist perspective
(Mead, 1934) a person with a substance use disorder may avoid the debilitating effects of self-stigma by focusing on areas in his life in which he has
been, or is, successful. We believe that three problems exist with this model
of resisting stigma for people with a substance use disorder. First, societal attitudes about the chronic use of illegal substances are extensive and would be
difficult to ignore. Indeed, they may, as we have argued, be part of the moral
fabric of our society. Second, it is likely that, over time, the person with an
active substance use disorder will have fewer and fewer successes in other
areas. Third, self-esteem, like other attitudes, may not be as ephemeral as
Crocker and Quinn (2000) assert. When society continually reminds one

about a problem, and one has that problem, negative attitudes about the self, leading to negative self-esteem, may become highly accessible (Fazio, 1989) because of the continual reminders.

As one way to protect their self-esteem, individuals with substance use disorders may engage in another psychological mechanism, that of denial. The term "denial" may refer to a number of cognitive processes, including rationalization, minimization of problems, comparison with others who have worse problems, and defocusing from the disorder or its consequences (Gorski & Grinstead, 2000; White, 1996). The concept of denial itself might be thought of as stigmatizing, in that it implies that the denial is a conscious or volitional act. One might better think of denial as a lack of insight.

The connection between social stigma and denial can be partially explained in terms of a process that Goffman (1963) characterized as stigma management. People may protect themselves from the pain of identification with a stigmatized condition by denying the condition or its impact on their lives and the lives of others (Williams, 1976). The more extreme or objectionable the associations connected with the stigma, the harder it is to identify with the condition and the easier it is to defend the denial (Woll, 2001). Comparison with people who have more serious problems than one's own is also a self-esteem protecting mechanism.

Although it protects one's self-esteem from the onslaught of external or internal stigma, denial is also a barrier to seeking or benefiting from treatment. In both the addiction treatment field and many mutual-help recovery movements, denial of addiction and its effects has long been considered a formidable obstacle to entry, engagement, and success in treatment and recovery (Alcoholics Anonymous World Services, 1976; Vaillant, 1983; White, 1996, 1998). Sixty percent of respondents to a survey of people in recovery identified denial as a major obstacle to recovery (Hart & Associates, 2001).

Social structures often help people defend against stigma by helping them deny their substance-related problems. The concept of "co-dependency" gained considerable attention in the addiction treatment field in the 1980s, with its exploration of the motives and mechanisms behind friends', family members', employers', and others' attempts to protect people from the consequences of their addictive use. Protection from these consequences often provides some protection from the acknowledgment of substance-related problems, and therefore from the stigma that surrounds these problems.

Isolation from "normals" and identification with drinking and drug using subcultures often may shield against stigma. The subculture creates its own value system, rewards addictive use, reinforces denial, and discredits the society that is the source and keeper of the stigma (Williams, 1976). Self-concept and the substance use disorder both remain intact.

Denial and identification with subculture values are not the only mechanisms by which stigma interferes with people's desire and ability to seek help for substance-related problems. As the consequences of these problems mount and awareness grows, the shame and guilt reinforced by the stigma may lead some to conclude that their conditions are hopeless (Watson & Corrigan, 2001), or that they do not deserve help. A time-honored concept in addiction treatment and recovery circles is that of "hitting bottom," reaching a low point at which people are compelled to seek help. However, many people who have a long history of several deeply entrenched problems have learned to "live on the bottom" (White, 1998). In these cases one may speculate that the experience of stigma and discrimination related to multiple life circumstances might compound the feelings of helplessness, hopelessness, and worthlessness that often spring from the circumstances themselves.

COUNTERING THE EFFECTS OF STIGMA

We have described the stigma associated with substance use disorders in some detail, focusing on multiple causes ranging from social values to individual psychology. We have also discussed the impact of stigma on people with these disorders. However satisfying it is to have shown the complexities of a problem, a great measure of dissatisfaction results if one cannot provide, or at least suggest, some solutions. Because we began at the societal level in our discussion of the problem, we will start there in our discussion of solutions.

Many of the difficulties experienced by those with substance use disorders may come from policies governing the legality of the substance and the criminal sanctions attached to its use. If these restrictive policies were to change, and society were to accept the legalization and controlled distribution of addictive substances, no doubt some of the stigma would be lessened (MacCoun & Reuter, 2001). Some forms of collateral damage to the health and welfare of people with substance use disorders, and to other members of society affected by crimes associated with the illegal status of many addictive substances, would be diminished. Depending on how such policies were enacted, more people might become addicted to these substances, just as the unrestricted availability of alcohol to adults after prohibition led to more serious problems associated with alcohol (Musto, 1987). Although the stigma of substance use disorders may be decreased, thereby decreasing some social problems, others might be created in its place.

There have been ongoing efforts to uncover biological factors that increase susceptibility to substance use disorders and make recovery difficult, and significant progress has been made in mapping the neurochemical manifestations of these disorders. These efforts should have the effect of taking substance use disorders out of the moral realm and putting them into the realm of medicine (White, 1998). However, White reminds us that treating substance use disorders as a medical disease is not something new (Courtwright, 1982; Gerstein & Harwood, 1990) and suggests that moralistic elements are at work trying to undermine this view. Unfortunately, some of the evidence reviewed indicates that some addiction treatment providers hold stigmatizing attitudes toward clients, which may affect clients' self-esteem and the quality and effectiveness of treatment. This certainly is a serious problem that must be addressed, especially because treatment of substance use disorders can be effective.

Stigma is often the result of fear and ignorance. Corrigan and his associates (2001, 2002) have conducted two experiments that showed that education programs and contact with a person with a mental illness can reduce stigma. It is possible that these two techniques will also serve to reduce stigma associated with substance use disorders. Some evidence from a study done by Penn, Kommana, Mansfield, and Link (1999) suggests that this is the case. They found that people held less negative attitudes toward those afflicted with substance use disorders after an education program. Contact with people in successful recovery might be another way of challenging stereotypes and reducing stigma.

Corrigan and Lundin (2001) describe a number of techniques aimed at changing self-stigma. These include reviewing the myths and challenging self-stigma, using cognitive therapy to counter self-stigmatizing attitudes, educating people fully about the risks and benefits of disclosure of the stigmatized condition, and educating people about confidentiality laws. They also suggest a number of ways of fostering empowerment. These include involving consumers in collaboration on their treatment plans; measuring consumer satisfaction with services and using that information to improve services; providing services in home or community settings; using recovering consumers as service providers; encouraging the use of mutual-help options; and involving consumers as collaborators in participatory research. Although these techniques and suggestions were aimed at people with mental illnesses, they may also be helpful to those with substance use disorders.

Woll (2001) offers treatment providers a number of suggestions for avoiding the reinforcement of stigma in treatment programs. These include assessing and addressing the individual service provider's own attitudes toward people with substance use disorders; avoiding judgmental, confrontational, or moralistic treatment methods, language, and approaches; focusing on strength, resiliency, recovery, hope, and respect; using culturally competent materials and approaches; teaching consumers about the neurochemical roots of addiction; and treating recurrence (relapse or return-to-use) as a symptom of the addictive disease, rather than as an infraction of treatment rules.

Activities in which people tell their own stories without self-judgment or -censure may provide another powerful tool in healing the effects of stigma (White, 1996). People might be encouraged to look at their life experiences not as collections of symptoms and diagnoses, but as rich and often contradictory tales that include both serious mistakes and moments of great strength and courage.

Finally, it should be noted that not everyone with a stigmatized disorder experiences the stigma. Some are unaware of the stigma, others choose to ignore it, and still others act out against it in empowerment (Corrigan & Watson, 2002). To a certain extent, stigma is a mixed blessing. As Link and Phelan (1999) remind us, labeling is often what qualifies a person for treatment. That treatment may make an enormous difference in the person's life. Unfortunately, labeling also results in stigma, which generally has a negative effect, especially in the case of substance use disorders, where fear of stigmatization may feed denial of the problem. However, stigma associated with a behavior may keep others from engaging in the behavior (Braithwaite, 1989). Thus stigma may in some cases be a factor in prevention of substance use disorders. Whereas we generally believe that stigma does more harm than good, we mention these positive effects to stress the complexity of the phenomenon.

CONCLUSION

People with substance use disorders face a substantial challenge in our society. Individualist and Puritan elements in our culture drive social institutions to discriminate against them, even to the point of not providing the treatment that will help them. They are harshly treated by the criminal justice system and sometimes face discrimination and stigma by the health provider community, the very people who should be trying to help them.

Public attitudes toward people with substance use disorders are generally negative. Although public sentiment may be shifting toward a treatment orientation, substantial support still exists for criminal sanctions (Lock, Timberlake, & Rasinski, 2002). An examination of the way in which the federal drug budget is allocated indicates that criminal justice and interdiction efforts continue to get the lion's share, whereas the amount given to treatment is small by comparison and becoming proportionally smaller (Lock, Timberlake, & Rasinski, 2002).

Unless changes are made at the societal level, beginning with changes in public policies that emphasize treatment and de-emphasize punishment, people with substance use disorders will continue to face the social problems associated with stigma. Unless the public is educated about the nature and course of substance use disorders, those afflicted will be the easy targets of stereotyping on the basis of public psychological motivations. Finally, unless treatment providers are educated and trained to recognize the negative effects of stigma, treatment programs will be less effective than those persons with the disorder deserve.

REFERENCES

Alcoholics Anonymous World Services. (1976). *Alcoholics Anonymous*. New York: Author.

Alisky, J. M., & Iczkowski, K. A. (1990). Barriers to housing for deinstitutionalized psychiatric patients. *Hospital and Community Psychiatry, 41*, 93–95.

Biernat, M., & Dovidio, J. F. (2000). Stigma and stereotypes. In T. F. Heatherton, R. E. Kleck, M. R. Hebl, & J. G. Hull, (Eds.), *The social psychology of stigma* (pp. 88–125). New York: Guilford Press.

Braithwaite, J. (1989). *Crime, shame, and reintegration*. Cambridge, England: Cambridge University Press.

Caplehorn, R. M., Irwig, L., & Saunders, J. B. (1996). Physicians' attitudes and retention of patients in their methadone maintenance programs. *Substance Use and Misuse, 31*, 663–677.

Center for Substance Abuse Treatment. (2000). *Changing the conversation: The national treatment plan initiative*. Rockville, MD: Author.

Centers for Disease Control and Prevention. (2002a). Policy issues and challenges in substance abuse treatment. *IDU/HIV Prevention*. Retrieved December 31, 2002, from http://www.cdc.gov/idu/facts/PolicyFin.pdf

Centers for Disease Control and Prevention. (2002b). Substance abuse treatment for injection drug users: A strategy with many benefits. *IDU/HIV Prevention*. Retrieved December 31, 2002, from http://www.cdc.gov/ idu/facts/PolicyFin.pdf

Corrigan, P., & Lundin, R. (2001). *Don't call me nuts: Coping with the stigma of mental illness*. Tinley Park, IL: Recovery Press.

Corrigan, P. W., & Penn, D. L. (1999). Lessons from social psychology on discrediting psychiatric stigma. *American Psychologist, 54*, 765–776

Corrigan, P. W., River, P., Lundin, R. K., Penn, D. L., Wasowski, K. U., Campion, J., et al. (2001). Three strategies for changing attributions about severe mental illness. *Schizophrenia Bulletin, 27*, 187–196.

Corrigan, P. W., Rowan, D., Green, A., Lundin, R., River, P., Uphoff-Wasowski, K., et al. (2002). Challenging two mental illness stigmas: Personal responsibility and dangerousness. *Schizophrenia Bulletin, 28*, 293–309.

Corrigan, P. W., & Watson, A. C. (2002). The paradox of self-stigma and mental illness. *Clinical Psychology: Science and Practice. 9*(1), 35–53.

Courtwright, D. T. (1982) *Dark paradise: Opiate addiction in America before 1940*. Cambridge, MA: Harvard University Press.

Courtwright, D. T. (1997). Morality, religion, and drug use. In A. M. Brandt & P. Rozin (Eds.), *Morality and health* (pp. 231–250). New York: Routledge.

Crocker, J., & Major, B. (1989). Social stigma and self-esteem: The self-protective properties of stigma. *Psychological Review, 96*, 608–630.

Crocker, J., & Quinn, D. M. (2000). Social stigma and the self: Meanings, situations, and self-esteem. In T. F. Heatherton, R. E. Kleck, M. R. Hebl, & J. G. Hull (Eds.), *The social psychology of stigma* (pp. 153–183). New York: Guilford Press.

Duke, L. L. (1990). Urban neighborhoods and the war on drugs. In A. S. Trebach & K. B. Zeese (Eds.), *The great issues of drug policy*. Washington, DC: The Drug Policy Foundation.

Fazio, R. (1989). On the power and functionality of attitudes: The role of attitude accessibility. In A. Pratkanis, S. Breckler, & A. Greenwald (Eds.), *Attitude structure and function*. Hillsdale, NJ: Erlbaum.

FYI: Fairness in treatment. (2001). *National Council on Alcoholism and Drug Dependence facts and information*. Retrieved June 12, 2001, from http://www.ncadd.org/facts/fyiparity.html

Gerstein, D. R., & Harwood, H. J. (1990). *Treating drug problems: A study of the evolution, effectiveness, and financing of public and private drug treatment systems* (Vol. 1). Washington, DC: National Academy Press.

Goffman, E. (1963). *Stigma: Notes on the management of spoiled identity*. Englewood Cliffs, NJ: Prentice Hall.

Gorski, T. T., & Grinstead, S. F. (2000). *Denial management counseling workbook*. Independence, MO: Herald House/Independence Press.

Heider, F. (1958). *The psychology of interpersonal relations*. New York: Wiley.

Jost, J. T., & Banaji, M. R. (1994). The role of stereotyping in system-justification and the production of false consciousness. *British Journal of Social Psychology, 33*, 1–27.

Kassanda, J. D., & Williams, T. (1989). Drugs and the dream deferred. *New Perspective Quarterly, 6*, 16–25.

Kessler, R. C., McGanagle, K. A., Zhao, S., Nelson, C. B., Hughes, M., Eshleman, S., et al. (1994). Lifetime and 12-month prevalence of *DSM–III–R* psychiatric disorders in the United States. *Archives of General Psychiatry, 127*(2), 8–19.

Kurzban, R., & Leary, M. (2001). Evolutionary origins of stigmatization: The functions of social exclusion. *Psychological Bulletin, 127*(2), 187–208.

Link, B. G. (1987). Understanding labeling effects in the area of mental disorders: An assessment of the effects of expectations of rejection. *American Sociological Review, 52*, 96–112.

Link, B. G., & Phelan, J. C. (1999). The labeling theory of mental disorder (II): The consequences of labeling. In A. V. Horwitz & T. L. Scheid (Eds.), *A handbook for the study of mental health: Social contexts, theories, and systems*. New York: Cambridge University Press.

Link, B. G., Phelan, J. C., Bresnahan, M., Stueve, A., & Pescosolido, B. (1999). Public conceptions of mental illness: Labels, causes, dangerousness, and social distance. *American Journal of Public Health, 89*, 1328–1333.

Link, B. G., Struening, E. L., Rahav, M., Phelan, J. C., & Nuttbrock, L. (1997). On stigma and its consequences: Evidence from a longitudinal study of men with dual diagnoses of mental illness and substance abuse. *Journal of Health and Social Behavior, 38*, 177–190.

Lock, E. D., Timberlake, J. M., & Rasinski, K. A. (2002). Battle fatigue: Is public support waning for "war"-centered drug control strategies? *Crime and Delinquency, 48*, 380–398.

MacCoun, R. J., & Reuter, P. (2001). *Drug war heresies: Learning from other vices, times, and places.* Cambridge, England: Cambridge University Press.

Marks, A. (2002, June 4). Jobs elude former drug addicts [Electronic version]. *Christian Science Monitor.* Retrieved August 23, 2004, from http://www.csmonitor.com .2002/0604/po2s02-ussc.html

Marsden, G. M. (1991). *Understanding fundamentalism and evangelicalism.* Grand Rapids, MI: Eerdmans.

Mead, G. H. (1934.). *Mind, self, and society.* Chicago: University of Chicago Press.

Mid-Atlantic ATTC. (2000). *Addiction Exchange, 2*(1). Retrieved December 10, 2002, from http://www.mid-attc.org/addex/addex1(20).pdf

Milliman and Robertson, Inc. (1997). Treatment Premium Estimates for Substance Abuse Parity for Commercial Health Insurance Products, for The Coalition for Nondiscriminatory Coverage of Addiction.

Musto, D. F. (1987). *The American disease: Origins of narcotic control.* New York: Oxford University Press.

National Evaluation Data and Technical Assistance Center. (1999). *Outcome and effectiveness in substance abuse treatment: Selected bibliography of national evaluations.* Fairfax, VA: Author.

National Institute on Drug Abuse. (1999). *Principles of drug addiction treatment: A research-based guide.* Bethesda, MD: Author.

Penn, D. L., Kommana, S., Mansfield, M., & Link, B. G. (1999). Dispelling the stigma of schizophrenia: II. The impact of information on dangerousness. *Schizophrenia Bulletin, 25,* 437–446.

Peter D. Hart Research Associates, Inc. (2001). *The face of recovery.* Retrieved September 13, 2002, from http://www.facesandvoicesofrecovery.org/pdf/hart_ research.pdf

Ragin, A., Rasinski, K. A., Cerbone, F., & Johnson, R. A. (1999). *The relationship between mental health and substance abuse among adolescents.* Washington, DC: Department of Health and Human Services, Substance Abuse and Mental Health Services Administration, Office of Applied Studies.

Regier, D. A., Farmer, M. E., Rae, D. S., Locke, B. S., Keith, S. J., Judd, L. L., et al. (1990). Comorbidity of mental disorders with alcohol and other drug abuse. *Journal for the American Medical Association, 264,* 2511–2518.

Rozin, P., & Brandt, A. M. (Eds.). (1997). *Morality and health.* Florence, KY: Taylor & Francis/Routledge.

Sidanius, J. (1993). The psychology of group conflict and the dynamics of oppression: A social dominance perspective. In W. McGuire & S. Iyengar (Eds.), *Current approaches to political psychology.* Durham, NC: Duke University Press.

Steadman, W. G. (1981). Critically reassessing the accuracy of public perceptions of the dangerousness of the mentally ill. *Journal of Health and Social Behavior, 22,* 310–316.

Steele, C. M. (1997). A threat in the air: How stereotypes shape intellectual identity and performance. *American Psychologist, 52,* 613–629.

Struening, E. L., Perlick, D. A., Link, B. G., Hellman, F., Herman, D., & Sirey, J. A. (2001). Stigma as a barrier to recovery: The extent to which caregivers believe most people devalue consumers and their families. *Psychiatric Services, 52,* 1633–1638.

Sturm, R. (1997). How expensive is unlimited mental health care coverage under managed care? *Journal of the American Medical Association, 12,* 1533–1537.

Substance Abuse and Aging Task Force. (2001). *Substance abuse and aging.* Proceedings from the May 10, 2001 symposium. Chicago: Great Lakes Addiction Technology Transfer Center.

Substance Abuse and Mental Health Services Administration. (1998). *The cost and effects of parity for mental health and substance abuse insurance.* Ruckville, MD: Author.

Substance Abuse Network of Ontario. (1999). *The stigma of substance use: A review of the literature.* Retrieved December 30, 2002, from http://sano.camh.net/stigma/litrev.htm

The ghost haunting methadone. (1996, Spring/Summer). *Addiction Treatment Forum, 5*(2). Retrieved January 2, 2003, from http://www.atforum.com/siteroot/pages/current_pastissues/VolVS96.shtml

Treatment spending shrinks. (n.d.). Retrieved December 31, 2002, from http://alcoholism.about.com/library/weekly/aa00721a.htm

Trebach, A. S. (1988). *The heroin solution.* Cambridge, MA: Yale University Press.

Vaillant, G. E. (1983). *The natural history of alcoholism.* Cambridge, MA: Harvard University Press.

Watson, A. C., & Corrigan, P. W. (2001). *The impact of stigma on service access and participation.* Tinley Park, IL: University of Chicago, Center for Psychiatric Rehabilitation.

Weinberg, T. S., & Vogler, C. C. (1990). Wives of alcoholics: Stigma management and adjustments to husband-wife interaction. *Deviant Behavior, 11,* 331–343.

Weiner, B. W. (1995) *Judgments of responsibility: A foundation for a theory of social conduct.* New York: Guilford Press.

Weiner, C. (1981). *The politics of alcoholism: Building an arena around a social problem.* New Brunswick, NJ: Transaction Publishers.

White, W. L. (1996). *Pathways from the culture of addiction to the culture of recovery.* Center City, MN: Hazelden Press.

White, W. L. (1998). *Slaying the dragon: The history of addiction treatment and recovery in America.* Bloomington, IL: Lighthouse Institute.

White, W. L. (2001). *A day is coming: Visions of a recovery advocacy movement.* Bloomington, IL: Lighthouse Institute.

Williams, J. R. (1976). Effects of labeling the "drug-abuser:" An inquiry. *NIDA Research Monographs*, 6. Bethesda, MD: National Institute on Drug Abuse.

Wills, T. A. (1981). Downward comparison principles in social psychology. *Psychological Bulletin*, 90, 245–271.

Woll, P. (2001). *Healing the stigma of addiction: A guide for treatment professionals.* Chicago: Great Lakes Addiction Technology Transfer Center.

Woll, P., & Gorski, T. T. (1995). *Worth protecting: Women, men, and freedom from sexual aggression.* Independence, MO: Herald House/Independence Press.

Woods, J. (2001). Methadone advocacy: The voice of the patient. *Mount Sinai Journal of Medicine*, 68(1), 75–78

III
CHANGING MENTAL ILLNESS STIGMA

11

STRATEGIES FOR ASSESSING AND DIMINISHING SELF-STIGMA

PATRICK W. CORRIGAN AND JOSEPH D. CALABRESE

As discussed in an earlier chapter, self-stigma seems to be represented by a paradox. First impressions about the stigma of mental illness suggest people with psychiatric disability, living in a society that widely endorses stigmatizing ideas, will internalize these ideas and believe that they are less valued because of their psychiatric disorder. Self-esteem suffers, as does confidence in one's future (Corrigan, 1998; Holmes & River, 1998). Given this research, models of self-stigma need to account for the deleterious effects of prejudice on an individual's conception of him or herself. However, research also suggests that instead of being diminished by the stigma, many persons become righteously angry because of the prejudice that they have experienced (Chamberlin, 1978; Deegan, 1990). This kind of reaction empowers people to change their roles in the mental health system, becoming more active participants in their treatment plan and often pushing for improvements in the quality of services (Corrigan, 2002). And yet a third reaction exists that needs to be considered in describing the impact of stigma on the self. The sense of self for many persons with mental illness is neither hurt, nor energized by social stigma; persons instead seem to be indifferent to it altogether.

Although many people with mental illness do not experience ill effects to the self because of stigma, there are others who are harmed by internalizing stigma. This chapter focuses on ways people with mental illness might deal with stigma so it does not harm the self. The chapter begins with a practical consideration of assessing self-stigma. Several measurement approaches have been tested for assessing self-stigma; strengths and weaknesses of these strategies are reviewed. Self-stigma might then be addressed in two ways: (a) From a social–cognitive perspective, self-stigma may be viewed as negative self-statements and schemas that arise from mental illness stereotypes that are prominent in one's culture (read more about this perspective in chap. 4 of this volume by Ottati, Bodenhausen, & Newman). Cognitive–behavioral therapy strategies that have been effective in changing these schemas are reviewed in terms of their relevance to diminishing their impact on self-esteem; and (b) self-stigma has been described as the opposite pole of personal empowerment. Hence, services that promote empowerment may diminish self-stigma. Several examples of consumer empowerment approaches are reviewed in this chapter.

Because the condition that yields the stigma of mental illness may be concealed, self-stigma is influenced by an individual's concern that others will discover the stereotype applies to him or her. Hence, considerations about disclosure may affect the self-stigma related to mental illness. Chapter 12 more thoroughly considers this issue.

ASSESSING SELF-STIGMA

One of the assumptions behind asserting that self-stigma is an important experience in the lives of some people with mental illness is that it can be identified and measured. This kind of measurement allows individuals to make qualitative and quantitative sense of their self-stigma. Moreover, assessment of self-stigma may provide an approach for evaluating the success of individual self-stigma change strategies. Self-stigma has been assessed in several ways in the literature. It has been equated with low self-esteem and self-efficacy, examined as the internalization of public stigma, and viewed as the opposite of empowerment. The strengths and limitations of each of these approaches are reviewed here.

Self-Stigma as Diminished Self-Esteem and Self-Efficacy

Self-stigma may lead to negative emotional reactions; prominent among these is low self-esteem and self-efficacy. *Self-esteem* is operationalized in research that examines this assumption as ratings of personal worth on Likert-type scale items (Corrigan, Faber, Rashid, & Leary, 1999). Perhaps best known among these scales is the Rosenberg Self-Esteem Scale (Rosenberg, 1965). When employing this scale, participants use a four-point Likert-type scale to self-report their agreement with ten items that represent self-worth. The Rosenberg scale frames self-esteem as a unitary construct that might be assessed on a continuous scale. More complex models have argued that self-esteem may comprise such multiple and independent factors as self-deprecation and self-confidence (Owens, 1994) or self-competence and self-liking (Tafarodi & Swann, 2001). Moreover, previous research has treated self-esteem as a personality variable, whereas more recent studies have included situational variables as an important element in understanding self-esteem. Further research into self-stigma and self-esteem needs to consider the evolution of constructs in this area.

Self-efficacy is defined as the expectation that one can successfully cope with life demands so that individual goals are achieved (Bandura, 1977, 1989). As such, self-efficacy is a cognitive appraisal of past experiences leading to future outcomes. Those who do not believe they will be efficacious in pursuing specific goals will likely avoid situations where achievement of these goals is dominant. Although several measures of general self-efficacy that frame the construct as a personality variable have been developed and tested (McDermott, 1995; Sherer & Adams, 1983; Tipton & Worthington, 1984), Bandura argues that self-efficacy is also likely to differ by specific situations (Bandura, 1977). For example, people are likely to view their possible success in work situations different from independent living settings. Hence, those measuring self-efficacy in self-stigma may also need to consider the situation in which efficacy is to be considered.

The Problem With Self-Esteem as an Indicator of Self-Stigma

The assumption here is that decrements in self-esteem are due to the harm caused by self-stigma. Hence, measures of self-esteem will represent the impact of self-stigma (Allport, 1954/1979). Although this hypothesis might be reasonable in many stigmatized populations, some experiences specific to mental illness make the relationship between diminished self-esteem and self-stigma more difficult to test. How can we know whether decrements in self-esteem are reactions to self-stigma or the direct results of the disease and disabilities that result from many psychiatric disorders (Corrigan & Watson, 2002)? Let us consider the question specifically as it relates to people with serious mental illness.

Most individuals with affective and schizoaffective disorders report low self-esteem; it is one of the diagnostic indicators of these syndromes (American Psychiatric Press, 1994). In addition, persons with schizophrenia often experience comorbid depression that could manifest itself as low self-esteem (DeLisi, 1990; Siris, 1995). Finally, subclinical depression and low self-esteem are common in persons who are not able to achieve their life goals and report a poor quality of life as a result (Corrigan & Buican, 1995; Estroff, 1989). Further complicating this question is the way self-esteem varies across diagnostic subgroups. People with schizophrenia may show diminished self-esteem as a result of reactive depression (Siris, 1995), individuals with borderline personality disorder may experience problems with self-esteem because of emotional dysregulation (Linehan, 1993), and those with narcissistic personality disorder may show poor self-esteem because their overvalued self-worth is not validated by the social environment (Millon, 1981). Hence, future research in this area needs to incorporate carefully considered diagnostic strategies that independently assess self-esteem.

Given these concerns, researchers must develop a measurement strategy that distinguishes the diminished self-esteem that results from the psychiatric disorder per se from that which emerges from internalizing stigma. Three considerations will facilitate development of this kind of measure. First, cognitive–behavioral models suggest low self-esteem and depression are manifested in negative self-statements about the person, his or her world, and his or her future (Beck, 1967; Clark, Beck, & Alford, 1999). Diminished self-esteem due to self-stigma might be especially evident in two of these three groups of statements: those about the self and the future.

It is conceivable, however, that persons whose diminished self-esteem arises from depression might also endorse these negative statements; hence, they are not unique to persons who self-stigmatize. A second factor would help determine whether endorsement of these statements represents self-stigma or depression. To yield self-stigma, people must be *aware* of the public stigma that corresponds with the negative self-statement ("Yes, I realize most people think the mentally ill can't take care of themselves!") and agree that it is true ("Most people are correct. The mentally ill can't take care of themselves!"). These assumptions are supported by research that suggests many persons with psychiatric disability are aware of the stigma about their group and agree with it (Hayward & Bright, 1997).

A third factor may further distinguish diminished self-esteem due to a psychiatric disorder from that which arises from self-stigma. The symptoms of depression, including low self-esteem, are frequently episodic (Gruenberg & Goldstein, 1997), though the waxing and waning of symptoms is less apparent in persons with dysthymic disorder. Hence, one might attribute low self-esteem to a person's psychiatric disorder when negative self-statements increase and decrease with the dysphoria commensurate with the individual's affective disorder. Moreover, treatments of the depressive syndrome (e.g., medication and some psychotherapies) will lead to improving the low self-esteem that results from psychiatric disorders, but not self-stigma. Poor self-esteem due to self-stigma should not show this kind of variable course.

Although self-stigma does not change with the course of depression, we do not mean to imply that self-stigma is an unvarying trait. The low self-esteem caused by self-stigma is constructed in the situation and hence better described as a state. Wright, Gronfein, and Owens (2000) found substantial flux in feelings of self-worth related to stigma in a sample of persons with mental illness. Thus, the impact of self-stigma on self-esteem may show a variable course dependent on situational features as opposed to illness course. This realization further confounds the development of a self-stigma measure and needs to be included into research considerations.

Self-Efficacy and Self-Stigma.

Similar problems occur when self-efficacy is used as a proxy for self-stigma. The defining factor that turns a mental illness into a psychiatric disability is poor skills and low self-efficacy that interfere with the attainment of social goals (Corrigan, 2002). Many people with mental illness are not successful in meeting work and other independent living goals. Hence, it is unclear whether poor self-efficacy is due to the limitations imposed by stigma or the skill deficits that result from psychiatric disabilities. This poses a methodological conundrum for assessing an efficacy-based model of self-esteem and stigma (McDermott, 1995). The problem may be resolved in a manner similar to discerning the effects of depression and stigma on self-esteem. Namely, problems with personal success that *covary* with the individual's awareness of public stigma might be attributed to an efficacy-based model of self-esteem and stigma.

Self-Stigma as Internalized Public Stigma and Fear of Rejection

Link and colleagues (Link & Phelan, 2001; Link, Struening, Neese-Todd, Asmussen, & Phelan, 2001) have framed self-stigma as internalizing public stigma; their model circumvents many of the problems of equating self-stigma with losses in self-esteem and self-efficacy. According to this model, people develop views of mental illness in early childhood from family lore, personal experience, peer relations, and the media's portrayal of mental illness. Based on these conceptions, public stigma develops that yields rejection and devaluation of those with mental illness. These beliefs have little personal relevance for those who never develop mental illness or can avoid the public label. However, such beliefs may possibly harm those with mental illness. That person may fear the possible rejection and devaluation of others who find out they bear the stigmatizing mark. This kind of fear may lead to strained relations with potential stigmatizers (Farina & Felner, 1973), poorer life satisfaction (Rosenfield, 1997), and unemployment (Link, 1982, 1987).

Link and colleagues have developed assessment strategies sensitive to internalized stigma and fear of rejection. The Devaluation-Discrimination Scale (Link, 1982; Link, Mirotznik, & Cullen, 1991) includes 12 items that research participants complete on a Likert-type scale of agreement. Statements reflect beliefs that the public generally devalue psychiatric patients by perceiving them as failures, less intelligent than most, and as individuals whose opinion need not be taken seriously. The Stigma-Withdrawal Scale (Beard, Malamud, & Rossman, 1978) assesses the extent to which a research participant endorses withdrawal as a way to avoid rejection. An example from the nine item scale is, "If a person thought less of you because you had been in psychiatric treatment, you would avoid him or her." Both scales have satisfactory test-retest reliability and construct validity (Angermeyer, Link, & Majcher-Angermeyer, 1987). A series of papers in a recent issue of *Psychiatric Services* edited by Deborah Perlick (2001) tested Link's model using these scales. One study showed that about 70% of caregivers believe devaluation is common (Struening et al., 2001). A second study found the two scales predicted self-esteem at 6 month follow-up when baseline self-esteem, depression, demographics, and diagnoses were controlled (Link, Struening, Neese-Todd, Amusen, & Phelan, 2001). A third study showed that concerns assessed by the Devaluation-Discrimination Scale predicted social adaptation in people diagnosed with bipolar disorder (Perlick et al., 2001).

We have attempted to expand on Link's ideas by elaborating on the social–cognitive component of the model (Corrigan & Watson, 2002). Although there are several benefits to Link's model and corresponding scales, they fail to distinguish the key elements of a social–cognitive model of self-stigma (see chap. 6, this volume, by Watson & River for a more complete discussion of this model). The three components of the social–cognitive model are awareness of stereotypes (which the Link model addresses well), concurrence of stereotype in terms of one's self, and diminished self-esteem–self-efficacy because of stereotype self-concurrence. Research by the Center for Psychiatric Rehabilitation at the University of Chicago is developing and testing the Measure of Self-Stigma in Mental Illness (MSSMI) to assess these three factors. Items for *Factor 1: Stereotype Awareness* reflect the major dimensions representing the stereotypes relevant to mental illness found in previous factor analyses: dangerousness, incompetence, and character weakness (Brockington, Hall, Levings, & Murphy, 1993; Taylor & Dear, 1980). Items are worded in active voice as statements about people with mental illness (e.g., "People with mental illness are unable to care for themselves"). Four expert judges (two researchers and two advocates) have generated additional items for a preliminary pool of 60. Added to this pool will be a second set of 40 items about other stigmatized groups. These items are added for purposes of *discriminant validation* and will show that results represent endorsement of specific stereotypes and not merely a willingness to endorse negative self-statements. Items will be drawn from research on stereotypes of other groups (Crocker, Major, & Steele, 1998). A second, independent group of experts will rate each of these items on a seven-point scale: How representative is this item in terms of the prominent stereotypes of mental illness? Based on these ratings, we plan to pare the test down to 60 items representing stereotype awareness: 40 items rated highest in terms of representativeness and 20 items rated lowest.

Two-part items representing *Factor 2: Stereotype Self-Concurrence* will be written to correspond with the 60 items representing stereotype awareness. The first clause in the statement will recapitulate the general stereotype and the second part will apply it to the individual. For example, "Like most people with mental illness, I am unable to care for myself." Finally, 60 two-part items that correspond with stereotype awareness will be written to represent *Factor 3: Self-Concurrence Esteem Decrement*. The first clause will represent a statement about low self-esteem or self-efficacy and the second clause will attribute this decrement to the stereotype. For example, "I respect myself less because I am unable to care for myself."

We believe the MSSMI is an important extension of Link's model because of the information that Factors 2 and 3 uniquely provide to our understanding of stereotype awareness. Although work on the MSSMI is in progress, we hypothesize that analyses of the data will yield the following patterns. Multiple regression analyses are expected to show *Factor 1: Stereotype Awareness* to be positively associated with a measure of general social awareness; people who are more cognitively aware of their social surroundings should also be more cognizant of the stereotypes that describe these surroundings. We also expect Factor 1 to be associated with the psychiatric symptom of thought disorder. Thought disorder greatly diminishes social awareness such that people who are cognitively disorganized or disoriented are less likely to be aware of the stereotypes that describe mental illness. Of special note, no significant relationship is expected between Stereotype Awareness and measures of self-esteem, self-efficacy, and righteous anger.

A different pattern is expected for the remaining factors of the MSSMI. We expect our data to show that *Factor 2: Stereotype Self-Concurrence* is significantly associated with disease awareness. Many persons with psychotic disorders are *unaware* of the nature of their mental illness or its impact on the breadth of life functioning domains (Amador et al., 1994; Amador & Seckinger, 1997). Hence, some persons with mental illness may not realize they belong to a group of people who are stigmatized. This would diminish group identification such that they may be relatively immune to self-stigma. Hence, we expect a specific association between disease awareness and stereotype self-concurrence. Moreover, stereotype self-concurrence will show relatively small associations with the measures of self-esteem, self-efficacy, and righteous anger. MSSMI-2 *Factor 3: Self-Concurrence Esteem Decrement* will show fairly robust associations with self-esteem, self-efficacy, and righteous anger. Moreover, these associations will remain significant after symptoms related to depression are partialed out. Regression analyses will also show that the relationships of the self-concurrence esteem decrement on self-esteem, self-efficacy, and righteous anger will be further moderated by thought disorder and disease awareness.

Self-Stigma as the Opposite of Personal Empowerment

Crocker and colleagues (Crocker & Lawrence, 1999; Crocker & Major, 1989) highlighted an amazing trend in stigma and self-esteem. Contrary to what might be expected, several stigmatized groups showed *higher* self-esteem than the majority; participants in these studies included persons of color (Hoelter, 1983; Jensen, White, & Gelleher, 1982; Porter & Washington, 1979) and people with disabilities (Fine & Caldwell, 1967; Willy & McCandless, 1973). It seems that in some people, being stigmatized somehow stimulates psychological reactance (Brehm, 1966; Corrigan & Watson, 2002). As applied to this discussion, reactance suggests that rather than complying with the perceived threat of stigma and viewing one's self poorly, an individual opposes the negative evaluation and positive self-perceptions emerge.

Research on *empowerment* in persons with mental illness has illustrated this point (cf. chap. 6., this volume, for a more complete discussion of this issue). This research represents empowerment and self-stigma as opposite poles on a continuum (McCubbin & Cohen, 1996; Rappaport, 1987; Speer, Jackson, & Peterson, 2001; Zimmerman & Rappaport, 1988). At the negative end of the continuum are persons who report being unable to overcome all the pessimistic expectations about mental illness. They have low self-esteem and little confidence in their future success. These are the self-stigmatized. At the positive end, however, are persons with psychiatric disability who, despite this disability, have positive self-esteem and are not significantly encumbered by a stigmatizing community. Instead, they seem to be energized by the stigma to righteous anger (Corrigan, 2002). Hence, assessment of personal empowerment may be a proxy for the self-stigma that specifically arises from being a person with mental illness. People high on personal empowerment may be viewed as relatively low on self-stigma.

Two measures have been developed and tested that represent facets of empowerment in mental health. Rogers, Chamberlin, Ellison, and Crean (1997) used a participatory action research design and developed the Empowerment Scale. In step one of their work, several consumers of psychiatric services identified 15 attributes of empowerment. The investigators then wrote 48 Likert-type scale items (a four-point agreement scale) that reflected these attributes (e.g., "I generally accomplish what I set out to do," to "I feel powerless most of the time"). Results of initial item analyses pared the list to 28. A subsequent factor analysis of responses from 271 people with mental illness yielded five factors: self-esteem–efficacy; power–powerlessness; community activism and autonomy; optimism and control over the future; and righteous anger. Corrigan and colleagues (1999) further examined the factor structure in a separate analysis of the Empowerment Scale. Completing a hierarchical factor analysis, the Empowerment Scale items yielded two higher order factors: a self-orientation to empowerment—confidence that one is worthy and effective in light of societal stigma—and a community orientation to empowerment, interest in affecting one's community to diminish the impact of stigma and to open up various life opportunities.

An independent research program has showed a similar split between internal and external empowerment. Segal, Silverman, and Temkin (1995) developed two instruments that represented the experiences of client-run self-help agencies. The Personal Empowerment Scale reflects perceived choice in one's personal life and includes two sections. The first section asks research participants to respond to 10 items on personal choice using a four point Likert-type scale (4 = a lot of choice). Sample items include "How much choice do you have about how you will spend your free time?" and "How much choice do you have about which town or city you will live in?" Section two assesses perceptions about having sufficient resources to meet basic needs (e.g., "How likely is it that you will have enough money to spend next month for necessities like food, shelter, and clothing?"). The second scale is called Organizationally Mediated Empowerment and assesses perceptions about authority roles in various agencies or organizations in which consumers may have participated (e.g., "Have you joined or kept membership in a club? If yes, have you voted in an election for officers?"). Research on 310 long-term users of self-help agencies have shown that summary scores from these scales were stable over time, had construct validity, and were sensitive to the kind of change that might result from participating in self-help (Segal, Silverman, & Temkin, 1995).

FACILITATING CHANGE IN SELF-STIGMATIZING COGNITIVE SCHEMATA

Recent developments in the area of cognitive therapy suggest that self-stigma may be understood as resulting from maladaptive self-statements or cognitive schemata of mental illness. These cognitive schemata have developed largely as a result of socialization and may be altered using the techniques of cognitive therapy. Interpersonal differences in cognitive schemata may help explain why, given the same social situation, one person may feel significantly "stigmatized" by its informational content, whereas a second may not feel stigmatized, and a third is motivated to action. The adverse effects of stigma are "located" not only in the social situation, but in the cognitive process of the stigmatized individual (i.e., the way an individual perceives and understands the social situation such that disrespectful messages emerge [Crocker & Quinn, 2000]).

Cognitive therapy has been shown to be an effective strategy for helping people change cognitive schemata that lead to anxiety, depression, and the consequences of self-stigma. Although some readers might be concerned that people with serious psychiatric disorders might not benefit from cognitive therapy, British clinicians have documented its benefits for psychotic disorders (Chadwick & Lowe, 1990; Drury, Birchwood, Cochrane, & Macmillan, 1996; Kuipers et al., 1997; Tarrier et al., 1993;). This approach targets distressing psychotic symptoms and maladaptive understandings of mental illness using a collaborative empirical framework. The therapist helps the client explore his or her distressing and often delusional cognitions, attempting to reframe them as belief rather than fact, empathically discussing how one might arrive at such beliefs (but also recognizing their emotional costs), reviewing evidence for and against the beliefs, and trying to find less distressing alternative interpretations (Chadwick, Birchwood, & Trower, 1996; Garety, Fowler, & Kuipers, 2000).

The primary targets of this approach have been the cognitive schemata underlying delusional beliefs and delusional attributions regarding auditory hallucinations. Changes in these schemata have been shown to yield improvement in psychiatric symptoms. For example, in a randomized controlled trial of cognitive therapy for acute psychosis, Drury and colleagues (1996) found a marked decline in positive symptoms after cognitive therapy; at a 9-month follow-up, only 5% of the cognitive therapy group showed moderate to severe residual symptoms compared to more than half the control group. Gould, Mueser, Bolton, Mays, and Goff (2001) conducted a meta-analysis of cognitive therapy for psychosis and found an effect size of 0.65 across seven controlled studies. They concluded that cognitive therapy represents a promising strategy for decreasing the severity of persistent psychotic symptoms.

The most promising studies of this line of research in relation to stigma were initiated by two other British researchers: David Kingdon and Douglas Turkington. These researchers (Kingdon & Turkington 1991, 1994) expanded the cognitive therapy of psychosis beyond the content of specific symptoms, also targeting the person's catastrophic interpretation of his or her symptoms and the stigma attached to mental illness generally. Following Strauss' (1969) finding that psychotic symptoms represent points on continua of function, the authors attempt to *normalize* the symptoms of therapy participants by comparing them to normal experiences such as deprivation states. Similarly, in their recent research, Garety, Kuipers, Fowler, Chamberlain, and Dunn (2000) strive for an understanding of psychosis that promotes social functionality and relapse prevention. In their initial uncontrolled study with 64 participants, Kingdon and Turkington (1991) revealed high acceptability and low readmission rate with no suicides or homicides over a 7-year period. They subsequently conducted two randomized controlled trials comparing this intervention to a similar amount of therapist hours using a supportive "befriending" intervention. The first published trial (Sensky et al., 2000) found that both interventions resulted in a significant reduction in positive and negative symptoms and depression but, at the 9-month follow-up, participants in the cognitive therapy group continued to improve, whereas those in the control did not. The second trial (Turkington & Kingdon, 2000) found that symptoms improved significantly for the cognitive therapy group but not for the control group and that the cognitive therapy group also had shorter periods of hospitalization during the follow-up period.

Several other lines of research converge to suggest that such destigmatizing cognitive interventions are feasible and potentially useful. Steele and colleagues (Shih, Pittinsky, & Ambady, 1999; Steele, 1997; Steele & Aronson, 1995) have documented the effects of "stereotype threat" on various stigmatized out-groups, suggesting that cognitive functioning improves when stereotype threat is minimized. In line with this research, Levy (1996) demonstrated that subliminal exposure to positive stereotypes of aging tended to improve the memory performance of elderly individuals, as well as improving sense of memory self-efficacy and views of aging. In contrast, exposure to negative stereotypes of aging tended to worsen memory performance, memory self-efficacy, and views of aging. A similar method applied to people with serious mental illness may diminish the effects of self-stigma.

FOSTERING PERSONAL EMPOWERMENT

Another approach to changing self-stigma builds on a definition of self-stigma made earlier in this chapter; that is, personal empowerment is the opposite of self-stigma (also see chap. 6, this volume). Being empowered means having control over one's treatment and one's life (Rappaport, 1987). Persons who have a strong sense of personal empowerment can be expected to have high self-efficacy and self-esteem. They are not overwhelmed by their symptoms and psychiatric labels but have a positive outlook and take an active role in their recovery. Empowerment approaches may be considered among the best ways to deal with self-stigma. Though the active involvement of the consumer is essential to this goal, communities and health service providers can foster personal empowerment among mental health consumers in a variety of ways that involve giving consumers greater control over their own treatment and reintegration into the community. Research findings indicate that programs that include the person with disabilities in all facets of intervention are conducive to the attainment of vocational and independent living goals (Corrigan, Faber, Rashid, & Leary, 1999; Corrigan & Garman, 1997; Rappaport, 1990; Rogers et al., 1997).

At the most general level, fostering empowerment involves adopting a collaborative approach to treatment planning in which the consumer ceases to be merely a passive recipient of services. At the very least, programs should form a treatment partnership, seeking feedback from consumers as to their satisfaction with the services offered and their suggestions for improvement. The emphasis is based on the strengths and potential of the consumer rather than his or her weaknesses. Beyond this, truly empowering services promote the self-determination of consumers in relation to employment opportunities, housing, and other areas of social life. Rather than a stigmatizing and coercive removal from the community, these new approaches provide community-based support for the consumer's continuing efforts to adapt to community living. This approach is typified in the Assertive Community Treatment (ACT) of Stein and Test (1980). In ACT, services are brought directly to the consumer's home, workplace, or other meaningful community setting. A recent review of research on ACT by Mueser, Bond, Drake, and Resnick (1998) found moderate to good effects on hospitalization, housing stability, symptoms, and quality of life. Supported employment and supported education are also methods used to facilitate the inclusion of persons with disabilities into the fabric of society. These approaches, which were given increased priority with the passage of the ADA in 1990, encourage the prompt placement of clients into employment or educational settings and provide supportive services for their continuing success in these activities. This approach contrasts with traditional approaches that focus on *preparing* clients for independent social functioning rather than on *supporting* them in actual community involvement.

Consumers can also empower themselves by becoming staff members of traditional treatment programs (Mowbray, Moxley, Jasper, & Howell, 1997), or they can create and run their own services. Services where consumers have a central role in operation may include lodges and clubhouses as well as self-help and mutual assistance groups. The Fountain House clubhouse in New York is a paradigmatic example of consumer empowerment through mutual help. This first clubhouse was founded in the 1940s by a group of former inpatients from Rockland State Hospital yearning for a place to gather and support one another. Fountain House, and the field of psychosocial rehabilitation that it influenced, destigmatized the recovering person by focusing on his or her strengths rather than weaknesses and by developing social competence through involvement in the very activities that constitute community integration (employment, housing, education, etc.).

The Fountain House model contrasts with traditional treatment in many ways. This program does not focus on providing treatment for mental illness but rather on developing the skills and talents of its members. Participants in Fountain House are called "members," which is a much less stigmatizing and more empowering label than "patient." It also implies an element of responsibility, as members are expected to take supportive and leadership roles in groups and in teams to accomplish the tasks required to maintain the clubhouse (Beard, Propst, & Malmud, 1982; Fountain House, New York City, 1999). Members and staff have equal status and work together to serve the clubhouse community. All elements and activities of the clubhouse are designed to ensure that each member experiences a strong sense of ownership in the clubhouse, feels expected each morning, has a sense of being wanted and needed by the members and staff, and can recognize that his or her contribution is critical to the functioning of the house. However, participation in the clubhouse community is strictly voluntary. Services like these greatly increase the consumer's sense of power, thereby challenging any stigma with which he or she might be struggling.

THE PARADOX OF TRYING TO FIX SELF-STIGMA

A paradox exists in trying to change self-stigma of which service providers and advocates need to be wary. Namely, focusing on self-stigma may frame the prejudice and discrimination that results as a problem of people with mental illness. Like the disabilities that arise from their illness, stigma is another unfortunate result of having mental illness with which people afflicted with the disease must learn to live. This kind of perspective may ignore the public's responsibility in creating and maintaining stigma. Although value exists in consumers of mental health services and others victimized by stigma learning how to deal with its harm for themselves, this should not release the public from its responsibility. Link and colleagues (1991) argued that because stigma is powerfully reinforced by culture, its effects are not easily overcome by the coping actions of individuals. Citing C. Wright Mills' (1967) distinction, they conclude that labeling and stigma are "social problems" that need to be addressed by public approaches, not "individual troubles" that are addressed by individual therapy. Although Link and colleagues' formulation risks being one-sided in limiting itself to interventions aimed only at the society at large (research supports the conclusion that both individual-level and society-level interventions can be useful), it is true that the self-stigma experienced by some people with mental illness is less likely to thrive when society as a whole refuses to nurture stereotypes, prejudice, and discrimination.

REFERENCES

Allport, G. W. (1979). *The nature of prejudice.* New York: Doubleday. (Original work published 1954)

Amador, X. F., Flaum, M., Andreasen, N. C., Strauss, D. H., Yale, S. A., Clark, C. C., et al. (1994). Awareness of illness in schizophrenia and schizoaffective and mood disorders. *Archives of General Psychiatry, 51,* 826–836.

Amador, X. F., & Seckinger, R. A. (1997). The assessment of insight: A methodological review. *Psychiatric Annals, 27,* 798–805.

American Psychiatric Association. (1994). *Diagnostic and statistical manual of mental disorders* (4th ed.). Washington, DC: Author.

Angermeyer, M. C., Link, B. G., & Majcher-Angermeyer, A. (1987). Stigma perceived by patients attending modern treatment settings: Some unanticipated effects of community psychiatry reforms. *Journal of Nervous and Mental Disease, 175,* 4–11.

Bandura, A. (1977). Self-efficacy: Toward a unifying theory of behavioral change. *Psychological Review, 84*, 191–215.

Bandura, A. (1989). Human agency in social cognitive theory. *American Psychologist, 44*, 1175–1184

Beard, J. H., Malamud, T. J., & Rossman, E. (1978). Psychiatric rehabilitation and long-term rehospitalization rates: The findings of two research studies. *Schizophrenia Bulletin, 4*, 622–635.

Beard, J. H., Propst, R. N., & Malamud, T. J. (1982). The Fountain House model of psychiatric rehabilitation. *Psychosocial Rehabilitation Journal, 5*, 47–53.

Beck, A. T. (1967). *Depression: Causes and treatment.* Philadelphia: University of Pennsylvania Press.

Brehm, J. W. (1966). *A theory of psychological reactance.* San Diego, CA: Academic Press.

Brockington, I., Hall, P., Levings, J., & Murphy, C. (1993). The community's tolerance of the mentally ill. *British Journal of Psychiatry, 162*, 93–99.

Buchremer, G., Klingberg, S., Holle, R., Shulze Monking, S., & Hornung, W. P. (1997). Psychoeducational psychotherapy for schizophrenic patients and their key relatives or care-givers: Results of a 2-year follow-up. *Acta Psychiatrica Scandinavica, 96*, 483–491.

Chadwick, P. D. J., Birchwood, M., & Trower, P. (1996). *Cognitive therapy for delusions, voices and paranoia.* New York: Wiley.

Chadwick, P. D. J., & Lowe, C. F. (1990). Measurement and modification of delusional beliefs. *Journal of Consulting and Clinical Psychology, 58*, 225–232.

Chamberlin, J. (1978). *On our own: Patient-controlled alternatives to the mental health system.* New York: McGraw-Hill.

Clark, D. A., Beck, A. T., & Alford, B. A. (1999). *Scientific foundations of cognitive theory and therapy of depression.* New York: Wiley.

Corrigan, P. W. (1998). The impact of stigma on severe mental illness. *Cognitive and Behavioral Practice, 5*, 201–222.

Corrigan, P. W. (2002). Empowerment and serious mental illness: Treatment partnerships and community opportunities. *Psychiatric Quarterly, 73*, 217–228.

Corrigan, P. W., & Buican, B. (1995). The construct validity of subjective quality of life in the severely mentally ill. *Journal of Nervous and Mental Disease, 183*, 281–285.

Corrigan, P. W., Faber, D., Rashid, F., & Leary, M. (1999). The construct validity of empowerment among consumers of mental health services. *Schizophrenia Research, 38*, 77–84.

Corrigan, P. W., & Garman, A. N. (1997). Considerations for research on consumer empowerment and psychosocial interventions. *Psychiatric Services, 48*, 347–352.

Corrigan, P. W., & Watson, A. C. (2002). The paradox of self-stigma and mental illness. *Clinical Psychology: Science and Practice, 9*, 35–53.

Crocker, J., & Lawrence, J. S. (1999). Social stigma and self-esteem: The role of contingencies of worth. In D. A. Prentice & D. T Miller (Eds.), *Cultural divides: Understanding and overcoming group conflict* (pp. 364–392). New York: Russell Sage Foundation.

Crocker, J., & Major, B. (1989). Social stigma and self-esteem: The self-protective properties of stigma. *Psychological Review, 96,* 608–630.

Crocker, J., Major, B., & Steele, C. (1998). Social stigma. In D. Gilbert, S. T. Fiske, & G. Lindzey (Eds.), *The handbook of social psychology* (4th ed., Vol. 2, pp. 504–553). New York: McGraw-Hill.

Crocker, J., & Quinn, D. M. (2000). Social stigma and the self: Meanings, situations, and self-esteem. In T. F. Heatherton, R. E. Kleck, M. R. Hebl, & J. G. Hull. (Eds.), *The social psychology of stigma* (pp. 153–183). New York: Guilford Press.

Deegan, P. E. (1990) Spirit breaking: When the helping professions hurt. *Humanistic Psychologist, 18,* 301–313.

DeLisi, L. (Ed.). (1990). *Depression in schizophrenia.* Washington, DC: American Psychiatric Press.

Drury, V., Birchwood, M., Cochrane, R., & Macmillan, F. (1996). Cognitive therapy and recovery from acute psychosis: A controlled trial I. Impact on psychotic symptoms. *British Journal of Psychiatry, 169,* 593–601.

Estroff, S. E. (1989). Self, identity, and subjective experiences of schizophrenia: In search of the subject. *Schizophrenia Bulletin, 15,* 189–196.

Farina, A., & Felner, R. D. (1973). Employment interviewer reactions to former mental patients. *Journal of Abnormal Psychology, 82,* 268–272.

Fine, M. J., & Caldwell, T. E. (1967). Self evaluation of school related behavior of educable mentally retarded children: A preliminary report. *Exceptional Children, 33,* 324.

Fountain House, New York City. (1999). *The wellspring of the clubhouse model for social and vocational adjustment of persons with serious mental illness.* Center City, MN: Hazelden Press.

Garety, P., Fowler, D., & Kuipers, E. (2000). Cognitive–behavioral therapy for medication-resistant symptoms. *Schizophrenia Bulletin, 26,* 73–86.

Garety, P. A., Kuipers, L., Fowler, D., Chamberlain, F., & Dunn, G. (1994). Cognitive behavioural therapy for drug-resistant psychosis. *British Journal of Medical Psychology, 67,* 259–271.

Gould, R. A., Mueser, K. T., Bolton, E., Mays, V., & Goff, D. (2001). Cognitive therapy for psychosis in schizophrenia: An effect size analysis. *Schizophrenia Research, 48,* 335–342.

Gruenberg, A. M., & Goldstein, R. D. (1997). Depressive disorders. In A. Tasman, J. Kay, & J. Lieberman (Eds.), *Psychiatry* (pp. 990–1015). Philadelphia: W. B. Saunders.

Hayward, P., & Bright, J. A. (1997). Stigma and mental illness: A review and critique. *Journal of Mental Health, 6,* 345–354.

Hoelter, J. W. (1983). Factorial invariance and self-esteem: Reassessing race and sex differences. *Social Forces, 61,* 834–846.

Holmes, P., & River, L. P. (1998) Individual strategies for coping with the stigma of severe mental illness. *Cognitive and Behavioral Practice, 5,* 231–239.

Jensen, G. F., White, C. S., & Gelleher, J. M. (1982). Ethnic status and adolescent self-evaluations: An extension of research on minority self-esteem. *Social Problems, 30*, 226–239.

Kingdon, D., & Turkington, D. (1991). The use of cognitive behavior therapy with a normalizing rationale in schizophrenia: a preliminary report. *Journal of Nervous and Mental Disease, 179*, 207–211.

Kingdon, D. G., & Turkington, D. (1994). *Cognitive–behavioral therapy of schizophrenia*. New York: Guilford Press.

Klingberg, S., Buchremer, G., Holle, R., Monking, H., & Hornung, W. (1999). Differential therapy effects of psychoeducational psychotherapy for schizophrenic patients—Results of a 2-year follow-up. *European Archives of Psychiatry and Clinical Neuroscience, 249*, 66–72.

Kuipers, E., Garety, P., Fowler, D., Dunn, G., Bebbington, P., Freeman, D., et al. (1997). London-East Anglia randomised controlled trial of cognitive-behavioural therapy for psychosis: I. Effects of the treatment phase. *British Journal of Psychiatry, 171*, 319–327.

Levy, B. (1996). Improving memory in old age through implicit self-stereotyping. *Journal of Personality and Social Psychology, 71*, 1092–1107.

Linehan, M. M. (1993). *Cognitive-behavioral treatment of borderline personality disorder*. New York: Guilford Press.

Link, B. G. (1982). Mental patient status, work, and income: An examination of the effects of a psychiatric label. *American Sociological Review, 47*, 202–215.

Link, B. G. (1987). Understanding labeling effects in the area of mental disorders: An assessment of the effects of expectations of rejection. *American Sociological Review, 52*, 96–112.

Link, B. G., Mirotznik, J., & Cullen, F. T. (1991). The effectiveness of stigma coping orientations: Can negative consequences of mental illness labeling be avoided? *Journal of Health and Social Behavior, 32*, 302–320.

Link, B. G., & Phelan, J. C. (2001). Conceptualizing stigma. *Annual Review of Sociology, 27*, 363–385.

Link, B. G., Struening, E. L., Neese-Todd, S., Asmussen, S., & Phelan, J. C. (2001). Stigma as a barrier to recovery: The consequences of stigma for the self-esteem of people with mental illnesses. *Psychiatric Services, 52*, 1621–1626.

McCubbin, M., & Cohen, D. (1996). Extremely unbalanced: Interest divergence and power disparities between clients and psychiatry. *International Journal of Law and Psychiatry, 19*, 1–25.

McDermott, B. E. (1995). Development of an instrument for assessing self-efficacy in schizophrenic spectrum disorders. *Journal of Clinical Psychology, 51*, 320–331.

Millon, T. (1981). *Disorders of personality: DSM–III: Axis II*. New York: Wiley.

Mills, C. W. (1967). *The sociological imagination*. New York: Oxford University Press.

Mowbray, C. T., Moxley, D. P., Jasper, C. A., & Howell, L. L. (Eds.). (1997). *Consumers as providers in psychiatric rehabilitation*. Columbia, MD: International Association of Psychosocial Rehabilitation Services.

Mueser, K. T., Bond, G. R., Drake, R. E., & Resnick, S. G. (1998). Models of community care for severe mental illness: A review of research on case management. *Schizophrenia Bulletin, 24*, 37–74.

Owens, T. J. (1994). Two dimensions of self-esteem: Reciprocal effects of positive self-worth and self-deprecation on adolescent problems. *American Sociological Review, 59*, 391–407.

Perlick, D. (2001). Special section on stigma as a barrier to recovery: Introduction. *Psychiatric Services, 52*, 1613–1614.

Perlick, D. A., Rosenheck, R. A., Clarkin, J. F., Sirey, J. A., Salahi, J., Struening, E. L., et al. (2001). Stigma as a barrier to recovery: Adverse effects of perceived stigma on social adaptation of persons diagnosed with bipolar affective disorder. *Psychiatric Services, 52*, 1627–1632.

Porter, J. R., & Washington, R. E. (1979). Black identity and self-esteem: A review of studies of black self-concept, 1968–1978. *Annual Review of Sociology, 5*, 53–74.

Rappaport, J. (1987). Terms of empowerment/exemplars of prevention: Toward a theory for community psychology. *American Journal of Community Psychology, 15*, 121–148.

Rappaport, J. (1990). Research methods and the empowerment social agenda. In P. Tolan, C. Key, F. Chertok, & L. Jason (Eds.), *Researching community psychology: Issues of theory and methods* (pp. 51–63). Washington, DC: American Psychological Association.

Rogers, E. S., Chamberlin, J., Ellison, M. L., & Crean, T. (1997). A consumer-constructed scale to measure empowerment among users of mental health services. *Psychiatric Services, 48*, 1042–1047.

Rosenberg, M. (1965). *Society and the adolescent self-image*. Princeton, NJ: Princeton University Press.

Rosenfield, S. (1997). Labeling mental illness: The effects of received services and perceived stigma on life satisfaction. *American Sociological Review, 62*, 660–672.

Segal, S. P., Silverman, C., & Temkin, T. (1995). Measuring empowerment in client-run self-help agencies. *Community Mental Health Journal, 31*, 215–227.

Sensky, T., Turkington, D., Kingdon, D., Scott, J. L., Scott, J., Siddle, R., et al. (2000). A randomized controlled trial of cognitive-behavioral therapy for persistent symptoms in schizophrenia resistant to medication. *Archives of General Psychiatry, 57*, 165–172.

Sherer, M., & Adams, C. H. (1983). Construct validation of the Self-Efficacy Scale. *Psychological Reports, 53*, 899–902.

Shih, M., Pittinsky, T. L., & Ambady, N. (1999). Stereotype susceptibility: Identity salience and shifts in quantitative performance. *Psychological Science, 10*, 80–83.

Siris, S. G. (1995). Depression in schizophrenia. In C. L. Shriqui & H. A. Nasrallah (Eds.), *Contemporary issues in the treatment of schizophrenia* (pp. 155–166). Washington, DC: American Psychiatric Press.

Speer, P. W., Jackson, C. B., & Peterson, N. A. (2001). The relationship between social cohesion and empowerment: Support and new implications for theory. *Health Education & Behavior, 28*, 716–732.

Steele, C. M. (1997). A threat in the air: How stereotypes shape intellectual identity and performance. *American Psychologist, 52*, 613–629.

Steele, C. M., & Aronson, J. (1995). Stereotype threat and the intellectual test performance of African Americans. *Journal of Personality and Social Psychology, 69*, 797–811.

Stein, L. I., & Test, M. A. (1980). Alternative to mental hospital treatment: I. Conceptual model, treatment program, and clinical evaluation. *Archives of General Psychiatry, 37*, 392–397.

Strauss, J. S. (1969). Hallucinations and delusions as points on continua function: Rating scale evidence. *Archives of General Psychiatry, 21*, 581–586.

Struening, E. L., Perlick, D. A., Link, B. G., Hellman, F., Herman, D., & Sirey, J. (2001). The extent to which caregivers believe most people devalue consumers and their families. *Psychiatric Services, 52*, 1633–1638.

Tafarodi, R. W., & Swann, W. B. (2001). Two-dimensional self-esteem: Theory and measurement. *Personality and Individual Differences, 31*, 653–673.

Tarrier, N., Beckett, R., Harwood, S., Baker, A., Yusupoff, L., & Ugarteburu, I. (1993). A trial of two cognitive-behavioural methods of treating drug-resistant residual psychotic symptoms in schizophrenic patients: I. Outcome. *British Journal of Psychiatry, 162*, 524–532.

Tarrier, N., Yusupoff, L., Kinney, C., McCarthy, E., & Gledhill, A. (1998). Randomised controlled trial of intensive cognitive behaviour therapy for patients with chronic schizophrenia. *British Medical Journal, 317*, 303–307.

Taylor, S. M., & Dear, M. J. (1980). Scaling community attitudes toward the mentally ill. *Schizophrenia Bulletin, 7*, 225–240.

Tipton, R. M., & Worthington, E. L. (1984). The measurement of generalized self-efficacy: A study of construct validity. *Journal of Personality Assessment, 48*, 545–548.

Turkington, D., & Kingdon, D. (2000). Cognitive–behavioural techniques for general psychiatrists in the management of patients with psychoses. *British Journal of Psychiatry, 177*, 101–106.

Willy, N. R., & McCandless, B. R. (1973). Social stereotypes for normal educable mentally retarded, and orthopedically handicapped children. *Journal of Special Education, 7*, 283–288.

Wright, E. R., Gronfein, W. P., & Owens, T. J. (2000). Deinstitutionalization, social rejection, and the self-esteem of former mental patients. *Journal of Health Social Behavior, 41*, 68–90.

Zimmerman, M., & Rappaport, J. (1988). Citizen participation, perceived control, and psychological empowerment. *American Journal of Community Psychology, 16*, 725–750.

12

DEALING WITH STIGMA THROUGH PERSONAL DISCLOSURE

PATRICK W. CORRIGAN

One of the distinguishing features of the stigma of mental illness is that the mark that specifically signals harm may not be readily apparent. Unlike race and gender, for example, no externally manifest cues signal that an individual belongs to the group stigmatized as "mentally ill." Put another way, people with mental illness may be able to escape some of the harm caused by both public and self-stigma by not letting other people know they belong to this stigmatized group. Hence, one way to avoid stigma is by not disclosing one's experience with mental illness and mental health services. Concluding, however, that it is best to conceal one's psychiatric history suggests that disclosure yields only harm with no benefits. In reality, neither the definition of what is disclosure nor the comparative costs and benefits of disclosure is clear.

In some ways the lesson of contact and mental illness stigma may parallel the experiences of the gay and lesbian community. Most individuals can hide membership in either group should they so choose. Gays and lesbians have discovered that they and their community benefit when individuals choose to disclose their sexual orientation and come out of the closet. In this chapter, I argue that the community of people with mental illness may similarly benefit from disclosing their illness to the public at large.

The purpose of this paper is to review the research literature on what is known about personal disclosure in terms of sexual orientation. In the process, we will highlight some recurring themes that may inform similar decisions that are faced by people who are stigmatized by mental illness. I wish the reader to recognize the purpose of this comparison task. I do not mean to imply that homosexuality and mental illness are transposable any more than that gays and lesbians have the same kind of experiences as people of color. Nevertheless, important similarities exist between the experience of being gay and having a mental illness in America. Gays and lesbians have benefited from decisions regarding coming out. It is not unreasonable, given the similarities, that people with mental illness can benefit from the lessons learned by gays and lesbians about coming out.

LESSONS LEARNED ON COMING OUT

Three specific issues that emerge from this literature are discussed here. First, I consider issues related to identity development and how that influences decisions and behaviors related to coming out. Second, the advantages and disadvantages of coming out are considered. This kind of cost–benefit analysis may inform individual decisions about disclosing experiences with mental illness. Finally, a behavioral definition of coming out is offered. The goal here is to debunk the notion that coming out is a unitary, all-or-nothing phenomenon; instead, disclosure may occur in multiple ways. As stated earlier, we seek to better understand ways in which people might manage the stigma of mental illness by comparing their experiences to those of gays, lesbians, and bisexuals. For this enterprise to be fruitful, we have to demonstrate that the comparison is valid. Table 12.1 outlines four characteristics of stigma that are similar across groups.

First, the mark that signals the stigma of homosexuality or mental illness is not readily transparent. Goffman (1963) distinguished stigmatized groups like these from groups whose stigmatizing mark is readily observed (e.g., the skin color that signals ethnic minority groups or the physical characteristics that signal gender). This notion may seem contrary to naive psychological ideas that gays and people with mental illness are easily recognizable. Members of the general public may list several cues that are thought to be characteristic of each group but in fact lead to mistaken identification. For example, labeling effeminate or persnickety men as gay will lead to false positives (Brookey, 2000). Similarly, tagging disheveled or eccentric people as mentally ill is often wrong (Corrigan, 2000). Because individuals in both sets may choose to conceal their membership in a stigmatized group, disclosure and coming out are key elements of identity for these groups.

Yet another commonality lies in the vagaries of categorical distinctiveness between the stigmatized group (gays or people with mental illness) and

TABLE 12.1
A Comparison of the Stigmatizing Experiences of
Gays, Lesbians, and Bisexuals Versus People With Mental Illness

Social characteristic of stigma	Similarities between gays and people with mental illness
The mark that signals the prejudice	Largely concealable: several cues that lead to false positives.
Perceived cause	Condition that represents socially abnormal behavior; treatment can eradicate it.
Categorical distinctiveness	On one hand, public views both groups as homogeneous and grossly different from norm. On the other hand, both are not readily comprehensible as binary phenomena.
Onset of experience	Frequently identity problems emerge in adolescence or young adulthood where first experience with homosexuality or mental illness emerge.

the majority. On one hand, naive psychological notions might suggest that homosexuality (or mental illness) distinguishes a unique category from the rest of the population (straight people or non-mentally ill). They are frequently described as binary groups (Cover, 2000): A person is either straight or gay, mentally ill or sane. This kind of duality accentuates the "we versus they" qualities that augment stigma (Link & Phelan, 2001). Note however, that the idea of duality is false for both groups. Although many people characterize themselves as either gay or straight, this is not an unequivocal categorization. Many self-identify as heterosexuals and have had gay or lesbian experiences. Conversely, gays and lesbians exist who have had sex with the opposite gender. Finally, a significant group of people exist who are bisexual altogether (Bronn, 2001; Rust, 2001) identifying with elements of the lifestyle of both heterosexuals and homosexuals. The line between gay and straight is much fuzzier than first impressions might suggest.

Similarly, the boundary between mental illness and "normal" is fuzzy. First, epidemiological research suggests that the prevalence rate of major mental illnesses like schizophrenia, major depression, and bipolar disorder is as high as 20%, thereby debunking the idea that mental illness is a rare occurrence that strikes a tiny minority (Narrow, Rae, Robins, & Regier, 2002). Second, and more germane to my point here, many of the characteristic symptoms of mental illness including depression and anxiety are quite common, albeit at subclinical levels. Hence, like gay versus straight, a transparent distinction between the sane and mentally ill is not borne out by the data.

Another commonality between homosexuality and mental illness is the way in which experiences with stigma emerge. This similarity can be understood by contrasting it to the experiences of those whose stigma are readily manifest from birth (e.g., women and ethnic minorities). People of color and women are born into families and communities who typically bear the same marks, are clearly aware of potential prejudice that results from the stigma, and provide some guidance for how people should respond to prejudice when it occurs. The life experiences that result in someone calling themselves gay or mentally ill typically occur in adolescence and young adulthood rather than at birth (Fisher & Akman, 2002; Weiser et al., 2001). They are developmental processes that are often experienced as alien. Gays and lesbians do not understand their homoerotic orientations in light of the dominant heterosexual world in which they are raised. Similarly, people with mental illness do not understand their experiences with depression, anxiety, or psychosis in normal "nonsymptomatic" society. These are foreign experiences not only to the individual, but also to his or her family and support system. At the worst, family members and others ostracize the person who is struggling with either their gay or mentally ill identity (Savin-Williams, 2001). More commonly, parents and other mentors are unable to provide any clarity to this alien experience, such that the person feels all the more estranged from what seemed familiar.

Finally, both groups have been stigmatized because of similar, society-wide misperceptions. In earlier times, homosexuality and mental illness were viewed in moral terms. According to this perspective, homosexuality represented a volitional decision to opt for a sinful lifestyle (Zachary, 2001). Mental illness embodied the demon-possessed individual who did not have sufficient moral backbone to hold off Lucifer (Kinzie, 2000). The 19th and 20th centuries replaced the religious models with views that medicalized the conditions (Duberman, 1993; Foucault, 1980). The *Diagnostic and Statistical Manual of Mental Disorders* (*DSM–I*) listed homosexuality among the sociopathic personality disturbances and defined it as a sexual deviation involving pathological behavior (American Psychiatric Association, 1952). *DSM–II* cut the category of sociopathic personality disturbances but continued to list homosexuality among deviant sexual practices (American Psychiatric Association, 1968). At the same time, most of what we consider to be major mental illnesses—schizophrenia, bipolar disorder, major depression—have been defined as medical conditions (American Psychiatric Association, 1952, 1968, 1980). Homosexuality per se was removed as a psychiatric disorder from *DSM–III* (American Psychiatric Association, 1980).

Implicit in the medicalizing of a phenomenon is *also* the idea that it can be corrected through treatment. Earlier in the twentieth century, some mental health professionals believed homosexuality could be cured through intensive psychotherapy. Hence, those who opt not to seek treatment or to obtain the cure are somehow to blame for their aberrant lifestyle. Most social scientists and health care professionals now recognize gays and lesbians as having an alternative lifestyle that is not an appropriate target of psychotherapy (Davies & Neal, 2000). Just as health care providers would not support an intervention to teach African Americans to ignore their heritage and act White, so it is no longer appropriate to view homosexuality as something that needs to be eradicated. It is interesting to note that some groups typically associated with the religious right still maintain that homosexuality is an appropriate target for behavior change and that providers associated with these groups have methods that will effectively help the person give up their gay or lesbian lifestyle. However, research generally seems to be unable to support its efficacy.

In some ways, parallels between gay life styles and mental illness diminish here. Unlike homosexuality, mental illnesses continued to be construed by the psychiatric community as medical conditions (American Psychiatric Association, 1987, 1994, 2000). Nor do I mean to imply, as did Thomas Szasz (1974), that mental illnesses are not medical conditions. Quite the contrary, evidence is clearly compelling that the primary cause of most major mental illnesses is genetic (Holzman, 1992; Tsuang & Faraone, 1996), *in utero* (Brown & Susser, 2002; Kendell & Kemp, 1989), or in some other way biological in origin (McClure & Weinberger, 2001). The parallel between homosexuality and mental illness also diminishes when considering issues related to treatment. Although several mental health survivor groups question the legitimacy of psychiatric treatment (Crossley, 1998), empirical research generally suggests that most people with mental illness are better able to cope with harmful symptoms or accomplish life goals that are impeded by disabilities when partnering with competent mental health care providers and receiving evidence-based pharmacotherapy and psychosocial services (Drake et al., 2001). Hence, unlike gays and lesbians, frequently treatment has a central role in the lives of many people with major mental disorders.

One other difference seems to emerge between gays and people with mental illness: choice. Most advocates and researchers agree that essential to the psychological well-being of gays, lesbians, and bisexuals is embracing their sexual orientation (Besner & Spungin, 1995). They need to recognize their innate preferences and identify themselves accordingly. At first appearances, the parallel does not seem to hold for people with mental illness. Rare would be the advocate or the researcher who would suggest that the person with mental illness needs to embrace his or her symptoms. Instead, it appears that the number one goal of membership in the mental illness group is to get out of it. Some clinicians and advocates assert, however, that a necessary part of recovery is identifying the role that one's experience with mental illness and psychiatric services plays in defining the self (Fisher, 1994; Mosher & Burti, 1992). Persons with serious mental illness need to admit that recurring aspects of the disorder are part of who they are. Despite the reasonableness of this perspective, a review of the literature yielded no empirical studies on identity development as a person with mental illness; in other words, how does experience with psychiatric symptoms, disabilities, and treatment affect the person's understanding of who they are vis-à-vis their mental illness (Blanch, Penny, & Knight, 1995)? Instead, the professional literature mostly views mental illness as a pathogen that interferes with identity development. This difference in viewpoints is ripe for conceptual development and empirical testing in two ways. First, does mental illness as an experience have significance for identity development in ways other than disruption? If yes, then what models might explain identity and identity development in people with mental illness? Some models of identity development relevant to gays and lesbians are reviewed in the next section as possible candidates.

Nevertheless, medicalizing mental illness, like gay and lesbian lifestyles, may lead to stigma in some ways. Implied in the medical model is the idea that people associated with mental illness are less than normal or somehow aberrant. The confusion between less than common behaviors that are statistically rare and the person who exhibits these behaviors as abnormal leads to prejudice and discrimination.

IDENTITY DEVELOPMENT

Fundamental to personal disclosure and coming out is the realization that someone is in the closet (i.e., that they belong to a stigmatized group about which they may choose not to disclose). Hence, individuals need to develop the realization that "I am mentally ill" before questions about in or out of the closet are relevant. Researchers of gay and lesbian lifestyles have developed a series of models that represent identity development in this population (McCarn & Fassinger, 1996; Rosario, Hunter, Maguen, Gwadz, & Smith, 2001; Vincke, De Rycke, & Bolton, 1999); see Table 12.2 for examples. Like other developmental models, researchers have struggled with stage models, developmental benchmarks, or some other theory that represents how people react over time to the realization that they differ from the status quo. Nevertheless, these models may serve as analogous ways to understand how people with mental illness come to identify themselves as "mentally ill."

One model with a fair amount of empirical support has described the process of integrating a lesbian and gay identity into the self-concept by dividing it into six stages (Brady & Busse, 1994; Cass, 1979, 1984; Sophie, 1985). The left hand column of Table 12.2 reviews those stages as applied to identity development in gays and lesbians. I extrapolate these stages here in the text to issues related to identity development for people with mental illness.

During the first two stages, identity confusion and comparison, people begin to question their sanity. They are keenly aware of their psychiatric symptoms and feel alienated from the seemingly "normal" population, which appears to be unbothered by similar experiences. Slowly, people in this situation learn to tolerate this new identity and seek out others with mental illness to better accept this newly discovered part of themselves. Research has shown that, first, many people with mental illness have diminished social support networks (Bengtsson-Tops & Hansson, 2001) in part that may arise

TABLE 12.2
Two Stage Theories of Identity Development

Integrating a lesbian–gay identity into the self-concept (Cass, 1979)	Describing the negro to Black conversion (Cross, 1971)
Identity confusion: questioning assumptions about one's sexual orientation	**Pre-encounter:** political naivete and dependence on White dominance
Identity comparison: feelings of isolation and alienation from both prior assumptions and nongay others	**Encounter:** a challenge to the individual's view of self and other Blacks
Identity tolerance: seeking out other gay people and tolerating a gay identity	**Immersion-Emersion:** immersion in the Black world and hostility toward Whites
Identity acceptance: selective identity disclosure to others	**Internalization:** the incorporation of learnings into the self-concept
Identity pride: immersion in gay culture and rejection of heterosexual values	**Internalization-Commitment:** a transformation to conscious anger, self-love, and Black communalism
Identity synthesis: gay identity is one aspect of the self instead of an overriding independent entity	

because of stigma (Wahl, 1999) and second, that the psychological well-being of people with mental illness improves with the support of peers (Davidson et al., 1999). At the identity acceptance stage of identity development, people decide to disclose to selected others, those who would not seem likely to react to such information with disapproval. Concern and fear about one's mental illness may be replaced by pride. People become immersed in the culture of consumer, survivor, and ex-patient groups (Frese & Davis, 1997; Trainor, Shepherd, Boydell, Leff, & Crawford, 1997). Moreover, a rejection of values in the dominant culture occurs; one way this shows is the anti-psychiatry movement, which eschews psychopharmacology and psychotherapy for the mental health needs of people (Crossley, 1998). According to this model, the relative extremism of identity pride is replaced by identity synthesis where the person's identity as mentally ill becomes only one aspect of a unique identity.

Cass's (1979) model of identity integration as outlined in Table 12.2 assumes statements like "I am gay and proud of it!" are an essential element of developing a self-concept that promotes psychological well-being. It is still unclear whether a parallel exists in mental illness: "I am mentally ill and proud of it!" Is this a necessary part of the self that needs to be recognized and included into an integrated view of one's self? Research needs to continue to identify the necessary components of experience that make them relevant to self-identity. For example, several other parts of the human experience appear, like eye color, foot size, and the frequent presence of colds, that do not typically lead to identity statements in Western cultures.

An alternative way to view statements like "I am mentally ill and proud of it!" may be as a necessary political assertion. Namely, because people with mental illness are discriminated by the majority, they may need to identify their similarities as a stigmatized group and obtain greater social power through identity and association within the group. In this case, an identity model like Cross's (1971)—summarized in the right hand column of Table 12.2—may be illustrative of the development process. Several studies have empirically validated aspects of this paradigm (Hall, Cross, & Freedle, 1972; Mio & Iwamasa, 1993; Parham, 1989; Ponterotto & Sabnani, 1989; Ridley, Mendoza, & Kanitz, 1994). This model seeks to map identity development in African Americans as they move from a "Negro" identity, which included some of the stereotypes about the group and was typically imposed by the majority, to a "Black" identity, which represents views that emerge from the African American community. Once again, we consider how this model might apply to people with mental illness. During the pre-encounter stage, people with mental illness are unaware of their political plight and of the way that assumptions by the seemingly "normal" majority influence attitudes about them. The subsequent encounter stage brings into awareness these subtle assumptions in two ways. First, people experiencing early signs of significant psychiatric symptoms are challenged by their view of normalcy. Second, people struggling with psychiatric symptoms encounter advocates who are out of the closet and seemingly dealing with the prejudice that mental illness entails. These challenges lead to immersion, in which some people steep themselves in the consumer-ex-patient-survivor movement. This immersion leads to hostility toward the "normal" majority and rejection of psychiatric services.

During the internalization phase, ideas that are learned as the result of interacting with the consumer-ex-patient-survivor community become part of the person's self-identity. People transition from statements about "them" ("The consumer community is supportive and artistic because of its common bond with mental illness") to about "me" ("I am supportive and artistic because of my mental illness"). In the last stage of Cross' model—internalization-commitment—the identity statements yield affective products including righteous anger and self-love.

BENEFITS AND COSTS TO DISCLOSING

Both costs and benefits exist to disclosing one's experiences with mental illness (Chin & Kroesen, 1999; Hays et al., 1993). Given a list of positive and negative outcomes to disclosing, opting whether and how to disclose is not a transparent decision that all people stigmatized with mental illness should pursue in a set manner. Rather individuals should weigh personal perceptions of the costs against the benefits to decide about disclosure. This kind of decisional comparison has been discussed extensively in both social (Ajzen & Fishbein, 1980) and clinical psychology (Miller & Rollnick, 1991) as a mechanism for opting how to proceed in terms of a specific behavioral goal.

What are specific advantages and disadvantages to identifying with a stigmatized group and opting out of the closet? Perhaps most sobering among the risks of coming out is bodily harm. The news regularly reports on hate crimes in which gay men in particular are the victims of extreme violence. The case of Matthew Shepard is perhaps best known. This 21-year-old Denver resident was tortured and beaten to death outside of Laramie, Wyoming on Columbus Day, 1998 because he was gay. Unfortunately, this is not a rare occurrence. Results of one study showed 41% of a sample of lesbians and gay men reported being victim of a bias-related crime since age 16 and another 9.5% reported an attempted bias crime against them (Herek & Gillis, 1997). Data provided by Human Rights Watch (2001) has shown that more than 80% of gay and lesbian students report incidents of name-calling and other forms of verbal harassment in a single year.

On one hand, there does not seem to be a facile comparison between these kinds of hate crimes and the experiences of people with mental illness. No body of evidence clearly suggests that people with mental illness who disclose are frequently victims of crime and other abuse in retaliation for their "mentally ill" life style. There may be some guilt by association; one group with which people with mental illness are frequently associated, homeless individuals, has been the victim of hate crimes. The National Coalition for the Homeless (2001) reported 43 murders and 23 other violent acts against people because of their homeless status. Alternatively, some advocates believe physical abuse against people with mental illness comes in a more subtle form (Chamberlin, 1998; Fisher & Ahern, 2000). Namely, the prescription of mandated treatments, such as involuntary inpatient commitment, outpatient commitment, and mandated medication has been used as a violent measure against people with mental illness. Research has shown that some people with mental illness who have been the target of mandated or coercive treatment experience these treatments as harmful and abusive (Svensson & Hansson, 1994).

Other examples exist of less violent, but still punitive, consequences to disclosing. Many members of the general public may choose to avoid people who come out. Experiences of social disapproval may negatively impact the self-esteem of people who are out. Of even greater concern, the effort to avoid people who are out may translate into job and housing discrimination. Individuals who are out of the closet in terms of their psychiatric conditions are far less likely to obtain or maintain jobs because of stigma (Corrigan & Watson, 2002). Such egregious acts as being victimized by crime or job discrimination are only the most flagrant examples of a society that views gays and lesbians with opprobrium. The kind of stress that results from this culture will have negative psychological effects on gays living in it. Research suggests that teens struggling with gay identity are more likely to attempt suicide (Savin-Williams, 2001) or a variety of other risky behaviors including running away, substance abuse, and prostitution (Saphira & Glover, 2001; Savin-Williams, 1994). In like fashion, we would be concerned abut the effects of public disclosure of a person's mental illness on his or her self-esteem and self-efficacy (Corrigan & Watson, 2002).

Despite the disadvantages, research has clearly shown multiple benefits to disclosing one's sexual orientation, benefits that might be equally applicable to people with mental illness who disclose. Perhaps key among these is the removal of the stress that results from having to no longer keep a secret on such an important part of one's identity (Rosario et al., 2001). Diminished stress leads to better interpersonal relationships (Beals & Peplau, 2001) and improved job satisfaction (Day, 2000; Day & Schoenrade, 1997). Moreover, people who come out report greater support from their families (Kadushin, 2000). Hence, in the abstract, coming out seems to yield many benefits. Moreover, as a group, the community of gays and lesbians seemed to have embraced coming out as beneficial for the political and socioeconomic needs of its communities. Advocacy groups repeatedly urge individuals to come out at all levels. Although the benefit for the community seems clear, the impact on individuals within that community is less transparent. No algorithms suggest how the costs and benefits of coming out will add up to affect an individual. Hence, the individual must consider these advantages and disadvantages for themselves in deciding whether to disclose. Moreover, disclosure is not a black or white decision such as, "I'm either out to the world or in the closet." In the next section, several levels of disclosure and its impact on people making the disclosure decision are reviewed.

DIFFERENT LEVELS OF DISCLOSURE

Given the costs and benefits of coming out, several strategies exist for disclosing. Qualitative studies have interviewed people in the gay community and individuals with mental illness to uncover the variety of ways in which this may occur. Results of these studies are summarized in Table 12.3. Cain (1991) interviewed 38 gay men and generated two lists of functions served by either coming out or choosing to stay in the closet. In some ways, Cain's work on the functions of coming out provides an alternative way of viewing the costs and benefits of disclosure. However, his work is presented here because it more directly captures places, settings, and behaviors that actually describe the coming out process.

Cain believes people choose to disclose because it meets six needs: (a) Research has shown that maintaining a secret about an important aspect of

TABLE 12.3
Different Ways to Deal With Coming Out and Staying Out

General disclosure strategies (Herman, 1993; Corrigan & Lundin, 2001)	Situation-based disclosure approaches (Cain, 1991)	Types of concealment (Cain, 1991)	Strategies for those who are out
Social avoidance: altogether keep away from persons and places where prejudice may be experienced who are out	**Therapeutic disclosure:** Telling someone to enhance one's self-esteem	**Inappropriateness:** disclosure in specific situation would be irrelevant or incorrect	**Advocacy groups and support centers:** Join in communities that can provide information and support for those
Secrecy: don't tell persons at places you work or live	**Relationship-building:** motivated by respondent's desire to improve relationship with specific person	**Deference:** concealed experience out of respect for another's beliefs	**Appropriate stigmatizing terms:** Use terms like queer and mad as symbols of pride
Selective disclosure: tell some persons who may be supportive	**Problem-solving:** a way to resolve a situational or interactional problem	**Avowal of responsibility:** person does not have the courage to do so	**Outing people:** publicly disclose a person who chooses to remaining the closet
Indiscriminatory disclosure: don't be concerned about who knows; tell everyone encountered	**Preventive:** people disclose to avoid anticipated problems	**Political:** hide sexual orientation because of concerns about political retribution	
Broadcast: Purposefully and publicly communicate your experiences	**Political:** a public effort to increase the visibility and power of the gay community		
	Spontaneous: not all disclosures are planned		

one's identity is inversely related to psychological well-being (Rosario et al., 2001). Hence, disclosing the secret serves the therapeutic purpose of enhancing one's self-esteem. (b) Disclosing may enhance relationships with some people. Many people reported great difficulty in developing close relationships with others when the closeted secret was between them. This kind of disclosure was essential for building mutual and trusting relationships and most typically focused on family members and friends. (c) Sometimes people disclosed as a way to resolve interpersonal problems. One specific example with relevance to mental illness was coming out to avoid constant questions about one's whereabouts when covertly involved in the gay world (or mental health community). (d) Preventive disclosures attempt to avoid worse outcomes that might occur by accidentally discovering that a person is gay. Examples obtained by Cain included people who were concerned that acquaintances might see them coming out of a gay establishment so he told these key people first. (e) Disclosure may serve an individual's political agenda. Some people opt to publicly announce their sexual orientation because they believe the more people that are out, the more the homophobic majority will diminish their prejudice. (f) Finally, Cain noticed that disclosure sometimes serves a spontaneous function. Examples include on-the-spot decisions or slips of the tongue. Alternatively, gay men in Cain's survey noted that sometimes unforeseen yet opportune moments emerge when the person decides to disclose on the spot.

Cain (1991) noted that just as reasons exist why people opt to disclose, so too functions keep people in the closet. Called concealment, four examples are also summarized in Table 12.3: (a) Often, people believe that disclosure is neither appropriate nor relevant to the situation. For example, several people reported it would be improper to share their sexual orientation with parents who have discouraged any discussion whatsoever on sexual matters. (b) Some people opt to conceal their homosexuality out of deference to a significant other. Age was often cited as reason to defer and not tell someone. People like aging parents or grandparents were perceived as unable to comprehend the disclosure message. (c) Some people stay in the closet, despite believing disclosure is the noble and necessary act, because they lack the necessary resources to do so. They are personally responsible for concealing because they are not brave enough for the challenge. (d) Finally, some people opt not to disclose because of concerns about political retribution. At the most pragmatic level, they are concerned that people in positions of power might use the information against them (e.g., an employer who does not give the person a promotion after that person has disclosed).

In an ethnographic study of 146 people with mental illness, Herman (1993) identified several specific ways in which people might disclose. On the basis of our work with mental health advocates (Corrigan & Lundin, 2001), we summarized her work into five specific levels of disclosure summarized in Table 12.3. These levels show that the actual behavior of disclosure is complex and multi-leveled. A person's decision about these matters is not limited to either "Yes, I am out entirely!" or "No, I will tell no one!" Multiple levels exist, in between which serve the functions of disclosure and concealment outlined by Cain (1991). According to Herman (1993), at the most extreme level, people may stay in the closet through *social avoidance*. This means keeping away from situations where people may find out about one's mental illness. People who are victimized by stigma may choose to not socialize with, live near, or work alongside persons without disabilities. Instead, they only associate with other persons who have mental illness. This may include persons with mental illness living in a therapeutic community, working in a sheltered or supported work environment, or interacting with friends in a social club developed for mental illness. In this way, the person can avoid the "normal" population that may disapprove of their disabilities or actively work to keep them out.

No need exists to avoid work or community situations to keep one's experiences with mental illness private. Many persons choose to enter these worlds but not share their experiences with others. *Secrecy* provides a means to do this. An alternative version of this is *selective disclosure*. Some people take a chance and disclose their mental illness to selected coworkers or neighbors. These people are taking a risk, however; those who find out may shun them. With the risk comes opportunity. Persons who disclose may find people who are supportive. Moreover, they do not have to worry about keeping a secret near those to whom they have disclosed.

Selective disclosure means both a group of people with whom private information is disclosed *and* a group from whom this information is kept secret exist. More than likely, the latter group is much larger than those to whom the information has been shared. This means a considerable number of people still exist to be wary of—individuals who are not in on the information. Moreover, this means a secret still exists that could represent a source of shame. People who choose *indiscriminant disclosure* abandon the secrecy. They choose to disregard any of the negative consequences of people finding out about their mental illness. Hence, they make no active efforts to try to conceal their mental health history and experiences. Note, however, that the decision to no longer conceal mental illness is not the same as telling everyone one's story. *Broadcasting* one's experience means educating people about mental illness. It's similar to the political goals of coming out of the closet in the gay community. This kind of disclosure is much more than dropping one's guard and throwing away any notion of secret. The goal here is to seek out people to share past history and current experiences with mental illness. Broadcasting has the same benefits as indiscriminant disclosure. The person no longer needs to worry about keeping a secret. However, people who choose to broadcast their experience seem to derive an additional benefit. Namely, it fosters their sense of power over the experience of mental illness and stigma. No longer must they cower because of feelings of inferiority.

The qualitative research described here has been fruitful for obtaining an overall sense of the variety and complexity in opting to come out. However, largely absent from the literature have been quantitative studies that might test the hypotheses that emerge from these findings. In particular, researchers have asserted that different forms of disclosure will yield different kinds of benefits as well as limitations. Cross-sectional and panel research can examine questions like these. What actually happens to people as they come out in the varying fashions listed is in Table 12.3.

Ways in Which Coming Out Has Been Supported

Although the decision to come out is a personal one, disclosure has been facilitated by a variety of institutions and social movements. Three of these are summarized in the right-hand column of Table 12.3.

The Reappropriation of Stigmatizing Labels

What's in a label—can queer by another name be less pejorative? Several examples to diminish the affect of a bad label are apparent from the commercial world where businesses sought to escape prejudice by changing their names. USAir became USAirways and Valujet morphed into Air Tran after major accidents. The Tories became Conservatives in Britain after major electoral reform in 1832 threatened its ability to command a majority. Colored went to Negro went to Black (Smith, 1992). Learning from these lessons, perhaps one way to deal with prejudice and discrimination is to find words that are less pejorative to describe a stigmatized group. An alternative, more aggressive action has been just the opposite, to reappropriate stigmatizing labels. In the latter instance, a stigmatized group revalues what was a negative label by self-consciously referring to itself in terms of that label (Galinsky, Hugenberg, Groom, & Bodenhausen, in press). Queer is an example of this phenomenon in the gay community. In 1990 four members of ACT-UP dubbed itself Queer Nation with the slogan "We're here. We're Queer. Get used to it." What used to be a disrespectful way of referring to gays and lesbians has been embraced by the community. Other lesbians and gay men have adopted the pink triangle as a symbol of gay pride. Nazi Germany used this figure as a way of identifying gays and lesbians for persecution. Some evidence exists of label reappropriation in the consumer survivor community, too. Perhaps the best example is MadNation. Established in 1997 in St. Louis, MadNation is now comprised of more than 800 members "working together for social justice and human rights in mental health." It can be found at www.networksplus.net/fhp/madnation/announce.htm.

Galinsky and colleagues (in press) identified several benefits to label reappropriation. Perhaps most obvious, the public can no longer use the term against the group. Galinsky and colleagues provide an example from a Simpson's episode where Homer becomes angry with a gay character for using the word queer to describe himself: "And another thing. You can't use the word queer . . . that is our word for you!" Second, reappropriation implies that deviance or abnormality is not a bad thing. Lastly, the reappropriation of a term like queer or mad actually becomes a source of pride for people who are out. In turn, this kind of pride enhances the self-esteem of individuals who willingly wear it.

Galinsky and colleagues (in press) described three levels to reappropriation of a label. At the most basic, charismatic individuals decide to use a potentially derogatory label to describe themselves. Examples include Dick Gregory and Richard Pryor who described themselves as "nigger" in their respective work. Note that although this label may be used by individuals, it does not seem to be a term that has gained widespread use in African American advocacy groups. Second, the individual descriptor moves to the collective; a stigmatized group may collectively decide that widespread reappropriation of a term is needed. As alluded to earlier, this happened in the gay community when prominent advocacy groups referred to themselves as queer. A similar phenomenon has occurred in the mentally ill community in people who have reappropriated "mad" to describe themselves. Reappropriation is most successful at its third level where the term has achieved widespread reappropriation (i.e., when the majority respectfully refers to the stigmatized group with this term). It is not clear that this level has been achieved in the gay community; I could find no data or anecdotal evidence that the straight majority affectionately refers to the gay community as queer. However, reapporpiration, and its relationship to diminished prejudice, is most evident when widespread acknowledgement of the proud label is evident.

Advocacy and Support Groups

A second social phenomenon that facilitates disclosure is the advocacy and support groups made up of people who are out. These groups sometimes adopt a reappropriated name and become a prominent resource in the community for people of a stigmatized group. An example in the gay community is the Gay and Lesbian Alliance. Groups like these provide a broad range of services and opportunities including support for those who are struggling with being out of the closet, recreation and shared experiences that foster a sense of community within a larger hostile culture, and advocacy–political efforts to further promote gay pride (Kates & Belk, 2001). Clearly, such communities have a measurable influence on the broader society too. For example, they become a market place with power over a sizeable portion of the business world that desires its consumers (Bowes, 1996). This kind of involvement positively affects the individual, too. Research suggests the quality of gay and lesbian relationships improves when partners are involved in the gay community (Beals & Peplau, 2001).

Several forces have converged over the past century to foster consumer-operated services for persons with psychiatric disabilities. Some reflect dissatisfaction with society's reaction to mental illness—its propensity to stigmatize and discriminate—and with mental health services that disempower persons by providing services in restrictive settings or with paternalistic attitudes. Others represent a natural tendency of persons to seek others with similar problems to make sense of their experience. Clifford Beers' description of his experiences as a patient in a psychiatric hospital in *A Mind That Found Itself* (1908) led to the founding of the National Mental Health Association, a group seeking to improve the quality of services for persons with mental illness. In the late 1940s, people released from New York city's state hospitals gathered on the steps of the Public Library to provide support and counsel to one another, creating *We Are Not Alone* (WANA), which later evolved into Fountain House and the clubhouse model of psychosocial rehabilitation (Flannery & Glickman, 1996). About the same time, a mutual-help program called GROW began in Australia when former mental patients sought a group of peers in a sharing and caring community.

More recently, a wide variety of consumer-operated service programs have developed, many of which have been described by Van Tosh and Del Vecchio (2000). These have included drop in centers, housing programs, homeless services, case management, crisis response, benefit acquisition, anti-stigma services, advocacy, research, technical assistance, and employment programs. To better understand the similarities and differences of consumer-operated services, we compare and contrast them to traditional mental health services they seek to augment. Traditional services (as outlined in state-of-the-art practice guidelines; e.g.,Torrey et al., 2001) and consumer-operated services share some *goals* (e.g., recovery, empowerment, improved role functioning, better housing and work opportunities, diminished symptoms, decreased costs), *settings* (essential focus on services in the person's community rather than distant institutions), and *processes* (e.g., interpersonal support, information exchange). These similarities have led to a call for greater linkages between traditional providers and consumer-led programs (Borkman, 1990; United States Surgeon General, 1988). Nevertheless, clear differences remain between consumer organizations and traditional services; these differences are fundamental to each paradigm. Consumer-operated services value empowerment and community, whereas traditional treatment focuses on symptom reduction and role attainment (Carling, 1990; Corrigan, 2003). They differ in the way settings are governed and controlled: Traditional treatment settings tend to be operated by providers, whereas consumer-operated services are open communities owned by its members (Galanter, 1990). They differ in processes: Consumer-operated organizations are hypothesized to facilitate change through sharing and caring among its members (Kaufman, Freund, & Wilson, 1989), whereas traditional treatment combines the impact of medication, psychoeducation, counseling, and in vivo support.

A significant number of empirical studies of consumer-operated services have yielded two recent reviews of the literature (Davidson et al., 1999; Solomon & Draine, 2001). Rather than summarize these reviews, we briefly consider key trends. Most of the prior studies on consumer-operated services have been descriptive or qualitative, seeking to identify the characteristics of people who choose to participate in these programs, the processes that lead to change, and the consumer's perspective on benefits of program participation (Chamberlin, Rogers, & Ellison, 1996; Kaufman, Schuldberg, & Schooler, 1994; Luke, Rappaport, & Seidman, 1991; Mowbray, Chamberlain, Jennings, & Reed, 1988; Mowbray & Tan, 1993; Segal, Silverman, & Temkin, 1995). An interesting example of this involved the findings from a Center for Mental Health Services (CMHS) multisite study on consumer-operated programs. CMHS funded 14 consumer services in 1988 with the goal of demonstrating and evaluating their efficacy. Results of a qualitative evaluation showed that participants in these programs reported improvements in self-reliance and independence, coping skills and knowledge, and feelings of empowerment (Van Tosh & del Vecchio, 2000).

Additional studies have sought to understand the perceived benefits of consumer-operated services by completing outcomes studies with control conditions. For example, research on peer support programs, using nonrandomized control groups or pretest scores as comparisons, has shown that participation in these services yields improvement of psychiatric symptoms and decreased hospitalization (Galanter, 1988), larger social support networks (Carpinello, Knight, & Jarulis, 1992; Rappaport et al., 1985), and enhanced self-esteem and social functioning (Kaufman et al., 1994; Markowitz, 1998). On the basis of this research, one might conclude that substantial preliminary evidence exists supporting consumer-operated services. However, the standard of internally valid, evidence-based outcomes research and random-controlled trials has not been completed on consumer-operated services. Without this kind of research, the impact of history and other variables that might confound interpreting the benefits of consumer-operated services cannot be ruled out. Moreover, research in this category needs to target a broad list of outcomes that are likely to improve because of participation in consumer services. Finally, future research needs to isolate the active ingredients of consumer-operated services that lead to positive change. A list of these common ingredients juxtaposed with putative outcomes will provide a comprehensive test of the assumptions that underlie consumer-operated services.

Outing

A third phenomenon related to disclosure is outing. In the past decade, some gay and lesbian advocates have called for outing people in the closet as a way to advance an antiprejudice agenda. Outing means publicizing the fact that a specific person is gay or lesbian when that person has actively tried to stay in the closet. Outing generates strong ethical debate (Chekola, 1994; Mayo & Gunderson, 1994; McCarthy, 1994) and may vary from what is frequently considered the most justified (e.g., publicly outing a conservative politician who takes an antigay stand on important public issues) to the least (e.g., outing a private citizen who chooses to keep all facets of his or her life private and who will clearly be harmed by the disclosure). In a parallel fashion, people active in the mental illness community might opt to out individuals who are in the closet about their psychiatric problems. There have been examples of the psychiatric problems of famous people being disclosed for political agenda. Perhaps best known of these was Thomas Eagleton's experiences with depression, which were leaked to the press. Senator Eagleton, a democrat from Missouri, was George McGovern's running mate in the 1972 general presidential election. In this instance, however, outing Eagleton was not to serve mental health pride but rather to fan the flames of prejudice.

Research on the effects of outing is limited. One study showed outed gay men manifest the traumatic stress response (Tobias, 1996). I do not think the personal egregious effects of outing would either surprise or dissuade most proponents supporting it. Lacking from the research literature is a sociological study that shows that outing has improved the lot of the gay and lesbian community. In particular, no evidence exists yet to my knowledge that outing has somehow diminished either prejudicial attitudes or discriminatory behaviors toward gays. This needs to be the focus of future research.

CONCLUSION

The gay and lesbian community seems to have realized that coming out has significant advantages for individuals within the community as well as the community as a whole. However, what it means to come out is more complex than the simple notion of letting people know "I am gay," and having that disclosure result in acceptance by others. I argued in this chapter that the experiences of stigma are similar in many ways between people with mental illness and gays/lesbians. Hence, what the gay community has learned about coming out may inform a similar movement in the community of people who identify themselves as mentally ill. In the process, the research that has examined some of the questions related to identity development and disclosure in the gay community may inform similar experiences in people with mental illness. This review has provided a preliminary understanding of the coming out process. It has also illustrated some methods for further examining research questions in this area. In particular, research needs to continue to examine the ways in which the various methods to come out impact the individual as well as the community as a whole.

REFERENCES

Ajzen, I., & Fishbein, M. (1980). *Understanding attitudes and predicting social behavior.* Englewood Cliffs, NJ: Prentice-Hall.

American Psychiatric Association. (1952). *Diagnostic and statistical manual of mental disorders* (1st ed.). Washington, DC: Author.

American Psychiatric Association. (1968). *Diagnostic and statistical manual of mental disorders* (2nd ed.). Washington, DC: Author.

American Psychiatric Association. (1980). *Diagnostic and statistical manual of mental disorders* (3rd ed.). Washington, DC: Author.

American Psychiatric Association. (1987). *Diagnostic and statistical manual of mental disorders* (3rd ed., revised). Washington, DC: Author.

American Psychiatric Association. (1994). *Diagnostic and statistical manual of mental disorders* (4th ed.). Washington, DC: Author.

American Psychiatric Association. (2000). *Diagnostic and statistical manual of mental disorders* (4th ed., revised). Washington, DC: Author.

Beals, K. P., & Peplau, L. A. (2001). Social involvement, disclosure of sexual orientation, and the quality of lesbian relationships. *Psychology of Women Quarterly, 25,* 10–19.

Beers, C. W. (1908). *A mind that found itself: An autobiography.* New York: Longmans, Green, & Co.

Bengtsson-Tops, A., & Hansson, L. (2001). Quantitative and qualitative aspects of the social network in schizophrenic patients living in the community. Relationship to sociodemographic characteristics and clinical factors and subjective quality of life. *International Journal of Social Psychiatry, 47,* 67–77.

Besner, H. F., & Spungin, C. I. (1995). *Gay and lesbian students: Understanding their needs.* Philadelphia, PA: Taylor & Francis.

Blanch, A. K., Penney, D., & Knight, E. (1995). "Identity politics" close to home. *American Psychologist, 50,* 49–50.

Borkman, T. (1990). Self-help groups at the turning point: Emerging egalitarian alliances with the formal health care system? *American Journal of Community Psychology, 18,* 321–332.

Bowes, J. E. (1996). Out of the closet and into the marketplace: Meeting basic needs in the gay community. *Journal of Homosexuality, 31,* 219–244.

Brady, S., & Busse, W. J. (1994). The Gay Identity Questionnaire: A brief measure of homosexual identity formation. *Journal of Homosexuality, 26,* 1–22.

Bronn, C. D. (2001). Attitudes and self images of male and female bisexuals. *Journal of Bisexuality, 1,* 5–29.

Brookey, R. A. (2000). Saints or sinners: Sociobiological theories of male homosexuality. *International Journal of Sexuality & Gender Studies, 5,* 37–58.

Brown, A. S., & Susser, E. S. (2002). In utero infection and adult schizophrenia. *Mental Retardation and Developmental Disabilities Research Reviews, 8,* 51–57.

Cain, R. (1991). Stigma management and gay identity development. *Social Work, 36*, 67–73.

Carling, P. J. (1990). Major mental illness, housing, and supports: The promise of community integration. *American Psychologist, 45*, 969–975.

Carpinello, S. E., Knight, E. L., & Jarulis, L. L. (1992). *A study of the meaning of self-help, self-help group processes, and outcomes.* Proceedings of the Annual Conference on State Mental Health Agency Services Research and Program Evaluation. Alexandria, VA: National Association of State Mental Health Program Directors Research Institute, Inc.

Cass, V. C. (1979). Homosexual identity formation: A theoretical model. *Journal of Homosexuality, 4*, 219–235.

Cass, V. C. (1984). Homosexual identity formation: Testing a theoretical model. *Journal of Homosexuality, 20*, 143–167.

Chamberlin, J. (1998). Citizenship rights and psychiatric disability. *Psychiatric Rehabilitation Journal, 21*, 405–408.

Chamberlin, J., Rogers, E., & Ellison, M. (1996). Self help programs: A description of their characteristics and their members. *Psychiatric Rehabilitation Journal, 19*, 33–42.

Chekola, M. (1994). Outing, truth-telling, and the shame of the closet. *Journal of Homosexuality, 27*, 67–90.

Chin, D., & Kroesen, K. W. (1999). Disclosure of HIV infection among Asian/Pacific Islander American women: Cultural stigma and support. *Cultural Diversity and Ethnic Minority Psychology, 5*, 222–235.

Corrigan, P. W. (2000). Mental health stigma as social attribution: Implications for research methods and attitude change. *Clinical Psychology: Science and Practice, 7*, 48–67.

Corrigan, P. W. (2003). Towards an integrated, structural model of psychiatric rehabilitation. *Psychiatric Rehabilitation Journal, 26*, 346–358.

Corrigan, P. W., & Lundin, R. K. (2001). *Don't call me nuts! Coping with the stigma of mental illness.* Tinley Park, IL: Recovery Press.

Corrigan, P. W., & Watson, A. C. (2002). The paradox of self-stigma and mental illness. *Clinical Psychology: Science and Practice, 9*, 35–53.

Cover, R. (2000). First contact: Queer theory, sexual identity and "mainstream" film. *International Journal of Sexuality & Gender Studies, 5*, 71–89.

Cross, W. E. (1971). Toward a psychology of Black liberation: The Negro-to-Black conversion experience. *Black World, 20*, 13–27.

Crossley, N. (1998). R. D. Laing and the British anti-psychiatry movement: A sociohistoric analysis. *Social Science and Medicine, 47*, 877–889.

Davidson, L., Chinman, M., Kloos, B., Weingarten, R., Stayner, D., & Tebes, J. K. (1999). Peer support among individuals with severe mental illness: A review of the evidence. *Clinical Psychology: Science and Practice, 6*, 165–187.

Davies, D., & Neal, C. (Eds.). (2000). *Therapeutic perspectives on working with lesbian, gay and bisexual clients.* Philadelphia, PA: Open University Press.

Day, N. E. (2000). The relationship among reported disclosure of sexual orientation, anti-discrimintation policies, top management support and work attitudes of gay and lesbian employees. *Personnel Review, 29*, 346–364.

Day, N. E., & Schoenrade, P. (1997). Staying in the closet versus coming out: Relationships between communication about sexual orientation and work attitudes. *Personnel Psychology, 50*, 147–163.

Drake, R. E., Goldman, H. E., Leff, H., Lehman, A. F., Dixon, L., Mueser, K. T., et al. (2001). Implementing evidence-based practices in routine mental health service settings. *Psychiatric Services, 52*, 179–182.

Duberman, M. (1993). *Stonewall*. New York: Dutton.

Fisher, B., & Akman, J. S. (2002). Normal development in sexual minority youth. In B. E. Jones & M. J. Hill (Eds.), *Mental health issues in lesbian, gay, bisexual, and transgender communities: Review of psychiatry*. Washington, DC: American Psychiatric Press.

Fisher, D. B. (1994). Health care reform based on an empowerment model of recovery by people with psychiatric disabilities. *Hospital and Community Psychiatry, 45*, 913–915.

Fisher, D. B., & Ahern, L. (2000). Personal Assistance in Community Existence (PACE): An alternative to PACT. *Ethical Human Sciences and Services, 2*, 87–92.

Flannery, M., & Glickman, M. (1996). *Fountain House portraits of lives reclaimed from mental illness*. New York: Hazelden Information and Educational Services.

Foucault, M. (Ed.). (1980). *Herculine Barbin: Being the recently discovered memoirs of a nineteeth-century French hermaphrodite*. New York: Pantheon.

Frese, F. J., & Davis, W. W. (1997). The consumer-survivor movement, recovery, and consumer professionals. *Professional Psychology: Research and Practice, 28*, 243–245.

Galanter, M. (1988). Zealous self-help groups as adjuncts to psychiatric treatment: A study of Recovery, Inc. *American Journal of Psychiatry, 145*, 1248–1253.

Galanter, M. (1990). Cults and zealous self-help movements: A psychiatric perspective. *American Journal of Psychiatry, 147*, 543–551.

Galinsky, A. D., Hugenberg, K., Groom, C., & Bodenhausen, G. (in press). The reappropriation of stigmatizing labels: Implication for social identity. In M. A. Neale, E. A. Mannix, & J. Polzer (Eds.), *Research in managing on teams and groups*. Greenwich, CT: Elsevier Science.

Goffman, E. (1963). *Stigma: Notes on the management of spoiled identity*. Englewood Cliffs, NJ: Prentice-Hall.

Hall, W. S., Cross, W. E., & Freedle, R. (1972). Stages in the development of a black identity. *Act Research Reports No. 50(21)*.

Hays, R. B., McKusick, L., Pollack, L., Hilliard, R., Hoff, C., & Coates, T. J. (1993). Disclosing HIV seropositivity to significant others. *AIDS, 7*, 425–431.

Herek, G. M., & Gillis, R. (1997). Hate crime victimization among lesbian, gay, and bisexual adults. *Journal of Interpersonal Violence, 12*, 195–207.

Herman, N. J. (1993). Return to sender: Reintegrative stigma-management strategies of ex-psychiatric patients. *Journal of Contemporary Ethnography, 22,* 295–330.

Holzman, P. S. (1992). A new path to the genetics of schizophrenia. In D. J. Kupfer (Ed.), *Reflections on modern psychiatry.* Washington, DC: American Psychiatric Press.

Human Rights Watch. (2001). *World report.* New York: Author.

Kadushin, G. (2000). Family secrets: Disclosure of HIV status among gay men with HIV/AIDS to the family of origin. *Social Work in Health Care, 30,* 1–17.

Kates, S. M., & Belk, R. W. (2001). The meanings of Lesbian and Gay Pride Day: Resistance through consumption and resistance to consumption. *Journal of Contemporary Ethnography, 30,* 392–429.

Kaufman, C., Freund, P., & Wilson, J. (1989). Self-help in the mental health system: A model for consumer-provider collaboration. *Psychosocial Rehabilitation Journal, 13,* 6–21.

Kaufman, C. L., Schulberg, H. C., & Schooler, N. R. (1994). Self-help group participation among people with severe mental illness. *Prevention in Human Services, 11,* 315–331.

Kendell, R. E., & Kemp, I. W. (1989). Maternal influenza in the etiology of schizophrenia. *Archives of General Psychiatry, 46,* 878–882.

Kinzie, J. (2000). The historical relationship between psychiatry and the major religions. In J. K. Boehnlein (Ed.), *Psychiatry and religion: The convergence of mind and spirit issues in psychiatry.* Washington, DC: American Psychiatric Press.

Link, B. G., & Phelan, J. C. (2001). Conceptualizing stigma. *Annual Review of Sociology, 27,* 363–385.

Luke, D. A., Rappaport, J., & Seidman, E. (1991). Setting phenotypes in a mutual help organization: Expanding behavior setting theory. *American Journal of Community Psychology, 19,* 147–167.

Markowitz, F. E. (1998). The effects of stigma on the psychological well-being and life satisfaction of persons with mental illness. *Journal of Health and Social Behavior, 39,* 335–348.

Mayo, D. J., & Gunderson, M. (1994). Privacy and the ethics of outing. *Journal of Homosexuality, 27,* 47–65.

McCarn, S. R., & Fassinger, R. E. (1996). Revisioning sexual minority identity formation: A new model of lesbian identity and its implications. *Counseling Psychologist, 24,* 508–534.

McCarthy, J. (1994). The closet and the ethics of outing. *Journal of Homosexuality, 27,* 27–45.

McClure, R. K., & Weinberger, D. R. (2001). The neurodevelopmental hypothesis of schizophrenia: A review of the evidence. In A. Breier & P. V. Tran (Eds.), *Current issues in the psychopharmacology of schizophrenia.* Philadelphia, PA: Lippincott Williams & Wilkins Publishers.

Miller, W. R., & Rollnick, S. (1991). *Motivational interviewing: Preparing people to change addictive behavior.* New York: Guilford Press.

Mio, J. S., & Iwamasa, G. (1993). To do, or not to do: That is the question for White cross-cultural researchers. *Counseling Psychologist, 21*, 197–212.

Mosher, L. R., & Burti, L. (1992). Relationships in rehabilitation: When technology fails. *Psychosocial Rehabilitation Journal, 15*, 11–17.

Mowbray, C. T., Chamberlain, P., Jennings, M., & Reed, C. (1988). Consumer-run mental health services: Results from five demonstration projects. *Community Mental Health Journal, 24*, 151–156.

Mowbray, C. T., & Tan, C. (1993). Consumer-operated drop-in centers: Evaluation of operations and impact. *Journal of Mental Health Administration, 20*, 8–19.

Narrow, W. E., Rae, D. S., Robins, L. N., & Regier, D. A. (2002). Revised prevalence based estimates of mental disorders in the United States: Using a clinical significance criterion to reconcile 2 surveys' estimates. *Archives of General Psychiatry, 59*, 115–123.

National Coalition for the Homeless. (2001). *HATE: A compilation of violent crimes committed against homeless people in the U.S.* Washington, DC: Author.

Parham, T. A. (1989). Cycles of psychological Nigrescence. *Counseling Psychologist, 17*, 187–226.

Ponterotto, J. G., & Sabnani, H. B. (1989). "Classics" in multicultural counseling: A systematic five-year content analysis. *Journal of Multicultural Counseling and Development, 17*, 23–37.

Rappaport, J., Seidman, E., Toro, P. A., McFadden, L. S., Reischl, T. M., Roberts, L. J., et al. (1985). Collaborative research with a mutual help organization. *Social Policy, Winter*, 12–24.

Ridley, C. R., Mendoza, D. W., & Kanitz, B. E. (1994). Multicultural training: Reexamination, operationalization, and integration. *Counseling Psychologist, 22*, 227–289.

Rosario, M., Hunter, J., Maguen, S., Gwadz, M., & Smith, R. (2001). The coming-out process and its adaptational and health-related associations among gay, lesbian, and bisexual youths: Stipulation and exploration of a model. *American Journal of Community Psychology, 29*, 113–160.

Rust, P. C. (2001). Two many and not enough: The meanings of bisexual identities. *Journal of Bisexuality, 1*, 31–68.

Saphira, M., & Glover, M. (2001). The effects of coming out on relationships and health. *The Journal of Lesbian Studies, 5*, 183–194.

Savin-Williams, R. C. (1994). Verbal and physical abuse as stressors in the lives of lesbian, gay male, and bisexual youths: Associations with school problems, running away, substance abuse, prostitution, and suicide. *Journal of Consulting and Clinical Psychology, 62*, 261–269.

Savin-Williams, R. C. (2001). *Mom, dad, I'm gay. How families negotiate coming out.* Washington, DC: American Psychological Association.

Segal, S. P., Silverman, C., & Temkin, T. (1995). Measuring empowerment in client-run self-help agencies. *Community Mental Health Journal, 31*, 215–227.

Smith, T. W. (1992). Changing racial labels: From "Colored" to "Negro" to "Black" to "African American." *Public Opinion Quarterly, 56*, 496–514.

Solomon, P., & Draine, J. (2001). The state of knowledge of the effectiveness of consumer provided services. *Psychiatric Rehabilitation Journal, 25*, 20–27.

Sophie, J. (1985). A critical examination of stage theories of lesbian identity development. *Journal of Homosexuality, 12*, 39–51.

Svensson, B., & Hansson, L. (1994). Patient satisfaction with inpatient psychiatric care: The influence of personality traits, diagnosis and perceived coercion. *Acta Psychiatrica Scandinavica, 90*, 379–384.

Szasz, T. S. (1974). *The myth of mental illness: Foundations of a theory of personal conduct*. New York: Harper & Row.

Tobias, R. G. (1996). The relationship between the "coming-out" process and traumatic stress responses in gay males. *Dissertation Abstracts International, 57*(2-B), 1457.

Torrey, W. C., Drake, R. E., Dixon, L., Burns, B. J., Flynn, L., Rush, A. J., et al. (2001). Implementing evidence-based practices for persons with severe mental illnesses. *Psychiatric Service, 52*, 45–50.

Trainor, J., Shepherd, M., Boydell, K. M., Leff, A., & Crawford, E. (1997). Beyond the service paradigm: The impact and implications of consumer/survivor initiatives. *Psychiatric Rehabilitation Journal, 21*, 132–140.

Tsuang, M. T., & Faraone, S. V. (1996). Epidemiology and behavioral genetics of schizophrenia. In S. J. Watson (Ed.), *Biology of schizophrenia and affective disease*. Washington, DC: American Psychiatric Press.

United States Surgeon General. (1988). *Surgeon General's workshop on health promotion and aging*. Washington, DC: Author.

Van Tosh, L., & del Vecchio, P. (2000). *Consumer/survivor-operated self-help programs: A technical report*. Rockville, MD: Department of Health and Human Services.

Vincke, J., De Rycke, L., & Bolton, R. (1999). Gay identity and the experience of gay social stress. *Journal of Applied Social Psychology, 29*, 1316–1331.

Wahl, O. F. (1999). Mental health consumers' experience of stigma. *Schizophrenia Bulletin, 25*, 467–478.

Weiser, M., Reichenberg, A., Rabinowitz, J., Kaplan, Z., Mark, M., Bodner, E., et al. (2001). Association between nonpsychotic psychiatric diagnoses in adolescent males and subsequent onset of schizophrenia. *Archives of General Psychiatry, 58*, 959–964.

Zachary, A. (2001). Uneasy triangles: A brief overview of the history of homosexuality. *British Journal of Psychotherapy, 17*, 489–492.

13

CHALLENGING PUBLIC STIGMA:
A TARGETED APPROACH

AMY C. WATSON AND PATRICK W. CORRIGAN

Common stereotypes about persons with mental illness include ideas that they are incompetent, irresponsible, dangerous, unpredictable, at fault for their illness, and unlikely to recover (Brockington, Hall, Levings, & Murphy, 1993; Corrigan et al., 2000; Hyler, Gabbard, & Schneider, 1991; Taylor & Dear, 1981; Wahl, 1995). These stigmas permeate society at all levels. They are located within individuals in the form of negative stereotypes and discriminatory behaviors (Corrigan, Markowitz, Watson, Rowan, & Kubiak, 2003; Corrigan & Penn, 1997; Corrigan & Penn, 1999; Corrigan et al., 2000, 2002; Link, Cullen, Frank, & Wozniak, 1987; Link, Phelan, Bresnahan, Stueve, & Pescosolido, 1999). They are broadcast to us through the media in the form of representations of persons with mental illness as crazed killers, incompetent children, or wild rebellious spirits (Hyler, Gabbard, & Schneider, 1991; Wahl, 1995). They are reflected in laws and institutions that limit the opportunities of persons with mental illness.

The breadth and depth of mental illness stigma make challenging it appear to be an overwhelming task. Yet, in recent years, advocacy groups have made reducing stigma a priority, implementing campaigns aimed at the public and the media. These efforts have targeted various components of stigma with a variety of strategies, few of which have been formally evaluated. However, social psychological research on ethnic minority and other group stereotypes provides important insight on the effectiveness of these strategies for reducing mental illness stigma (Corrigan & Penn, 1999). In this chapter, we borrow from the social psychological literature on reducing stigma related to ethnicity and review what is currently known about reducing mental illness stigma. We then juxtapose this research with existing anti-stigma efforts and discuss how they fit into a targeted model of stigma change. Implications for research and practice are discussed.

STRATEGIES FOR CHANGING STIGMA

Although the research on changing mental illness stigma is limited, social psychologists have developed a particularly rich body of research on strategies to improve intergroup attitudes related to race and ethnicity. On the basis of our review of this literature, we grouped the various approaches to changing public stigma into three processes: protest, education, and contact (Corrigan & Penn, 1999).

Protest

Protest strategies highlight the injustice of specific stigmas and lead to a moral appeal for people to stop thinking that way: "Shame on you for holding such disrespectful ideas about mental illness!" Ironically, this kind of attitude suppression may yield a rebound effect so that prejudices about a group remain unchanged or actually become worse (Corrigan et al., 2001; Macrae, Bodenhausen, Milne, & Jetten, 1994; Penn & Corrigan, 2002). Although both cognitive and social explanations of this kind of rebound exist, perhaps the simplest is the construct of psychological reactance (Brehm & Jones, 1970): "Don't tell me what to think!" Hence, protest may have limited impact for changing public *attitudes* about people with mental illness.

This does not mean protest has no role in affecting stigma. Largely anecdotal evidence exists that protest can change some *behaviors* significantly (Wahl, 1995). For example, National Alliance for the Mentally Ill (NAMI) StigmaBusters is an e-mail alert system that notifies members about stigmatizing representations of persons with mental illness in the media and provides instructions on how to contact the offending organization and its sponsors (NAMI StigmaBusters, 2002). In 2000, StigmaBusters played a prominent role in getting ABC to cancel the program "Wonderland," which portrayed persons with mental illness as dangerous and unpredictable. In the first ten minutes of the first episode, a person with mental illness shot several police officers and stabbed a pregnant psychiatrist in the abdomen with a hypodermic needle. StigmaBusters' efforts not only targeted the show's producers and several management levels of ABC, they encouraged communication with commercial sponsors including the CEOs of Mitsubishi, Sears, and the Scott Company. This suggests that organized protest can be a useful tool for convincing television networks and other media outlets to stop running stigmatizing programs, advertisements, and articles rather than alienate an important advertising demographic.

Research might show protest to be effective as a punishing consequence to discriminatory behavior that decreases the likelihood that people will repeat this behavior. Research might also consider other types of punishing consequences such as legal penalties prescribed by the Americans With Disabilities Act (ADA) and the Fair Housing Act. For example, what is the effect of judgments ordering punitive damages be paid by employers who discriminate in hiring or communities that design zoning laws to keep group homes for persons with mental illness out (Stefan, 2001)? Do such penalties prevent future discrimination? In like manner, research might identify reinforcing consequences to affirmative actions that undermine stigma and encourage more public opportunities for people with mental illness (e.g., government tax credits for employers who hire and provide reasonable accommodations to people with psychiatric disabilities).

Education

Educational approaches to stigma change attempt to challenge inaccurate stereotypes about mental illness and replace these stereotypes with factual information. This can be accomplished by providing basic facts about mental illness to an audience, or by contrasting myths with facts about mental illness. The goal is not to make the audience experts on mental illness, but rather to provide simple facts so that many of the myths about mental illness crumble (Watson & Corrigan, 2001).

The evidence about educational strategies targeting racial and other minority group stereotypes is mixed and suggests that effects of educational interventions may be limited (Devine, 1995; Pruegger & Rogers, 1994). This research indicates that stereotypes provide a template for encoding subsequent information that may disconfirm them. Thus, if a person endorses the stereotype that people with mental illness are dangerous, they may be less attentive to information that these individuals are "no more dangerous than the general population" than they are to the latest news story about a violent crime committed by a person with mental illness. As a result, stereotypes may be particularly resistant to change on the basis of new information (Fyock & Stangor, 1992; Stangor & McMillan, 1992).

Despite this consistency effect, however, individuals may learn to inhibit these stereotypes by using more cognitively controlled personal beliefs (Devine, 1995). Individuals motivated not to stigmatize persons with mental illness may automatically assume dangerousness and experience fear when meeting a person with mental illness. However, these same people can consciously override the initial stereotype and replace their reaction with one based on more accurate information that most people with mental illness are not violent. Thus, their initial reaction may activate a stereotype about a member of a stigmatized group. However, the individual may purposefully replace that thought with more accurate beliefs and behave accordingly.

Educational strategies aimed at reducing mental illness stigma have used public service announcements, books, flyers, movies, videos and other audio visual aids to dispel myths about mental illness and replace them with facts (Bookbinder, 1978; National Mental Health Campaign, 2002; Pate, 1988; Smith, 1990). Evidence from education studies suggests that people with a better understanding of mental illness are less likely to endorse stigma and discrimination (Brockington et al., 1993; Link & Cullen, 1986; Link et al., 1987; Roman & Floyd, 1981) and that education programs do produce short-term improvements in attitudes (Corrigan et al., 2001; Corrigan et al., 2002; Holmes, Corrigan, Williams, Canar, & Kubiak, 1999; Keane, 1991; Morrison & Teta, 1980; Penn et al., 1994; Penn, Kommana, Mansfield, & Link, 1999). Although education can be a useful strategy, the magnitude and duration of improvement attitudes and behavior may be limited (Corrigan & McCracken, 1997; McCracken & Corrigan, in press). Further research is needed to determine its long-term effects and to examine the effectiveness of different mediums of delivery (Public Service Announcements [PSAs], classroom lecture, movies, etc.) and content.

Contact

The third strategy for reducing stigma is interpersonal contact with members of the stigmatized group. Contact has long been considered an effective means for reducing intergroup prejudice (Allport, 1954/1979; Pettigrew & Tropp, 2000). In formalizing the "contact" hypothesis, Allport (1954/1979) contended, and more recent research supports (Cook, 1985; Gaertner, Dovidio, & Bachman, 1996; Pettigrew & Tropp, 2000), that "optimal" contact interventions must contain four elements.

1. *Equal status between groups.* In the contact situation, neither the minority nor the majority group members occupy a higher status. Neither group is in charge. This differs from the type of contact certain power groups typically have with persons with mental illness (e.g., doctor–patient, landlord–resident, employer–employee).
2. *Common goals.* Both groups should be working toward the same ends. Some studies of "optimal" contact have used contrived tasks such as completing a puzzle (Desforges et al., 1991). In more natural settings, this might include working together on a community project or solving a neighborhood problem.

3. *No competition.* The tone of the contact should be a joint effort, not a competitive one.
4. *Authority sanction for the contact.* This might mean the contact intervention is sponsored or endorsed by management of an employment organization, or by particular community organizations (e.g., the Board of Education, Better Business Bureau).

Furthermore, contact's benefits are enhanced when it is with a person who moderately disconfirms the stereotypes about his or her group (Johnston & Hewstone, 1992; Reinke & Corrigan, 2002; Weber & Crocker, 1983). Individuals who highly disconfirm prevailing stereotypes may not be believed or might be considered "special exceptions," whereas contact with persons who behave in ways consistent with the stereotypes about their group may reinforce stigmatizing attitudes or make them worse.

A recent meta-analysis (Pettigrew & Tropp, 2000) of more than 200 studies of intergroup contact further supports its effectiveness for reducing prejudice. The 44 studies in the meta-analysis that consisted of a structured program that maximized the four "optimal" conditions listed previously yielded consistently larger reductions in prejudice. Additionally, the authors found that contact interventions were most effective if they involved face-to-face interactions and if they occurred in work or organizational settings. Smaller but still significant effect sizes were found for reducing prejudice against older adults and persons with mental illness. The authors note that several of the studies on these populations included only brief contact with individuals with severe disabilities and emphasize the importance of structured contact situations that counter prevailing negative stereotypes.

Several studies specifically focusing on contact's effect on mental illness stigma have produced promising findings. Corrigan and colleagues found that contact with a person with mental illness produced greater improvements in attitudes than protest, education, and control conditions (Corrigan et al., 2001). In a subsequent study, contact again produced the greatest improvements in attitudes and participant willingness to donate money to NAMI (Corrigan et al., 2002). Improvements in attitudes seem to be most pronounced when contact is with a person who moderately disconfirms prevailing stereotypes (Reinke & Corrigan, 2002). Contact effects are not limited to adults. Research with school children suggests that education combined with contact leads to greater attitude improvements than education alone (Pinfold et al., 2002).

On the basis of these studies, contact appears to be among the best strategies for changing mental illness stigma. Although less amenable to widespread distribution than educational programs, carefully structured and strategically implemented contact interventions could have significant impact. Future research should further elaborate factors that augment the effect of contact on stigma.

Many of the existing antistigma campaigns use an educational approach, either by itself or in conjunction with protest or contact. And many, hoping to reduce the blame associated with mental illness, have focused on a biological model of mental illness. One example is NAMI's "Mental Illness is a Brain Disease" campaign in which they distributed posters, buttons, and literature that provided information about the biological basis of serious mental illness. Evidence exists that this type of message does reduce blame for psychiatric illness (Corrigan et al., 2002; Farina, Fisher, Getter, & Fischer, 1979; Fisher & Farina, 1979). However, framing mental illness in biological terms may increase other negative attitudes about mental illness (Mehta & Farina, 1997). For example, Farina and colleagues (Farina, Fisher, Getter, & Fischer, 1978; Fisher & Farina, 1979) found that when provided with a disease-based explanation for mental illness, participants viewed persons labeled mentally ill as less able to help themselves than when they were provided with a psychosocial explanation for the same problems. In a later study, Mehta and Farina (1997) found that disease explanations for mental illness reduced blame, but also provoked harsher behavior toward an individual with mental illness.

Biological explanations of mental illness may also yield unintended consequences by supporting the benevolence stigma; namely, the belief that persons with mental illness are innocent and childlike and as such, must be taken care of by a parental figure (Brockington et al., 1993). Although well-intentioned, this type of stigma can be disempowering, leading persons with mental illness (and others) to view themselves as different from other people, less competent, and less acceptable as a friend. Biological explanations may also imply that persons with mental illness have no control over their behavior, and therefore are unpredictable and violent (Read & Law, 1999).

In contrast to the biological message, several studies have found that psychosocial explanations of mental illness can be effective for increasing positive images of persons with mental illness and reducing fear. Instead of arguing that mental illness is like any other medical illness, psychosocial explanations of mental illness focus on environmental stressors and trauma as causal factors. These may include childhood abuse, poverty, and job stress. The idea is to reframe psychiatric symptoms as understandable reactions to life events (Read & Law, 1999). Demythologizing seminars that present a psychosocial model of mental disorder have been shown to be effective with students and health professionals (Morrison, 1980; Morrison, Becker, & Bourgeois, 1979; Morrison & Teta, 1979, 1980). A more recent study conducted in New Zealand also suggests that information about psychosocial causes and treatments for mental illness is effective for improving attitudes, particularly those related to dangerousness and unpredictability (Read & Law, 1999). Although the previously mentioned studies of educational interventions focusing on a psychosocial model did not include control or comparison groups, they do suggest that this type of message can be useful for challenging stigma. Combined with the evidence of mixed effects of interventions limited to biological explanations, this suggests an approach that frames mental illness as a disorder with both biological and psychosocial components, and that people can and do recover from.

Although the psychosocial model has been shown to reduce fear and perceptions of dangerousness, neither of the approaches directly addresses this particularly pervasive stigma. Other studies examined stigma change interventions that specifically address dangerousness. Penn and colleagues (1999) found that research participants given information on prevalence rates of violent behavior among persons with mental illness perceived individuals with mental illness as less dangerous than participants not given this information. A study conducted by our group compared educational approaches focused on dangerousness (accurate information about the rates of violence among persons with mental illness) or causes and treatments of mental illness (Corrigan et al., 2002). Although both conditions produced improvements in perceptions of dangerousness, desired social distance, and willingness to donate money to NAMI, the dangerousness condition increased blame, whereas the cause and treatment condition decreased blame.

Clearly, the content of the educational message is important and needs to be tailored to the specific component(s) of stigma and behavior(s) and group(s) being targeted (Byrne, 2000). For example, addressing the biological causes of mental illness with a group of neighborhood residents may improve some of their attitudes about persons with mental illness. However, unless dangerousness is addressed, their unwillingness to welcome a group home to the neighborhood may go unchanged. Conversely, addressing only dangerousness with police officers may make them less likely to use undue force, but not influence their willingness to assist a victim with a mental illness.

Legislators are another group that makes important decisions that may limit or expand the opportunities and resources available to persons with mental illness. For example, they decide how tax money is distributed among various types of services. Research on attributions and helping behavior indicates that people are more willing to help and give resources to people whom they do not blame for their problems (Corrigan & Watson, 2003; Skitka & Tetlock, 1992, 1993; Weiner, 1995; Zucker & Weiner, 1993). Thus, when addressing legislators regarding funding for mental health services or health insurance parity, it might prove most fruitful to focus on a biological message. Including information that people with mental illness do recover and lead meaningful lives may enhance the positive effect of the message. Clearly, if time and resources allow, strategies should address multiple stereotypes. More realistically, the content of the message may need to be selectively targeted to the stereotypes most relevant to the goals of the intervention.

EXISTING EFFORTS AT CHANGING PUBLIC STIGMA

In recent years, major advocacy groups in the United States, such as NAMI and the National Mental Health Association, have launched anti-stigma campaigns. Other groups, including the National Stigma Clearing-house and the Resource Center to Address Discrimination and Stigma Associated with Mental Illnesses, have made the stigma of mental illness its sole focus. Both federal and state governments have also joined the fray. In the past couple of years, the U.S. Substance Abuse and Mental Health Services Administration (SAMHSA) and the National Institute of Mental Health have supported nationwide conferences on stigma. SAMHSA produced and disseminated an antistigma kit that included posters and brochures challenging common stereotypes. Tipper Gore and Alma Powell joined with other national leaders to form the National Mental Health Awareness Campaign (NMHAC) that developed a multilevel effort to challenge stigma.

Similar efforts are evident elsewhere in the world. The World Psychiatric Association has launched "Schizophrenia: Open the Doors." The program is currently active on three continents: Asia, Europe, and South America. Prominent among these demonstration projects is "Changing Minds" by the British Royal College of Psychiatrists. Like other efforts of its ilk, Changing Minds includes multiple levels of public education to change stigma about mental illness. Central to this effort is focusing on family education as key to changing stigma.

The goals and tactics of these advocacy groups neatly fall into the education, protest, and contact distinctions described by researchers. Many of these programs rely on public education to dispel the stigma of mental illness. Television and other media have become a central vehicle for these education programs. The NMHAC, for example, developed 30-second PSAs concentrating on the attitudes of adolescents (National Mental Health Campaign, 2002). Called "Change Your Mind," the PSAs send two messages that challenge important stereotypes: people with mental illness are not responsible for their problems and they are "just like everyone else." Being mindful of their audience, the NMHAC has widely aired the PSAs on such teen outlets as MTV, as well as VH1, ESPN, ABC, Fox, and Channel One. The specific goal of the NMHAC program is to increase adolescent use of mental health services when needed. The PSAs end with a web address where interested teens can learn more about mental illness and corresponding services. Although it is difficult to determine the depth and breadth of this campaign's penetration, as of October, 2001 the Web site reported more than 12 million hits.

Now numbering more than 4,000 members, NAMI StigmaBusters have been an important source of protest (NAMI StigmaBusters, 2002). Among its many efforts, StigmaBusters identify disrespectful and inaccurate images of mental illness in the popular media and coordinate letter-writing campaigns to get producers of these images to stop. The NAMI group had a prominent role in removing an ABC show called "Wonderland" from the air in 2000. As a result of these efforts, ABC pulled the show after a couple of episodes at a substantial financial loss.

About 2 years ago, NAMI developed a contact-based antistigma program called *In Our Own Voice: Living With Mental Illness*. Particularly remarkable about the program is its combination of carefully crafted exercises and information base that helps consumers teach civic and other groups about the experience of mental illness. To date, they have provided the program to law enforcement, schools, businesses, and other community groups. NAMI is currently planning an evaluation of this program in conjunction with researchers from the Chicago Consortium for Stigma Research.

Several examples also exist of state governments using contact to diminish stigma and enhance consumer empowerment. New York (Blanch & Fisher, 1993; Knight & Blanch, 1993), Florida (Loder & Glover, 1992), and Illinois (Corrigan, Lickey, Schmook, Virgil, & Juricek, 1999) have arranged formal dialogues between persons with mental illness and mental health care professionals as a way to change insidious attitudes in the mental health system that undermine empowerment. These dialogues provided a forum for consumers and health care professionals to exchange perspectives about mental illness and challenge latent stigmatizing attitudes. Moreover, the U.S. Center for Mental Health Services has an intramural office on consumer empowerment and funds consumer-based, extramural projects that attempt to discount stigma. Many state departments of mental health hire consumer advocates whose job, in part, includes vigilance to misrepresentations of mental health issues.

A TARGETED MODEL OF STIGMA CHANGE

These are just some of the examples of how education, protest, and contact can be used to reduce prejudice and discrimination. The reader should note the common feature to these examples that further augments program impact: *Each program targets a specific group and corresponding attitudes and behaviors for change.* The NMHAC is attempting to increase service use among *adolescents* who may be experiencing mental health-related problems. NAMI's StigmaBusters seeks to stop the *popular media* from perpetuating disrespectful images in their TV shows and movies. States are trying to change entrenched and disempowering attitudes in their *mental health systems* by pairing consumers with providers. The logic of a target-specific approach is all the more compelling when compared to the alternative—a generic effort to change the attitudes of the population as a whole. Consider, for example, a video that promotes the idea that mental illness affects 20% of the citizenry and hence is neither rare nor bizarre. Although this effort is well intentioned and poignant, such mass appeal suffers because it is not particularly relevant to specific elements of the populace. It is unclear who exactly is supposed to take note of this message. Moreover, the expected products of these efforts are fuzzy; it is unclear exactly how the population should change regarding the highlighted stereotypes and prejudice. People might think, "Okay, so 20% of the population may be mentally ill in their lifetime. Now, what should I do about it?"

The goal of improving attitudes about mental illness in general is laudable, yet too amorphous to achieve. A targeted approach that focuses on changing specific discriminatory behaviors of specific groups lends itself to the practical approach outlined in Table 13.1. First, antistigma programs target specific power groups that make important decisions about the resources and opportunities available to persons with mental illness. These include employers, landlords, police officers, legislators, and media executives. Individuals acting out these power roles are significantly influenced by institutional and organizational factors (Link & Phelan, 2001; Oliver, 1992; Pincus, 1999; Scott, 1995) and may be more likely to rely on stereotypes about a group than persons in less powerful roles (Fiske, 1993). For each group, we identify the discriminatory behavior and corresponding attitudes we would like to change. For example, we may want to address employers' unwilling-

TABLE 13.1
Targeted Model of Stigma Change

Targets	Discriminatory behavior	Attitudes
Employers	Fail to hire No reasonable accommodation	Dangerousness Incompetence
Landlords	Fail to lease No reasonable accommodation	Dangerousness Irresponsibility
Criminal justice professionals	Unnecessarily coercive Fail to refer to mental health services	Dangerousness Responsibility—Blame
Policy makers	Insufficient resource allocation Unfriendly interpretation of regulations	Dangerousness Responsibility—Blame
The media	Perpetuation and dissemination of stigmatizing images	Dangerousness Responsibility—Blame Incompetence Irresponsibility

ness to hire persons with mental illness. The corresponding attitudes might relate to incompetence and danger to other employees.

Once the target group, behavior(s), and attitude(s) are identified, the most appropriate strategy can be selected. Although the effect of protest on attitudes is unclear, it seems to be useful for eliminating undesirable behaviors such as negative images in the media and discriminatory housing and labor practices. Education appears to improve attitudes on a short-term basis and can be implemented relatively inexpensively. Contact appears to be the most promising strategy, especially when it is structured to include "optimal" conditions. This may be difficult to achieve on a broad scale unless more people become willing to disclose their illness in work and other social situations. That, however, could be risky for those individuals.

Note that antistigma campaigns may use a combination of strategies to address the attitudes and behaviors of a particular group. Note also that in addition to targeting power groups, campaigns may target groups that may be hesitant to access services because of stigma. Take, for example, the NMHAC's program aimed at teens who may be struggling with mental health issues. The targeted model is useful for these programs as well.

Many organizations are jumping into the ring to fight stigma. As the examples in this chapter suggest, some of these efforts appear to be heeding the existing evidence and stand a good chance of winning a few rounds against stigma. Before we can win the fight, however, more research is needed to clarify the effects of different combinations of content, medium, and strategy on the attitudes and behaviors of various groups. This does not mean we have to wait for more research to act. Instead, consumers, advocates, and researchers can partner to develop, implement, and evaluate targeted antistigma programs on the basis of their joint experience and knowledge.

REFERENCES

Allport, G. W. (1979). *The nature of prejudice*. New York: Doubleday. (Original work published 1954)

Behavior Health Recovery Management. (2001). The impact of stigma on service access and participation. Retrieved May 18, 2002, from http://www.bhrm.org

Blanch, A., & Fisher, D. (1993). Consumer-practitioners and psychiatrists share insights about recovery and coping. *Disability Studies Quarterly, 13*, 17–20.

Bookbinder, S. R. (1978). *Mainstreaming—What every child needs to know about disabilities*. Providence: Rhode Island Easter Seal Society.

Brehm, J. W., & Jones, R. A. (1970). The effect on dissonance of surprise consequences. *Journal of Experimental Social Psychology, 6*, 420–431.

Brockington, I. F., Hall, P., Levings, J., & Murphy, C. (1993). The community's tolerance of the mentally ill. *British Journal of Psychiatry, 162*, 93–99

Byrne, P. (2000). The stigma of mental illness and ways of diminishing it. *Advances in Psychiatric Treatment, 6*, 65–72.

Cook, S. W. (1985). Experimenting on social issues: The case of school desegregation. *American Psychologist, 40*, 452–460.

Corrigan, P. W., Lickey, S. E., Schmook, A., Virgil, L., & Juricek, M. (1999). Dialogue among stakeholders of severe mental illness. *Psychiatric Rehabilitation Journal, 23*, 62–65.

Corrigan, P. W., Markowitz, F. E., Watson, A. C., Rowan, D., & Kubiak, M. A. (2003). An attribution model of public discrimination towards persons with mental illness. *Journal of Health and Social Behavior.*

Corrigan, P. W., & McCracken, S. G. (1997). *Interactive staff training: Rehabilitation teams that work.* New York: Plenum Press.

Corrigan, P. W., & Penn, D. L. (1997). Disease and discrimination: Two paradigms that describe severe mental illness. *Journal of Mental Health, 6*, 355–366.

Corrigan, P. W., & Penn, D. L. (1999). Lessons from social psychology on discrediting psychiatric stigma. *American Psychologist, 54*, 765–776.

Corrigan, P. W., River, L., Lundin, R. K., Penn, D. L., Uphoff-Wasowski, K., Campion, J., et al. (2001). Three strategies for changing attributions about severe mental illness. *Schizophrenia Bulletin, 27*, 187–195.

Corrigan, P. W., River, L., Lundin, R. K., Uphoff-Wasowski, K., Campion, J., Mathisen, J., et al. (2000). Stigmatizing attributions about mental illness. *Journal of Community Psychology, 28*, 91–102.

Corrigan, P. W., Rowan, D., Green, A., Lundin, R., River, L., Uphoff-Wasowski, K., et al. (2002). Challenging two mental illness stigmas: Personal responsibility and dangerousness. *Schizophrenia Bulletin, 28*, 293–310.

Corrigan, P. W., & Watson, A. C. (2003). Factors that explain how policy makers distribute resources to mental health services. *Psychiatric Services, 54*, 501–507.

Desforges, D. M., Lord, C. G., Ramsey, S. L., Mason, J. A., Van Leeuwen, M. D., West, S. C., et al. (1991). Effects of structured cooperative contact on changing negative attitudes toward stigmatized social groups. *Journal of Personality and Social Psychology, 60*, 531–544.

Devine, P. G. (1995). Prejudice and out-group perception. In A. Tessor (Ed.), *Advanced social psychology* (pp. 467–524). New York: McGraw-Hill.

Farina, A., Fisher, J. D., Getter, H., & Fischer, E. H. (1978). Some consequences of changing people's views regarding the nature of mental illness. *Journal of Abnormal Psychology, 87*, 272–279.

Fisher, J. D., & Farina, A. (1979). Consequences of beliefs about the nature of mental disorders. *Journal of Abnormal Psychology, 88*, 320–327.

Fiske, S. T. (1993). Controlling other people: The impact of power on stereotyping. *American Psychologist, 48*, 621–628.

Fyock, J., & Stangor, C. (1992). The role of memory biases in stereotype maintenance. *British Journal of Social Psychology, 33*, 331–343.

Gaertner, S. L., Dovidio, J. F., & Bachman, B. A. (1996). Revisiting the contact hypothesis: The induction of a common ingroup identity. *International Journal of Intercultural Relations, 20*, 271–290.

Hamburger, Y. (1994). The contact hypothesis reconsidered: Effects of the atypical outgroup member on the outgroup stereotype. *Basic and Applied Social Psychology, 15*, 339–358.

Holmes, E., Corrigan, P. W., Williams, P., Canar, J., & Kubiak, M. A. (1999). Changing attitudes about schizophrenia. *Schizophrenia Bulletin, 25*, 447–456.

Hyler, S. E., Gabbard, G. O., & Schneider, I. (1991). Homicidal maniacs and narcissistic parasites: Stigmatization of mentally ill persons in the movies. *Hospital and Community Psychiatry, 42*, 1044–1048.

Johnson, D. W., Johnson, R. T., & Taylor, B. (1994). Impact of cooperative and individualistic learning on high-ability students' achievement, self-esteem, and social acceptance. *Journal of Social Psychology, 133*, 839–844.

Johnston, L., & Hewstone, M. (1992). Cognitive models of stereotype change: III. Subtyping and the perceived typicality of disconfirming group members. *Journal of Experimental Social Psychology, 28*, 360–386.

Keane, M. C. (1991). Acceptance vs. rejection: Nursing students' attitudes about mental illness. *Perspectives in Psychiatric Care, 27*, 13–18.

Knight, E., & Blanch, A. (1993). *A dialogue on recovery: Tips for structuring a recipient dialogue.* Albany: New York State Office of Mental Health.

Link, B. G., & Cullen, F. T. (1986). Contact with the mentally ill and perceptions of how dangerous they are. *Journal of Health and Social Behavior, 27*, 289–302.

Link, B. G., Cullen, F. T., Frank, J., & Wozniak, J. F. (1987). The social rejection of former mental patients: Understanding why labels matter. *American Journal of Sociology, 92*, 1461–1500.

Link, B. G., & Phelan, J. C. (2001). Conceptualizing stigma. *Annual Review of Sociology, 27*, 363–385.

Link, B. G., Phelan, J. C., Bresnahan, M., Stueve, A., & Pescosolido, B. A. (1999). Public conceptions of mental illness: Labels, causes, dangerousness, and social distance. *American Journal of Public Health, 89*, 1328–1333.

Loder, A., & Glover, R. (1992). New frontiers: Pioneer dialogue between consumers/survivors and commissioners. *Mental Health Statistics Improvement Program Updates*, 13–14.

Macrae, C., Bodenhausen, G. V., Milne, A. B., & Jetten, J. (1994). Out of mind but back in sight: Stereotypes on the rebound. *Journal of Personality and Social Psychology, 67*, 808–817.

McCracken, S. G., & Corrigan, P. W. (in press). Staff development in mental health. In H. E. Briggs (Ed.), *Evidence-based social work practice.* Chicago: Lyceum Books.

Mehta, S., & Farina, A. (1997). Is being "sick" really better? Effect of the disease view of mental disorder on stigma. *Journal of Social and Clinical Psychology, 16*, 405–419.

Morrison, J. K. (1980). The public's current beliefs about mental illness: Serious obstacle to effective community psychology. *American Journal of Community Psychology, 8*, 697–707.

Morrison, J. K., Becker, R. E., & Bourgeois, C. A. (1979). Decreasing adolescents' fear of mental patients by means of demythologizing. *Psychological Reports, 44,* 855–859.

Morrison, J. K., & Teta, D. C. (1979). Impact of a humanistic approach on students' attitudes, attributions, and ethical conflicts. *Psychological Reports, 45,* 863–866.

Morrison, J. K., & Teta, D. C. (1980). Reducing students' fear of mental illness by means of seminar-induced belief change. *Journal of Clinical Psychology, 36,* 275–276.

NAMI Stigma Busters. (2002). NAMI *Stigma Busters alert.* Retrieved May 18, 2002, from www.nami.org/campaign/20000405.htm

National Mental Awareness Health Campaign. (2002). Retrieved May 18, 2002, from www.nostigma.org

Oliver, C. (1992). The antecedents of deinstitutionalization. *Organization Studies, 13,* 563–588.

Pate, G. S. (1988). Research on reducing prejudice. *Social Education, 52,* 287–289.

Penn, D. L., & Corrigan, P. W. (2002). The effects of stereotype suppression on psychiatric stigma. *Schizophrenia Research, 55,* 269–276.

Penn, D. L., Guynan, K., Daily, T., Spaulding, W. D., Garbin, C., & Sullivan, M. (1994). Dispelling the stigma of schizophrenia: What sort of information is best? *Schizophrenia Bulletin, 20,* 567–578.

Penn, D. L., Kommana, S., Mansfield, M., & Link, B. G. (1999). Dispelling the stigma of schizophrenia: II. The impact of information on dangerousness. *Schizophrenia Bulletin, 25,* 437–446.

Pettigrew, T. F., & Tropp, L. R. (2000). Does intergroup contact reduce prejudice: Recent meta-analytic findings. In S. Oskamp (Ed.), *Reducing prejudice and discrimination* (pp. 93–114). Mahwah, NJ: Erlbaum.

Pincus, F. L. (1999). From individual to structural discrimination. In F. L. Pincus & H. J. Ehrlich (Eds.), *Race and ethnic conflict: contending views on prejudice, discrimination, and ethnoviolence* (pp. 120–124). Boulder, CO: Westview Press.

Pinfold, V., Huxley, P., Thornicroft, G., Farmer, P., Toulmin, H., & Graham, T. (2002). *Reducing psychiatric stigma and discrimination: Evaluating an educational intervention with the police force in England.* Unpublished manuscript.

Pruegger, V. J., & Rogers, T. B. (1994). Cross-cultural sensitivity training: Methods and assessment. *International Journal of Intercultural Relations, 18,* 369–387.

Read, J., & Law, A. (1999). The relationship of causal beliefs and contact with users of mental health services to attitudes to the mentally ill. *International Journal of Social Psychiatry, 45,* 216–229.

Reinke, R., & Corrigan, P. W. (2002). *Examining media's use of contact on the stigma of mental illness.* Unpublished manuscript.

Roman, P., & Floyd, H. (1981). Social acceptance of psychiatric illness and psychiatric treatment. *Social Psychiatry, 16,* 16–21.

Scott, R. W. (1995). *Institutions and organizations.* Thousand Oaks, CA: Sage.

Skitka, L. J., & Tetlock, P. E. (1992). Allocating scarce resources: A contingency model of distributive justice. *Journal of Experimental Social Psychology, 28,* 491–522.

Skitka, L. J., & Tetlock, P. E. (1993). Of ants and grasshoppers: The political psychology of allocating public assistance. In B. Mellers & J. Baron (Eds.), *Psychological perspectives on justice: Theory and applications.* New York: Cambridge University Press.

Smith, A. (1990). Social influence and antiprejudice training programs. In J. Edwards, R. S. Tindale, L. Heath, & E. J. Posavac (Eds.), *Social influence processes and prevention* (pp. 183–196). New York: Plenum Press.

Stangor, C., & McMillan, D. (1992). Memory for expectancy-congruent and expectancy-incongruent information: A review of the social and social developmental literatures. *Psychological Bulletin, 111,* 42–61.

Stefan, S. (2001). *Unequal rights: Discrimination against people with mental disabilities and the Americans With Disabilities Act.* Washington, DC: American Psychological Association.

Taylor, S., & Dear, M. J. (1981). Scaling community attitudes toward the mentally ill. *Schizophrenia Bulletin, 7,* 225–240.

Wahl, O. F. (1995). *Media madness: Public images of mental illness.* New Brunswick, NJ: Rutgers University Press.

Weber, R., & Crocker, J. (1983). Cognitive processes in the revision of stereotypic beliefs. *Journal of Personality and Social Psychology, 45,* 961–977.

Weiner, B. (1995). *Judgments of responsibility: A foundation for a theory of social conduct.* New York: Guilford Press.

Worchel, S. (1986). The influence of contextual variables on interpersonal spacing. *Journal of Nonverbal Behavior, 10,* 230–254.

Zucker, G. S., & Weiner, B. (1993). Conservatism and perceptions of poverty: An attributional analysis. *Journal of Applied Social Psychology, 23,* 925–943.

14

CHANGING STIGMA THROUGH THE MEDIA

MARGARET SULLIVAN, THOMAS HAMILTON,
AND HERBERT ALLEN

Research that explores the presentation of people with mental illness as characters in media driven stories such as television programs or films, or as points of focus in journalism stories such as news stories or feature articles in newspapers and magazines, is important because it examines the results of media projects and can be used to analyze their intended or unintended consequences. Ultimately, because "art happens," these examples are difficult for mental health advocates to respond to. Should Hollywood create two positive mental illness films for every one that contains a serial killer whose chief character quality is his mental illness? Should newspapers be required by a governing body to report treatment efficacies or stories of recovery? Should media be required to counteract its own impressions with contradictory or healing impressions aimed at a parallel or similar audience?

This chapter will review various options in this regard, focusing on media sources that are clear and direct about their intention to manipulate. We will study the media role in manipulating the public's impression of people with mental illness through marketing communication and the broad arena of media channels it uses. Every film, television program, magazine, and newspaper uses marketing communication programs to create and maintain their audiences. And, as this chapter will demonstrate, every marketing communication program uses film, television, and print media to create and maintain its message. If a marketing communication message or its creative strategy can be effectively managed to promote a positive image of mental illness, then argument exists to launch that campaign. If film, television programs, and print media content can be analyzed for their imbedded marketing communication messages, then responsibility can be more appropriately identified, and the sources of stigma can be influenced clearly.

Marketing communication professionals use social marketing, cause marketing, marketing for not-for-profits, stealth marketing, buzz marketing, public relations issues management, and cultural seeding to present manipulative information programs to audiences for which traditional sales oriented business-to-consumer messages are not appropriate or believable. These terms, and their importance for media and stigma, are defined more fully throughout this paper. The successful application of these marketing styles, together with the trend toward integrated marketing campaigns, has made these methods increasingly attractive in solving advertising problems in traditional markets. Ries and Ries (2002) proposed "positioning" as the successful movement away from traditional advertising toward more culturally intrusive and culturally coordinated models. These new campaigns use methods parallel to ordinary advertising campaigns, but are different in that they tend to engage a broader set of media forms; they do not appear to be sales oriented to the viewer; they are more likely to use media forms that have established credibility; they implement intrusive multisensory engagement; their messages do not appear to be self serving; and they are not restrained by the ethical requirements of advertising, which is bound to federal law, its own professional code, and an implicit contract with the consumer. We will now examine some specific examples of positioning, highlighting its relevance for diminishing mental illness stigma.

CULTURAL SEEDING

Consider the example in the novel *The Bulgari Connection* by Fay Weldon. In 2001, the Italian jewelry company Bulgari commissioned a successful novelist to create a story giving a Bulgari retail site a significant presence. This seems to be the first time a client elected to use the creation of a novel as part of an integrated marketing communication program. The publishing industry (in this case, Grove/Atlantic) is apparently open to such influence, perhaps because of its own marketing challenges. Although at this writing the book has not reached the market, it is possible to anticipate the effects this novel will have in establishing Bulgari—semiotically and literally—

squarely in the position its owners strive for. Media analysts who would heretofore have considered novels exempt from the influences of marketing communication now must consider the world of literature in their assessment of media influence. This reality suggests that all art and communication forms may be available to penetration by marketers. Any group that strives to understand or to penetrate the media world must be informed by the industry developments in cultural seeding.

Cultural seeding is a strategic attempt to integrate products and services into the lifestyles of its targeted consumer audiences. It intends to expand the marketplace to include all cultural content. All cultural creation becomes a potential media channel to be used in an integrated marketing communication campaign. Culturally seeded messages are more powerful than messages delivered in advertisements alone because they are realized through channels the audience already respects; they do not appear to be manipulative; they demonstrate the products or services in ideal use; and they support a product in seamlessly becoming part of the cultural landscape.

An obvious cultural preparation for cultural seeding, or a hint that the expansion of the marketplace and the integration of commerce and culture was inevitable, was in the children's market. Popular characters from the "commercial world" have been brought into storybooks since the Second World War years. An American child's world could include the same character appearing on the cereal box, the television screen, the sheets on the bed, and the image decorating the lunchbox. These impressions were not considered or understood to be advertising messages, but they did communicate a marketing message.

Given the advances in the marketing and advertising industry, the convergence of culture and commercialism is increasingly relevant. Consider a parallel example to the Fay Weldon novel described earlier in the creation of *Breakfast at Tiffany's*. Would Truman Capote have accepted a commission from Tiffany marketing executives in 1958? What marketing positioning or place in the world did Tiffany's realize as a result of the novel and subsequent film? In today's marketing industry, which has been traditionally prescient about the power of convergence, such messages can be imbedded, and their effectiveness quantified.

It is possible to bring this example of an integrated marketing communication program with reducing the stigma of mental illness as an objective. What if Larry King invited a prominent psychologist to appear on his television program? Perhaps the topic could be "Four Warning Signs of Overstress," or "Recovering from Severe Depression." What could Oprah Winfrey do to establish the brand "The Promise of Mental Health?" What if National Public Radio sponsored a reading series led by authors who have a mental illness? Perhaps the subject areas in their writing could sensitize the public to stories of recovery and the complexities of living with mental illness. Jacki Leyden, host of the NPR program "All Things Considered," has recently published a memoir, *Daughter of the Queen of Sheba* (Penguin Books, 1997), which focuses on her mother's mental illness. Although the author was not paid by advocacy groups to write a story with that angle, the advancement of the story would disseminate the memes that feed a cultural seeding campaign. Indeed, Ms. Leyden was invited to appear on *Oprah* with her mother when this book was being introduced.

Ultimately, these campaigns are aimed at creating a contagious idea. Therefore, mental health advocates would do well to support the popularity of art and culture that supports the cause, whether or not they participated in commissioning it. In a small example, Patrick W. Corrigan is working with a mental health advocate to create a public symposium that will acknowledge excellence in filmmaking and highlight films that contain characters with mental illness. This award could connect the filmmaking community with the subject of mental illness and heighten awareness of the issue among authors of popular culture.

CAUSE MARKETING

Cause marketing is a marketing initiative that attempts to attach products and services to specific popular sociopolitical causes with the expectation that the audience will attribute the values of their chosen cause to the product or service itself. These campaigns are thoughtfully matched, and are a result of market research about crossover in the existing or desired target audience for the product or service and the audience that purports to have or has demonstrated interest in the cause. Cause marketing is a way for corporations to publicly advocate for causes that support their identity. Done well, these marketing campaigns create "good corporate citizens."

Consider the example of MAC cosmetics' "Viva Glam" campaign. MAC claims to donate all revenue realized from the sales of one of its lipstick colors to foundations and other non-profit organizations that are dedicated to AIDS prevention. Hence, consumers who support this initiative can feel they are supporting research for AIDS prevention. At once they can (a) derive some degree of altruistic fulfillment from an activity as self-indulgent and comparatively trivial as purchasing makeup, (b) feel they are confronting an ominous disease that potentially threatens them and those close to them, and (c) facilitate their engagement with, and immersion in, their generational, social, and economic world of concern.

Every promotional and advertising message for this MAC campaign uses celebrity endorsements from Elton John, Ru Paul, Mary J. Blige, Shirley Manson, and K. D. Lang. At this writing, Viva Glam sales alone have delivered $23 million to AIDS research. It would be possible to use cause marketing to inform a campaign to reduce the stigma of mental illness.

SOCIAL MARKETING

Social marketing uses integrated marketing techniques to manipulate an audience's beliefs, usually in a direction that the creators of the message consider a general societal improvement (Kotler & Zalman, 1971). Unlike cause marketing, cultural seeding, or traditional marketing–advertising campaigns, a social marketing campaign is not driven by a profit motive, but rather by the welfare of the client group or all of society. The audience is "sold" on the idea that society cannot afford *not* to participate in the attitude or behavior change the campaign calls for. An attempt to increase awareness of the quality of the natural environment is a typical example of a social marketing problem. One behavior it may attempt to change in a target market would be recycling habits. The audience would be motivated to believe that society cannot afford the consequences if the general public does not improve its recycling practices.

In some ways, reducing the stigma of mental illness presents a good social marketing problem. The issue is not profit driven, and the target market could be convinced to understand that society is missing out on the potential of people with mental illness. The possibility invites a number of interesting questions that could be used to inspire future research. For example, What is a standard for mental health? At what point is the failure to meet that standard classified as illness? How does the society in general, or the target market in particular, define "normal" behavior? At what point does a target audience begin to feel threatened by unusual behavior? What are the best target audiences for this social marketing campaign? This last question may suggest that reducing stigma of mental illness is too complex for a social marketing campaign. Consider the fact that one of a marketer's first concerns is the selection of the target audience. Marketers use research to discover which constituencies in a group have the most impact. They build creative strategies around reaching those people who are most likely to respond to their message, and they decide to approach groups of people who are most likely to fulfill their objectives.

Many ways exist to segment groups of people: by values, demographics, and income, to name a few. One extremely successful organizing system used to select a target audience is product use. Heavy users of a product may be targeted to ensure their continued brand loyalty or to introduce the expanded use of a product. Medium users may be targeted to motivate an increase in their purchasing trends. Low or nonusers could be approached to build new markets. How would a social marketing campaign for the reduction of mental illness stigma be targeted if product use were the organizing system? This question invites more suggestions for new research. Are some groups more fearful of people with mental illness than others? Is regular exposure to people with mental illness a factor in stigmatizing? Does media exposure (heavy, moderate, or light) reflect a pattern?

ALTERNATIVE MARKETING FORMS

Buzz marketing and stealth marketing are examples of widely used alternative marketing techniques. As is the reality with all integrated marketing communication forms, alternative methods can serve to create or reduce stigma. Buzz marketing exploits the certain realities of word of mouth transmission by manipulating an audience through trusted others. Indeed, word of mouth becomes an invisible marketing network. The mother who gets paid to talk about a laundry detergent at a Little League game is delivering buzz marketing communication. If the stigma around mental illness were treated as a buzz marketing problem, clinical psychologists might be offered incentives—for example, release time from work and travel expenses—to make presentations to neighborhood groups, in schools, or at religious gatherings. They would be trained to present positive and personal stories about people with mental illness. The psychologist speaking to his or her own community becomes the trusted other who does not appear to be selling anything. A buzz is created around the success and openness of the mental health world and the lives of people with mental illness. In another possibility, a community centered creative nonfiction writing contest funded by an advocacy group could award prizes and recognitions for stories about mental illness.

Stealth marketing suggests more aggressive tactics (e.g., the deliberate mention of drug success stories presented by celebrities appearing on talk shows). It includes a variety of tactics that deliver extremely imaginative messages to an audience. For example, one stealth marketing campaign for a beverage manufacturer involved filling trash receptacles in glamorous neighborhoods with empty cans of the product, thereby creating the impression that the product was used by those who lived in that area. The credibility of the neighborhood was attributed to the product. The advantages of these alternative forms are that they do not appear to come from a corporation. The messages therefore seem more informative than manipulative, as they come from sources the audience trusts. Alternative methods allow the advertiser to get around the fact that consumers have learned to avoid commercials through technology; video recorders, for example, allow them to bypass what they understand to be manipulation. Alternative marketing tactics could be used to reduce the stigma around mental illness.

PUBLIC RELATIONS ISSUES

Public relations (PR) are the efforts to establish attitudes through media that people trust. This is to be contrasted with the paid, highly produced messages advertising creates. A PR effort is centered in trying to create a narrative that is stronger than any competing narratives. PR does not attempt to create separate entities or truths, but works holistically. In a certain sense, PR is the only marketing program that does not thrive on the identifications of branding. Branding creates a categorical perception, like a commodity with a special wrapper. PR is different from other marketing forms in that it does not address attributes of a product, but prefers the sphere of public opinion.

Consider the example of a campaign that discourages smoking among teenagers. The PR problem is that kids think smoking is cool. This is the result of a set of circumstances, in this case delivered over decades through the very glamorous world of film, the public lives of celebrities, and the richly entertaining characters created for endorsement in cigarette advertising (Joe Camel, to name one). The PR program would not attempt to change the real world circumstances that created that understanding, but would attempt to reframe narratives so that attitudes would change accordingly.

Perceptions of mental illness are especially appropriate for a public relations campaign because the circumstances are infinitely flexible, and because the competing narratives are so familiar. In this case, we can understand the stigma as having been created long ago. Mocking the "village idiot" is perhaps as old as storytelling. Thus, the competing narratives are in place in the world culture, available to be challenged by a more interesting set of stories.

In another sense, the subject of mental illness is flexible in that the boundaries are not, and perhaps never have been, properly understood. One person's psychiatric symptom could be another person's idiosyncratic quirk. The "them and us" dynamic is therefore weaker. It would be different if it were permanent and the boundaries were fixed, as in the examples of religious, class, or lingual differences. The implications to understand and create new contexts for mental illness is as important to people with the illness as it is to the rest of society.

MARKETING FOR NOT-FOR-PROFITS

Marketing for not-for-profits is a category that implements the same marketing principles as a traditional marketing campaign, but in response to an environment with an agenda that goes beyond selling products and services. Not-for-profit clients are usually more interested in increasing market share, engaging new users, creating awareness, or encouraging a target market to try something. Not-for-profit clients are often foundations whose marketing message or public face must stay consistent across a broad variety of services, events, and national activities and their community-based subsets.

Consider a typical marketing issue for a library. Perhaps the target audience is infrequent library users who would be motivated through a not-for-profit campaign to participate in events or explore the video loaning area. This market has sampled, but they have not used the services in a way that fulfills the potential of a library. Perhaps the creative approach in such a campaign would be to emphasize the sense of community that libraries provide, thereby inspiring the light user of the library to increase usage. Matters of consistency are particularly relevant in a national campaign to increase the number and depth of library visits.

INTEGRATED MARKETING COMUNICATION

Marketing communication is a central topic in understanding changing stigma through the media because the marketplace has expanded to infiltrate every media form, and, arguably, nearly every cultural form; therefore, marketing communication is the most inclusive media example, content, and vehicle, of deliberate opinion influence. Integrated Marketing Communication (IMC) is a concept that integrates all of the communication vehicles that an organization employs so that a clear and consistent message can be delivered to its target audiences. IMC is not a new concept. Sophisticated marketers have been employing it for more than forty years. What has allowed the legitimacy of IMC is the move away from traditional marketing communication (broadcast, print, sales promotion, and infrequent use of PR) to today's environment where available marketing communication tools have expanded vastly (Internet, cable, special events, sponsorships, cultural seeding, stealth marketing, and buzz marketing, to name a few). The fragmentation and communication needs of an audience for any product or service have propelled the proliferation of media channels. The proliferation has forced marketers who want to be successful to embrace IMC. These campaigns are planned and implemented through traditional marketing plans using long established guidelines for creating and developing brands.

Branding

In the mid-19th century, Harley Procter burned an image of a moon on the soap crates he was shipping, not to build an external reputation or make a brand for Procter and Gamble (P&G), but to differentiate his crates from the others on the dock. He branded his product the way a rancher branded livestock. It was not until 1905 that Congress legally attached trademarks to ownership. And it was not until the mid 1990s that branding became the central focus of any marketing strategy. Today, marketing managers at P&G attend an Assistant Brand Manager's College as part of their executive training. Branding has become a universal rallying point.

Students of marketing communication are taught that a brand evolves, that it should be considered a living thing. Marketing professors teach prospective marketing managers that products are like things, but that brands are like people. Brands represent personalities, thereby differentiating their uniqueness, and qualifying their ongoing development. Objectively, a brand is a name or a mark intended to identify the product or service of a seller or group of sellers and differentiate it from competing products. But as the earlier descriptions of marketing techniques in this chapter demonstrate, brands have vitality and permeate the culture.

In an interesting sense, branding and stigma are alike. The issue of studying media through marketing communication and stigma invites the parallel. Stigma can be seen as a negative version of branding because a stigma and a brand effectively accomplish the same thing. Think of the words Gandhi and Hitler and consider the following: The suggestion of the names creates an immediate image; the images these words suggest are subject to cultural evolution; the wearers of the sign can feel identified with the image (for example, wearers of a Gandhi or Hitler T-shirt are associating themselves with an image); an immediate association of value or quality appears; the words themselves discourage any further analysis of a subject; these names are easily understood and recognized; the names differentiate certain types of goodness and evil in others, and each has become a descriptive concept, a personification.

We would propose that Gandhi is a brand and Hitler has a stigma. But given the conditions of society, both could be either. The use they are put to is the personification of certain attributes. Brand and stigma represent each end of a continuum.

Consider the physicality of branding and stigma. Branding began as a physical marking of a product. Stigma was once represented similarly, as in the examples of physically branding felons, requiring adulterers to wear representative signs in public, or the physically recognizable fact of a thief who had lost a hand. Both branding and stigma were introduced as physical representations, but have moved to more conceptual and far reaching applications.

Mental Illness as Stigma or Brand

In a marketing sense, the term "mental illness" unfairly groups many conditions and behaviors. Improper judgments are evoked. Consider a parallel example in the branding of Alzheimer's disease. Most readers of this chapter can probably remember a time when the broad set of conditions and behaviors presently described as early Alzheimer's were confused with the ordinary decline associated with old age. People likely used informal expressions to attempt to describe someone who was experiencing what we presently use a brand name for. So, terms like "around the bend," "(s)he's out of it," and "old geezer" became familiar. These terms are stigmatizing in the same manner as expressions like "psycho," "nut case," and the like. It seems that, in the absence of intentional branding, the room for stigmatization is wide open. Research could examine through word association devices how people respond to the words "Alzheimer's," "senile," and "elderly."

TOWARD A MARKETING PLAN TO BRAND THE SUBJECT AREA OF MENTAL ILLNESS

A brand helps the seller build a complete story about the special qualities of a product or service. It provides the foundation for promotion. Consider an IMC marketing plan to reduce or eliminate mental illness stigma. A typical format for a marketing plan consists of six logical components: Fact base (current situation); problems and opportunities; objectives; strategies; budget; and forecast.

The Fact Base

Everything in a marketing plan depends on correct understanding of the facts. Here are some of the considerations that would contribute to a fact base for a plan to reduce stigma.

Broadcast networks allege to exist in the cause of public interest. Yet research demonstrates that television media is hostile toward mental illness. Some of the research that explores the representation of people with mental illness draws these conclusions about characters in television programs: Characters with mental illness in television programs have an undeveloped social identity (Wahl & Roth, 1982). Their primary existence is in their illness. They are most often dangerous, childlike, and unpredictable (Wilson et al., 1999). They are characteristically violent (Diefenbach, 1997).

Every network has a statement of broadcast standards and practices. Ethical standards in broadcast are informed by and represented in Federal Communications Commission (FCC) requirements, the National Association of Broadcasters standards, and the individual guiding ethics of the network.

News coverage exploits and sensationalizes mental illness. It vilifies people who are mentally ill. Research in journalism notes an absence of stories of recovery in newspaper articles that involve people with mental illness (Wahl, Wood, & Richards, in press). Many other studies demonstrate an unbalanced number of stories about people with mental illness that mention violence.

Efficacy of mental illness therapy and other treatment methods have low visibility, especially the new treatment methods. In an interview published in the *New York Times* (August 27, 2002), Harvard psychiatrist Allan Hobson observed that in his early training, he was advised to control psychosis with psychoanalysis alone. Later, when psychopharmacology became an established trend, "the pendulum swung the other way" (p. F6) Mental health practitioners could be more responsive to media in the stages of change in such practices and in treatment efficacies, so that the general public feels more advised.

Mental health practitioners have low visibility and are not accountable to society in the manner of physicians. When the public school systems announce a reduction in recess time, psychologists could come forward to express their concern about stress in the daily lives of children in coordinated messages informed by publicists and media relations experts, especially in a time when teen suicide is an everyday event. In another example, an organized group of psychologists could demonstrate concern over the prevailing content in daytime television programs that sensationalize family problems. Further, popular culture does not appear to have many psychology "heroes." By contrast, the police and other law enforcement officials have such heroes on top rated shows such as *Law and Order*. As professions, psychology, psychiatry, social work, and psychiatric nursing are vulnerable to stigma. Research should explore the manner in which the general public perceives them.

Advertising is, by tradition, off limits to most mental health advocates. Although legislation has made it acceptable for those in legal and medical practice to advertise, it is only recently that it has become common. And a professional community still exists that elects to avoid advertising because of a perception that advertising for health practices is inappropriate. Nor can one make the product claims typical of other advertising messages. No money-back guarantees exist in the world of legal or medical practice. Consider the parallel example of lawyers who use television advertising. In one interview, a prominent lawyer commented that because law firms are more institutional than entrepreneurial, when he sees a firm advertising, he concludes that they are not very well respected. Thus, the possibility that a psychologist or team of mental health professionals could become strategically positioned and familiar to the culture through advertising is extremely limited. In advertising messages, the treatment of mental illness depends on the images created by pharmaceutical companies or hospitals.

Problems and Opportunities

If all of the relevant facts are clearly stated in the fact base, a complete listing of problems and opportunities will emerge. Often, a problem leads to an opportunity. However, occasions appear when there may not be a corresponding opportunity. To more carefully analyze problems and opportunities, a separate listing for each is appropriate. Here are examples of likely problems and opportunities that would be delivered in such a plan.

Problems

Television programs contain content that exacerbates, and possibly creates, stigma. News coverage of mental illness related stories encourages the public to fear mental illness. Hollywood's representation of mental illness is inconsistent. The general public is underexposed to stories of treatment efficacies and receives little media content about the treatment of mental illness.

Opportunities

Networks can be held accountable to their own published standards. Journalists would be interested in their treatment of this subject, as they would be in research findings about such areas as the treatment of the mentally ill by law enforcement workers. The film production process is widely reported. Critical points exist at which stigmatizing occurs in the production process. Psychologists could become a strong humanistic presence.

Objectives

The specific objectives of the marketing plan are a natural outgrowth of the listings of problems and opportunities. Objectives, in essence, are the core of the marketing plan, because everything preceding leads up to the objectives, and everything that follows aims at achieving them.

Objectives must be precise, measurable, and have realistic deadlines for results. Additionally, it is far better to have several objectives that can be achieved, rather than numerous ones that dissipate energy and resources without hard results. It should be noted that before stating objectives, a list of working assumptions should be created.

A typical assumption could be: Network executives are not concerned with the stigma issue, as evidenced by their portrayal of people with mental illness. A typical objective could be: Create an awareness of the stigma problem among 80% of appropriate major network executives by the end of the year.

Strategies

Whereas objectives establish desired results, strategies outline the actions to be taken to achieve these results. A strategy to achieve the aforementioned objectives could be: Provide a prominent guest to be a keynote speaker at a premier major television conference. This speaker would create the desired awareness.

Budget

This is, as it implies, a listing of the attendant costs to deliver the plan results.

Forecast

A forecast focuses on what will be achieved by the plan. The forecast could include numbers of "eliminate mental illness stigma" CDs delivered to high school guidance counselors, for example.

Summary

Creating and implementing a marketing plan is an interactive effort that should be a result of shared thinking and discussion by the organization and the person or group creating the plan. It is a roadmap to lead the organization to results. It should not be created and shelved as "evidence of industry," but must be treated as a living, breathing document that may require monitoring and adjusting from time to time.

IMPORTANT CONSIDERATIONS IN CREATING A BRANDING STRATEGY TO REDUCE THE STIGMA OF MENTAL ILLNESS

The image and resulting stigmatization of people with mental illness cannot be viewed as separate and apart from the image and perceptions of the efficacy of mental health practice. Whether viewed in syntax or paradigmatically, the mental patient is viewed in significant part as a product of mental health practice or treatment. Thus, the stigmatization accorded to people with mental illness implicitly rubs off on the profession itself. This suggests that any effort to reduce stigmatization should include focus on the profession's need to reposition itself, its efficacy, and its credibility in the minds of the general public. It must also be remembered that the public at large does not make a major distinction between psychology and psychiatry. This suggestion, in turn, points to the applicability of branding strategies for repositioning the practice of psychiatry and psychology as components within the overall scope of an effort aimed at reducing stigmatization. A branding strategy should include the following considerations and processes.

Brand Psychology as a Reliable Service

Establish psychology's association with health and prevention to demonstrate its functional benefits. Also, assert the profession's efficacy parity with other fields of medicine, despite the quiescent nature of its effectiveness.

Brand Psychology as an Organized and Accountable Service

Establish that mental health practitioners are accountable to the efficacy and ethical standards of the professional community or organizations that oversee practice.

Brand Psychology Practitioners as a Personality

Establish the personality characteristics of the mental health practitioner as an archetype on its own terms and, thus, as a personality image different from that of physicians.

Brand Psychology as a Symbol

Establish symbolic representations that posit key attributes of psychology and its practitioners and the related services and benefits to achieve the desired connotative recall. What is psychology's logo? What is psychology's benefit imagery? What is psychology's practitioner imagery?

To achieve these branding goals, it is necessary for psychology as a profession to research issues related to its image perception and the possible contribution of that image perception to the stigmatization of people with mental illness. It should define how psychology is perceived among key segments—meaning both internal and external segments—such as the following: internal public–psychiatrists and psychiatric social workers; and external public–general public and professional public, such as medical practitioners, social workers, Employee Assistance Program (EAP) executives, insurance executives, funding publics (both philanthropic and government), and legislative publics. A campaign could then be developed to address the education needs of these segments.

Some possible messages would likely be that psychology works, that it is continually evolving, and that it is more powerful than you think.

To the extent that any meaningful conclusions can be drawn, an effective marketing communication strategy with inherent popular culture appeal should reposition people with mental illness; reposition psychiatrists and psychologists as humanistic healers; explicate treatment efficacies; educate and sensitize creators of media in all phases of image making, from lighting directors to casting agents; and promote the promise of mental health as a brand.

Stigma of mental illness is an issue that refers not only to people with mental illness, but also to the entire community of psychiatric, psychological, physical, legal, educational, religious, and personal professional healers who serve the cause of mental health. Further, as a social marketing problem, stigma denies the entire society lost productivity and valuable connection with an important group of citizens.

Marketing communication is essential communication and can infiltrate every media form, thereby broadly influencing culture. Stigma can be seen as a marketing—or, more specifically—as a branding problem. An IMC program can discourage stigmatization of persons with mental illness using the techniques and strategies practiced in solving a marketing problem.

Research questions that define stereotyping of psychiatrists and psychologists should be answered in literature to inform a situational analysis of the forces that have created stigma. Further, research forms that advise the world of marketing should be discovered and adapted by psychology to more fully explore this issue. For example, media use studies, focus group techniques, and analyses of target audiences, to name a few, could inform this and other problems commonly attached to the world of medical or academic research. The roles of creative directors, art directors, designers, casting agents, and copywriters should be explored by marketers and psychiatrists together to advise on the subtleties of stigmatization in media. The consortium that created the concept for this chapter was forward thinking to consider inviting a panel of marketers to discuss this issue.

Creators of media have, at the very minimum, a voice in the representation of mental illness and can use the same tools, forces, and opportunities to control media that helped develop the problem of stigma in the first place.

Already, some progress seems imminent. For example, in a recent *New York Times* review titled "The Psychology of *The Sopranos*," it was noted that "Tony is good for business." The reviewer was responding to reports from therapists that they believed that their base of male clients was expanding because of the representation of psychotherapy in the television program. It is hoped that this sort of popularization of mental health will help reduce stigma in other ways.

REFERENCES

Bendinger, B. (2001). *Advertising, the business of branding.* Chicago: The Copy Workshop Press.

Diefenbach, D. L. (1997). The portrayal of mental illness on prime time television. *Journal of Community Psychology, 25,* 289–302.

Dreifus, C. (2002, August 27). A rebel psychiatrist calls out his profession. *New York Times,* p. F6.

Kelly, D. (2002, September 15). Deconstruct this! *New York Times,* p. 8.

Kirkpatrick, D. (2001, September 7). Fay Weldon writes a book commissioned by a jeweler. *New York Times,* p. A1.

Kotler, P., & Zalman, G. (1971, July). Social marketing: An approach to planned change. *Journal of Marketing, 35,* 3–12.

Neff, J. (2002, September 30). Back to school for P&G, competition a core requirement, but advertising isn't in the canon. *Advertising Age, 3.*

Ries, A., & Ries, L. (2002). *The fall of advertising and the rise of PR.* New York: Harper Business.

Rosen, E. (2000). *The anatomy of buzz.* New York: Doubleday.

Wahl, O., & Roth, R. (1982) Television images of mental illness: Results of a metropolitan media watch. *Journal of Broadcasting, 26,* 599–605.

Wahl, O., Wood, A., & Richards, R. (in press). Newspaper coverage of mental illness: Is it changing? *Psychiatric Rehabilitation Skills Journal.*

Wilson, C., Naim, R., Coverdale, J., & Panapa, A. (1999). Mental illness depictions in prime time drama. *Australian and New Zealand Journal of Psychiatry 33,* 232–239.

IV
CONCLUSION

15

MENTAL ILLNESS STIGMA AS SOCIAL INJUSTICE: YET ANOTHER DREAM TO BE ACHIEVED

PATRICK W. CORRIGAN

As academics, we have dissected the idea of mental illness stigma across the various chapters of this book and framed it as a major public health problem. We used basic behavioral science models to make sense of the experience. We advocated for carefully controlled research studies to test the hypotheses that emerged from these models. As a result, we have given credence to the idea that mental illness stigma is largely a phenomenon to be studied and treated much like the other foci of mental health research. If this is all we have done, it would be our mistake and a distraction from an essential message: The stigma of mental illness is first, foremost, and only an issue of social injustice! As such, it needs to be understood in the same light as the other forms of prejudice and discrimination that have hounded the modern world: racism, sexism, and ageism, to name a few. As a social injustice, mental illness stigma is largely the responsibility of the societies that created it. Hence, it is up to the people and institutions that populate these societies to recognize the harm caused by stigma and embrace their duty to erase it.

So what's the point of research in all this? After all, Martin Luther King, Jr. and the civil rights heroes of the 1960s shook up racism through the sweat and toil of protest, not the knowledge of science. No doubt their legacy is a watershed moment in erasing prejudice in the United States. However, forty years later Americans are left to realize the dream by breaking down the more subtle barriers that define racial lines and are the legacy called modern racism. To this end, social science is needed. One example illustrates this assertion: Classic social psychological theory maintains that contact between minority and majority groups should significantly decrease prejudice and discrimination, especially when contact is individualized, equal-status, cooperative, and supported by authorities (Allport, 1954/1979). Hence, racially integrated schooling seemed to hold great promise for diminishing racial prejudice at its roots among children. Unfortunately, short term effects of contact at integrated schools is mixed at best (Aboud & Levy, 2000; Schofield, 1995). In a comprehensive review of school desegregation, Stephan (1999) concluded that Black students were more likely to become positive, whereas White students actually seemed more negative. Additional research, however, identified mediating factors that seem to augment contact's antiprejudice effects. Prominent among these is positive peer relationships. Having a cross-race friend as a child leads to more positive interactions in adolescence and augments contact effects right on through into adulthood (Ellison & Powers, 1994). Hence, school officials should not only bring together majority and minority children in the classroom, but actively foster positive interactions that lead to friendship.

This brief example shows that social science plays a necessary role in informing a community's policy for stopping the roots of prejudice. We end this book with two examples that illustrate how certain obvious approaches to stigma might be limited despite their intentions, and how research might suggest solutions to these limitations.

ELIMINATING THE SYMPTOMS DOES NOT ERASE THE STIGMA

Some people have argued that curing mental illness will reduce its stigma (Liberman & Kopelowicz, 2005). As a person's disabilities vanish, prejudice against him or her because of his or her mental illness also disappears. Some proponents of this approach note how the stigma of leprosy, for example, has been erased because the illness has been eradicated (Sartorius, Byrne, & Smith, 2003). Researchers in some third world countries, however, might disagree with both the assertion that leprosy has been controlled or that the stigma of people with the illness is minimal (Chatterjee et al., 1989; Krishnatray & Melkote, 1998). Others who promote "treating the stigma away" argue that what is labeled stigma may be a "normal" response to frightening behaviors exhibited by people who are psychotic (Torrey, 1994; Torrey

& Zdanowicz, 2001). Hence, putting the symptoms, and hence the disease, under cover will decrease the stigma that signals prejudice and discrimination. We would argue that this approach might not only be feckless in terms of the antistigma agenda, but might actually make the prejudice worse.

Treating the stigma by hiding the symptoms has a counterpoint in the history of stigma and ethnicity; namely, racism can be fought by becoming color blind (Brown, Carnoy, Currie, Duster, & Oppenheimer, 2003). Some activists in the 1960s believed that Americans should be oblivious to outward signs that distinguish White from Black from other ethnic groups (e.g., skin color). Instead, we should identify and cherish a common set of supraracial values that serve as the benchmarks by which an individual's worth is judged. Unfortunately, the search for these supraracial values frequently led to Western European standards, so that African Americans, for example, were still being judged by White American values.

The notion of erasing mental illness implies that being "normal" is somehow better. A disease-orientation to mental illness stigma misplaces the responsibility for prejudice. It suggests that people who are not hiding their symptoms are somehow to blame for them, perhaps because they are not fully participating in treatment. This kind of perception is a distraction from the fundamental reality: Stigma is a social construction, not a product of the person. Hence, we must look to society to implement solutions, not the individual struggling with his or her mental illness and the stigma it entails.

PARITY, NOT PITY

Research suggests programs that focus on the biological causes of mental illness may increase pity for people with mental illness (Corrigan, River, et al., 2001; Corrigan et al., 2002; Watson, Otey, Corrigan, & Fenton, 2003), which may yield both positive and negative results. Weiner (1995) has argued that sympathetically viewing a person as victimized by a health condition is associated with willingness to provide help to that person. Research has shown that members of the general public who pity individuals with mental illness are more willing to offer a helping hand to them (Corrigan, Markowitz, Watson, Rowan, & Kubiak, 2003).

However, pity may also produce negative effects. Viewing people with mental illness as pitiful is likely to be associated with the benevolence stigma (Brockington, Hall, Levings, & Murphy, 1993; Cohen & Struening, 1962; Corrigan, Edwards, Green, Diwan, & Penn, 2001; Madianos, Madianou, Vlachonikolis, & Stefanis, 1987); that is, because people with mental illness are unable to competently handle life's demands, they need a benevolent authority who can make decisions for them. Mental health advocates and researchers have argued that a major problem with the mental health system is disempowering practices that prevent people with psychiatric disabilities from pursuing life goals (Beers, 1908; Chamberlin, 1978; Rogers, Chamberlin, Ellison, & Crean, 1997). For example, the traditional mental health system has set up a continuum of care that often acts as barriers to accomplishing life goals rather than facilitating rehabilitation (Corrigan, 2001). Hence, antistigma advocates need to be very cautious about programs that promote sympathy. People with mental illness need parity, not pity.

FINAL THOUGHT

On the steps of the Lincoln Memorial more than forty years ago, Martin Luther King Jr. gave the defining speech of our time. He said:

> I have a dream that one day this nation will rise up and live out the true meaning of its creed: "We hold these truths to be self-evident: that all men are created equal." . . . I have a dream that my four children will one day live in a nation where they will not be judged by the color of their skin but by the content of their character. I have a dream today. (August 28, 1963)

His message has similar relevance to the goals of this book. Some readers might blanch at using Dr. King's noble verse to make sense of the vision needed to overcome mental illness stigma. But for many advocates, the prejudice related to psychiatric illness is no less insidious or heinous. Hence, just as Dr. King's message continues to be a dream for all people of color, so is his vision a similar clarion call for people with mental illness. I dream of a time when people are judged by the merit of their character, not by the diagnosis in their chart or the symptoms with which they struggle.

REFERENCES

Aboud, F. E., & Levy, S. R. (1999). Reducing racial prejudice, discrimination, and stereotyping: Translating research into programs. *Journal of Social Issues, 55.* 621–787

Allport, G. W. (1979). *The nature of prejudice.* New York: Doubleday. (Original work published 1954)

Beers, C. (1908). *A mind that found itself.* New York: Longmans, Green.

Brockington, I. F., Hall, P., Levings, J., & Murphy, C. (1993). The community's tolerance of the mentally ill. *British Journal of Psychiatry, 162,* 93–99.

Brown, M. K., Carnoy, M., Currie, E., Duster, T., & Oppenheimer, D. B. (2003). *Whitewashing race: The myth of a color-blind society.* Berkeley: University of California Press.

Chamberlin, J. (1978). *On our own: Patient-controlled alternatives to the mental health system*. New York: McGraw-Hill.

Chatterjee, R., Nandi, D., Banerjee, G., Sen, B., et al. (1989). The social and psychological correlates of leprosy. *Indian Journal of Psychiatry, 31*, 315–318.

Cohen, J., & Struening, E. L. (1965). Opinions about mental illness: Hospital differences in attitude for eight occupation groups. *Psychological Reports, 17*(1), 25–26.

Corrigan, P. W. (2001). Getting ahead of the data: A threat to some behavior therapies. *Behavior Therapist, 24*(9), 189–193.

Corrigan, P. W., Edwards, A. B., Green, A., Diwan, S. L., & Penn, D. (2001). Prejudice, social distance, and familiarity with mental illness. *Schizophrenia Bulletin, 27*, 219–225.

Corrigan, P. W., Markowitz, F. E., Watson, A. C., Rowan, D., & Kubiak, M. A. (2003). An attribution model of public discrimination towards persons with mental illness. *Journal of Health and Social Behavior, 44*(2), 162–179.

Corrigan, P. W., River, L., Lundin, R. K., Penn, D. L., Uphoff-Wasowski, K., Campion, J., et al. (2001). Three strategies for changing attributions about severe mental illness. *Schizophrenia Bulletin, 27*(2), 187–195.

Corrigan, P. W., Rowan, D., Green, A., Lundin, R., River, P., Uphoff-Wasowski, K., et al. (2002). Challenging two mental illness stigmas: Personal responsibility and dangerousness. *Schizophrenia Bulletin, 28*, 293–310.

Ellison, C. G., & Powers, D. A. (1994). The contact hypothesis and racial attitudes among Black Americans. *Social Science Quarterly, 75*, 385–400.

Krishnatray, P. K., & Melkote, S. R. (1998). Public communication campaigns in the destigmatization of leprosy: A comparative analysis of diffusion and participatory approaches. A case study in Gwalior, India. *Journal of Health Communication, 3*, 327–344.

Liberman, R. P., & Kopelowicz, A. (2005). Recovery from schizophrenia: A criterion-based definition. In R. Ralph & P. Corrigan (Eds.), *Recovery in mental illness: Broadening our understanding of wellness*. Washinton, DC: American Psychological Association.

Madianos, M., Madianou, D., Vlachonikolis, J., & Stefanis, C. (1987). Attitudes towards mental illness in the Athens area: Implications for community mental health intervention. *Acta Psychiatrica Scandinavica, 75*, 158–165.

Rogers, E. S., Chamberlin, J., Ellison, M. L., & Crean, T. (1997). A consumer-constructed scale to measure empowerment among users of mental health services. *Psychiatric Services, 48*, 1042–1047.

Sartorius, N., Byrne, P., & Smith, M. (2003, October). *Roundtable discussion: Fighting stigma: Is it necessary to make diagnostic distinctions?* Paper presented at the World Psychiatric Association Second International Conference, Kingston, Ontario, Canada.

Schofield, J. W. (1995). Promoting positive intergroup relations in school settings. In W. D. Hawley & A.W. Jackson (Eds.), *Toward a common destiny: Improving race and ethnic relations in America* (pp. 257–289). Pittsburgh, PA: University of Pittsburgh.

Stephan, W. (1999). *Reducing prejudice and stereotyping in schools*. Las Cruces: New Mexico State University.

Torrey, E. F. (1994). Violent behavior by individuals with serious mental illness. *Hospital and Community Psychiatry, 45*, 653–662.

Torrey, E., & Zdanowicz, M. (2001). Outpatient commitment: What, why, and for whom. *Psychiatric Services, 52*, 337–341.

Watson, A., Otey, E., Corrigan, P. W., & Fenton, W. S. (2003). *The Science of mental illness: Evaluation a middle school curriculum's impact on mental illness stigma*. Unpublished manuscript.

Weiner, B. (1995). *Judgments of responsibility: A foundation for a theory of social conduct*. New York: Guilford Press.

AUTHOR INDEX

Numbers in italics refer to listings in the reference sections.

Cacioppo, J. T., 113, *121*
Cain, N. M., 55, 56, *62*
Cain, R., 266, 267, 268, 269, *276*
Calabrese, J. D., 154, 156, *158*
Caldwell, T. E., 27, *37*, 116, *121*, 148, *159*, 246, *253*
Caldwell-Smith, G., *93*
Callahan, L., 191, *192*
Camp, D. L., 56, *62*
Campana, K. A., 56, *63*
Campbell, D., 100, *121*
Campel, D., 201, *212*
Campion, J., *63*, *176*, *193*, *212*, *232*, *292*
Canar, J., 284, *293*
Cantor, J. C., 21, *34*
Cantor, N., 185, *196*
Caplehorn, R. M., 226, *232*
Carling, P. J., 18, *34*, 272, *276*
Carlson, M., 104, *124*
Carpinello, S., 273, *276*
Cass, V. C., 262, 263, *276*
Cathey, C., 107, *126*, 200, *215*
Center for Substance Abuse Treatment, *232*
Centers for Disease Control and Prevention, 225, *232*
Cerbone, F., 220, *234*
Chadwick, P. D. J., 248, *252*
Chaiken, S., 17, *36*, 107, 114, *120*, *121*
Chaikin, A. L., 105, *121*
Chamberlain, F., 248, *253*
Chamberlain, J., 88, *93*, 318, *318*, *319*
Chamberlain, P., 273, *279*
Chamberlin, B. W., 114, 116, *121*, *125*
Chamberlin, J., 27, *42*, 145, 151, 153, 155, *158*, *163*, 239, 246, *252*, *255*, 265, 273, *276*
Chandler, C., *196*
Chassin, L., 147, *163*
Chatterjee, R., 316, *319*
Chekola, M., 274, *276*
Chiles, J. A., 20, *38*, 199, *213*
Chin, D., 264, *276*
Chinman, M., *276*
Chuang, H. T., 208, *212*
Cirincione, C., 190, *192*
Claiborn, W. L., 191, *192*
Claire, T., 154, *159*
Clark, C. C., *251*
Clark, D. A., 242, *252*
Clarkin, J. F., *162*, *255*
Clausen, J., 15, *38*
Cleary, P., *37*
Clifford, E., 147, *158*

Clifford, M., 147, *158*
Clore, G. L., 101, 103, 104, *123*, *125*, *127*
Coates, T. J., *277*
Cochrane, R., 248, *253*
Cocozza, J. J., 168, *179*
Coen, J., 182, 184, 187, *192*
Cogan, J., 56, *62*
Cohen, D., 246, *254*
Cohen, J., 317, *319*
Cohen, P. S., 33, *34*
Colella, A., 209, *216*
Collins, A., 101, *125*
Cook, J., 57, *65*
Cook, S. W., 284, *292*
Cooley, C. H., 130, *142*
Cornwell, B., 153, *159*
Corrigan, P. W., 13, 17–20, 23–27, 32, *35*, *44*, 49, 54, *63*, 71, 78, 90, *93*, 100, 115, *121*, *126*, 130, 136, *142*, 145, 146, 148, 149, 151, 154–156, *158*, 168, 169, 174, 175–*177*, 184, 187, 189–191, *193*, 201, 208, 209, *212*, 217, 219, 223, 224, 226, 227, 229–232, 235, 239–244, 246, 249, 252, 258, 265–268, 272, *276*, 281–287, 289, 292–294, 317–320
Courtwright, D. T., 221, 229, *232*
Cover, R., 259, *276*
Coverdale, J., *312*
Crandall, C. S., 151, *158*
Crank, J. P., 206, *212*
Crawford, E., 263, *280*
Crean, T., 27, 33, *40*, *42*, 155, *163*, 246, *255*
Creswell, J. W., 55, *63*
Crocetti, G., 15, *35*
Crocker, J., 17, 26, 27, *35*, 113, *121*, 147–154, *157–163*, 191, *193*, 204, *212*, 223, 227, *232*, 244, 246, 247, *252*, 285, *295*
Croizet, J., 154, *159*
Cronbach, L. J., 46, *63*
Cross, W. E., 263, 264, *276*, *277*
Crossley, N., 261, 263, *276*
Crow, T. J., 167, *177*
Cullen, F. T., 13, 15, 28, 39, 53, *63*, 71, 96, 100, 111, *124*, 133, 136, *142*, *143*, 146, *161*, 168, *177*, 191, *194*, 243, *254*, 281, 284, *293*

Dahl, A., 19, *37*, 100, *122*
Daily, T., 13, *41*, *294*
Dalby, J., 208, *212*

Fazio, R. H., 103, 112, *121*, *125*, 228, *233*
Feldman, S., 32, *37*
Felner, R. D., 19, *36*, 101, *121*, 191, *193*, 243, *253*
Fenn, D. S., 30, *38*
Filson, C. R., 167, *178*
Finchilescu, G., 153, *159*
Fine, M. J., 27, *37*, 148, *159*, 246, *253*
Fink, P. J., 23, *37*
Finkel, S., 138, *142*
Finlay, W. M. L., 56, *62*
Finn, M. A., 208, 209, *213*, 216
Fischer, E. H., *37*, 286, *292*
Fishbein, M., 265, *275*
Fisher, B., 260, *277*
Fisher, D. B., 261, 265, *277*, 289, *291*
Fisher, J. D., *37*, 286, *292*
Fiske, S. T., 99, 109, *121*, 191, *193*, 196, 199, 203, 204, *213*, 290, *292*
Flannery, M., 272, *277*
Flaum, M., *251*
Floyd, H., 19, *42*, 100, *126*, 284, *294*
Flynn, L., *280*
Foucault, M., 260, *277*
Fountain, D., *177*
Fountain House, 250, *252*, *253*
Fowler, D., 248, *253*, *254*
Fox, L., 77, *94*
Frable, D. E., 155, *160*
Francis, C., 58, 59, 60, *63*
Frank, J., 13, 15, *39*, 100, 111, *124*, 133, *142*, 146, *161*, 191, *194*, 281, *293*
Franklin, C., 183, *196*
Freedle, R., 264, *277*
Freeman, D., *254*
Frenkel-Brunswik, E., 106, *119*, 200, *211*
Frese, F. J., 77, *94*, *95*, 263, *277*
Freud, A., 116, *122*
Freund, P., 272, *278*
Frey, J., 18, *42*
Friedman, S. J., *43*, *163*
Fuchs, L., *95*
Fultz, J. T., 210, *213*
Furnham, A., 151, *160*
FYI: Fairness in treatment, *233*
Fyock, J., 283, *292*

Gabbard, G. O., 23, *37*, *160*, 281, *293*
Gabbard, K., 23, *37*, *160*
Gabriel, S., 112, *120*
Gaertner, S. L., 173, *177*, 284, *292*

Gagne, C., 70, *93*, *94*, *96*, *97*
Gaillard, P., 208, *212*
Galan, P. A., 187, *193*
Galanter, M., 272, 273, *277*
Galinsky, A. D., 270, 271, *277*
Gallo, K. M., 25, *37*, 70, 72, 76, *95*
Ganim, A. R., *95*
Ganju, V. K., *179*
Garbin, C., *294*
Gardner, W. L., 107, 113, *120*, *121*
Garety, P. A., 248, *253*, *254*
Garfield, S. L., 28, *37*
Garman, A. N., 249, *252*
Garrett, B., *95*
Gatsonis, C. A., 21, *34*
Geis, K. J., 140, *144*
Gelleher, J. M., 26, 27, *38*, 147, *160*, 246, *254*
Geller, J. L., 56, *64*
Gerstein, D. R., 229, *233*
Getter, H., 286, *292*
Gibbons, F. X., 147, *160*
Gifford, R. K., 109, *122*
Gillis, R., 265, *277*
Gledhill, A., *256*
Gleick, J., 183, *193*
Glickman, M., 272, *277*
Glover, M., 266, *279*
Glover, R., 289, *293*
Goetz, R. R., 30, *38*
Goff, D., 248, *253*
Goffman, E., 4, *7*, 13–15, 22, *37*, 55, *63*, *95*, 129–131, 139, *142*, 190, *193*, 228, *233*, 258, *277*
Goldinger, S. D., 106, *122*
Goldman, H. E., *277*
Goldstein, R. D., 242, *253*
Gordon, A. K., 184, *194*
Gorski, T. T., 228, *233*, 236
Goto, S. G., 107, *128*
Gould, R. A., 248, *253*
Gove, W. R., 15, *37*, 100, *122*, 133, *142*
Govender, R., 114, *120*
Gracia, G., 175, *177*
Graham, S., 187–189, *193*, *196*
Graham, T., *294*
Granat-Goldstein, J., 77, 78, 86, *95*
Green, A., 17, *35*, *63*, 176, *193*, 209, *212*, 232, *292*
Green, M., 60, *64*
Green, M. F., 154, *160*
Green, T. M., 207, *213*
Greenberg, D. F., 138, *142*

Koch, R., 38
Koehler, M., 93, 94, 96, 97
Koegel, P., 14, 39
Kommana, S., 230, 234, 284, 294
Kotler, P., 301, 311
Kreisman, D., 15, 39
Krishnatray, P. K., 316, 319
Kroesen, K. W., 264, 276
Krosnick, J. A., 103, 123, 128
Krueger, J., 16–17, 39, 100, 123, 186, 194
Krumholz, H. M., 21, 36, 39
Kubiak, M. A., 142, 175, 176, 189, 193, 209, 212, 281, 284, 292, 293
Kuipers, E., 248, 253, 254
Kurzban, R., 119, 124, 224, 233

Lagos, J., 167, 177
LaGrange, T., 20, 39
Lally, S. J., 95
Lamb, H. R., 20, 39, 197, 198, 199, 210, 213
Lampe, J., 56, 62
Langan, P. A., 166, 177
Langer, E. J., 109, 124
Lanquetot, R., 95
Larson, D. B., 184, 194
Laska, E. M., 38
Lauer, M. S., 21, 39
Law, A., 286, 294
Lawn, S., 63
Lawrence, J. S., 27, 35, 148, 158, 246, 252
Lazarus, R. S., 101, 124
Leaf, P. J., 19, 28, 38, 39
Leary, M. R., 26, 35, 119, 124, 155, 158, 224, 233, 240, 249, 252
Lee, Y.-T., 100, 109, 124, 126, 201, 214
Leete, E., 76, 78, 87, 88, 96
Leff, A., 263, 280
Leff, H., 277
Lefkowits, J. Y., 202, 217
Lefley, H. P., 22, 39, 80, 88, 93–97, 191, 194
Lehman, A. F., 15, 18, 25, 39, 161, 277
Lehman, S., 15, 18, 25, 39
Leiebelt, R. A., 187, 193
Leigland, S., 185, 192, 194
Leisse, U. K., 107, 123
Lemert, E., 130–132, 142
Lemperiere, T., 208, 212
Lenski, G. E., 200, 214
Leonard, M. M., 155, 162
Lerner, M. J., 25, 39, 105, 106, 124
Levings, J., 19, 34, 100, 120, 157, 244, 252, 281, 291

Levinson, D. J., 106, 119, 200, 211
Levy, B., 154, 161, 249, 254
Levy, J. A., 191, 192
Liberman, R. P., 319
Lickey, S. E., 289, 292
Lieberman, P., 163
Lin, Z., 53, 63
Lindeman, M., 186, 194
Linehan, M. M., 242, 254
Link, B. G., 5, 7, 12–15, 19, 20, 22, 25, 26, 28, 29, 32, 39, 40, 41, 50, 53, 54, 63, 64, 70, 71, 73, 90, 96, 97, 100, 101, 109, 111, 124, 126, 130, 133–138, 141, 142, 143, 146, 147, 161, 165, 168–170, 173, 177–179, 191, 194, 195, 201, 202, 211, 214, 215, 220, 224, 227, 230, 231, 233–235, 243–245, 251, 254, 256, 259, 278, 281, 284, 290, 293, 294
Lippmann, W., 111, 124
Liu, X., 59, 65
Livermore, G., 177
Lloyd, C., 56, 62
Lock, E. D., 231, 233
Locke, B. S., 234
Loder, A., 289, 293
Loevinger, J., 46, 64
Logan, H., 112, 120
Lord, C. G., 49, 63, 292
Lorion, R. P., 28, 40
Louis Harris & Associates, 18, 40
Lovejoy, M., 78, 86, 96
Lovern, J. D., 19, 37, 191, 193
Low, P. W., 190, 194
Lowe, C. F., 248, 252
Luhtanen, R., 151, 159
Luke, D. A., 273, 278
Lundin, R. K., 23–25, 35, 63, 130, 142, 176, 193, 212, 226, 230, 232, 267, 268, 276, 292
Lurigio, A. J., 197, 199, 214
Lyass, A., 33, 40
Lyden, J., 96
Lynch, K., 78, 88, 96
Lynn, A. R., 103, 123
Lyons, E., 56, 62, 161
Lyons, M., 161, 201, 214

Maccoby, E. E., 26, 40, 147, 161
MacCoun, R. J., 221, 222, 229, 234
MacDonald-Wilson, K. L., 33, 40

Mace, F. C., 185, *194*
Macmillan, J. F., 167, *177*, 248, *253*
Macrae, C. N., 111, 112, 115, 116, *120,
    124, 127*, 282, *293*
Madey, S. F., 106, *121*
Madianos, M. G., 19, *40*, 100, *124*, 317, *319*
Madianou, D., 19, *40*, 100, *124*
Maehr, M. L., 111, *127*
Magnetti, S. M., *162*
Magnusson, J., 53, 65, 187, *196*
Maguen, S., 262, *279*
Majcher-Angermeyer, A., 244, *251*
Major, B., 17, 26, 27, *35*, 113, *121*, 147, 148,
    152, 153, 154, *159, 161, 163*, 191,
    193, 223, 232, 244, 246, *253*
Malamud, T. J., 244, *252*
Male, A., 18, *44*
Malle, B. F., 200, *215*
Malmud, T. J., 250
Malt, U., 19, *37*, 100, *122*
Manderscheid, R. W., 18, 28, *42, 44*
Mangone, D., *37*, 191, *193*
Manning, P. K., 206, *214*
Mansfield, M., 230, *234*, 284, *294*
Manstead, A. S. R., 152, *160*
Manus, M., 16, *38*
Marcia, J. E., 47, *62*
Marcus-Newall, A., 104, *124*
Mark, M., *280*
Mark, T., 21, *40*
Markowitz, F. E., 18, 19, *40*, 54, 64, 129, 138,
    139, *142, 143*, 146, *161*, 175, *176,
    189, 193, 209, 212*, 273, *278*, 281, *292*
Marks, A., *234*
Markus, H., *38, 160*
Marley, J., 209, *214*
Marsden, G. M., 221, *234*
Marshall, T. B., 92, *96*
Martin, J. K., 13, 20, *40, 41*, 136, *143*
Martin, L. L., 105, *124*, 205, *214, 215*
Martin-Stanly, C., 190, *193*
Mason, J. A., *63, 292*
Masota, L., 18, *42*
Massaro, J. M., 33, *40*
Mastrofski, S. D., 21, *40*, 208, *214*
Matas, M., 60, *64*
Mathisen, J., *176, 193, 292*
Matsueda, R. L., 140, *143*
Matthews, S., *177*
Maxwell, C. D., 208, *214*
Mayer, A., *161*
Mayer, C., 191, *192*

Mayo, D. J., 274, *278*
Mays, V., 248, *253*
McAlpine, D., 15, *40*
McCandless, B. R., 27, *44*, 147, 148, *164,
    246, 256*
McCarn, S. R., 262, *278*
McCarthy, E., *256*
McCarthy, J., 274, *278*
McCarty, D. W., 20, *43*, 198, *216*
McCauley, C., 100, *124, 125, 126*
McClelland, G. M., 20, *43*, 197, 198, *216*
McClintock, C., 106, *123*
McClure, R. K., 261, *278*
McConahay, J., *119*
McCracken, S. G., 284, *292, 293*
McCubbin, M., 246, *254*
McDermott, B. E., 241, 243, *254*
McFadden, L. S., *279*
McFarland, S. G., 107, *125*, 167, *178*, 200, *214*
McGanagle, K. A., *233*
McGrath, M. E., 76, 87, *96*
McGregor, I., 114, *125*
McGuire, W. J., 99, *125*
McKusick, L., *277*
McMillan, D., 283, *295*
Mead, G. H., 130, *143*, 226, 227, *234*
Mechanic, D., 15, 28, 33, *37, 40*
Meehl, P. E., 46, *63*
Mehta, S. I., 22, *40*, 286, *293*
Melick, M. E., 168, *179*
Melkote, S. R., 316, *319*
Mendoza, D. W., 264, *279*
Meyer, J. P., 190, *194*
Meyers, B. S., *163*
Mid-Atlantic ATTC, *234*
Mikulincer, M., 116, *125*
Miles, M. B., 46, *64*
Miller, A. G., 184, *194*
Miller, C. E., 152, *162*
Miller, D. T., 38, 105, *127, 160*, 185, *194*
Miller, M., 30, *38*
Miller, N., , 104, *121, 124, 126*
Miller, W. R., 265, *278*
Millman and Robertson, Inc., 225, *234*
Millon, T., 242, *254*
Mills, C. W., 251, *254*
Milne, A. B., 115, *124*, 282, *293*
Milner, S., 30, *38*
Mio, J. S., 264, *279*
Mirabi, M., *162*
Mirotznik, J., *143*, 146, *161*, 243, *254*
Mirowsky, J., 140, *144*

SUBJECT INDEX

ABOUT THE EDITOR

Patrick W. Corrigan, PsyD, is professor of psychiatry at the University of Chicago where he directs the Center for Psychiatric Rehabilitation, a research and training program dedicated to the needs of people with serious mental illness and their families. Dr. Corrigan has been principal investigator of federally funded studies on rehabilitation, team leadership, and consumer-operated services. In 2000, Dr. Corrigan became principal investigator of the Chicago Consortium for Stigma Research (CCSR), the only research center examining the stigma of mental illness funded by the National Institute of Mental Health. The CCSR comprises more than two dozen basic behavioral and mental health services researchers from nine Chicago-area universities and currently has more than 20 active investigations in this area. Dr. Corrigan is a prolific researcher, having published more than 150 articles and 7 books including *Don't Call Me Nuts! Coping With the Stigma of Mental Illness,* coauthored with Robert Lundin.